Hitchcock's Romantic Irony

D1611771

Film and Culture Series
John Belton, General Editor

Hitchcock's Romantic Irony

Richard Allen

 Columbia University Press   *New York*

Columbia University Press
Publishers Since 1893
New York   Chichester, West Sussex

Library of Congress Cataloging-in-Publication Data
Allen, Richard, 1959–
Hitchcock's romantic irony / Richard Allen.
p. cm. — (Film and culture)
Includes bibliographical references and index.
ISBN 978-0-231-13574-0 (cloth : alk. paper) — ISBN 978-0-231-13575-7
(pbk. : alk. paper) — ISBN 978-0-231-50967-1 (ebook)
1. Hitchcock, Alfred, 1899–1980—Criticism and interpretation. I. Title. II. Series.

PN1998.3.H58A73 2007
791.4302'33092—dc22
2007012808

Columbia University Press books are printed on permanent and
durable acid-free paper.

Printed in the United States of America

c 10 9 8 7 6 5 4 3 2 1
p 10 9 8 7 6 5 4 3 2 1

Reproduction of color stills was made possible with a generous grant from the
Tisch School of the Arts, New York University.

Portions of the following work have been published in slightly different form and
are reprinted with the permission of the editors and publishers: "Hitchcock, or the
Pleasures of Metaskepticism," *October* 89 (Summer 1999): 69–86; "*The Lodger* and the
Origins of Hitchcock's Aesthetic," *Hitchcock Annual* (2001–2002): 38–78; "Hitchcock
and Narrative Suspense: Theory and Practice," in Richard Allen and Malcolm Turvey,
eds., *Camera Obscura, Camera Lucida: Essays in Honor of Annette Michelson* (Amsterdam: Amsterdam University Press, 2003); "Daphne du Maurier and Alfred Hitchcock,"
in Robert Stam and Alessandra Raengo, eds., *A Companion to Film and Literature*
(New York: Blackwell, 2004), 298–325; and "Sir John and the Half-Caste: Identity and
Representation in Hitchcocks's *Murder!*," *Hitchcock Annual* 13 (2004–2005): 92–126.

In memory of
Tom Keavy (1991–2003)

Their faces were not made for wrinkles, their
Pure blood to stagnate, their great hearts to fail.
The blank grey was not made to blast their hair,
But like the climes that know nor snow nor hail
They were all summer: lightning might assail
And shiver them to ashes, but to trail
A long and snake-like life of dull decay
Was not for them—they had too little clay.

—LORD BYRON

Contents

In America … you respect him because he shoots scenes of love as if they were scenes of murder. We respect him because he shoots scenes of murder like scenes of love. Anyway, it's the same man we are talking about, the same man, and the same artist.

—FRANÇOIS TRUFFAUT

It seemed to me, as much from certain precise points made in the conversation as from statements gathered from Hitchcock's collaborators, that he had a permanent notion of mise-en-scène, that of a tension in the interior of a sequence, a tension that one would not know how to reduce either to dramatic categories or plastic categories but which partakes of both at the same time. For him it is always a question of creating in the mise-en-scène, starting from the scenario, but mainly by the expressionism of the framing, the lighting, or the relation of the characters to the décor, an essential instability of image. Each shot is thus for him like a menace, or at least an anxious waiting. . . . One recognizes at a glance the most banal still from one of his films, in the admirably determined quality of this disequilibrium.

—ANDRÉ BAZIN

Preface

For over ten years I have regularly taught Alfred Hitchcock's films in a university setting, and more recently I have edited, with my colleague Sid Gottlieb, the *Hitchcock Annual*, a journal of "Hitchcock Studies." My thinking about Hitchcock's work has been shaped, for better or worse, by these experiences, in particular by my attempt to digest the plurality of commentaries his work has supported and spawned since the critics of *Cahiers du cinéma* first acknowledged his significance as a director in the 1960s. Hitchcock's work has yielded critical approaches as divergent as the argument of Lesley Brill, who understands Hitchcock as an essentially conventional director of "romances," and "queer theorist" Lee Edelman, who conceives of Hitchcock's films as an attack on "heteronormativity." The Hitchcock criticism of Robin Wood is actually self-divided between his first book, which views Hitchcock's films as therapeutic in their effect, confronting us with the dark side of human existence in order to affirm conventional morality, and his later writings, which understand Hitchcock as a critic of conventional morality, particularly as it is embodied in the values of heterosexual romance. Unless these critics are completely misguided rather than simply selectively biased, there are surely properties of Hitchcock's films that explain this divide, that can explain how it is that Hitchcock's works yield the divergent interpretations that they do.

Preface

Of course, part of the explanation for this contrasting emphasis and "selective bias" in critical writings on Hitchcock stems from the fact that studies of Hitchcock are often driven by a specific theoretical or ideological agenda wherein the critic discovers in the works of Hitchcock what he or she wants to see in them and disregards the potential counterexamples. This problem is compounded by the fact that critics of Hitchcock often discuss at most a dozen or so films—and frequently fewer—out of the fifty-three feature films he made during his long career. I began my research on Hitchcock by setting out to write a book that would be structured around individual films or groups of films, and this research has resulted in a number of published essays that I refer to from time to time in this volume. However, as I conceived the broader contours of the project in response to the wide range of literature in the field, I began to think of this book in terms of a series of thematically organized chapters that encompass a greater span of Hitchcock's work.

The problem of "selective bias" is not simply one of the *scope* of critical inquiry, but of the *nature* of critical inquiry, where film criticism is primarily conceived of as an activity of interpretation. I do not agree with David Bordwell that interpretation is intrinsically an act of "making" (rather than "discovering") meaning;[1] however, I do agree that it is an activity that is prone to the making of meaning, especially when interpretation is conceived as a practice that exists to confirm a theory which the critic applies to the text. In bad interpretation meaning is made; in good interpretation meaning is discovered. One test of a good interpretation is the agreement that a good interpretation commands from informed viewers, while a bad interpretation largely reflects back from a film the assumptions of the critic. While I would not wish to see the activity of interpretation abandoned— indeed, I regularly practice it in the pages of this book—I agree with Bordwell that interpretation must be answerable to the practice of what he calls "poetics" in order to yield critical insights of lasting value.

Poetics is not primarily an interpretative practice, but a practice of descriptive generalization that clarifies the patterns of style (what are the cinematic ways in which Hitchcock's story is conveyed?); content and theme (what kinds of stories does Hitchcock tell and what are his recurring motifs?); and form (how does Hitchcock structure the spectator's experience of his stories?). There are many places where description meets interpretation. Even in such a simple case as characterizing what happens in a story, one often needs to interpret what one sees and hears in order to understand it: for example, what exactly happens in the "memory" flashback which concludes Hitchcock's film *Marnie*? Nonetheless, much of what takes place in a film *can* be described—from the canonical story types in Hitchcock's films and his characteristic stylistic patterns and visual motifs, to the role and function of narrative suspense. Few studies of Hitchcock have placed poetics at center stage in the interpretation of his works. Notable exceptions are Susan Smith's book on Hitchcock (subtitled *Suspense, Humor, and Tone*), and Michael Walker's *Hitchcock's Motifs*, which came out just in time for me to at least reference it in these pages.[2] This book is a poetics-driven study, and that is, I hope, one of the contributions it makes to the literature.

One of the main advantages of poetics in the study of film is that it forces the critic to pay attention to style and form. As Bordwell notes, interpretation-based criticism is too often thematic, or pays attention to style only selectively and opportunistically. My assumption in this book, one that is shared with the first important critical work on Hitchcock's films by Claude Chabrol and Eric Rohmer,[3] is that the significance of Hitchcock's films is indissolubly wedded to the form and style in which they are told. However, at the same time, the study of "poetics" need not, it seems to me, entail a formalism that simply studies patterns of style for their own sake, or construes the themes of a work as merely occasion for indulging in certain rhetorical strategies or experiments in style. The critical debate over Hitchcock's status as an auteur has been traditionally framed as a question about whether he was merely a director of technically and rhetorically brilliant works of entertainment or whether his works actually express a moral point of view. My answer in this book is that this opposition poses a false dichotomy, for Hitchcock's depth lies in the visual (and aural) surface of his works, and in this way they express a distinctive viewpoint. This outlook is neither moral nor immoral: it is the *amoral* point of view of the romantic-ironist or aesthete.

This book is organized into two distinct but interrelated parts, each of which comprises three chapters. Part I, Narrative Form, is framed by the concept of romantic irony that is introduced and anatomized in chapter 1. Chapter 2 develops the argument that Hitchcock's particular brand of suspense that is imbricated with black humor is the privileged mode of romantic irony in his work. Chapter 3 investigates the way in which romantic irony informs Hitchcock's plots that are structured around the problems of recognition and misrecognition, knowledge and skepticism, and whose consequences differ according to gender. Part II, Visual Style, is framed in chapter 4 by the concept of aestheticism, which is the way in which romantic irony is expressed through style in Hitchcock's work. Chapter 5, on expressionism, explores the specific film style in which aestheticism is manifest in Hitchcock's work. Chapter 6 extends the discussion of chapter 5 into the domain of color, where the influence of surrealism, an heir of aestheticism, is manifest in Hitchcock's work. All the chapters circle back to romantic irony, which serves as an introduction to the whole, and just as questions of aestheticism and style emerge when introducing the concept of romantic irony and articulating suspense, the forms and content of Hitchcock's work remain important for part II.

The idea of romantic irony I develop in chapter 1 is a "descriptive generalization" that seeks to encompass the vast majority of works directed by Hitchcock. *Romantic irony* is a concept that at once accounts for the divergent interpretations of the role of the romantic ideal in Hitchcock's work but also provides an explanation of the relationship between form and content that defines Hitchcock's emplotment and subversion of that ideal. The concept of romantic irony describes the *both/and* rather than the *either/or* logic that governs the universe of Hitchcock's films, and it explains how it is that critics could construe Hitchcock's work both as an affirmation of the ideal of heterosexual romance and as a critique of that ideal. The concept of romantic irony also explains why Hitchcock's films are not simply elaborate works of self-conscious formal dexterity that incorporate a consistent reflection upon their own conditions of existence, but the manner in which their formal dexterity is a product of and entwined with the content of the work; indeed, it is, in part, the expression of that content. Finally, romantic irony describes what at once unifies and differentiates Hitchcock's works. I shall describe three main types of romantic irony in Hitchcock's work according to whether the "dialectical" logic of both/and creates an atmosphere of perpetual transformation and renewal that is characterized by his romantic thrillers such as *North by Northwest* (1959), whether it creates an environment of pervasive ambiguity, as in *Suspicion* (1941), or whether it fosters a downward spiraling trajectory of negation and descent, as in *Vertigo* (1958).

Chapter 2 addresses the role and function of suspense which, together with the black humor that informs it, is Hitchcock's signature mode of narration and the primary vehicle of romantic irony. I begin by outlining two key forms of suspense in Hitchcock's work—classical suspense and suspenseful mystery—and I describe the ways that these different forms of suspense are implicated in Hitchcock's control of the spectator's access to the narrative world and his orchestration of character point of view. These distinctions are a prelude to showing how suspense is one of the central ways in which Hitchcock complicates the narrative resolution that favors the formation of the couple by manipulating the relationship between narrative point of view and character point of view. Finally, this chapter demonstrates how the goal of Hitchcockian suspense is, as a form of black humor, to subvert the coordinates of conventional morality and to foster audience allegiance with the sources of human perversity.

Chapter 3 continues the concerns of chapter 2 with the role of knowledge from the standpoint of investigating Hitchcock's signature recognition narratives. Given the way in which Hitchcock's romantic irony involves orchestrating the deceptiveness of visual appearances and the misattribution of guilt to innocent protagonists in his famous "wrong man" or "wronged man" motif, it is tempting to conclude that Hitchcock is a radical skeptic. However, this conclusion ignores the frequency with which guilt and innocence are resolved in Hitchcock's works. Knowledge is a problem in Hitchcock's films not primarily because it is infected by doubt, but because of the way it is keyed to the incipiently coercive force of sexual desire that drives the formation of the couple and binds them in love. Where the couple are both outsiders to power, as in Hitchcock's romances like *The 39 Steps* (1935), the object of knowledge takes the form of what Hitchcock terms a "MacGuffin," that is, it is essentially a plot pretext for the quest that will unite the couple. However, where the quest for knowledge is to redeem one who is desired or loved, the quest to attain knowledge, while successful, is often coercive, as in *Marnie* (1964), or disillusioning, as in *Shadow of a Doubt* (1943), or both, as in *Vertigo*.

Chapter 4 opens part II of the book by exploring aestheticism as the stylistic mode of Hitchcock's romantic irony. In Hitchcock's work, human sexuality, deemed by definition perverse, is self-consciously displaced into style in the manner of a Freudian joke that at once disguises and reveals its sexual content. Tracing some of the historical antecedents of Hitchcock's style in British fin de siècle aestheticism, this chapter focuses on the manner in which Hitchcock's visual style is allied to those forces of human perversity, in particular a homosexuality deemed "perverse," which disrupts the romance, while acknowledging that Hitchcock's narratives of romantic renewal (discussed in chapter 1) also bear the hallmarks of aestheticism. This chapter concludes by developing an overarching distinction that is derived, in part, from the distinction between classical suspense and suspenseful mystery. This distinction is one that contrasts Hitchcock's "masculine aesthetic," where style registers perverse sexual content and holds it at arm's length in the manner of a joke, as in *Rope* (1948), and his "feminine aesthetic," where visual style registers the sublime allure of human perversity, as in *Rebecca* (1940).

Chapter 5 complements chapter 4 by exploring the way that Hitchcock's aestheticism is inflected by the influence of the works of German expressionist filmmakers who rework the idioms of German romanticism in a manner that is in some ways comparable to the way in which fin de siècle aestheticism reworks the idioms of English romanticism. It demonstrates at once how the theme of the double or the shadow world is the central trope of romantic irony in Hitchcock's work and how that theme is centrally articulated through visual narration: framing, mise-en-scène, and editing. Given the fact that visual expressionism articulates the subversive force of the double or the shadow world, this chapter, like the previous one, focuses on narratives where the formation of the romance is wholly or partly subverted, rather than upon Hitchcock's narratives of romantic renewal.

Chapter 6 continues the argument of chapter 5 by treating in detail a topic that has been neglected in the study of Hitchcock and of cinema as a whole: namely, color. Far from being a peripheral element of Hitchcock's visual style, I argue that color design is central to the character of his later works. By affording a more differentiated range of expression than black and white, color expands the vocabulary of black-and-white expressionism beyond the articulation of the double. Hitchcock's uses of color gestures toward a surrealist aesthetic where the shadow world supervenes completely upon the world of the everyday or the ordinary through the use of color symbolism, such as the reds of *Marnie* or *Vertigo*. Yet, at the same time, color gives a remarkable unity to Hitchcock's thematic concerns by affording the articulation both of patterns of complementarity that define the narratives of romantic renewal and of the logic of opposition that characterizes the double in Hitchcock's black-and-white expressionism.

Preface

A book like this could not have been written without the works of others. The influence of Lesley Brill's book, *The Hitchcock Romance*, on chapter 1 is evident, even as my argument departs from it. Chapter 2 is indebted to the writings of Susan Smith and Noel Carroll on suspense. Part of the argument of chapter 3 is indebted to my reading of Stanley Cavell's writings in a manner that I have made explicit elsewhere,[4] as well as those critics, such as Tania Modleski and Paula Marantz Cohen, who have drawn attention, in different ways, to the role of female agency in Hitchcock's work. Chapter 4 is influenced by Thomas Elsaesser's essay "The Dandy in Hitchcock" and by Raymond Durgnat's study of the director, as well as the writings of queer theorists such as Lee Edelman and D. A. Miller. Chapter 5 is indebted to William Rothman's pioneering investigation into Hitchcock's expressionism. My understanding of the relationship between sexuality and style is influenced by Hitchcock's psychoanalytic critics, most of all Slavoj Žižek, and by Tom Leitch's conception of Hitchcock as a ludic director whose mode of address to the audience is a playful one. However, my profoundest, if more diffuse, debt is to the work of Robin Wood, who first applied the idea of the shadow world, or what he calls "the chaos world," to Hitchcock's works and, in spite of the moralism which is oddly ill-attuned to his object of admiration, surely remains the most perceptive of all Hitchcock's critics.

By absorbing these diverse influences, I have sought to craft a work that can serve both as a reliable introduction to Hitchcock and as an in-depth study. Most of all, I hope this book will inspire students or general readers alike to turn to and return to Hitchcock's films.

Acknowledgments

It is my pleasure to thank the many people who have helped bring this book to fruition. First, I wish to thank my film teachers, all of whom taught me about Hitchcock and some of whom are Hitchcock scholars in their own right: Charles Barr, Don Ranvaud, and Thomas Elsaesser at the University of East Anglia; Janet Bergstrom, Nick Browne, and Steve Mamber at UCLA. At an early stage in my study of Hitchcock, the late Bill Everson shared his enthusiasm and his wonderful 16mm prints. Ann Harris, Cathy Holter, and Mai Kiang in the George Amberg Study Center at New York University have facilitated my research in numerous ways. Funds for the research and publication of this book have been provided in the form of Faculty Development Grants from the Tisch School of the Arts, and I thank Dean Mary Schmidt Campbell and Dean Randy Martin for their support. My work has also been sustained by the constant support and encouragement of the former Chair of Department, Chris Straayer. I thank Bill Simon for allowing me to poach his teaching territory and for the many undergraduate and graduate students who, over the years, have shared my enthusiasm for Hitchcock and contributed to the development of my thought.

Among the individuals who have invited me to speak or publish on Hitchcock, and who have contributed conversation and criticism, I wish to thank David Bordwell, James Chandler, Peter Evans, Ben Gibson,

Acknowledgments

Tom Gunning, Miriam Hansen, Andrea Kern, Tom Leitch, Adam Lowenstein, Annette Michelson, Patrick McGilligan, Brian Price, Alessandra Raengo, Walter Raubicheck, John David Rhodes, Steven Schneider, Ben Singer, Murray Smith, Walter Srebnick, Robert Stam, Ravi Vasudevan, Rebecca Walkowitz, Thomas Wartenberg, Susan White, Federico Windhausen, and Slavoj Žižek. I am especially grateful to the late Joe Stefano and Evan Hunter for extended conversations on their collaboration with Hitchcock.

Several people have played a significant role in the development of my arguments. I benefited, in the early stages, from conversations with Sam Ishii-Gonzales, who collaborated with me on two Hitchcock anthologies; Malcolm Turvey read with his customary acuity early drafts of chapter 1 and helped me to clarify the conceptual foundations of my argument; Phil Kennedy inspired me to write chapter 3, and I have benefited from my conversations with him on the topic of recognition in storytelling; Ira Bhaskar shared her wide knowledge of romantic literature and sharpened my understanding of romanticism and expressionism at a key phase of the project; Ken Mogg has saved me over the years from countless errors and supplied more useful references than I could possibly incorporate into this book; Sid Gottlieb thoughtfully criticized (and proofread!) many drafts of my work and has proved an inestimable colleague throughout our collaboration on the *Hitchcock Annual* and in the classroom; Columbia University Press's Film and Culture series editor John Belton read drafts of the first three chapters, and I benefited from his rigorous and unsparing criticism of them; Elizabeth Weis provided helpful suggestions on the manuscript as I embarked upon a final draft; and by reading the entire work at a late stage, my colleague Dana Polan expedited final completion. However, my greatest debt is to my friend and colleague, Bill Paul. Bill carefully read two versions of this manuscript and on both occasions gave me pages of insightful suggestions about structure and content that contributed substantially to the argument of each chapter and to the improvement of the whole. Needless to say, I am solely responsible for the faults that remain.

I am particularly grateful to my editor at Columbia University Press, Jennifer Crewe, for providing such a hospitable environment for this book, and I also wish to thank the rest of the editorial team: Juree Sondker, Anne McCoy, and especially Roy Thomas. Thanks also to Priyadarshini Shanker for her careful proofreading, and Renata Jackson for her copious index.

Acknowledgments

Finally, it is my pleasure to thank my friends, Alfie Graham, Robin Hart, James Saynor, Jim Shafland, Ken Sweeney, Frank and Louise Wallace, Harvey Siegel, Peter Newman, and Kevin Weldon, for their conversation and support, and my family, Bridget, Sophie, and James, for living with Hitchcock, as well as myself, for so long.

Hitchcock's Romantic Irony

I

Narrative Form

1
Romantic Irony

Alfred Hitchcock is widely acknowledged as a "reflexive" or "self-reflexive" filmmaker who inscribes himself within his own works through cameos and authorial surrogates, orchestrates the narrative world as a world of self-conscious artifice, and acknowledges and invokes the role of the audience in his films, most notably in the spectatorial role assigned to L. B. Jefferies (James Stewart) in *Rear Window* (1954). However, it seems to me that in order to understand the nature of Hitchcock's formal dexterity, the idea of "reflexivity" or "self-reflexivity" is insufficient. First, it is a concept that tends to emphasize overt moments of authorial interpolation or audience address as against the more pervasive, invisible presence that Hitchcock sustains in his work. Second, the concept tends to privilege the role of the author in self-consciously fabricating the fictional world over the quality and significance of the world that is fabricated. However, is it my contention that Hitchcock's formal dexterity does not operate "in a void" to quote John Belton, quoting Bosley Crowther.[1] Rather, Hitchcock's formal dexterity is constitutive of a "worldview" articulated by his works.

It is for this reason that I have turned in this book to the concept of romantic irony in order to understand the nature of Hitchcock's work. The concept of romantic irony, though elusive, accounts for both vertical and horizontal form—that is, for both the inscription of authorial self-consciousness and the organization of narrative meaning, which the idea of self-reflexivity alone fails to adequately explain. Furthermore, it is a concept that allows us to understand Hitchcock's relationship to romanticism, one that is mediated by fin de siècle aestheticism and by European modernism, German expressionism in particular. Romantic irony has wide, indeed ever-widening, currency in the field of literature, but its application to understanding film has been minimal, and to my knowledge the term has never been applied to films of Hitchcock. The purpose of this chapter is to introduce the concept of romantic irony, to explain in detail how romantic irony in Hitchcock's work involves at once a specific kind of self-conscious narration and a particular attitude or stance toward the emplotment of romantic love, and to describe the basic forms that romantic irony takes in Hitchcock's films. This chapter begins with a discussion of the origins of the concept of romantic irony in romantic philosophy. Readers who wish to move straight to the explication of Hitchcock's romantic irony should skip to page 11.

The Concept of Romantic Irony

Any critic who seeks to employ the term *romantic irony* is faced with the necessity of defining a term whose usage is so amorphous and wide-ranging as to appear inchoate. What do the words *romantic* and *ironic* mean in "romantic irony"? Do they have a separate reference, that is, does "irony" in "romantic irony" serve to qualify the term *romantic* and describe a specific inflection of "the romantic"? Finally, to what aspects of a text does the term apply? Is it a worldview or a way of thinking, or is it an aesthetic category, a narrative mode or form? The concept of romantic irony is taken from the writings of Friedrich Schlegel (1772–1829) where it is formulated, at least implicitly, for the first time. Schlegel discusses irony extensively in his early published writings, which consist of trenchant aphoristic fragments whose form itself seeks to express or reflect his philosophy, and he develops a theory of romantic poetry in which the concept of irony plays a central role. However, Schlegel did not actually use the term "romantic irony" at all in his published writings.

For Schlegel, the concern of philosophy is the relationship between the relative and finite, which are chaotic, and the absolute or infinite, which are unified and complete: "Only in relationship to the infinite is there meaning and purpose; whatever lacks such a relation is absolutely meaningless and pointless." For Schlegel, irony is not merely a local rhetorical ploy in which you mean the reverse of what you say: it is nothing less than a cognitive instrument through which the relationship of the finite to the infinite may be grasped. Subjectively, Schlegel's concept of irony may be understood in relationship to Johann Gottlieb Fichte's idealist philosophy. For Fichte, reality is created by the subject as an external constraint against which it defines itself. This self-definition consists in a ceaseless dialectical opposition or self-division between the empirical, finite self, and the self that, aspiring to the absolute, constantly confronts, overcomes, and confronts again its own finitude. Schlegel states that irony is "constant alternation of self-creation and self-destruction,"[2] and "by its means one transcends oneself."[3] The role irony plays as an instrument for objectively grasping this mobility is defined in Schlegel's romantic, rhetorical logic in which the either/or Aristotelian logic of non-contradiction (something cannot be both a and not-a) is replaced by the both/and principle of a "romantic logic" or "a = a and a $\neq$ a."[4] Schlegel writes, "An idea is a concept perfected to the point of irony, an absolute synthesis of absolute antithesis, the continual self-creating interchange of two conflicting thoughts" (A 121).

Schlegel captures the active, transforming nature of this "self-creating interchange" with the term *wit*. Wit is "an explosion of the confined spirit" (L 90) and "the outward lightning bolt of the imagination."[5] In all its manifestations" wit is at once the "principle" and the "organ" of "universal philosophy" (A 220). Schlegel describes wit as partaking of a "logical chemistry." The witty juxtaposition of opposites functions like the then recently discovered processes of chemical combination whereby elements separate out of compounds and join to form new compounds which are more than the sum of their parts. Thus, sodium carbonate (Na_2CO_3) mixed with hydrochloric acid (HCl) forms sodium chloride (Na_2Cl), that is, salt and carbonic acid (H_2CO_3). This in turn breaks down into water (which is hydrogen plus oxygen, H_2O) and carbon dioxide (CO_2).[6] Schlegel writes, "Whoever has a sense for the infinite and knows what he wants to do with it sees here the result of eternally separating and uniting powers, conceives of his ideals at least as being chemical, and utters, when he expresses himself decisively, nothing but contradictions" (A 412).

Philosophical irony achieves its realization, for Schlegel, in romantic poetry. As Hans Eichner has made clear, the term "romantic poetry" in this context should be treated with care. Romantic is opposed to classical by Schlegel, and he applies the term "romantic poetry" to "any work of fiction, primarily 'modern,' that did not belong to any of the three classical genres—the epic, the drama, and the lyric."[7] In contrast to classical fiction that, for Schlegel, was dictated by prescribed forms and hence "objective," romantic poetry is an "arabesque" that mixes together different genres, modes, or styles in a manner that creates contradictory perspectives, a sense of fragmentation, and moments of self-conscious authorial commentary. Romantic poetry fuses "poetry and prose, inspiration and criticism, the poetry of art and the poetry of nature" (A 116). Ideal modern fiction is "fragmentary both in form and content, simultaneously completely subjective and individual, and completely objective and like a necessary part in a system of all the sciences" (A 77).

Romantic poetry for Schlegel "is in the arts what wit is in philosophy" (A 238). Indeed, it perhaps provides an ideal realization of philosophical irony or wit at the level of both "horizontal" and "vertical" form. "Horizontally" across the text, wit is manifest in the self-creating interchange of opposed ideas that Schlegel describes as "artfully ordered confusion" and "a charming symmetry of contradictions," which yields that "wonderfully perennial alternation of enthusiasm and irony."[8] "Vertically," wit is manifest in the irony of self-transcendence. Romantic poetry hovers "at the midpoint between the portrayed and the portrayer … and can raise that reflection again and again to a higher power, can multiply it in an endless succession of mirrors" (A 116). In summary:

> There is a kind of poetry whose essence lies in the relation between the ideal and real, and which therefore, by analogy to philosophical jargon, should be called transcendental poetry. It begins as satire in the absolute difference of ideal and real, hovers in between as elegy, and ends as idyll with the absolute identity of the two. But just as we wouldn't think much of an uncritical transcendental philosophy that doesn't represent the producer along with the product and contain at the same time within the system of transcendental thoughts a description of transcendental thinking: so too … this poetry should describe itself, and always be simultaneously poetry and the poetry of poetry. (A 238)

Schlegel defines irony as "divine," yet, in the same breath, as "transcendental buffoonery," and he compares it to the "mimic style of the averagely gifted buffo." That is, the author is like the buffoon in the Italian comic opera who is constantly laughing at his own histrionic performance and the world of the play.

The idea of irony as wit also serves to link Schlegelian irony to the self-conscious invocation of the reader or listener as interlocutor for the author. For Schlegel explicitly compares the imaginative, creative function of irony, in the form of wit, to the spark of conversation between old friends. "Wit," Schlegel writes, is "logical sociability" and "many witty ideas are like the sudden meeting of two friendly thoughts after a long separation." Wit is not simply like communication but it stems, as Gary Handewerk points out, from seeking to overcome a sense of communicative isolation.[9] Schlegel speaks at once of "the impossibility and necessity of complete communication" (*L* 108). The "explosion" of the confined spirit in wit breaks out of communicative isolation and expresses the desire to solicit a response from the reader, listener, or spectator. But it is not a question of simply blurting out everything one has to say and imposing oneself on the other. Nor is it a matter of making a calculated impression. Rather, it involves making the reader or listener an interlocutor: "The synthetic writer constructs and creates a reader as he should be; he doesn't imagine him calm and dead, but active and critical. He allows whatever he has created to take shape gradually before the reader's eyes, or else he tempts him to discover it himself" (*L* 112).

In the first half of the twentieth century, the interpretation of romantic irony centered upon a debate as to whether romantic irony was essentially subjective or objective in character. The question at stake was whether romantic irony is to be equated with the kind of authorial self-consciousness or self-reflexivity to be found in the works of Laurence Sterne and Schlegel's friend and contemporary Ludwig Tieck. This kind of subjective romantic irony, it was argued, was not what Schlegel had in mind. Instead, Schlegel's model for romantic irony was the kind of objective romantic irony to be found in the works of Shakespeare, where the hand of the author is evenly and essentially "invisibly" distributed, like the presence of God that is immanent within every aspect of his creation according to the Pauline doctrine.[10] "Objective romantic irony" was deemed superior to "subjective romantic irony" in which the text was merely an occasion for flaunting the presence or dexterity of the author, and content is ceded to the play of form. While this debate seems largely to have been forgotten, it does receive an echo in the way in which romantic irony has been treated by contemporary commentators.

One group of literary theorists and critics continues to define romantic irony primarily in terms of subjective romantic irony. D. C. Muecke, in *The Compass of Irony*, equates what he calls "proto-romantic irony" with formal self-reflexivity or "artistic irony," where an author draws attention to the fictional status of the artwork by a deliberate destruction of the fictional illusion, in the manner of Sterne's authorial interpellations in *Tristam Shandy*.[11] Lilian Furst contrasts romantic irony with traditional irony. In traditional irony, of the kind to be found in the novels of George Eliot, irony is used as a weapon to discriminate truth from falsity in a way that preserves a consistent texture for the fictional world. The knowing narrator guides the reader to the correct meaning that lies beneath a form of words that might appear to say the reverse. Romantic or modern irony is situated not between the narrator and the reader, but between the narrator and his narrative, where the storyteller openly manipulates the elements of his story to reflect upon the nature of his tale and himself as a writer. The storyteller becomes a "narrative gamesman" who "delights in sporting with his creation, exploiting it as a medium for displaying the fireworks of his creativity."[12] Rather than guide the reader to certainty, the reader is made to realize the unattainability of truth and the pervasiveness of paradox.

However, other critics such as Anne Mellor and Clyde de L. Ryals have noted that the equation of romantic irony with self-reflexivity tends to downplay the way in which romantic irony may be inscribed in a text laterally or horizontally rather than vertically.[13] The orchestration of competing or dichotomous voices that refuses to choose between one and the other but adopts Schlegel's logic of both/and, and tonal ambiguity, such as the juxtaposition of seriousness and humor, is central to romantic irony. Romantic irony always displays a playful authorial self-consciousness with its accompanying sense of address to the spectator—an attitude of hovering or hesitating between two competing views in suspended judgment—but this attitude need not (though it might) involve the breaking of fictional illusion or an overt display of authorial voice. Furst's definition implies the idea of radical paradox or uncertainty that privileges the nature of the telling over the story that is told in a manner that seems inspired by contemporary writers such as Donald Barthelme, Jr., Samuel Beckett, and Jorge Luis Borges. Raymond Immerwahr pointed out many years ago in his subtle analysis of the debate between subjective and objective romantic irony that while romantic irony is not to be equated with the disguise of the narrator in and through his creation in the manner that the theorists of objective romantic irony maintain, neither can it simply be equated with self-reflexivity. Rather "the ironic poet exercises 'objective' restraint by not losing himself in his poetic inspiration but consciously shaping and ordering its diverse products. His 'subjective' license or caprice is a constant readiness to turn from one element of this inspiration to the other."[14]

From this brief review of the literature we can extract two dimensions to the problem of understanding romantic irony which cut across the opposition between "objective" and "subjective." The first dimension involves the relationship between horizontal and vertical form, that is, the nature and role of authorial self-consciousness or self-reflexivity. The second involves the character of the horizontal form, that is, whether it is unitary, divided, or plural in perspective or point of view. On this basis, we can define romantic irony in contrast to two other narrative modes, and here I adapt the conclusions of John Francis Fetzer.[15] In traditional, preromantic irony, irony functions as a rhetorical device where the writer or filmmaker invites the reader to choose between conflicting viewpoints, through presenting the correct viewpoint in the guise of its opposite. The traditional ironist is self-conscious rather than self-reflexive and therefore preserves a unified point of view within the text. In romantic irony, the writer or filmmaker presents competing, opposed perspectives in unstable equilibrium, following Schlegel's both/and logic, with the author self-consciously hovering between them. The articulation of this double perspective entails the insistent presence of a self-conscious or commentative narrator, who will be manifest, periodically, in formal moments of self-reflexivity or metafiction that invoke the relationship between the author and the reader or viewer. In postromantic or modern irony (that Furst confusingly wishes to call romantic irony), the text is not merely bifurcated in point of view but fragmented into paradox and uncertainty. This horizontal dispersal of meaning becomes a product of a narration where the telling is privileged over what is told, narrative collapses into narration, and self-reflexivity is the dominant mode.

Some discussions of romantic irony seem to break off at precisely this point of formal definition. However, it seems to me that a question that is equally fundamental to defining romantic irony is the relationship that the concept bears to a romantic worldview. Most critics seem to agree that the concept has an extension beyond the literature of the romantic period and this is certainly in accordance with Schlegel's definition of romantic poetry. But romantic irony in Schlegel is linked to a romantic attitude or stance that involves the aspiration or quest for the ideal or the absolute following the logic of Fichte's subjective idealism. I shall define the romantic component in romantic irony as *the propensity to measure what is real and finite against what is ideal and absolute*. Thus the orchestration of competing voices in romantic irony has a specific purpose and tone, and that is to foster a sense of the perpetual transcendence of limits and hence of the aspiration toward the ideal.

However, as Furst points out, Schlegel's conception of romantic irony is a double-edged sword. Instead of ascending to an ideal, Schlegel's dialectical irony that relentlessly de-creates and re-creates might provoke a spiral of descent into dejection, melancholy, or nihilism. Instead of creatively transcending the real in self-transformation, the ideal may collapse or implode back into it. According to Ernst Behler, this is precisely the direction the philosophy of irony took in Germany in the early to middle period of the nineteenth century. He quotes philosopher Karl Wilhelm Ferdinand Solger: "Immeasurable sadness must seize us when we see the most glorious entities dissolved into nothingness because of their necessarily earthly existence.... This moment of transition when the idea is destroyed must be the true seat of art.... Here the mind of the artist must combine all directions into one synoptic view. We call this view, soaring above everything and destroying everything, irony."[16] Here the shape of the romantic ironic text orchestrates incompatible or contrasting viewpoints not with a view toward transcendence but in a downward dialectic or spiral of descent.

But there is a third possibility. This would be a form of romantic irony that in terms of its attitude to the ideal is neither positive nor negative but rather holds that ideal itself in suspended judgment. This form of romantic irony would, in Morton L. Gurewitch's terms, blend "a romantic ardor with an anti-romantic animus."[17] Furst criticizes this formulation as one that naively splits off the romantic and ironic components of romantic irony rather than conceiving romantic irony as a composite mode. However, suspended between the ideal and its opposite, this form of romantic irony remains a composite mode. It is just that in this form of romantic irony, the dialectical relationship between the ideal and its opposite remains suspended between its component parts rather than integrated into an upward or downward spiral of descent. Indeed, a text that is structured in this way can be understood as one that hovers between the upward dialectic of transcendence and the downward dialectic of descent. In this sense, the romantic irony of suspended judgment can be viewed as the primary form of romantic irony from which the positive dialectic of transcendence and the downward spiral of descent are generated. As we shall see, these three forms of romantic irony circumscribe the parameters of Hitchcock's romantic irony.

The concept of romantic irony serves both to define and unify Hitchcock's otherwise diverse body of work, which ranges from a romantic thriller like *North by Northwest*, a black comedy like *The Trouble with Harry* (1955), to a horror film like *Psycho* (1960). The romantic ideal in Hitchcock's work is articulated through the value placed upon the realization of love between a man and a woman as a narrative goal. Of course, the story of the formation of the couple is a commonplace convention of popular fiction, and it is a fallacy simply to equate romanticism and the romantic quest for the ideal or for transcendence with romantic love. Yet among romantic writers like Byron, Shelley, and Keats, not to mention Schlegel himself in his unfinished novella *Lucinde*, the romantic ideal *is* expressed in terms of romantic love. Heterosexual romantic love provides an image at once of opposites uniting in a third term, the couple, that is greater than the sum of its parts, and of an ecstatic transcendence that is at once spatial (it goes beyond the world of the ordinary and the everyday) and temporal (it cleaves toward a future of romantic enchantment). Hitchcock's films articulate and emphasize romantic love as an ideal in a manner that is emblematized by his staging of the kiss: Dr. Constance Petersen (Ingrid Bergman) kissing John Ballantine (Gregory Peck) in *Spellbound* (1945) as doorways fly open behind them to infinity, John "Scottie" Ferguson (James Stewart) kissing Judy Barton (Kim Novak) in *Vertigo* as the camera pans around them 360 degrees, Roger Thornhill (Cary Grant) and Eve Kendall (Eva Marie Saint) in *North by Northwest* kissing in a moving train while turning in the manner of a waltz, to give but three examples.[18]

Yet what defines Hitchcock's presentation of heterosexual romance as an ideal is the manner in which it is entwined with its opposite—human perversity. It is as if, in a very Freudian way, sexuality is a source of profound anxiety for Hitchcock. We may speculate about Hitchcock's personal biography, but my concern in this book is the way that the form taken by Hitchcock's work arises from his preoccupation with human perversity. In a literal sense, perversity is associated in Hitchcock's work with the fact of human sexuality itself, considered as the uninhibited expression of impulse that is free of any moral or social restraint, as in Freud's phrase "polymorphous perversity." Human perversity is therefore associated with death—that is, with the potential at once for the annihilation of the other and for self-dissolution. Often in Hitchcock's films, lurking within the gentleman-hero, lies a sexual predator or a murderer of women, like Cary Grant's character, John Aysgarth ("Johnnie"), in *Suspicion*, who seems intent on murdering his wife. And beneath the ostensibly pure or virginal heroine lies the sexually promiscuous woman or the "whore" that is suggested by Ingrid Bergman's character in *Notorious* (1946) or by Grace Kelly's character in *To Catch a Thief* (1955). Both these heroines are cool Hitchcock blondes who harbor incipient promiscuity beneath their ladylike exterior. The formation of the couple and the portrayal of the kiss are haunted by a sense of perversity and incipient deadliness that is captured in the advertising tagline for *Suspicion*: "Each time they kissed, there was the thrill of love . . . The threat of murder!" The logic that unites romantic love and human perversity or life and death in Hitchcock's works is the both/and logic of romantic irony in which romantic love and human perversity are at once utterly opposed to one another and yet also, paradoxically, closely identified.

In general, Hitchcock, the narrator, self-consciously draws attention to the force of perversity by suggesting rather than by showing it. Hitchcock is an aesthete in the very precise sense that the extraordinary formal realization of his works functions as a displaced expression of human sexuality. Raymond Durgnat has spoken of Hitchcock as a democratic rather than aristocratic aesthete.[19] In Hitchcock's cinema, all human sexuality carries the aura of perversity; its secret pleasures are not condemned but are made available to all; and they are not cordoned off for the subtle delectation of a knowing few. Hitchcock's aestheticism may collude in the articulation of the romantic ideal, as in the frenzied fireworks' montage of the deliriously romantic *To Catch a Thief*; it may ambiguously connote romance as an ideal or as an idealization that harbors destruction, as in the romantic/vampiric kiss in *The Lodger* (1926); or it may evoke the frenzy of annihilation, as in the tour de force shower scene montage in *Psycho*.

These possibilities encapsulate the way in which the three kinds of romantic irony I have already outlined inform Hitchcock's work. The first kind of romantic irony, romantic irony as romantic renewal (or *romantic* irony), is

Regardless, Soviet montage did influence the German expressionists, who were a formative influence on Hitchcock during his stint in Germany in 1924 – 25, as well as works of the French avant-garde such as Fernand Léger's *Ballet mécanique* (1924), which was screened, alongside Weimar films, at the London Film Society, which Hitchcock habitually attended in the mid-twenties. These influences result in what I shall term Hitchcock's analytical expressionism, a technique of embedding the visual rhetoric of expressionism with the framework of analytical editing that characterizes the classical Hollywood style, in a manner that at once sustains the character-centered causal drive of cinematic storytelling and preserves a self-conscious commentary upon the events in the story world.

Orchestration of Internal and External Artifice

Hitchcock scholar Lesley Brill uses the terms "internal and external artifice" to describe the self-conscious theatricality and sense of fiction that is attached to the presentation and performance of character and star persona in Hitchcock's films (internal artifice), and to Hitchcock's orchestration of the stylistic elements of film such as editing, lighting, mise-en-scène, and camera movement to create a self-consciously theatricalized, aestheticized, or fictive aura (external artifice).[25] Furthermore, Brill points to a key distinction in Hitchcock's works between those films in which internal and external artifice function to create a world of playful fictiveness and those films in which the pervasive sense of theatricality and fictiveness is an index of a demonic or fallen world.

In this book I argue that Hitchcock's artifice is invariably associated with the presence of a human sexuality that is deemed to be incipiently perverse. But in those works where artifice is playful and benign, like *The 39 Steps* and *North by Northwest*, the lure of human "perversity" is one that spices up the romance and fuels the movement of the narrative toward romantic-ironic redemption. In his ambivalent works like *The Lodger*, *Suspicion*, or *Shadow of a Doubt*, the status of artifice and the lure of "perversity" it harbors are ambiguous, at best offering the promise of romantic renewal, and at worst potentially life-threatening. In his darker works, like *Vertigo* and *Psycho*, artifice and theatricality render the world a profoundly untrustworthy place. In both of these films the central protagonist is lured toward destruction by a character that plays someone else. In *Vertigo*, Judy Barton masquerades as the possessed wife of another man and, under his tutelage, lures the protagonist Scottie Ferguson to witness an apparent suicide. In *Psycho*, Norman Bates appears to be innocent of a crime that we believe his mother has committed, when all along he is the criminal whose personality is demonically fused with that of his mother whose clothes he wears. Hitchcock, the narrator, in temporary league with these incipiently demonic characters, disguises the truth of who these characters are.

Visual and Aural Expressionism: The Rhetoric of the Double

Hitchcock employs the rhetoric of the double articulated through the aesthetics of visual expressionism in order to evoke the presence of what Robin Wood calls "the chaos world," a world of human perversity that exists beneath the veneer of the everyday.[26] This shadow world appears as a psychological projection of a character's state of mind. For example, when Lina McLaidlaw (Joan Fontaine) fears that her husband Johnnie Aysgarth is going to murder her in *Suspicion*, her fears are registered by the spider webs' shadows on the walls of her house. But the shadow world is also, equally, in accordance with the logic of romantic irony, something that is wholly external to the character—a threatening and alien other. Johnnie in *Suspicion* may indeed be trying to murder his wife, and the analogy between his character and a spider suggests his predatory, murderous nature.

The protagonist of Hitchcock's films is typically doubled in a pattern that begins with the earliest films such as *The Pleasure Garden* (1925), *The Lodger*, and *The Ring* (1927). The straight, ostensibly moral hero is paralleled and contrasted to the figure of the incipiently perverse criminal, as in the contrast between Devlin (Cary Grant) and Alexander Sebastian (Claude Rains) in *Notorious*, or between Roger Thornhill and Phillip Vandamm (James Mason) in *North by Northwest*. In most cases, as in these films, the opposed protagonists are in love with the same woman, creating a triangular relationship that emphasizes the affinities between the two male leads. Furthermore, often the criminal is an alluring dandified figure like the flamboyant Bruno Anthony (Robert Walker) in *Strangers on a Train*, or even someone who elicits our sympathy, like the unfortunate Alex Sebastian in *Notorious*. Alex finds himself married to an American agent who exploits his evident feelings for her (though she, too, is in part a victim of circumstances). Occasionally, it is the female character who is doubled in this way, as in Hitchcock's first English film, *The Pleasure Garden,* where the showgirl protagonists are divided between the morally wholesome Patsy Brand (Virginia Valli) and the gold-digger Jill Cheyne (Carmelita Geraghty), and his first American film *Rebecca*, where the second wife of Maxim de Winter (Laurence Olivier) is the double of his first wife, Rebecca herself.

Tonal Ambiguity and Black Comedy

As James Naremore and Susan Smith have pointed out, Hitchcock's films are characterized by a seriocomic tonal ambiguity.[27] Hitchcock's romances, like *The 39 Steps* and *North by Northwest,* often treat the depredations undergone by their protagonists with humor. For example, when Roger Thornhill, abducted by the henchmen of the villain Vandamm, is set up for a murder that will look like a suicide, the circumstances of his "poisoning" with alcohol and perilous drive along the cliff and subsequent pursuit by the police are played for laughs and include a final comic collision with the police car that is reminiscent of the sight gags of silent comedy. In making light of something ostensibly bleak, black comedy epitomizes the both/and logic of romantic irony.

This use of black comedy as a relief from suspense can structure a whole work. Thus Hitchcock's late dark film, *Frenzy* (1972), is organized around a contrast between the story of an impotent and psychotic sexual murderer of women, Bob Rusk (Barry Foster), and the domestic melodrama of a henpecked detective, Chief Inspector Oxford (Alec McCowen) and his wife Mrs. Oxford (Vivien Merchant). Oxford resiliently survives his wife's sadistic, though comic, imposition of obscene gourmet food (undoubtedly substituting for sex in their marriage), while she solves the crime and blames him for imprisoning the wrong man.

However, in other contexts, black comedy can contribute to suspense, providing an excuse for allegiance with the villain in Hitchcock's film. Hitchcock not only invites our sympathy with the devil by endowing villains such as Bruno Anthony in *Strangers on a Train* or Bob Rusk in *Frenzy* with engaging character traits and aligning us with their point of view; in these contexts (as I shall explore in chapter 2), suspense itself becomes a species of black comedy.

Hitchcock's tonal ambiguity not only relieves us in moments of suspense or solicits identification with the villain, it often drives a wedge between the emotions that a scene ought to solicit and the way in which we are actually invited to respond, in a way that leaves the spectator anxious or uneasy. Often Hitchcock creates this effect by portraying and creating laughter where it is radically inappropriate to the dramatic context. For example, toward the conclusion of *Saboteur* (1942), the criminal Fry (Norman Lloyd), pursued by police, enters a "music hall" that evokes Radio City in New York, where a melodramatic love triangle plays out on a giant screen. A woman protests that her lover must leave before another man, presumably her husband, shoots him to death. But the audience responds in fits of laughter, apparently finding the idea that a man might get shot to be a joke. This inflects with comedy the deadly pursuit being played out with Fry and the police. Then Hitchcock himself compounds the tonal ambiguity by joking upon the idea of being shot in a film with a visual and aural pun. A man on the film screen, who claims he has a real gun, shoots. Then, apparently in response, a man in the auditorium appears to fall from a wound but is actually only laughing. Thus, we the audience is encouraged to laugh. Then Fry shoots his gun in silhouette in front of the large screen, looking as if he is a man in the movie, his shot disguised as a film shot. A policemen shoots back from the auditorium, and the man who previously only appeared to be shot is actually shot. Are we supposed to laugh or scream?

Multiple and Ambiguous Endings

Hitchcock's films often, even typically, end on a note of ambiguity or irresolution that reflects Hitchcock's commitment to the both/and logic of romantic irony. Different endings, often of profoundly different tone, exist for a number of Hitchcock films. Both the existence of these multiple endings, and the fact that Hitchcock often opts for the more unresolved or open-ended one, suggest the structuring ambiguity of Hitchcock's narratives. The ending of *The Pleasure Garden* exists in two different versions (along with a number of other significant scene differences). In the longer version of the film the conclusion is downbeat. The heroine Patsy Brand joins the delirious hero, Hugh Fielding (John Stuart), who has fallen victim to fever in the Far East: "We both suffered … what have either of us got to live for now?" declares Patsy. Hugh responds, "We have one of the greatest things of life … youth." Given the fact that Hugh has just risen like Lazarus from a stretcher, this declaration is decidedly unconvincing. In the shorter so-called Rohauer version of the film released in 1971 (named after the collector who saved and reconstructed it), the ending is much more conventional and upbeat as the hero returns with the heroine to her home to be greeted by the parental figures of her landlord and landlady, and by Patsy's beloved dog, who yaps at his heels with delight.

Vertigo also has two endings. The official-release ending leaves the hero of the film, Scottie, poised helplessly over the edge of a bell tower that the woman he loves, Judy, has plunged from moments before. This is a repetition of an earlier fall in the film, a staged event which Scottie witnessed but was helpless to prevent. The ending leaves the audience with an acute sense of loss and fails to tie up the loose ends. The second version of the ending returns us to the beginning as Scottie, in a state of shock, enters the apartment of his old friend Midge (Barbara Bel Geddes). We hear on a radio that the villain, Gavin Elster (Tom Helmore), is being sought by the police, and we also hear a strange tale about a cow being led up the steps of a college. This story at once evokes the college days of Midge and Scottie and also makes a darkly comic joke about Judy's prior ascent of the bell tower, dragged by Scottie, before her fall. Like the cow, Judy cannot get back down the steps. The scene ends with Scottie standing in silence overlooking the dark panorama of San Francisco. This alternative ending remains downbeat, but it at least allows the audience to imagine some kind of future for Scottie and Midge and suggests that Elster will be brought to justice.

Hitchcock scholar Bill Krohn has studied in detail the multiple endings of *Suspicion* in relation to the overall ambiguous structure of the work.[28] Krohn shows that Hitchcock toyed insistently with the possibility of an alternate ending in which Grant, the potential wife murderer, is shown to be guilty, even to the point of possibly shooting extra scenes during production that he could insert, if he so decided, to demonstrate Johnnie's guilt. The three endings he actually shot all show that Johnnie is, against the odds, an innocent man. However, the one he let stand preserves ambiguity. Johnnie, having "confessed" to Lina his innocence of an intent to kill, and vowing to mend his ways, is forgiven by Lina. The car in which he is driving her away from their home and back to her mother does a U-turn in front of the camera. As they drive back into the space of the frame, Johnnie coils his arm around Lina in a gesture that recalls the images of natural predation that have been associated with him throughout the film. Is this a romantic embrace or a snakelike coil of death?

Voyeruism and Self-reflexivity

As legions of critics have pointed out, Hitchcock's interest in the cinema is one that exploits the physical, objectifying, "pornographic" qualities of the medium that certain film theorists have claimed is inherent to it.[29] In this way, even the affirmation of romantic love has an aura of perversity about it. In his staging of the kiss, Hitchcock's camera dwells in tight close-up upon the intimacy of the couple as if it was, as Hitchcock described it, the third party in a *ménage à trois*.[30] In Hitchcock's home movie collection, there is a particularly revealing home movie in which Hitchcock himself puckishly acts out this *ménage à trois* on the set of *Blackmail* (1929) with Anny Ondra who plays the female lead and Cyril Ritchard who plays the attempted rapist she kills. Hitchcock himself presses the lips of the protagonists together and then playfully takes the place of the male protagonist and kisses Ondra himself![31]

Theories of voyeurism in the cinema tend to align the look of the camera with the look of a character within a film. For example, Robert Stam and Roberta Pearson argue that the audience is aligned through Hitchcock's use of the point-of-view shot with the voyeuristic look of the character L. B. Jefferies in *Rear Window*.[32] However, a film audience is never simply aligned with the voyeuristic gaze of a character, for only the fictional character is an actual voyeur; the film spectator is at best a camera-voyeur. *Rear Window* and other Hitchcock films exploit and explore the affinity and distance between voyeurism that may be evoked by looking at a film image and voyeurism. By inviting the audience to share the point of view of the character who is a voyeur, Hitchcock provides the spectator an excuse or pretext for engaging in camera voyeurism; after all, it is the character, not me, the spectator, who is really a voyeur. At the same time, the spectator is also in a position to reflect upon both the voyeurism of the character in the fiction and the position they are encouraged to occupy or refuse.

Romantic Irony

The Author in the Film

Hitchcock's cameos are a well-known feature of his work. They playfully draw attention to Hitchcock, the director, as a presence behind the work, by inscribing that presence, not as a character in his films but as the flesh-and-blood director himself who populates his own film as an extra. Following the example of Raymond Bellour, Michael Walker has analyzed these cameo appearances in detail and draws attention to their main characteristics. Often, though not always, Hitchcock's appearances occur at the beginning of his films, which is congruent with their role in playfully acknowledging Hitchcock's authorship. Hitchcock often appears in a public space "as a (usually unobserved) guest, fellow traveler or casual passer by"—for example, sitting on a train in *Blackmail*, getting on a train in *Spellbound*, and trying to get on a bus in *North by Northwest*.[33] In this way Hitchcock announces his allegiance with his audience as an ordinary member of the public. This is further reinforced by the fact that, as Susan Smith points out, Hitchcock often makes himself the butt of his own joke. She cites the cameo in *Blackmail* where he is assailed by an unruly boy and the Reduco advertisement in *Lifeboat* (1944), where the fat Hitchcock strikes a lively pose and the slim Hitchcock looks depressed.[34] This also applies to the scene in *Marnie* analyzed in detail by Bellour, where Hitchcock looks after Marnie Edgar (Tippi Hedren) and looks back at the camera, as if he has been caught out being a voyeur.[35]

Walker also notes that Hitchcock's cameos are often carefully timed interventions in the story which signal a decisive shift in the action as the protagonist "crosses a threshold" into the shadow world.[36] Thus, in *Psycho*, Hitchcock appears outside the office where Marion Crane (Janet Leigh) works just before she is tempted to steal the $40,000. In *Strangers on a Train*, Hitchcock gets on the train in which Guy Haines (Farley Granger) is bound for Metcalf to confront his estranged wife in a scene that provides Bruno with "symbolic" justification to murder Miriam Haines (Laura Elliott) on Guy's behalf. Hitchcock also carries a double bass, his own symbolic double, just as Bruno is the double of Guy. These appearances achieve their most self-conscious form when Hitchcock actually seems to acknowledge his role in orchestrating or precipitating the narrative action. This is nicely illustrated in his cameo appearance in *Rear Window*, where the attentive viewer will observe Hitchcock repairing the clock in the apartment of a composer who is struggling to write the song that will become the love theme of the film. As John Fawell has argued, Hitchcock, through this gesture, identifies himself with the composer as the orchestrator of his film (perhaps reminded by Jean Renoir's far more complex elaboration of this analogy in *Rules of the Game* [1939]).[37]

As some of these cameos suggest, Hitchcock also figures in his text in a more allegorical way as the double of his characters. When he appears holding the double bass in *Strangers on a Train*, Hitchcock is at once identified with Guy Haines, but equally with Bruno, his dark double. In *Rear Window*, the cameo aligns him with the composer, but Hitchcock is also identified with L. B Jefferies, who bestows names like "Miss Torso" and "Miss Lonely Hearts" upon the "characters" across the courtyard in the manner of a director. Sometimes Hitchcock casts a character in a film with whom he bears a clear physical resemblance, such as the saboteur Mr. Verloc (Oscar Homolka) in *Sabotage* (1936), who, as Susan Smith writes, "in his dual role as cinema proprietor and saboteur serves as a rather compelling, complex surrogate for Hitchcock."[38] More generally, as William Rothman points out, Hitchcock is aligned in his films with the figure of the "gamesman aesthete" who serves to orchestrate narrative events within the film, whether it is the figure of the ostensible hero, like the actor-writer-director Sir John Menier (Herbert Marshall) in *Murder!*, or the figure of the villain, like the duplicitous Gavin Elster in *Vertigo*, who orchestrates the web of deception in which the character of Scottie Ferguson is ensnared.[39]

However, Hitchcock's authorial surrogacy extends beyond male characters (hero and villain alike) to the female characters in his work. Paula Cohen has demonstrated the manner in which Hitchcock's use of his daughter (Patricia Hitchcock) as a kind of Hitchcock surrogate in three of his films—*Stage Fright* (1950), *Strangers on a Train*, and *Psycho*—suggests Hitchcock's alignment with the point of view of the young female character.[40] And Michael Walker has ingeniously pointed to a connection or identification between Hitchcock and Grace Kelly. In *To Catch a Thief*, Hitchcock appears on a bus on which John Robie (Cary Grant) is escaping the police, his face half-bisected as a kind of Janus face (see chapter 5). Walker points out that Hitchcock actually takes the place of the Grace Kelly character who is sitting on the bus in David Dodge's novel from which the film was adapted. Only this fact, it seems, can account for the strange look that Cary Grant gives the director. Would Hitchcock like to be Grace Kelly for Cary Grant?[41]

Most of these formal and stylistic aspects of romantic irony are evident in Hitchcock's remarkable third film, *The Lodger,* which I believe functions as a baseline work for understanding Hitchcock's subsequent films and provides a veritable anthology of his future filmmaking practice. In *The Lodger,* a mysterious man, the Lodger, played by matinee idol Ivor Novello with the aristocratic mannerisms and sartorial heir of a dandy and an aesthete, appears suddenly at the working-class household of the blonde heroine, who is courted by a dull but apparently dependable policeman, Joe Betts (Malcolm Keen). The Lodger's appearance coincides with a series of brutal murders of blonde women, of "golden curls," by "the Avenger," and his actions cast suspicion, especially in the mind of the landlady, Mrs. Bunting. The Lodger exhibits a curious fascination for and repulsion from the pictures of golden-curled women on his bedroom wall; he anxiously paces his room; he mysteriously enters and leaves the house; and his room contains a map of the murders. Yet while he is a suspected serial killer, Novello's lodger is also a romantic hero who becomes the object of affection to Daisy Bunting (June), the daughter of the house, who steadfastly protests his innocence.

Hitchcock creates competing, unambiguous points of view, both contradictory and undecidable, that focus on the identity of the Lodger. Is the Lodger an aristocratic, amateur sleuth seeking to capture the criminal who murdered his sister or is he that criminal himself? Is he a figure of threat or sympathy? Is he a gentleman or a sexual predator? In both roles, the Lodger appears as the figure of the "gamesman-aesthete" authoring the world of the film, either as the presumptively impotent aristocratic dandy-criminal ranging over the spaces of urban modernity like a vampire-alien preying on unwary victims, or as the dandy Holmesian detective who channels potentially antisocial impulses (he is, after all, perfectly able and willing to take the law into his own hands) toward the social good. Either way he is a figure who seeks to bring into being or "author" a certain kind of outcome in the social world, and thus in both roles he functions as an authorial surrogate for Alfred Hitchcock. Hitchcock appears early on in the film as a newspaper editor who gesticulates in animated fashion as news of another murder rolls off the presses. It is perhaps tempting to interpret this as Hitchcock's first self-conscious cameo that suggests the alignment of his own film, as part of a mass medium, with the role of the print media in whipping up public hysteria, as Tom Cohen does in a recent book. But Hitchcock himself rejects the idea that his role, at this stage, was an intentional cameo; rather he was filling in for a bit-part actor who failed to arrive: "It was strictly utilitarian; we had to fill the screen."[42]

Hitchcock orchestrates the relationship between objective and subjective point of view in *The Lodger* in the "macro" sense of orchestrating point of view in relation to suspense, but also in the "micro" sense of anticipating the rhetoric of analytic expressionism that became the hallmark of his mature style. Hitchcock's innovative use of what he termed "subjective suspense" is illustrated in a sequence in the film where the Lodger, creeping out for a nocturnal assignation (is he going out to kill a blonde or rescue her?), is overheard by the landlady, Mrs. Bunting, who eavesdrops at her bedroom door. Hitchcock creates a sustained pattern of alternation between Mrs. Bunting straining to hear him and the Lodger creeping down the stairs.[43] Because *The Lodger* is a silent film, the idea that Mrs. Bunting is listening to the Lodger is only conveyed through Hitchcock's editing, thereby foregrounding the hand of Hitchcock, the narrator, who *shows* the audience what the character can only (strain to) hear. In a broader sense, while we share the character's anxiety about the Lodger, the detachment from her point of view afforded by Hitchcock's analytical editing also ensures that we can respond to her reaction as a needless worry. We may view the Lodger's careful steps as motivated by the innocent desire to not wake and unduly disturb her rather than as a sign of his guilt and fear of discovery.

Furthermore, in *The Lodger*, a deadly serious question—"Is the Lodger a psychotic killer?"—becomes for Hitchcock a source of entertainment, of black comedy. Hitchcock playfully deploys the rhetoric of expressionist mise-en-scène and commentative editing to hint at a predatory vampirism and to evoke the shadow world of perverse desire. By subtle editing and visual symbolism, Hitchcock orchestrates a point of view of the character's motivation that differs from the point of view of the heroine, such that we imagine him entertaining predatory and murderous impulses that she appears not to see. Rather than share her suspense, as in the case of Mrs. Bunting, here we fear on Daisy's behalf. For example, when Daisy brings the Lodger his breakfast and, for the first time, they are in close proximity, we see the Lodger in close-up pick up a knife from the breakfast table. In a masklike profile shot, we see a gleam of light on the Lodger's teeth as his mouth is frozen slightly open. Beneath the controlled, gentlemanly veneer may lie a chaotic murderous desire. It turns out that the Lodger uses the knife, innocently, to flick an unsightly speck (of food?) from

Daisy's clothing, but even this gesture is ambiguous given the Lodger's intense preoccupation with the image of the feminine. Later, Daisy and the Lodger play chess in front of the fireplace. As Daisy reaches to pick up a chess piece, we see that the Lodger, unknown to her, has picked up a poker which is poised in the frame close to her head. At this moment, Hitchcock cuts to Joe, the erstwhile boyfriend, arriving at the house—he has just been put on the Avenger case—and when we return to the couple, the Lodger is stoking a raging fire with his poker. He puts the poker down and impulsively reaches to caress Daisy's hair. "Beautiful Golden Hair," he asserts, and they look into each other's eyes before they and the camera nervously pull back.

Hitchcock's visual narration suggests a motivation that the heroine does not share. And yet we cannot help asking why is it that the heroine is attracted to a man that her mother suspects is a serial murderer. In this way, it is as if Hitchcock's voyeuristic camera is inviting us to entertain a motivation possessed by the character that the character herself cannot acknowledge—namely, that the Lodger is alluring in virtue of his possession of these concealed predatory desires, desires that are romantic precisely to the extent that they remain contained and concealed within the mask of respectability. Hitchcock shoots the kiss between Daisy and the Lodger in a shot/reverse-shot. Daisy looks in medium shot with chest heaving and eyes glinting. The Lodger in reverse shot approaches the camera, his pallid face highlighted against a black background that abstracts the figure from space. His accentuated half-opened lips approach the camera in tight close-up (the lips of a vampire?). Hitchcock cuts to a medium two-shot as the Lodger hesitates, intoxicated by her golden curls. Is he afraid of the kiss and of the desires it awakens or is he overtaken by longing? Finally, slowly, in tight close-up, their white faces framed against a black background, the couple kiss, and Hitchcock cuts to an overhead shot as Daisy's head and eyes fall back in a swoon.

The ending of *The Lodger* is both doubled and ambiguous. After the Lodger has been exonerated, and the real murderer has ostensibly been caught, we see the Lodger in long shot languishing on a hospital bed where the doctor reports that while he has had a severe nervous strain his youth and energy will pull him through. He languidly puts out his arm, and Daisy, sitting beside him, clasps it. Then a title self-consciously announces, "All stories have an end." We are introduced to the Lodger's mansion. The

Lodger leads Daisy up a sweeping staircase and they embrace in front of a large window. Again, the Lodger is intoxicated by her hair, while outside the window a neon sign flashes "Tonight Golden Girls," a sign whose earlier display in the film signaled both the dance revue, the promise of romance, and the possibility of murder. While the sign, as seen through the window, is now diminished in size and "contained" within the scene, in a manner that might suggest, as Charles Barr contends, that the threat it represents has been finally neutralized,[44] it also connotes the sense that the threat has migrated into domestic space, in a way that anticipates Hitchcock's later narratives like *Rebecca* or *Suspicion*, where the figure of Jack the Ripper now becomes an incipient Bluebeard or wife murderer.

The Forms of Romantic Irony

Having identified the salient stylistic and narrational characteristics of Hitchcock's romantic irony, I shall now explore in more detail how the both/and logic of romantic irony in Hitchcock's work results in different forms of storytelling according to whether the romantic ideal is renewed, undercut, or viewed with ambivalence.

Romantic Irony as Romantic Renewal

As we have seen, Hitchcock's romantic irony is characterized by artifice: both internal artifice such as self-conscious references on the part of characters to the fact that they are performing roles, and external artifice that consists in Hitchcock's commentative, self-conscious narration. This artifice is linked to the pervasive presence of perversity, of those anarchic energies that are concealed beneath the often repressive veneer of human civilization and civility. In Hitchcock's narratives of romantic renewal, this sense of the arbitrariness or fictiveness of the story world and of anarchic energies that upset any sense of a stable ordered narrative universe gives vitality to the romance which thrives on the unreliability of appearances and draws upon the perverse or anarchic impulses that undermine stability and order. Hitchcock's male characters may be flawed, his female characters duplicitous and deceiving, and circumstances may conspire against them, but it is precisely out of these conditions that what Lesley Brill calls the "miracle" of romance is forged, its success always assured by the benign intervention of the narrator.[45]

The sensibility of romantic irony in the mode of romantic renewal is exemplified by the magical match on action that concludes Hitchcock's finest achievement in this mode, *North by Northwest*. On the sheer face of Mount Rushmore, Roger Thornhill holds Eve Kendall in one hand at full stretch by the wrist as she dangles below him, while he clings to the lip of a cliff with the fingertips of his other hand, which the foot of a villain has just crushed. In a sublime match on action, Hitchcock cuts from this situation of certain disaster—we imagine Thornhill unwilling to let go of the woman he loves and plunging with her to his death, or perhaps worse, surviving the fall for which he would blame himself—to a shot of Thornhill pulling Eve up to a cozy nuptial bed on a transcontinental express. Hitchcock concludes the sequence, and the film as a whole, with a final cut to the express train rattling into a tunnel.

Hitchcock's match on action perfectly illustrates how ironic juxtaposition provokes romantic transcendence in a Schlegelian manner, at once dramatizing and overcoming the contrast between the real and the ideal. The horror of separation and death, represented by the protagonists on the edge of extinction, is juxtaposed with the comedy of their coming together suggested by the train rattling into the tunnel as a metaphor of sexual intercourse. Formally, the sequence contrasts a high-angle, open-frame long shot down into the void over which the characters are suspended in a state of paralyzed limbo, with a low-angle shot that signifies ascent into the cozy nestlike space of the bunk. The transition consists of an ironic reversal in the sense that the second scene negates the first, but it is an ironic reversal associated with transcendence. Furthermore, it is made possible by what is self-evidently an authorial intervention, which takes the punning form of a match on action and a Freudian joke. All the salient features of romantic irony are thus evident: the internal "horizontal" structure of dialectical opposition between elements; the self-conscious intervention of the narrator that "vertically" orchestrates the dialectical opposition in a genuine moment of "transcendental buffoonery"; and the sense of romantic transcendence from the real to the ideal that in Hitchcock's work is embodied in the formation of the couple.

However, perhaps what most distinguishes this moment of romantic irony as distinctively Hitchcockian is the sense of human perversity that underlies it. The nature of the irony here lies not simply in the sense that the moment of romantic transcendence emerges in contrast to its opposite, but in the notion that romantic love emerges out of the situation of a man holding the woman he loves by her wrist while dangling from a precipice, and of a woman being held that way. In other words, it is not simply that the marital bed is a negation of the situation where a man kills the woman he loves, but it incorporates and continues that thought. Elsewhere, in Hitchcock's more ironically ambivalent works, the expression of human "perversity," where perversity is identified in Hitchcock's Edwardian sensibilities with the domain of human sexuality itself, works against the assertion of the heterosexual romantic ideal. But within the form of romantic irony that structures Hitchcock's narratives of romantic renewal, the force that may elsewhere be opposed to the binding of love actually makes love possible. Hence the sequence concludes with the delirious visual metaphor of the train violently entering the tunnel, which always, in my experience, provokes pleasant laughter in the audience.

The role of human perversity in Hitchcock's narratives of romantic renewal is further illustrated in two precursors of *North by Northwest*—*The 39 Steps* and *To Catch a Thief*. In *The 39 Steps*, Hitchcock adopts from the Scottish novelist John Buchan, who wrote the original story, the idea of the wrong man—the hero who is wrongly accused of a crime and traps the criminals to clear his name, in this case an organization of spies that poses a threat to national security. In Buchan's novel, the "wrong man" narrative is merely a plot device that underscores the thin line between civilization and chaos, and there is no heroine to foster a romantic interest. However, in Hitchcock's adaptation of the Buchan narrative, the wrong man becomes romantically desirable on account of his position in the fiction as an outlaw, even as we, the audience, know that he is innocent. Protest as she does about the hero's villainy, the heroine that Hitchcock and his collaborators added to Buchan's story protests too much, for we know that this protest only further sustains the fiction that the hero is an outlaw, a factor that is, in turn, the very source of his romantic allure. Trading on the audience's knowledge of the hero's innocence and the heroine's willful failure to acknowledge the fact, Hitchcock contrives circumstances in which the hero and heroine are literally handcuffed together in such a way that the heroine is "forced" to acknowledge the hero's charms, even as she protests to the contrary.

The concrete metaphor of the handcuffs in *The 39 Steps* precisely captures the logic of romantic irony in Hitchcock's redemptive romantic thrillers and the relationship between Hitchcock's fascination with human perversity and his self-consciously punning narration. First, out of an utterly random event a permanent union is forged. The romantic thriller turns contingency or arbitrariness to the advantage of the romance, rather than showing up its limitations. Second, the positive or regenerative dimension of the romance is created out of a negative constraint. The common idea of marriage as a prison is at once invoked and transcended by the thought that handcuffing places these strangers in delicious physical proximity. Third, as Hitchcock remarks to Truffaut: "There is also a sexual connotation, I think. When I visited the Vice Museum in Paris, I noticed there was considerable evidence of sexual aberrations through restraint."[46] That is, Hitchcock uses the handcuffs to suggest that it is the very threatening quality of the hero that renders him a source of (masochistic) desire, while the resistance of the heroine to the hero renders her a source of (sadistic) delight.

In *To Catch a Thief*, Hitchcock revisits the formula of *The 39 Steps* in a manner that divests the thriller narrative entirely of its national security framework and allows him to realize what is perhaps his most perversely romantic work. Hitchcock and screenwriter John Michael Hayes give the idea of the wrong man a further brilliant twist in a manner that fully exploits the Grant persona. Grant plays renowned jewel thief John Robie, called "The Cat," who has apparently retired from his trade. However, a spree of catlike crimes lead the police to believe that he has resumed his activities. Robie's identity as a "jewel thief" overtly consisted of stealing money from rich widows who languish on the French Riviera by sneaking into their hotel rooms at night, but the implication is clearly that he stole more than simply jewels. Although, as the story begins, Robie is, literally speaking, the wrong man— that is, he is not committing the crimes we witness at the beginning of the film—he is, in another sense, the culprit. Or rather, the film allows us (morally speaking) to have our cake and eat it. We know that an older, wiser Robie has retired and paid for his crimes; we also know that beneath the façade of the country gentleman who cultivates his vineyards is the roguish youth. Indeed, Cary Grant's own former occupation as an acrobat is playfully alluded to in the film when John Robie says to an insurance agent that it was his youthful training as a trapeze artist that prepared him for thieving.

The nature of Robie/Grant's allure is made explicit once Robie, in the risible disguise of Conrad Burns, an American lumberman from Oregon, seeks to preempt the new cat's activities by monitoring potential victims, including heiress Francie Stevens (Grace Kelly), who is immediately attracted to him. Francie insists that Grant is really "the Cat," for it gives her the necessary excuse to present herself to him as someone who wishes nothing more than for her jewels to be stolen. At the same time, he can insist (without lying) that he is not the cat and thereby preserve the veneer of respectability that is necessary to his allure. Just as Hitchcock exploits Grant's star persona, he exploits the persona of Kelly who, beneath her "clean" angelic exterior, was rumored to be sexually "promiscuous."[47] Thus the film presents what might appear to be a thoroughly ironic view of romance. As one critic has put it, their relationship appears based not on mutual understanding but mutual objectification.[48] But, of course, their mutual understanding lies in their mutual exploitation. It is their delight in artifice, disguise, and double-entendre—shared by Hitchcock, the narrator, who contrives this concoction—that creates and sustains erotic frisson. "You really want to see fireworks … it's better with the lights out," says Francie, as she begins turning out the lights in their hotel room. Ostensibly she wants to watch the fireworks show, but really she dims the lights to stage the display of her own "jewels." "I've a feeling that tonight you are going to see one of the Riviera's most fascinating sights … I was talking about the fireworks … [but] the way you looked at my necklace I didn't know." (By denying the connection between fireworks and jewelry she is, of course, also denying the connection implicitly made between jewelry and her own sexuality/genitalia, which she thereby draws attention to.) Robie, feigning disinterest, claims that he has the same interest in jewelry as he has "in women who need weird excitement." (Robie here connects his interest in the jewelry with perversion, in the context of disclaiming concern for either.) They sit down on a couch while white "male" fountain fireworks and red "female" starburst fireworks flare and burst behind them. "Look, John, hold them … diamonds … the only thing in the world you can't resist," Francie declares, as she places a "diamond" necklace in his hands and her neck at his disposal. "You know as well as I do this necklace is imitation," he responds, finally admitting his expertise as a thief. "Well, I'm not," she replies, as they both give in to desire and the fireworks fill the screen in a frenzied, self-consciously speeded-up explosion. As in *North by Northwest*, Hitchcock affirms the romance through an obscene visual pun.

Romantic Irony

Romantic Irony as Ironic Ambivalence

Where romantic irony takes the form of redemptive renewal, the anarchic forces of human perversity find expression within the framework of romantic love, providing a negative energy that refuels romance and, as we have seen, Hitchcock, the omniscient narrator, colludes in making this possible. In many of Hitchcock's films, however, the forces of human perversity lie outside the framework of romantic love, not simply working against its restoration but providing a competing center of entertainment and even allegiance.

As we have already seen, in the case of Hitchcock's film *The Lodger*, much of the competition is yielded by Hitchcock's mode of narration, where through strategies of humor, suspense, doubling, and expressionist visual style, he entertains the audience with the thought that the forces of corruption or immorality might be victorious, and even teases the audience into a temporary allegiance with those forces. In each case, Hitchcock's mode of narration reveals a perspective upon the narrative situation that goes beyond the limited point of view of the central character within it. These strategies are evident in *Suspicion*, which is in many ways a Hollywood remake of *The Lodger*, although now the "hero" is married to the heroine whose life he threatens and the presumption is one of his guilt rather than innocence. As in *The Lodger*, Hitchcock's romantic irony works at once "horizontally," creating conflicting interpretations upon what we see and hear, and "vertically," engendering a gap or distance between the playful stance of the narrator and the point of view of the central character within the fiction.

For example, at the beginning of the film Johnnie lures Lina out of the stuffy family domicile for a trip to church with a bunch of admirers, but before they enter, he whisks her away from the party (and from behind a policeman's back), to a hilltop where, after an abrupt ellipse we see them struggling in long shot as nature's wild wind billows around them. "What do you think I was trying to do? Kill you?" Johnnie asks. "Nothing less than murder could justify such violent self-defense! Look at you ... Oh, I'm just beginning to understand. You thought I was going to kiss you, didn't you." But what really happened on the hilltop? Perhaps what occurred was a romantic embrace, sharply curtailed by Lina's fear of her own sexuality, projected onto an essentially innocent Johnnie. However, the way the viewer perceives the event does not unambiguously support this interpretation, an interpretation which after all is essentially that of Johnnie, whom we already know to be a liar. The long shot is evasive, concealing as much as it reveals, and from where the spectator is placed it supports the worry that Johnnie actually harbors rapacious, murderous intentions. Hitchcock's visual style here forces the spectator into diametrically opposed interpretations of what he or she sees, which, at once, seem to affirm and call into question the opposite interpretations of both participants in the event.

It is also worth noting that since Johnnie would have nothing to gain at this point in the plot by murdering Lina because he is not yet married to her and hence could not claim life insurance money, this is a singularly perverse moment in the film.[49] It suggests that even where a character in Hitchcock appears to have other motives for assault or murder than psychosexual ones, sexual motivations underlie the surface motivations of the character. To put it in another way, the surface motivations of characters provide Hitchcock a pretext to dramatize or stage motivations that his characters themselves might not acknowledge, as we shall see again in *Rear Window*.

After the marriage, Lina's fears are intensified on account of Johnnie's duplicitous actions, which she tends to cast in the worst light. In the mise-en-scène of the family home, the hallway doubles as a gigantic spider's web, with Grant the predatory spider at its center. Is this a paranoid projection on Lina's part or do these shadows reveal the underlying truth? Later in the film, Johnnie climbs the staircase to Lina's bedroom carrying a glass of milk that is ominously enlarged and iridescent in a manner that suggests it houses the poison that Lina believes it to contain (fig. 21). The fact that believing it is poison, she refrains from drinking it, renders permanent our doubts about the contents of the glass, even while Lina later affirms her belief in Johnnie's innocence. Feeling her life is threatened, Lina decides to leave, and as Johnnie drives her along the cliff road where she earlier imagined him killing his friend, the car door flies open. In a montage of shots, we see what is possibly an attempt by Johnnie to prevent her falling out of the car, but what is equally plausibly understood as the action of pushing her out that she is struggling to resist. This scene reproduces exactly the ambiguity that characterized their earlier struggle on the heath outside the church. Lina believes he pushed, he claims he pulled, the audience is left undecided.

Unsurprisingly, Hitchcock had difficulty ending the film. As I have already noted, in the ending he chose we see Johnnie's hand romantically slide around Lina's shoulders in a snakelike coil that functions simultaneously to affirm and undermine the romance. Like the match on action that defines romantic irony as romantic renewal in *North by Northwest*, the visual metaphor that closes *Suspicion* and leaves the ending of the film open is an ideal representation of the artfully contrived suspension of judgment that characterizes this form of romantic irony. It is a visual pun that playfully and self-consciously at once asserts what it denies and denies what it asserts.

But while the deceptiveness of appearances is a central ingredient of Hitchcock's romantic irony, whether it is playfully embraced in the narrative of romantic renewal or whether it is a threat to the romance, as it is in *The Lodger* and *Suspicion*, the deceptiveness of appearances rarely leaves us in a situation of permanent doubt about who the hero is and who the villain is. In *Strangers on a Train*, we know that Bruno Anthony is a murderer, and we have no doubt that Uncle Charlie (Joseph Cotten) is the killer in *Shadow of a Doubt*. More often than not, Hitchcock will deploy strategies of doubling and the orchestration of narrative point of view not to sustain the audience in a state of uncertainty about the hero's motivations, but rather to suggest that a character's motivations are essentially contradictory and divided. This is a theme that I shall pursue in more detail in chapter 3.

In *Rear Window*, the central character, L. B. Jefferies, action photographer, confined to his wheelchair because of an accident, spends his time looking across the courtyard of his Greenwich Village apartment, through the windows of the apartment opposite, where by interpreting a series of visual clues he begins to suspect that a murder has taken place. Through the rigorous point-of-view structure of the film, the spectator is implicated in the look of the central character whom she also looks upon. At one level, as Paula Marantz Cohen has argued, *Rear Window* is about the education of L. B. Jefferies from a "playboy" man who defines himself by action and nonattachment to more rounded character.[50] Initially, he acts like a voyeur, ogling the woman doing her exercise routine, whom he labels "Miss Torso" (Georgine Darcy). At the same time, he is derogatory toward the profession of his girlfriend Lisa Fremont (Grace Kelly), and sympathetic to Lars Thorwald (Raymond Burr) as a victim of a nagging wife. However, forced to observe rather than act, Jefferies comes to recognize and identify both with the plight of Miss Lonely Hearts (Judith Evelyn), who longs for a soul mate, and with Mrs. Thorwald (Irene Winston) as the victim of domestic violence. As Cohen suggests, rather than a detached, skeptical, and voyeuristic gaze, he establishes through his look an emotional connection. Furthermore, as Lisa Freemont joins his quest their look becomes a shared look. When Lisa takes on the agency Jefferies cannot (one that he is previously skeptical of her displaying) and is caught in the act of seeking evidence that will incriminate Thorwald, he displays a sense of frantic concern that demonstrates his capacity for empathy. The spectator, it seems, has also been encouraged to move from an uncomfortable alignment with an ogling voyeur to a sympathetic alignment with his point of view.

Yet Cohen's interpretation of *Rear Window*, accurate though it is, ignores the pervasive tone of black comedy that hovers over the film. This centers upon contemplating the act of cutting up a woman's body and disposing of it, which is directly compared by Hitchcock to the objectification of the woman's body by the camera. Thus, when Thorwald is seen by Jefferies and the audience leaving the apartment with his briefcase in the middle of the night, Hitchcock's camera, following the gaze of Jefferies, pans from Thorwald to the "body" of Miss Torso cut off by the waist at the bathroom window, as Jefferies and the spectator are invited to meditate upon what it would be like to cut up a female body. The next evening Jefferies kisses Lisa while describing the evidence that leads to his hypothesis. But he is much more enthused about being a detective than with the immediate task at hand. Again he looks over, and the spectator too, at Miss Torso, framed by the window of her apartment that at once forms crosshairs upon her torso and divides it into four pieces (fig. 30). Now Jefferies explicitly meditates upon what it must be like to cut up a body, and it is most certainly a woman's body he is thinking about. Critics have argued that the murder of Mrs. Thorwald can be conceived as Jefferies' fantasy, as if Thorwald functions, expressionistically, as Jefferies' double, acting out Jefferies' own unacknowledged or unconscious wish toward Lisa. Cohen objects to these interpretations on the grounds that the murder is decidedly real, it is not a product of Jefferies' imagination. But once again, this is not an either/or proposition. If Jefferies comes to identify with the female victim, he is, equally, imaginatively invested in conceiving an event—the murder of Mrs. Thorwald—that happens to turn out to be true.

Indeed, the very scene that seems to clinch the argument for Cohen—when Jefferies has become an empathic spectator and reacts in panic to the scene of Lisa's assault—does no such thing. The reason lies, ironically, in precisely the same self-reflexive structure that, at the beginning of the movie, allows the spectator at once to vicariously share Jefferies' voyeurism (through sharing his point of view), but also to criticize it (by looking at him). Before the scene of the assault, the composer, who occupies an adjacent apartment, finally, successfully completes the song he is writing and plays it. Lisa has earlier noted that this tune is like their theme song, and Jefferies muses that the composer's failure to write it is indicative of their relationship. Now the completed "Lisa" score, heard for the first time, orchestrates the scene in which Jefferies witnesses Lisa's assault. On the one hand, Lisa has shown her mettle, proved her love, and L. B. Jefferies squirms in fear and sympathy for her plight. The spectator, fully identifying with his look, responds in kind. Yet, on the other hand, Hitchcock also invites us to see what is taking place in a very different, perverse light. What is pictured here is a woman under assault, orchestrated to a romantic accompaniment—as if Hitchcock, the narrator, registers here the aspiration of the character that remains unacknowledged by Jefferies, that is, to imagine Lisa being assaulted.

Ambiguity in *Rear Window* is also sustained at the "horizontal" level through the open-ended nature of the film's conclusion. On the far side of the courtyard, Miss Lonely Hearts is now friendly with the composer, and Miss Torso's boyfriend, Stanley, has come home from the army. But the newlyweds, who have spent most of the movie with their window blinds closed, save for cigarette breaks taken by the husband between sex, are now quarreling, and Stanley is more interested in what is in the fridge than in Miss Torso. On the near side of the courtyard, Jefferies now has two broken legs, the second broken after a struggle with Thorwald. Does the second broken leg resign him to a more sedentary life with Lisa or increase his resistance to it? Lisa reads *Beyond the High Himalayas* while Jefferies dozes, suggesting her preparation for an active life. Yet when she sees he is not watching she puts it down and picks up *Harper's Bazaar* instead, suggesting that she too is unwilling to compromise.

Romantic Irony as Ironic Inversion

North by Northwest, as we have seen, provides a paradigm for one type of romantic irony in Hitchcock's work. But romantic irony can also take the opposite path, that is, it can foster ironic inversion and downward descent rather than fostering upward mobility or ascent. Perhaps the supreme illustration of this form of romantic irony in Hitchcock's work is *Vertigo*. In *Vertigo*, the central character Scottie Ferguson is ensnared by an elaborate masquerade in which Judy Barton poses as the wife of an old acquaintance of Scottie's, Gavin Elster, possessed by a dead relative, Carlotta Valdes. The plan, successfully executed in the first half of the film, is to trap Scottie into witnessing Madeleine Elster's apparent suicide, in a state of possession, from a bell tower. Madeleine is in fact already dead and it is her corpse, not the body of the imposter, that falls from the tower. But in the meantime, Scottie, who is on a rescue mission, has fallen in love with the imposter Madeleine and she with him. In the second half of the film, Scottie, emerging from hospitalization a diminished figure, discovers a woman who seems to look like Madeleine called Judy Barton and begins to obsessively re-create her in the image of his ideal. Unbeknownst to him, Judy Barton is the imposter. Finally, slowly, as Judy caves in to Scottie's demand to be re-created as Madeleine (because she loves him), it begins to dawn on Scottie that she is Madeleine. The re-creation of the illusion serves to shatter the illusion.

The plot of *Vertigo* is as contrived as the plot of *North by Northwest*, but rather than conspiring to give a kind of immunity to the hero from the depredations of the everyday world and foster the realization of the romantic ideal, artifice in *Vertigo* works to cruelly expose and undercut that ideal. An equivalent moment at the end of *Vertigo* to Hitchcock's magical cut on action in *North by Northwest* occurs when the figure of the nun in black appears before Judy Barton, causing her to withdraw from Scottie's embrace and fall from the tower. Having realized that Judy was acting the part of Madeleine and his love is based on a fraud, Scottie drags "Madeleine" back to the bell tower, from which she was supposed to have fallen, in an effort to overcome the vertigo that his helplessness after witnessing the fall has reinforced. They arrive successfully at the top of the tower and they begin to embrace, as if there is still a faint possibility for Scottie to acknowledge and respond to Judy's love for him. "Oh Scottie please. Oh Scottie, you love me, keep me safe." "Too late" he responds, using the words that Madeleine had used with him earlier, when she left to climb the bell tower the first time, "It's too late, there is no bringing her back." But when Judy says "Please," again, he takes her into his arms. But just as they embrace, a black figure arises from the trap door in the bell tower. Judy turns away from Scottie in horrified reaction to this apparition and falls to her death, leaving Scottie standing on the edge of the bell tower, once again reduced to a state of limbo. Now, as Brill points out, he has not only lost Judy/Madeline for good, but he has also been robbed of his past, his memory of Madeleine. He is left with nothing.[51]

Romantic Irony

The figure of the nun is a deus ex machina on a par with Hitchcock's magical match on action in *North by Northwest*. Again there is an ironic reversal; again it takes the form of a visual pun: the nun is mistaken for an apparition or a ghostly figure of death. Here, however, the ironic reversal works to undercut the possibility of transcendence and the realization of the romantic ideal. The handmaiden of God arises as the agent of death and causes the man to lose hold of the woman he loves and for her to plunge to her death, in a precise reversal of the ending of *North by Northwest*. Often, in my experience, this ending causes consternation to audiences of the film, unlike the exuberant closure of *North by Northwest*, as if the characters and with them, the spectator of the film, have been arbitrarily robbed of happiness. But of course this is precisely Hitchcock's point. *Vertigo* has to end this way.

Vertigo is the apotheosis of melancholic romantic irony that borders on tragedy and therefore, as we have seen, it is the antithesis of *North by Northwest*. Yet it has been the burden of this chapter to demonstrate how these films that are polar opposites within Hitchcock's oeuvre are, together with the range of works that lie between them, actually profoundly alike in their form and sensibility. This sense of the unity across the disparate modes and genres of his work—comedy, tragedy, horror, melodrama—will be honed in the subsequent chapters of the book, but there is one mode that has privileged status in Hitchcock's films and that is suspense. The idea of suspense in Hitchcock goes beyond a merely generic definition to encompass the privileged idiom of narration in his cinema. It is the central mode through which the logic of romantic irony becomes expressed. This is not to say that suspense should simply be equated with the logic of romantic irony; rather, in Hitchcock's films, the idioms of suspense are transformed and stretched into a vehicle for the expression of romantic irony.

2
Suspense

Hitchcock is popularly known as the "Master of Suspense," a moniker assigned to him by a New York radio adman for his proposed "Suspense Radio" series in 1940.[1] Yet it is a remarkable fact that although numerous academic volumes have been written on Hitchcock, very few have treated seriously this dimension of the director's work.[2] I shall argue in this chapter that, far from being a superficial aspect of his work, the idiom of suspense is the primary vehicle of Hitchcock's romantic irony.

It is commonplace to point out the manner in which suspense involves the orchestration and control of narrative information. As Ian Cameron writes, all suspense involves "a channeling of the emotions so that one is entirely taken up with what is going to happen next."[3] This emotional focalization on what is going to happen next is created by the fact that we are forced to entertain the prospect of a narrative outcome that is contrary to the one that is desired. Indeed, we worry about the likelihood of an undesirable or threatening outcome and thereby experience the characteristic emotional state of suspense: anxious uncertainty. Thus both the "vertical" aspect of romantic irony, in which the spectator is made aware of the constructed or controlled nature of the fiction, and the "horizontal" aspect, which registers the copresence of opposing tendencies in the narrative world, are incipient features of the form. Hitchcock's deployment of suspense as a mode of ·

romantic irony foregrounds our sense of an orchestrated fiction by dramatizing the gap between character point of view and spectator point of view, by constantly shifting the forms and modes of suspense, and perhaps most distinctively, by exploiting and amplifying the ironic edge of suspense.

In Hitchcock's narratives of romantic renewal, the orchestration of situations of suspense contributes to the sense of artifice that governs the fiction by showing that his characters would not emerge unscathed from the circumstances in which they find themselves but for the grace of Hitchcock, who contrives their survival. It is not primarily Roger Thornhill's agency but the agency of Hitchcock, the narrator, that enables Thornhill to survive a drunken ride along a cliff edge, the attack of a crop-dusting plane, or a threatened fall from a cliff on Mount Rushmore. In his more ironic narratives, Hitchcock exploits suspense in order to foster in the spectator an allegiance to those forces that actually run counter to the resolution of the story that is ostensibly desired. In this way, Hitchcock turns the idiom of the thriller into a playfully perverse challenge to, and manipulation of, our customary moral responses.

Forms of Suspense

Anxious uncertainty about what is going to happen next lies at the core of suspense. How is this anxious uncertainty created? Noël Carroll has argued persuasively that, in what I shall call classical suspense, this state of anxious uncertainty is created in a narrative where the question "What happens next?" is dramatized through the representation of two alternate narrative outcomes of a specific kind: one is desirable and hence wished for but unlikely; the other is undesirable and hence feared, yet likely.[4] Carroll also argues that the outcome that is wished for or desired in suspense is the moral one. While I shall argue that Hitchcock's practice contests the necessary connection Carroll proposes between morality and suspense, he is right to emphasize that classical suspense is conventionally moral in structure. For example, in D. W. Griffith's *The Lonely Villa* (1909), the heroine and her children are trapped in her isolated house by villains. Will the absent husband rescue her before they overpower her? It seems unlikely. The villains are nearby and she seems defenseless, and since the hero is a long way off, how is he going to get back in time to rescue her?

In classical suspense, the temporal deadline created by the sense of an imminent catastrophe creates a ratio of probability in which, as time passes, the likelihood of a bad outcome increases relative to the likelihood of a good outcome.[5] In the rescue narrative, the narrator will augment the sense of time passing and decrease the likelihood of a positive outcome by building arbitrary delays into the progress of the rescue. In classical suspense the intensity of suspense is thus calibrated: the closer we are to the moment of impending doom, the more it becomes unavoidable and hence fearfully anticipated. In the typical suspense sequence, time is broken up into smaller and smaller units as the imminent catastrophe nears in order to prolong the moment of narrative irresolution and force the audience to hold out as long as possible before resolving opposed possibilities in favor of one or the other—usually, in Griffith and popular cinema in general, the moral one.

Griffith's suspense conforms to what Hitchcock in his "Lecture to Students" at Columbia University calls objective suspense. Hitchcock points out that his own approach to suspense differs from Griffith by introducing a "subjective factor." There are in fact two different aspects of his practice that Hitchcock refers to as the "subjective factor." One definition of subjective suspense he gives is "letting the audience experience it through the mind or eyes of one of the characters."[6] Here, it seems that the distinction between objective and subjective involves whether or not suspense is filtered through the point of view of a character. However, Hitchcock wishes to get at something else, for he suggests that subjective suspense contrasts with objective suspense not through the presence of character point of view per se, but in presenting the spectator with limited knowledge of the situation and hence "making the audience suffer":

> In the French Revolution, probably someone said to Danton, "Will you please hurry on your horse," but never show him getting on the horse. Let the audience worry whether the horse has even started, you see. That is making the audience play its part.
>
> The old way used to be that the audience was presented with just an objective view of this galloping horse, and they just said they hoped the horse got there in time. I think it should go further than that. Not only "I hope he gets there in time," but "I hope he has started off," you see. That is a more intensive development.[7]

Here, Hitchcock is concerned to pinpoint the role of narrative suppression in generating suspense, which he contrasts to Griffith's unrestricted narration.

What is distinctive about the way in which Hitchcock filters suspense through the mind of a character? Hitchcock never abandoned the protocols of "objective suspense," and part of what he seems to mean by adding a "subjective" factor in his films is simply that, as in the work of most suspense directors, the audience experiences suspense in part by identifying with the distressed situation of a character in the fiction. In fact, audience identification with the heroine in distress is a feature of Griffith's suspense. Furthermore, when, through parallel editing, Griffith cuts away from the narrative position of the heroine under threat to the ride to the rescue of the absent hero, he encourages the audience to root for the hero by putting various blockages in the way of the hero's rescue attempt. On the one hand, Griffith portrays a character under threat whose point of view we share. This character is in fear of her life and worries that her rescuer will not arrive in time. On the other hand, Griffith portrays the rescuer, who fears on behalf of the woman under duress and who thereby becomes a kind of surrogate for the director and for the audience.

Hitchcock's interest in subjective suspense consists, in part, in intensifying the kind of character identification that is already present in classical suspense, often by restricting us to the narrative point of view of a single character under duress and orchestrating that narrative point of view through the use of optical point of view, which is rare in Griffith's work. Thus when the crop-dusting plane attacks Roger Thornhill in *North by Northwest*, the narrative is almost entirely focalized through Roger's narrative point of view and orchestrated through point-of-view editing. In this kind of "shared suspense" the character himself is placed in the position of experiencing anxiety and the audience is aligned with him.[8]

A second way in which Hitchcock orchestrates the relationship between omniscience and character point of view is to place the spectator in a position of superior knowledge to that of the character. This is in fact how he defines suspense in the interview with Truffaut:

There is a distinct difference between "suspense" and surprise. . . . I'll explain what I mean. We are now having a very innocent little chat. Let us suppose that there is a bomb underneath the table between us. Nothing happens, and then all of a sudden, "Boom!" There is an explosion. The public is *surprised*, but prior to this surprise, it has seen an absolutely ordinary scene, of no special consequence. Now, let us take a *suspense* situation. The bomb is underneath the table and the public knows it, probably because they have seen the anarchist place it there. The public is aware that the bomb is going to explode at one o'clock and there is a clock in the décor. The public can see that it is a quarter to one. In these conditions the same innocuous conversation becomes fascinating because the public is participating in the scene. The audience is longing to warn the characters on the screen. . . . In the first case we have given the public fifteen seconds of *surprise* at the moment of the explosion. In the second we have provided them with fifteen minutes of *suspense*.[9]

Susan Smith aptly terms this form of suspense "vicarious suspense," in the sense that it is a form of suspense that is felt in the place of a character.[10] When Lila Crane (Vera Miles), sister of the murdered Marion Crane, approaches the house where Norman Bates lives in *Psycho*, she is trying to speak to the frail old woman who lives upstairs. However, we the audience believe that this old woman is in fact the murderer of both Marion Crane and the detective Arbogast (Martin Balsam) and is about to murder Lila herself. We thus feel excruciating tension and fear on behalf of the character as she approaches the mansion. Again, here, Hitchcock's practice is an intensification of aspects of Griffithian suspense. For when a character is placed under threat in Griffith's work, there is, characteristically, an initial phase in which we, the audience, perceive the threat before the protagonist does—for example, the would-be intruders who lurk outside the house in *The Lonely Villa*. Purely objective suspense that is experienced in a manner that is altogether independent of character is obviously a rare thing in character-driven narrative, for when the audience experiences a suspenseful situation that a character is unaware of, we still feel suspense on behalf of that character. For example, in *Notorious* we perceive (but Devlin does not) that, as he inspects the wine bottles in the cellar where he is looking for evidence of a conspiracy, one of them is about to fall to the ground in a manner that may alert the villains. The suspense is directed to the spectator, but we are concerned vicariously on Devlin's behalf.

Up until now I have understood "subjective suspense" to describe the way in which suspense involves character identification. However, Hitchcock's definition of subjective suspense as suppressive narration suggests not merely a qualification of the idea of classical suspense through the role that is played by character, but a form of suspense that is different in kind from classical suspense because it involves narrative suppression rather than narrative omniscience. This is an idea that Hitchcock is usually assumed to have rejected. When Truffaut, in the interviews with Hitchcock, suggested to him that suspense may rise out of a hidden danger, Hitchcock strenuously denied it: "To my way of thinking mystery is seldom suspenseful. In a whodunit for example, there is no suspense, but a sort of intellectual puzzle. The whodunit generates a kind of curiosity that is void of emotion, and emotion is an essential ingredient of suspense."[11]

Hitchcock is undoubtedly right about the whodunit lacking suspense, for what is involved is less a sense of hidden danger in the present that engenders a worry about what will happen but an intellectual puzzle about the past. There are multiple possible candidates for who is the murderer; the detective and the reader or audience must decide upon the right one. His distinction anticipates the distinction drawn by narrative theorist Meir Sternberg between curiosity and suspense. "Suspense," Sternberg writes, "derives from a lack of desired information concerning the outcome of a conflict that is to take place in the narrative future, a lack that involves a clash of hope and fear; whereas curiosity is produced by a lack of information that relates to the narrative past, a time when struggles have already been resolved, and as such it often involves an interest in the information for its own sake."[12]

However, the kind of mystery Hitchcock has in mind when he speaks of subjective suspense is not the intellectual puzzle of detective fiction but a situation in which the nature of the mysterious situation is one that does engender concern about the future on the part of the audience in the form of the anxious anticipation that characterizes suspense. How is this condition of anxious anticipation generated by mystery? Characteristically, as in the horror film, the mystery is not merely something that we are curious to resolve, but it contains something threatening. We want to find out the source of the mystery, in order to confront our fears, but we also fear the outcome, and hence we may also wish not to have the secret revealed. In suspenseful mystery, something more is at stake than merely curiosity about the answer to a question; rather, what is posed in the narrative is a hidden danger that we at once fear and desire to reveal and confront. Since we have this emotional stake in resolving the mystery, delay in revealing the outcome contributes to our anxiety. As Truffaut himself put it to Hitchcock, suspense in this form involves the "stretching out of an anticipation" in connection with a hidden danger. I shall call this form of suspense *suspenseful mystery*. There is a qualitative difference between this kind of suspense and classical suspense, which is the difference between "low-key ominous" and "climactic nail-biting."[13]

The creation of suspense through suppressive narration is ubiquitous in Hitchcock's work. It is typically fostered by aligning the audience with the restricted viewpoint of a character who anxiously desires and fears the resolution of a mystery (shared suspenseful mystery). For example, in *Rebecca*, when the second Mrs. de Winter arrives at Manderley, she has been primed to think of Rebecca, her husband's first wife, as a figure of awe and fascination, about whom she both desires to know more and fears to know more. By restricting us to the epistemic viewpoint of the character, Hitchcock suppresses our knowledge of who Rebecca really is and the nature of the "threat" she poses until Maxim reveals her true identity late in the story. During the second Mrs. de Winter's first encounter with Rebecca's housekeeper, Mrs. Danvers (Judith Anderson), she experiences the overwhelming presence of Rebecca in the house of Manderley. Leaving her bedroom with Danvers silently escorting her, Mrs. de Winter glides, with her back to Hitchcock's camera, toward the door of Rebecca's bedroom. They hesitate at the top of the stairs, framed from behind in two-shot as Danvers points out the doors of Mrs. de Winter's room. First Danvers, then the second Mrs. de Winter, peel off, leaving Hitchcock's camera to venture, to be lured, a little closer, until stopped from approaching by Rebecca's dog Jasper, who stands guard. The suspense that is invoked here is the fearful anticipation of something whose nature is wished to be known, and it is registered as a delay or forestalling of the moment of narrative disclosure.

Typically, Hitchcock restricts knowledge by aligning the audience with the limited viewpoint of a character, and thus it is easy to understand why Hitchcock used the term "subjective suspense" to cover both ideas. Nonetheless, it is possible for the suppression of narrative knowledge to be cued independently of character. Consider the final shot from the sequence I have just described in *Rebecca*. As Mrs. Danvers and the second Mrs. de Winter leave the frame, Hitchcock's camera ventures closer to the bedroom and stops in a manner that makes us aware of a yet-to-be-revealed secret. In an extraordinary shot just prior to the murder of Marion Crane in the shower in *Psycho*, Hitchcock places the camera behind the curtain in such a way that we see a dark figure looming whom we think is Norman's mother, although we cannot be absolutely sure.[14] The camera does not at this point take Marion's perceptual point of view, and we are not cued to think that this is what she sees, since she is busy cleansing herself in the shower. Our perception of this figure gives us knowledge that is superior to the character, and thus we worry on her behalf, but it does so only to alert us to a mystery. This mystery is sustained by the bird's-eye view position taken by Hitchcock's camera when Arbogast is attacked by "mother" on the staircase in a manner that conceals from the audience the real identity of Arbogast's assailant.

Classical suspense and suspenseful mystery are mutually exclusive forms and typically orchestrated by Hitchcock sequentially. For example, in *North by Northwest*, we initially share, through suppressive narration, the ignorance of Roger Thornhill as to the identity of George Kaplan and seek with him to unravel the mystery. Once we find out who George Kaplan is—or rather, that he was nonexistent until Thornhill filled his shoes and brought him into being—we fear vicariously on his behalf. Later, our experience of classical suspense is intensified by being aligned with the character's point of view in the crop-dusting sequence. Finally, at the denouement of the film, as Thornhill seeks to rescue Eve from the clutches of the villain, Vandamm, and throws his matchbook from the balcony where he is hidden in the hope of her discovering it, he is placed in the position of the spectator of a suspenseful situation and a shared classical suspense situation is created. In *Vertigo*, we are initially restricted to the point of view of the protagonist, who believes he is following a woman who is mysteriously possessed by a ghost from the past, and seek with him to grasp the mystery. Two-thirds of the way through the film, when we find out that the story of Madeleine possessed is a fiction and that Scottie has been framed, we worry vicariously on his behalf.

However, the different forms of suspense may overlap according to the aspect of the narrative information that is known or withheld. For example, as Lila Crane approaches the *Psycho* house we believe that someone in the house is about to swoop down and murder her. Yet we have been systematically excluded the sight of mother in the film, and the house exudes an aura of mystery, which is only compounded by the information imparted by Sheriff Chambers (John McIntire) that Mrs. Bates has been dead for the past ten years. Hitchcock shoots Lila's approach in a manner that combines a forward-tracking point-of-view shot and a backward-tracking reaction shot that creates a sense of shared suspenseful mystery. This is a signature combination that in *Vertigo* and elsewhere provides a concrete enactment or embodiment for the spectator of the sense of at once investigating but also being drawn into what is being seen. At the same time, knowing that whoever occupies the house is a vicious murderer, we also fear vicariously on Lila's behalf (vicarious classical suspense).

In Hitchcock's definition of suspense with which I started out, suspense is defined in contrast to surprise. This is certainly true of classical suspense, which Hitchcock is concerned to emphasize in that interview. As we have seen, classical suspense involves giving the audience information about the possible outcomes of the situation or story. Surprise, as Hitchcock emphasizes, depends upon the withholding of information. Of course, surprise may enter into structures of classical suspense, not because we lack information about what is going to happen, but through the manipulation of time. For example, in *Rear Window*, L. B. Jefferies sends the killer, Lars Thorwald, away from the apartment by telephoning him with the threat of blackmail. Thorwald leaves the apartment to go to the arranged rendezvous where Jefferies has agreed to meet him in fifteen minutes. In the meantime, Jefferies' girlfriend, Lisa Fremont, enters the apartment to retrieve incriminating evidence. A shared classical suspense situation is set up: will Lisa retrieve the evidence before Lars Thorwald returns? But my experience of viewing this scene is that Hitchcock also lulls the audience into a sense of false security by allowing us to think that it will be some time before Thorwald returns, given the time frame Hitchcock sets up for the rendezvous. It is thus a surprise when we see him cross the street so soon and enter the apartment. In terms of timing, surprise can enter into classical suspense and intensify it.

However, suspenseful mystery has a different relationship to surprise, for obviously both suspenseful mystery and surprise involve the suppression of narrative information. Suspenseful mystery differs from a situation of pure surprise (such as the murder of Marion Crane), only by cuing us to the fact that something is being suppressed. Mystery therefore prepares us to anticipate a surprising revelation. Typically, while suppressing knowledge of narrative events, Hitchcock will cue us to the probability of one conclusion, only to surprise us at the end with something that is totally contrary to our expectations. Thus in the conclusion of *Psycho*, we are prepared to encounter the murderous mother, whose identity has been suppressed, only to discover Norman Bates.

In *Rebecca*, where we share the restricted point of view of the second Mrs. de Winter with respect to what Rebecca was really like, we are, like the second Mrs. de Winter, fascinated by the enigma of Rebecca, and the apparent hold she has both on Maxim de Winter and Mrs. Danvers, the keeper of the house. However, we are also led to believe that Maxim de Winter was in love with his first wife when quite the contrary is the case. The revelation of Maxim's true feelings toward her, and his culpability in her death, are thus a surprise. Similarly, in *Vertigo*, a film that shares so much of the structure of *Rebecca*, Gavin Elster's plot to murder his wife is withheld from the audience just as it is withheld from Scottie. Alongside Scottie, we are ensnared in the mystery of why the woman whom we believe to be Elster's wife seems possessed by the ghost of a dead woman. However, his and our preoccupation with understanding this mystery only serves to conceal more completely the deeper secret that comes as a total surprise: the woman who appeared to be Elster's wife is an imposter who faked her possession.

In practice, especially in Hitchcock's later work where he has achieved such a complete mastery of form, the different kinds of suspense and surprise are entwined in complex ways. One signal sequence from *The Birds* (1963) provides a simple but striking example. Melanie Daniels (Tippi Hedren) sits in front of the jungle gym waiting for the kids to finish school (plate 10). At first she is oblivious to the alarming fact that the spectator is made aware of from the beginning of the scene: birds are gathering on the bars of the jungle gym behind her. Hitchcock cuts back and forth between Melanie nervously smoking in the foreground—mimicking, and thereby fuelling, the spectator's anxiety, with her own, slightly different, anxiety—and the birds progressively gathering in the background. This classic rendition of vicarious suspense is accompanied by the mesmerizing repetition of the children's song (from the classroom) that serves to mark out the passing of time. Finally, Melanie notices a single bird in flight, and Hitchcock cuts from a reaction shot of Melanie looking to a long point-of-view shot of the bird flying that, in the context of the sequence, serves to restrict our knowledge of what is going on and inclines us to anticipate with anxiety what she will see when the bird lands (shared suspenseful mystery). However, what she does see turns out to be a surprise, forged in part by a condensation of narrative time, for unknown to us, in the meantime, the birds have accumulated in quite massive proportions, an accumulation which the cut to Melanie's restricted point of view had occluded. The film then reverts again to a classical suspense structure, but one in which the knowledge of the character is now, in contrast to the earlier sequence, shared with that of the audience, and we fear for the schoolchildren's lives.

Morality and Classical Suspense

It is a critical commonplace about Hitchcock's work that he works almost wholly within the genre of the thriller, a narrative idiom that usually involves, among other things, the articulation of clear-cut moral coordinates that discriminate the good guys from the bad through the commission of a criminal action that usually involves murder. Suspense in Hitchcock's works is broadly structured around these moral coordinates and the allegiance they give rise to in the spectator. In *The 39 Steps*, Richard Hannay (Robert Donat) is framed for a killing he did not commit—will he be wrongfully arrested or escape? In *Notorious*, Alicia Huberman (Ingrid Bergman) is sent on a dangerous mission to penetrate a murderous German spy ring that is working on a nuclear bomb in Rio de Janeiro. Will the spy she marries in order to further the allied cause—Alex Sebastian (Claude Rains)—find out that she is trying to expose him and what will he do? In *Strangers on a Train*, the hero, Guy Haines, is caught up in a diabolical plot in which the villain, Bruno Anthony, kills his wife and threatens to frame him for the murder unless Guy kills Bruno's father. Will Guy fall victim to Bruno's web of blackmail or will he escape his snare?

Furthermore, in Hitchcock's work, the suspense generated around the plot involving the conflict between the hero (or heroine) and the villain (or villains) is linked to the suspense generated by the romance plot. Hitchcock himself insisted that suspense is as much a feature of the romance as it is of the pure thriller, although the emotional emphasis of romantic suspense is different.[15] In a thriller, our concern lies with the threat posed by the agents of evil and we fear for the hero's safety. The emotional emphasis of romantic comedy lies in our wish for a happy outcome and the way in which that wish is frustrated by obstacles placed in the way of the romance. By combining the elements of the thriller and the romance in his "wrong man" and, sometimes, "wrong woman" narratives of the 1930s and after, Hitchcock intensifies our emotional investment in the narrative outcome. For the romance narrative adds to the anticipation of a fearful outcome that is characteristic of the thriller or the horror film an intensification of the wish of a happy ending that characterizes the romance narrative. The obstacles placed in the way of the hero in a "wrong man" narrative such as *The 39 Steps*, where the hero is wanted for murder, are precisely the obstacles that need to be overcome for the romance to be cemented. For example, in *Strangers on a Train*, the "wrong man," Guy Haines, must clear his name in the murder of his wife in order for his romance with Anne Morton (Ruth Roman) to flourish. *Notorious* is a "wrong woman" narrative whose focus is upon the notoriety and hence apparent untrustworthiness of the woman who is required to prove herself to the man. By risking her life as a double agent, Alicia Huberman atones for her past in order to win the love of Devlin.

However, there is already an incipient irony in classical suspense when a narrator like Griffith augments suspense by prolonging the moment before the narrative is finally resolved. For it is as if the audience is invited to relish the situation of delay and the virtuoso orchestration of suspense for its own sake. It is as if, indeed, the purpose of securing the redemption of virtue has as its unacknowledged undercurrent a desire to see villainy victorious, or at least almost victorious. This is the ironic edge of suspense, wherein the structure of suspense threatens to undermine the moral rationale it ostensibly seems to support. As Susan Smith has suggested, this ironic dimension of suspense becomes particularly evident in Hitchcock's favored situation of vicarious suspense, where he flaunts the gap between what the character knows and what the spectator knows, and it is demonstrated in a prolonged sequence of suspense from *Sabotage*.

Stevie (Desmond Tester), a young mop-haired boy, is asked to deliver a package to its destination while, unbeknownst to him, it contains a bomb. First, Hitchcock establishes very clearly a deadline of 1:45 P.M., when the bomb will explode. When Stevie sets out on his journey, he is beset by delays—he gets lost in the market-day crowds, and he is lured into having his face cleaned and scrubbed by a street peddler. To remind us of the imminent catastrophe, Hitchcock periodically intercuts close-ups of the bomb under his arm and superimposes the instructions written by one of the saboteurs: "Don't forget the Birds will Sing at 1:45." But Stevie gets distracted again, this time by the Lord Mayor's show, and Hitchcock interposes a montage of a clock reading 1:00 P.M. with the inner cogs engaging in a manner that suggests the relentless momentum of time. Then a minute hand moves fast-forward onto 1:15. But Stevie continues to dillydally at the show.[16] He gets onto the bus and snuggles a puppy held by his neighbor, blissfully unaware. Indeed the puppy provides a concrete analogue of his innocence. He looks behind him at a clock outside and feels the package next to him. Indeed, Stevie constantly fidgets. In terms of the story, his fidgeting registers Stevie's worry that he is late delivering the package, but in terms of the orchestration of suspense it ironically evokes the much deeper anxiety of the audience, that, unknown to Stevie, the bomb is about to explode. Stevie's fidgeting, though it has a different motivation, still mimics the spectator's own burgeoning anxiety and thereby also serves to promote our awareness of it. As in the jungle gym sequence from *The Birds,* Hitchcock here uses the body of the actor as one of the expressive elements of the film. We pass a clock reading 1:30, then 1:35. Hitchcock cuts at an increasingly frantic pace between shots of Stevie petting the puppy and looking outside, shots of hands of the clock as the time of the explosion nears, shots of the bomb, shots of the conductor at the back of the bus (which has a diagonal bar across the window that evokes "No Entry" or a barricade), and shots of the bus caught up in a series of delays: it is stopped first by a policeman, then by a traffic jam, and then by traffic lights indicating STOP. When the lights change to GO, Hitchcock cuts rapidly from Stevie, to 1:45, then to a close-up of the clock's face moving to 1:46, then three shots in rapid succession of the bomb, then the explosion, as if detonated by the montage.

In many ways this is a tour-de-force sequence of classical suspense. All the cues given to the spectator conspire to make us worry on the boy's behalf that an imminent catastrophe is about to occur, and our anxiety is progressively ratcheted up by the orchestration of narrative elements. Delays are put in the way of Stevie reaching his destination, and our attention is drawn to increasingly small segments of narrative time as the probability of catastrophe increases. And yet, as Smith points out, Hitchcock in this sequence flaunts his mastery over the fate of the little boy. While the fact that we know what the character does not yields sympathy, it also has a distancing, ironizing effect. Smith writes:

> The epistemic gap that it inevitably opens up between him and ourselves also has the effect of preparing us for the eventual break from his character

at the point of the explosion. . . . Indeed, the more intense the suspense becomes . . . the more its own mechanisms and processes are laid bare. . . . The
incongruity between our serious level of suspense and Stevie's much milder
form of anxiety . . . produces a further degree of distance. For, in provoking
an intense frustration at being unable to communicate this much greater
threat to the character, it heightens our self-consciousness about being positioned outside of the narrative world.[17]

In this way Hitchcockian vicarious suspense pulls the spectator in two contradictory directions simultaneously—we sympathize with Stevie and the
catastrophe that is to befall him, but we are also made aware of the hand of
the director, who relishes the orchestration of the imminent catastrophe.

The problem here, as Hitchcock subsequently recognized, was that audiences of the time were not attuned to the hardness of an irony that issued
in the death of someone for whom one has been rooting, against the odds,
to survive. Given the way that we are invited to hope against hope that
Stevie will survive, this scene is an even more extreme violation of audience
expectations than the surprise and shock of Marion Crane's murder in
Psycho. We have subsequently come to associate this kind of violation of
our allegiance with the modern horror film, where, of course, it has become
a basic convention of the genre; but as Hitchcock recognized, the irony of
Sabotage was not something that the audience of the time could readily
appreciate: "The boy was involved in a situation that got him too much
sympathy from the audience, so that when the bomb exploded and he was
killed the public was resentful."[18]

However, the kind of ironic edge manifest in *Sabotage* is also used by
Hitchcock in a less sadistic context where it can be more readily shared
by the spectator. In the tour-de-force Albert Hall sequence in *The Man Who
Knew Too Much* (1956), we identify emotionally with Jo McKenna (Doris
Day), whose son has been kidnapped, as she struggles in indecision. If she
alerts the authorities to the fact that a murder is about to take place, it will
jeopardize her son's life; at the same time, she must try to prevent the crime
from taking place. Unlike the example from *Sabotage*, Hitchcock here presents us with a character who knows most of what we know, that an assassination is about to take place and that the more she delays, the probability
of the assassination increases. Arthur Benjamin's "Storm Cloud Cantata"
accompanies Hitchcock's visual representation of her emotional state and

augments its expression. Yet her response is nonètheless distinct from that of the spectator and remains itself an element in Hitchcock's overall rhetorical orchestration of suspense. For we know something crucial that she does not—namely, that the assassination is cued to the moment when the cymbals will crash at the climax of the cantata in order to disguise the sound of the shot, although we do not know how long it will take to get to this climax.

While our superior knowledge heightens our worry on her behalf about the impact of her indecision, the attention Hitchcock invites us to give to the music becomes self-referential, making us aware of how the melodrama of suspense is being self-consciously "orchestrated." The initial overture self-consciously announces a period of relative calm before the heightening of anxiety. The first and second violins are counterpointed aurally and visually to express Jo's vacillation. The rising crescendo, pace, and lyrics of the cantata narrate the gathering storm clouds as the suspense is heightened. The brass instruments and the voices of the male choir introduce the second movement, as Jo's husband Ben McKenna (James Stewart) arrives to help her foil the assassin. The female lead in the choir is a double for the heroine, who is herself a singer; she vocalizes the heroine's mute suffering. The conductor of the orchestra in the film is, we are told, none other than Bernard Herrmann, the composer for the film. Hitchcock provides us with a big close-up shot viewed from between the cymbals poised to crash together, and we are invited to follow the musical notation that leads to the cymbal crash from the point of view of the assassin, then the cymbalist, and then the conductor. Hitchcock's elaborate conceit draws attention to the way in which the devices that he employs—crosscutting, repetition, increasingly rapid editing, and tighter close-ups—also function in a self-conscious vein to ratchet up suspense.

These devices certainly do not invite us to wish for a negative outcome to the situation and for the assassin to succeed, but we are asked to savor the condition of being held in suspense, which is evidently not a response available to the character in the fiction. Crucially this response is enabled in part, as Cameron notes, by the way that Hitchcock deflects our attention from the primary worry, that Hank McKenna (Christopher Olsen) might be killed, which is the partial analogue here to Stevie dying, and which we know is not going to happen, to a secondary worry, the assassination of a foreign dignitary with whom we have only the most abstract moral allegiance, since he is not a character with whom we have been invited to sympathize.[19] Furthermore, even under these circumstances, Hitchcock orchestrates a benign resolution by ensuring that Jo "intuitively" screams just before the gun is fired, in a manner that causes the ambassador only to be grazed by the shot from the assassin's gun.

Hitchcock also uses structures of shared suspense as an occasion for undercutting our conventional moral responses by inviting us to experience a situation of suspense with a villainous character, to sympathize with his predicament, and thus to wish for a state of affairs that is contrary to the desirable narrative outcome. A famous example is provided by the scene in *Psycho*, cited by Hitchcock in his interview with Truffaut, where Norman Bates pauses in momentary trepidation when the car that contains the body of the dead Marion Crane fails, for a moment, to sink into the swamp.[20] Norman is here trying to cover up a horrendous crime. Through shared suspense we are invited to wish for the body of Marion Crane, with whom we have strongly identified until her untimely death, to disappear for good, although this wish runs utterly counter to the moral outcome of the story. Of course, Hitchcock has taken great pains to disguise to the spectator Norman's true identity and to endow him with sympathetic traits. We do not know that Norman is Marion's killer—we believe it is his mother—and Norman has been rendered a sympathetic character on account of the way he cares for her. The fact that he cleans up after her mess is an extension of his helpless dependency and we pity him. In this way, the moral iniquity of the character is disguised and we continue to feel sympathy with him right up until the end of the film, when his identity as "mother" is revealed and, subdued by Sam, he keels back in anguish.

However, while Hitchcock elicits sympathy for the devil by endowing him with endearing traits, this does not suffice to explain the role played by suspense in this sequence. For we do not simply sympathize with the character, and therefore feel suspense, though this may be a partial explanation; we are also made to feel anxiety on behalf of the character by being placed in his narrative situation and therefore sympathize with him. It is not simply that Hitchcock in this scene creates a sympathetic devil whose point of view we can then share; he creates sympathy for the devil by inviting us to share the devil's point of view.

In his interviews with Truffaut, Hitchcock claims that suspense is not intrinsically tied to moral evaluation, and he uses examples of vicarious suspense to illustrate his point. He argues that if an audience were cued to the fact that a bomb was ticking under a conference table waiting to explode, while Hitler was sitting at the table unawares, the audience would still feel suspense regardless of how they felt about the character. A second example supports this point:

> A curious person goes into somebody else's room and begins to search through the drawers. Now, you could show the person who lives in that room coming up the stairs. Then you go back to the person who is searching, and the public feels like warning him, "Be careful, watch out. Someone's coming up the stairs." Therefore, even if the snooper is not a likable character, the audience will still feel anxiety for him.[21]

The implication of these examples for understanding the relationship between morality and suspense is to question the assumption of Carroll and others that the outcome we desire is always the *morally* desirable one or that there is an intrinsically moral structure to suspense.

In his first essay on suspense, Carroll distinguishes between what he calls a "general" theory of suspense, which aligns suspense to morality, and a "universal" theory where suspense is not thus aligned. This distinction, which he formulates in response to a consideration of Hitchcock's works, seems to me largely correct, in that it conceives Hitchcock's films as an implicit counterexample to the idea that moral alignment to a character is a necessary condition for feeling suspense on his or her behalf.[22] However, in his later theory, Carroll liberalizes the conditions of moral approval to account for the anomalous cases of "sympathy with the devil." He claims that either these characters have morally redeeming character traits, such as the Grecian virtues of strength, fortitude, bravery, or beauty, or that the criteria of moral evaluation provided by a film encourages the viewer to identify with characters of limited virtue, because they are positively dis-criminated from other characters who have entirely negative attributes.[23]

However, Hitchcock's arguments point to the fact that our response to being in a character's situation is a more primitive or hardwired response, which our moral responses may support or counteract, but that is not reducible to them. They draw attention to a feature of identification in cinema that Hitchcock is keen to exploit—namely, the way in which audience identification in the cinema is manipulated by the orchestration of narrative and perceptual point of view. Hitchcock's obsession with "technique" is thus closely connected with the ironic subversion of morality in his work.

Identification is usually associated with the feelings of sympathy we may have for a character that is rooted in our evaluation of that character's moral worth. However, films may align the audience with the point of view of a character in the sense of encouraging us to see a narrative situation from their perspective, and sometimes literally through their eyes, irrespective of our judgment of their worth. Yet this identification with narrative point of view is not wholly divorced from our emotional responses because sharing the narrative situation of a character will itself evoke sympathetic emotional response. In the two situations of vicarious suspense described by Hitchcock, as well as the shared suspense situation of Norman Bates watching the car sinking, the narrative outcome is, from the point of view of the protagonists, an undesirable one, and this is the point of view the audience is encouraged to share. Suspense situations thus contribute to sympathy for the devil by severing our emotional responses to character from their customary moral anchor.

Ordinarily, the autonomy of suspense from moral evaluation will not be evident because the outcome that is desired will be the moral one and the structure of suspense will simply reinforce the coordinates of conventional morality. Furthermore, it is certainly not the case, as we have seen, that Hitchcock abandons the conventional moral coordinates of suspense entirely. Even where we sympathize with the devil, like Norman Bates in *Psycho*, it is in part because the true identity of the devil is disguised and the devil is endowed with morally sympathetic traits. But occasionally Hitchcock will use the situation of a character under threat to create identification with a character who is extremely unsympathetic. In *Frenzy*, the serial killer, Robert Rusk, tries desperately to retrieve a distinctive tiepin, which will implicate him as a murderer, from the clenched fist of the naked murder victim in the back of a potato truck. Hitchcock initially solicits our sympathy with Rusk by contrasting him to the negative qualities of the nominal hero, Richard Blaney (Jon Finch). Blaney is a fallen member of the upper middle class, egotistical, pusillanimous, and full of sour grapes. Rusk, a working-class Cockney, is a smooth, savvy, witty, mother-loving ladies' man. However, soon Rusk stands revealed as a psychotic killer who murders two sympathetic female protagonists. Yet as Rusk scrabbles around in the back of the potato truck, the audience is invited to identify with the situation of this character who has been victimized by circumstances and share his anxious uncertainty as he seeks against the odds to retrieve the tiepin. In this situation, the structure of suspense, as filtered through the narrative point of view of a morally reprehensible character, yields sympathy for that character, a sympathy which, temporarily at least, seems to trump our horror at his actions.

In both *Psycho* and *Frenzy*, these inversions of the moral coordinates of classical suspense take place in the context of narratives in which the possibility of romance is extinguished by killing off the heroine, although in the latter film a form of love, after romance has died, remains affirmed in the relationship between the detective and his wife, who between them corner the villain. However, in *Notorious* and *Strangers on a Train*, Hitchcock solicits our identification with the villain in a context where we are also clearly rooting for the hero. In both films, Hitchcock draws in part on a strategy of rendering the villain a sympathetic character by endowing him with desirable traits, but he also contrives, in different ways, to use shared suspense itself as a device to engender sympathy with a character whose narrative role is one that undermines the wished-for fulfillment of the romance.

The antihero in *Notorious*, Alex Sebastian, a German spy whom the heroine, Alicia Huberman, marries in order to penetrate the spy ring of which he forms a part, has many desirable qualities that the cold and wooden hero Devlin lacks. Alex is attentive, generous, and kind to Alicia, until he finally realizes that she is a double agent and conspires, at his mother's behest, to poison her. At the conclusion of the film, as Devlin saves Alicia from death at the hands of Alex's mother, Mme Sebastian (Madame Konstantin) and Alex meet them on the landing. Alex's coconspirators, roused by the commotion, open the door downstairs and look up at the scene on the staircase. When Mme Sebastian realizes that Devlin is on to them, she encourages Alex to play along with his escape plan. Hitchcock cuts rapidly across the look between Devlin (holding Alicia), Alex, and his mother, on the one hand, and between the group on the stairs and the Nazis below looking up at them, on the other, as Alex deliberates whether or not to save Devlin and Alicia.

The central thrust of this suspense sequence clearly turns on our wish for the couple to reach the bottom of the staircase and freedom, and our concern that Devlin's identity will not be betrayed by Alex is underscored by

Suspense

"crosscutting." Yet, at the same time, Hitchcock contrives to make hero and villain allies against a more sinister third party in a way that allows the audience to root for both. Devlin, Alicia, and Alex are placed together relative to the threatening gaze of the Nazi leader, Eric Mathis (Ivan Triesault), and the crosscutting serves to express their parallel positions rather than the opposition between them. The sense that they face a common enemy is confirmed once Alex resolves to help the couple, and furthermore, the voice of his associates below and his mother just above him echo in a manner that evoke a sense that he is, like Alicia, near delirium and victimized by circumstances. By the end of the sequence we thus root for all three of them to get out of the house in the face of a common enemy.

In *Strangers on a Train* two men meet by chance on a train, which is the archetypal space of *romantic* encounter in Hitchcock. One of them, the criminal-dandy Bruno Anthony, proposes to the other, Guy Haines, a plot whereby Bruno offers to get rid of Guy's wife, whom Guy hates, thus freeing him to marry a senator's daughter, if Guy will in turn get rid of Bruno's father, whom Bruno hates, thus allowing Bruno to assume his father's place. Later, Bruno actually commits the murder, while a horrified Guy does not. At the denouement, Bruno, who has turned against Guy, seeks to plant a lighter—an incriminating piece of evidence that will frame Guy for the murder—while Guy, watched by the police, attempts to finish a tournament tennis match in time so he can then foil Bruno's plan.

Hitchcock presents to us what is ostensibly a straightforward moral classical suspense structure in which he crosscuts between Guy Haines, who must win his tennis match and foil the villain in order to win the girl, and Bruno, who seeks to plant the incriminating lighter. However, this suspense is further complicated by the question: will Guy, by playing more aggressively to win the match, alert the cops who are watching him closely to the fact that something is awry, and thereby sabotage his plan? Even so, Hitchcock goes out of his way to encourage us to root for Bruno by having him drop the lighter down a sewage drain and then struggle with great difficulty, in excruciating close-up, to retrieve it. In this way, the opposition between the characters also takes the form of a parallel between them. But unlike the case of *Notorious*, the parallel is drawn between characters who are working for diametrically opposed goals. We want Guy to defeat his tennis opponent so that he can stop Bruno, and yet, at the same time, we are invited to root for Bruno to retrieve the lighter, even as the consequence of

57

this action may be that he will defeat Guy. Perhaps these ostensibly opposed sympathies can exist because, by focalizing on the local and essentially physical struggles of each of the protagonists in this sequence, Hitchcock actually distracts us from the larger moral framework and consequences of their actions. We are drawn to compare their physical struggles, which seem very much alike, and the intense focalization upon Bruno's action leads us to temporarily suspend consideration of its broader narrative consequences and the moral implications of our temporary allegiance.[24]

I have charted specific sequences in which conventional morality is undercut by suspense in Hitchcock's work. But there is one film in his canon, his "experimental narrative" *Rope*, which is structured around the inversion of the moral coordinates of traditional suspense for the first two-thirds of the film. In *Rope*, a man is murdered at the beginning of the film by the film's protagonists, a male couple, Brandon (John Dall) and Phillip (Farley Granger), and deposited in a caisson. The death of this character effectively kills off the possibility of the heterosexual romance, for he is the suitor of the film's nominal heroine Janet Walker (Joan Chandler), whom the couple has invited to a party that same afternoon. The suspense in the film is generated in large part by the fact that the audience is encouraged to wish for the murder to remain concealed to the "audience" of guests at the party in order to not spoil the party and effectively end the show that is the movie itself. Hitchcock encourages us to enjoy, alongside Brandon who orchestrates the party, the way in which the discovery of the corpse in the chest is postponed and deferred. As Victor Perkins has argued, it is only in the last third of the film that the conventional moral alignment of the spectator is restored through the fact that we are invited to identify with the figure of Rupert Cadell (James Stewart), who, as he comes to recognize that a terrible crime has been committed, also realizes his own complicity in their action, a complicity that has also been that of the audience itself.[25]

Is there an ironic edge to suspenseful mystery that is correlative to the manner in which classical suspense may elicit an appreciation for the ways in which the narrative conspires to undermine the desired outcome? I have described suspenseful mystery as the combination of a wish to find something out together with fear of what it contains, which engenders a competing wish for the mystery to remain concealed. But there may be another component to suspenseful mystery that is not easy to state in an uncontentious way. It is not simply that we wish to find out the content of a mystery because we need to *allay* our fears about the secret, where, as it were, our wish exists in spite of our fear. We may wish to find out the secret on account of the fear it causes. As in a taboo situation, we are drawn to the secret like a moth to a flame. Thus, Rebecca is a source of perverse allure to the second Mrs. de Winter, to whom she is irresistibly drawn. To state the full irony or paradox, the second Mrs. de Winter wishes to penetrate the mystery of Rebecca precisely because it is something that she senses is repellent to her, and the spectator is invited to share her fascination. A similar kind of fascination arguably propels Lila Crane or the spectator, for whom Lila Crane is a surrogate in the fiction, to the Bates house in *Psycho*. I shall return to this form of suspense at the conclusion of the chapter.

Black Humor and Suspense

In his discussion of black humor, Sigmund Freud cites the canonical example of a condemned man on his way to the gallows who is overheard to remark, "Well, the week's beginning nicely!"—which is perhaps better translated as "What a way to start the week!"—or who asks for a scarf around his neck in order to prevent his catching cold.[26] The essence of such humor, Freud suggests, "is that one spares oneself the affects to which the situation would naturally give rise and dismisses the possibility of such expressions of emotion with a jest."[27] He describes black humor as a triumph of the ego that refuses to be cowed by adverse circumstances, which thus lends it a tone of grandeur and elevation. The juxtaposition of laughter and morbidity in black humor distills the both/and logic that characterizes romantic irony. Many of the narrative and visual strategies I described in chapter 1 are forms of black humor: the ambiguously threatening gestures of the Lodger; the nun appearing at the end of *Vertigo*; the snakelike coil of Cary Grant's arm in *Suspicion*; Eve Kendall held by Roger Thornhill over the precipice of Mount Rushmore by one hand, while the other gets crushed by the villain in *North by Northwest*. However, here, I am particularly concerned with the relationship that black humor bears to suspense and the characteristic emotion of anxious uncertainty it solicits.

In situations of conventional suspense, black humor is used by Hitchcock to defuse anxiety and relieve us from the stress of the suspense situation in a manner that conforms to Freud's account of the role of black comedy. As

I noted in chapter 1, the deflationary effect of black humor is achieved through the simple device of having a character or characters in the fiction laugh in the context of an otherwise anxiety-inducing situation. A simple example is provided by the hilarious moment in the elevator in *North by Northwest*. Roger Thornhill's flighty mother Clara (Jessie Royce Landis), tired of Roger's silly story about being kidnapped within an inch of his life, says to the men who have been following him: "You gentlemen aren't really trying to kill my son, are you?" They begin to laugh, the mother joins in, and soon the elevator full of people, including the hoodlums chasing him, boisterously erupts, in a manner that creates a self-conscious hiatus in the suspense that at once draws our attention to the seriousness of his situation and also makes fun of it. If we can freely embrace the light-hearted tone of this laughter, it is because we ourselves never really believe that Thornhill is seriously in danger of his life. Another light moment of black comedy from the same film occurs when Grant is "framed" for the murder of Lester Townsend (Philip Ober) by being captured, knife in hand, in the lens of a press photographer. The pun on being "framed" turns the very nasty situation in which the character finds himself into a joke.

The use of humor as a comic relief for the anxiety generated by suspense often becomes a broader structuring principle of an entire narrative in Hitchcock's work, as in *Shadow of a Doubt*, *Rear Window*, and *Frenzy*. In *Shadow of a Doubt* the primary narrative that centers upon the dandy-murderer who holds a dangerous allure for the female protagonist is paralleled by a comic narrative where masculine *resentiment* takes a benign comic form.[28] Joe Newton (Henry Travers), the kind but timid father of the young heroine, and his friend Herb Hawkins (Hume Cronyn), the sensitive "mother's boy," joke about the different ways to commit the perfect murder, in ironic counterpoint to the real-life serial killer, Uncle Charlie or Charles Oakley (Joseph Cotten). The parallelism between the joking friends and Uncle Charlie evokes contrast between them, but it also suggests their affinity. Black humor is a benign outlet for murderous impulses. In a similar way, the fascination with the details of murder expressed by L. B. Jefferies' nurse, Stella (Thelma Ritter), in *Rear Window* provides comic relief from the suspense plot. *Frenzy*, as we saw in chapter 1, is structured by the contrast between the story of an alluring yet psychotic sexual murderer of women and a domestic melodrama of the hen-pecked detective husband who resiliently survives his wife's sadistic imposition of obscene gourmet food while she solves the crime and blames him for imprisoning the wrong man.

However, in cases where Hitchcock exploits the ironic edge of suspense, the relationship between humor and suspense is a more complex and parasitic one. Consider again the time-bomb suspense sequence from *Sabotage*. The way in which Hitchcock places obstacles in the way of the protagonist to increase the likelihood of a negative outcome is characteristic of all classical suspense. But it also seems that this way of orchestrating the story to court disaster and of crafting entertainment out of a dire situation is, incipiently, a species of black comedy. It becomes black comedy the moment we are aware of the irony that the protagonist's fate is being toyed with, that our emotions are being orchestrated, and our anxiety being exploited. As we have seen, Hitchcock's orchestration of this suspense sequence is marked by a high degree of self-consciousness, which serves to distance us from the fate of the boy.

If we concur with Freud that black humor diffuses the negative emotions that govern the circumstances in which it arises, then we might conclude that suspense, when successful as suspense, stops short of being comic, and that, conversely, ironic self-consciousness takes us out of suspense. To some extent, as I have argued, our identification with Stevie is challenged by Hitchcock's way of self-consciously orchestrating suspense. Our responses here are complicated by the fact that the very mechanisms that contribute to suspense are the self-same mechanisms that contribute to the ironic distance we experience toward Stevie's fate. Hitchcock thus drives a wedge into our customary moral responses, and to the extent we become self-conscious about Hitchcock's machinations we suffer, as it were, a second-order anxiety about how it is we are to respond. Should we laugh or not? What is the appropriate response? Here, the ironic edge created by black humor, rather than reducing our discomfort at the protagonist's predicament, undercuts our alignment with that predicament in a manner that creates a different level of anxiety, a kind of second-order anxiety which to some extent mimics the emotion yielded by first-order suspense but whose origins are distinct.

The conclusion of the sequence at once comments upon and compounds this discomfort. After Stevie is blown up, the sound and image of the explosion dissolves with laughter in the parlor of Mrs. Verloc (Sylvia Sydney), which, as James Naremore observes, "resembles nothing so much as the sound of broken glass or shattered debris."[29] The laughter this scene evokes in the spectator (and as Naremore suggests, audiences *do* laugh) is not simply the brittle laughter that characterizes black comedy, it is also the uncomfortable laughter that arises from the sense that the "joke" has been literally forced on us in a manner suggested by the way in which Hitchcock's dissolve juxtaposes two utterly dissociated events.

Where the moral coordinates of conventional suspense are inverted, a third kind of relationship between suspense and black humor is staged. Here, black comedy contributes to the creation of suspense, and suspense becomes a manifestation of black comedy. In *Rope*, our knowledge of the crime in contrast to the ignorance of the partygoers makes us complicit with wrongdoing, but as Thomas Bauso points out, our complicity is fostered by the fact that we are placed in a position to appreciate Brandon's macabre jokes, which are made at the expense of the partygoers. He writes: "We may be appalled at Brandon's 'warped sense of humor' but since we can't help getting the morbid jokes, we are compelled to laugh at them, and our laughter implicates us in the act of murder. We are thus continually being forced to identify with the killers, an identification that is, as [Raymond] Durgnat says, 'paradoxical and tension-charged.'"[30] In this way black humor provides a context for the moral inversion of suspense. But as we have seen, the moral inversion of suspense also contributes to our identification with the devil and thus is, itself, a species of black humor.

Consider the following justly celebrated long-take sequence from *Rope*. The guests have finished eating and the maid leaves them in the living room area and walks screen left to begin clearing the food that has been laid on top of the unlocked caisson containing the corpse. Hitchcock positions the camera just above the chest (which occupies the bottom left quadrant of the screen), while Rupert Cadell's arm frames the screen on the right. The guests, offscreen right, conduct a conversation about the whereabouts of the murder victim as we watch the maid walk to and from the kitchen door (visible in deep space), with the chest in the foreground and becoming ever more accessible to being opened as the dishes and tablecloth are cleared away. The suspense situation is a classical one that turns on the fact that we know, but the guests (and the maid) do not, that the corpse is in the trunk. However, our moral allegiance is inverted. We delight in the irony of the guest's conversation, knowing as we do where the body is hidden, even as we worry about the guests and the maid finding out about what is in the trunk, especially when we see the maid approaching with a pile of books, taken from the dining room table, that she intends to put in the trunk, where they belonged until they were moved to make room for the corpse. Our worry is brilliantly compounded by the way Hitchcock ingeniously embeds suppressive narration within the classical suspense situation. By denying us access to what Brandon and Phillip are seeing, Hitchcock makes us wonder whether they are looking in the direction of the chest and are as clued in as we are about what exactly is going on. Just as the maid is about to open the chest to place the books inside, the character who most suspects foul play, Rupert Cadell, steps up to help her and we watch anxiously as he begins to lift the lid. But thankfully for the spectator, who is surely at this stage appreciating the black comedy and at one level rooting for the villains, Brandon appears from offscreen in the nick of time and deftly averts discovery by placing his hand on the lid of the chest and smoothly intoning: "That's alright, Mrs. Wilson, you can put the books back when you come and clean in the morning."

Is this really a case where comedy enhances rather than diffuses the emotion of anxiety? The key aspect of this situation seems to be the role of black humor in creating the context for suspense. In the case of *Sabotage*, the suspense situation yields incompatible emotional responses in the spectator—anxiety on behalf of the protagonist and, if we get the "joke," delight in the manner that he is being set up, which causes us a sense of acute discomfort. However, in the case of *Rope*, it is the fact that we are made to feel anxiety on behalf of the villain that is a source of discomfort. This discomfort is mitigated by our awareness that Hitchcock is artfully contriving circumstances to put us in this situation. Thus black humor, here, sets the stage for the experience of suspense.

But while black comedy supports the subversion of our customary narrative allegiances in situations of suspense, it can also work at the same time as a counterweight to that identification. Smith shows how this black humor works in *Rope* to undermine the allegiance Hitchcock otherwise establishes with Brandon.[31] A similar effect is achieved in the aforementioned scene in *Frenzy* where we are aligned with a psychotic killer in his efforts to retrieve a tiepin off a corpse that is buried in a sack of potatoes in the back of a truck. Initially, a series of black jokes encourage our identification with Rusk as he places the corpse in the back of the truck. Hitchcock puns on the idea of the body "weighing like a sack of potatoes." Rusk's sense of relief is echoed in the license plate "FUW" on the truck and also by a melody that combines discordant strings with a playful trill on the piccolo accompanied by discordant laughter (cuing the black comedy). Suddenly Rusk realizes that the corpse clutches in her hand a tiepin that will incriminate him in the murder, and he is forced to return to the potato truck to retrieve it, inaugurating the sequence of shared suspense.

Individual moments of black comedy provide us with an alibi to watch his otherwise obscenely degrading behavior and even to sympathize with his predicament. Rusk scrabbles about in the "bowels" of the truck, rummaging among the potatoes, which resemble feces and are hard to distinguish from the flesh of the corpse itself. Rusk burrows his body into the potato sack, and when the driver brakes, his head is thrust up between the legs of the corpse. When Rusk finally uncovers the pin, he cannot release it from the corpse's deathgrip with his penknife, which breaks, and so with his bare hands he is forced to break each finger, which cracks with a loud, excruciating snap and only opens after a tremendous effort.

The way that Hitchcock invites us to root for Rusk during this ordeal is an extreme instance of black comedy combining with suspense to elicit sympathy with the devil. However, the sequence is much more complicated than it first appears. The humor not only works with Rusk but against him, both in the manner that the corpse holds the tiepin, but also in the way in which the corpse "assaults" Rusk. The content of this scene is lifted almost verbatim from Arthur La Bern's novel, *Goodbye Piccadilly, Hello Leicester Square*, from which the film was adapted, but the key difference is that, in the novel, Rusk engages in necrophilia. Here, while Hitchcock hints at necrophilia, he reverses its import; Rusk is forced, as it were, by the woman's corpse, to bury his head between her legs. Finally, even the action of breaking the corpse's fingers is double-edged: each loud crack of the finger cues immense relief from Rusk when he is successful, but is also a shocking reminder of the corpse's resistance to his actions.

Sexuality and Suspense

I have discussed in some detail how the ironic, darkly humorous edge of suspense in Hitchcock invites us to enjoy the process of being held in suspense, and I have suggested that suspenseful mystery may also be endowed with an ironic edge when the concealed threat is represented as alluring. In either case, Hitchcock provides an incentive to enjoy suspense by trading upon the allure of human perversity. Since Hitchcock typically treats human sexuality as incipiently perverse, it is implicitly linked to murderous or self-annihilating impulses. Sexuality itself is something that is at once to be feared and yet to be wished for, and it is therefore endowed with an aura of suspense or anxious anticipation that we are invited to savor. Hitchcock's suspense scenarios stage, in displaced or disguised form, a sexual content that renders the anticipation of an ostensibly immoral outcome perversely enjoyable.

The relationship between sexuality and style and the forms of aestheticism this relationship yields in Hitchcock's work is the subject matter of chapter 4. However, here I want to anticipate the argument of that chapter by drawing a distinction between the way in which the displaced expression of human sexuality contributes to the two types of suspense I have identified. Hitchcock's aestheticism characteristically involves at once invoking human perversity and holding it at bay as a kind of visual pun or darkly comic double-entendre. I call this ludic aesthetic a masculine one, after Hitchcock himself, who in the context of discussing his adaptation of Daphne du Maurier's novel, *Rebecca*, referred to his own distinctive brand of humor as a masculine one in contrast to the feminine characteristics of the novel, perhaps because of the way his humor functions to invoke human intimacy, only to hold that intimacy at arm's length in the manner that is culturally associated with men rather than women, and in a manner that contrasts with what he perceived to be the feminine concerns of du Maurier's novel.[32] André Bazin reports that Hitchcock complained to him about "the necessity of renouncing adult, masculine humor in order to satisfy American producers."[33] In the context of suspense, this masculine aesthetic is often manifest in sequences where Hitchcock manipulates the idioms of classical suspense in order to playfully register the perverse motivations of a male character.

The Lodger provides an early eloquent expression of this aesthetic. As we have seen, the central question posed in the film is whether or not the eponymous "hero," who appears to be in love with the heroine, is a serial killer. Hitchcock dramatizes this thought by consistently endowing his actions with ambiguity through editing, visual expressionism, and Ivor Novello's performance. Is he reaching for the poker to put out the fire or to strike the heroine? Is he approaching the bathroom to apologize for giving her a gift or to attack her? Is his look the look of love or annihilation? This orchestration of narrative ambiguity creates (classical) suspense of the conventional kind—we fear for the heroine's safety. However, it does so in a revealingly self-conscious way: Hitchcock teases us with the thought that the Lodger might be a sexual murderer rather than leading us to believe that such is the case. It is as if the "murderous" quality that informed the Lodger's attitude of admiration toward Daisy were something to be enjoyed. The rationale of suspense here seems to be that while the audience is invited to root for the heroine and fear on her behalf, we are also invited to enjoy the portrayal of a desire that is perverse and potentially deadly. The conventional moral coordinates of suspense are undermined by the invitation to enjoy the threat posed by the hero and the sexual tension it evokes.

A second, more straightforward example of this kind of sexualization of suspense is the scene from *Strangers on a Train* that is staged in the carnivalesque atmosphere of a fairground. Bruno Anthony stalks Miriam, the estranged wife of Guy Haines, having resolved to murder her on Guy's behalf. We know that Bruno is insane, and the pregnant Miriam herself is portrayed (misogynistically perhaps) as a wholly disreputable character, thus we feel little sympathy for her. But we do not know what exactly Bruno is going to do. We anxiously anticipate the probable outcome as Miriam flirts and Bruno stalks her in a provocative dance of proximity and distance that orchestrates the progressive building of sexual tension, until their final deadly embrace. Taken at face value, the immoral outcome of a sordid murder is scarcely wished for, although like Bruno, with whom we have been invited to identify, we can scarcely be disappointed at the demise of the shrill and manipulative Miriam. However, Hitchcock invites us to positively relish the suspense that the anticipation of this negative outcome solicits, because suspense is the pretext for enjoying a frank display of sexual desire. Hitchcock aligns us with Bruno's point of view and evokes, with extraordinary formal dexterity, the thrill of the sexual chase, laced with the aura of deadliness. Insofar as we are invited to sympathize with the devil, the whole sequence inscribes suspense as a form of black comedy, and individual comic moments provide an incentive for our allegiance: Bruno gratuitously pops a little boy's balloon (bursting his bubble); he suddenly appears right beside Miriam in her personal space just when she wasn't looking; his shadow appears to envelop and swallow Miriam as his boat follows hers in the tunnel of love.

Hitchcock also embeds suspense structures within scenarios of voyeurism or eavesdropping and in this way lends suspense an aura of perversity. In general, scenes of male voyeurism in Hitchcock playfully exploit the distinction between character and spectator, as well as their possible alignment. As we saw in chapter 1, pace those critics who align the spectator's voyeurism with that of the character within the fiction, the spectator is never a voyeur in the way a character in the fiction is a voyeur. They are at best a camera-voyeur. My discussion of *Rear Window* showed that while a character's voyeurism can be an excuse or pretext for the spectator's camera voyeurism, it can also be an identification that the spectator opts out of. However, Hitchcock also exploits the opposite possibility—namely, that an instance of spying in a suspenseful situation is endowed with an aura of perversity in spite of the ostensible innocence of the character involved.

In his interviews with Truffaut and elsewhere, Hitchcock fondly recounted the scene from *Easy Virtue* (1927) where the telephone operator eavesdrops on a marriage proposal. Will the proposal lead to marriage? Hitchcock cites this as a suspenseful circumstance involving romance that does not include the expectation of something fearful. We hope for the couple to marry and worry that the man might not pull it off. But the context of Hitchcock's discussion with Truffaut also suggests this may be a case of what he calls "suspense of situation" in contrast to the kind of suspense that involves "what happens next." Of course, "what happens next" is important to the representation of suspense in the scene;[34] nonetheless, Hitchcock's idea of "suspense of situation" is suggestive. The content of the suspense here is not perverse, but the suspense is embedded in a specific subjective situation, in particular one of eavesdropping on the private lives of strangers. In this way our engagement with the suspenseful "narrative" that we are privy to hear over the phone line is given an aura of "naughtiness." Rather more interesting than this anodyne example is the situation I described in chapter 1 that Hitchcock constructs in *Rear Window*. In a condition of acute anxiety and apparent concern, L. B. Jefferies looks upon Lisa Fremont under assault, but the spectator is invited to perversely relish this scene in a way that the character ostensibly does not.

There is a complex scene in *The Lodger* where both responses are evoked. Since the central character in *The Lodger* is himself ambiguously perverse, we at once respond to him as a perverse character from whom we can distance ourselves and as an innocent character who is a vehicle for our own perverse look. Perched at the top of a "Victorian" staircase, the Lodger peers down at the heroine, transfixed, as she struggles to free herself from her policeman boyfriend, who has handcuffed her at the culmination of a playful sexual chase. Unlike the situation portrayed in *Easy Virtue*, this has an implicit sexual content that links the sexual chase to domination and submission. However, in staging the scene in this way, Hitchcock authorizes the spectator to recognize the scene as a displaced expression of sexual perversity (sadomasochism) because we view it through a "pervert's" gaze. He also allows us to distance ourselves from this thought because of the "excuse" provided by the presence of the voyeuristic character. Yet, at the same time, we perceive the character as innocent, and this innocence provides us an excuse to appreciate the perversity of the scene.

What I shall call Hitchcock's feminine aesthetic emerges in his adaptation of Daphne du Maurier's *Rebecca*, where he was obliged by his producer, David Selznick, to direct a "faithful" adaptation. Although Hitchcock complained about the absence of his own masculine humor, he discovered a cinematic aesthetic that realizes the concerns of the novel, in particular the sense in which the novel suggests but does not state that the fascination the figure of Rebecca holds for the lesbian housekeeper Mrs. Danvers, and via Mrs. Danvers for the second Mrs. de Winter herself, is an erotic one. Hitchcock registers the presence of Rebecca through the mise-en-scène of shimmering rain and the looming shadows that are cast on the whitewashed walls of Manderley, and through the tokens of Rebecca's presence in the house that are lovingly preserved by Danvers. Manderley is at once a tomblike memorial to Rebecca and a womblike place of sublime beauty, and the second Mrs. De Winter, while repelled by Danvers, is irresistibly drawn by the allure Rebecca holds for her that is inscribed, in displaced fashion, in the sublime mise-en-scène of the film.

Hitchcock's feminine aesthetic operates in the context of suspenseful mystery to give expression to perverse allure through editing and visual style. This aesthetic, like Hitchcock's masculine ludic aesthetic, is an aestheticized expression of human sexuality, for sexuality is only indirectly expressed through visual style. However, Hitchcock's feminine aesthetic does not marshal editing and visual style in order to assert a sexual content through a form of visual punning. Instead, editing, camera movement, and mise-en-scène serve to register the object of desire, writ large in the visual and aural textures of the film, as something of overwhelming and sublime beauty whose mystery is a source of fear, awe, and desire. It bears comparison with what Gaylyn Studlar, discussing the films of Josef von Sternberg, has termed a "masochistic" aesthetic. For, in the context of suspenseful mystery, the aesthetic surface of the film invites the spectator to be enraptured by something that is incipiently harmful and to enjoy the prolongation of suspense.[35] In a comparable way, one could argue that Hitchcock's ludic masculine aesthetic, which fosters the inversion of our allegiance in classical suspense, is a "sadistic" aesthetic that is made possible by black humor.

Unlike Hitchcock's inscription of the male gaze, where voyeurism is at once registered and then criticized (as in *Rear Window*) or turned into something that can be denied (as in *The Lodger*), a female gaze of an explicitly sexual character is completely absent, here, as it is absent throughout Hitchcock's work, with the occasional exception, like the sexual come-on purveyed by Miriam to Bruno in *Strangers on a Train*, for which she is severely punished.[36] Instead, the second Mrs. de Winter's fascinated gaze upon the traces of Rebecca's presence in the house takes on the lure of something that is taboo through the manner in which it is governed and mediated by the figure of Mrs. Danvers, who clearly harbors an erotic attraction to Rebecca and is constantly spying and eavesdropping on the second Mrs. de Winter, though we never see her engaged in this activity from her point of view. Thus while suspenseful mystery in *Rebecca* inscribes a feminine aesthetic or gaze,[37] this gaze is defined not primarily by the fact that the person looking is a female character, the second Mrs. de Winter, but in the sublime nature of the visual array that holds her in thrall.

This distinction is important because in Hitchcock's later work, *Vertigo*, which is organized, like *Rebecca*, as a suspenseful mystery, the nominal owner of that gaze is a male character while at the same time the film is the fullest realization of Hitchcock's feminine aesthetic. I shall establish this argument in chapter 4, but let us note here some key features that link *Vertigo* to *Rebecca*. If Scottie is a voyeur in the first part of the film, it appears so only in retrospect. Scottie's goal is to find out what the woman he thinks is Madeleine is up to, and this involves him spying on her, but this spying, it seems to me, is never overtly sexual in the manner of L. B. Jefferies' spying in *Rear Window*. Furthermore, the object of his desire is a fiction, Judy as possessed by Madeleine, whose presence is itself a part of and manifest within the visual style and mise-en-scène of the work, in the same way that Rebecca's presence is in this way inscribed. Finally, as a consequence of this, the figuration of Judy as Madeleine, as someone to whom Scottie (and the spectator) is in thrall, is extended to the film as a whole, and which itself becomes an object of sublime fascination.

Suspense in Hitchcock thus ultimately reaches beyond the more obvious parameters of narrative form with which I began this chapter to mesh with Hitchcock's overall approach to visual style. Hitchcock's mastery of suspense consists in being an aesthete of suspense, and this involves, at once, giving perverse sexual content to the anticipated outcome in a suspenseful situation (often disguised) and prolonging that outcome (or the revelation of the disguise) through the self-conscious play of style. The sexual content of his masculine aesthetic is characteristically linked to predatory, phallic masculinity and is inscribed through visual and aural double-entendres. Furthermore, it usually involves the aestheticization of classical suspense. Hitchcock's feminine aesthetic, in contrast, idealizes human sexuality as a source of perverse, self-annihilating allure. This allure is expressed, in displaced fashion, through sublime form and is characteristically linked to the representation of female sexuality. In both cases, narrative form—the rhetorical structures of suspense—is thoroughly interwoven with style, via the role that the lure of (perverse) sexuality plays in both, and in a way that gives rise, once again, to the distinctive tone of Hitchcock's work.

In chapter 4, I shall come to modify this picture. For although what I have called Hitchcock's masculine aesthetic is contingently linked to the displaced representation of predatory or sadistic masculinity, and his feminine aesthetic is contingently linked to the idealization of a sublime femininity, other possibilities occur. Predatory masculinity is often inscribed in Hitchcock with a homoerotic character through the rhetorical analogies Hitchcock constructs between suspenseful mystery and homoerotic desire which idealize or render sublime anal-phallic masculinity. It is hard to think of Hitchcock's masculine aesthetic being given a feminine content; however, in his late works of horror, *Psycho* and *The Birds*, his feminine and masculine aesthetics arguably combine.

Before I turn in detail to exploring Hitchcock's aestheticism, I want to discuss a topic that has received even less treatment in studies of Hitchcock than the role of suspense, yet is, in part, complementary to that role; namely, recognition. If suspense involves the withholding of knowledge, recognition marks its achievement. As we have seen, Hitchcock engenders suspense at once by calibrating and controlling what a character in the fiction knows, and by orchestrating the spectator's relationship to what it is that a character knows. Recognition, in contrast, marks the moment of revelation, one which may sometimes be given to the spectator and not the character, and thereby yield further suspense. But what is the nature of the quest for knowledge whose outcome is dramatized by suspense? What kind of knowledge is sought, withheld, and subsequently revealed? And what are the moral consequences of the pursuit and achievement of knowledge in the lives of Hitchcock's protagonists. Chapter 3 will read Hitchcock's films not for in the way in which he tells his stories, but in the stories themselves, in order to trace the way in which the pursuit and achievement of knowledge at once makes romance possible and renders it a source of profound ambivalence.

3
Knowledge and Sexual Difference

In chapter 1, I defined the both/and logic of romantic irony in terms of two complementary aspects of the text. The "vertical" axis of romantic irony describes the way in which the author manifests himself as the organizing inspiration behind the work, orchestrating its self-evidently fictional elements. The "horizontal" aspect describes the organization of the romantic both/and logic across the film, particularly with respect to the opposition between the romantic ideal and the sources of human perversity which may support or derail it. In chapter 2, we saw how suspense is the primary mode of romantic irony in Hitchcock's work. Hitchcock uses suspense to control our knowledge about what is happening in the narrative vis-à-vis the knowledge of characters within the narrative, and he combines suspense with black humor to subvert our customary moral expectations, which are tied to our allegiance to the romantic ideal. In both chapters the emphasis has been on Hitchcock's self-consciously playful orchestration of the story in a manner that directly involves and addresses the spectator.

In the course of this discussion, I have had occasion to refer to Hitchcock's "wrong man" and sometimes "wrong woman" plots of mistaken identity. I have discussed the "wrong man" motif either as a benign criminal outsider masquerade, a pretext for emphasizing the romantic allure of the "wrong man" hero, or as something more threatening (even as it might be alluring), and hence as a source of both suspense and black comedy. But as Hitchcock himself recognized, there is something of more than entertainment value in these stories that pose the problem of how we are to discriminate virtue from villainy. In his 1956 film *The Wrong Man*, he sets out, he claims, to tell the real-life story of what happens to someone who is wrongly accused of a crime. It is a sad story of an ordinary man, Christopher Emmanuel "Manny" Balestrero (aptly and brilliantly played by Henry Fonda), who stoically suffers wrongful accusation, humiliating incarceration, a fruitless search to clear his name, and the slow descent into mental illness of his wife Rose (Vera Miles) that results from the failure of their joint quest to redeem him in the eyes of the law.

Hitchcock's claim that *The Wrong Man* is a real-life story is made in an opening prologue that is narrated by him in person in the manner of his television shows of the 1950s. Tellingly, he is only visible in a distant long shot and in silhouette. He thus both appears and fails to appear:

This is Alfred Hitchcock speaking. In the past, I have given you many kinds of suspense pictures. But this time I would like you to see a different one. The difference lies in the fact that this is a true story, every word of it. And yet, it contains elements that are stranger than all the fiction that has gone into many of the thrillers that I've made before.

The manner of this prologue might suggest to the spectator who is familiar with Hitchcock's introductions to his television shows in the 1950s that the idea that this film is a true story—"every word of it"—should not be taken at face value. Yet in fact the film cleaves closely to the fine details and order of events of the real-life story that had been published as "A Case of Identity" in *Life* magazine by Herbert Brean in 1953.[1]

However, like most of Hitchcock's films, *The Wrong Man* is fabricated around the ironic logic of parallelism and doubling, between the "wrong man" who is right and the "right man" who is wrong. Furthermore, *The Wrong Man* contains Hitchcock's characteristic ambivalence between the story of romantic renewal and ironic inversion. One place where Hitchcock does depart from the true story is that he exaggerates the weakness of Manny's alibis (all his witnesses are dead, unlike the real-life story), and the incompetence of his lawyer, in order to suggest the hopelessness of Manny's situation and prepare the way for his redemption through a momentous and sublime directorial intervention. In the real-life story Manny reports,

"It's a horrible feeling, having someone accuse you. You can't imagine what was inside of me. I prayed for a miracle," and Brean comments that a miracle of sorts occurred when there was a mistrial.[2] In the film, the answer to Manny's prayers is not the mistrial, but discovery of the villain on the street through a dissolve that links Manny's face to the face of the criminal. At the same time, Mrs. Balestrero's breakdown is dramatized by Hitchcock as an ironic twist to the story: Manny's redemption comes too late to preserve his wife's sanity.

The story of the film seems to end with Manny visiting a detached and distant Rose in an asylum, accompanied by Bernard Herrmann's haunting, Wagnerian-inspired theme. Manny and Rose's nurse close the door on her and walk away from the camera down a darkened corridor illuminated from the rear in a way that silhouettes them. It is a shot that anticipates the scene that concludes the first half of *Vertigo*. Then, suddenly, the tone of the music abruptly shifts to a sunny upbeat orchestration, and we are informed by a written title that two years later Rose has "completely recovered" and is now living happily in Florida with Manny and the boys. The image of the dark corridor dissolves to an extreme long shot of the family walking along a Florida avenue. This is a characteristically Hitchcockian double ending that is entirely consistent with the ambiguous or double endings that conclude a number of his films as well as the tacked-on happy endings in film noirs of the period.[3] For an audience familiar with Hitchcock's television shows, it recalls the way in which he would sometimes narrate, in the epilogue, a moral or happy ending after the content of the show had left an immoral or unhappy ending intact.[4]

However, irony is, characteristically, a double-edged sword. If *The Wrong Man* is not "real life" because it is like Hitchcock's other films, it is still, in comparison with Hitchcock's other works, very much modeled on "real life," not simply in the factual sense but also in the way that it is a serious exploration of the emotional consequences of wrongful imprisonment that lacks Hitchcock's customary entertainment values. It is shot in the semi-documentary style that had been popularized in police procedurals of the 1950s following the success of Jules Dassin's 1948 film *The Naked City* (produced by Mark Hellinger). If Hitchcock's films are characteristically, as he put it, slices of cake rather than slices of life,[5] *The Wrong Man* is a slice of life depicting in relentless detail the dehumanization of Manny through interrogation and incarceration. There is little dramatization of suspense in the film since, although we wish for Manny to be rescued from his plight, the prospects for the narrative outcome are relentlessly negative until

Hitchcock's deus ex machina dissolve. The film also lacks humor other than humor of the blackest kind. The signal instance of "laughter" occurs when Rose starts giggling in response to the fateful "metaphysical" irony that both witnesses who might support Manny's alibi have died. Her laughter signals her descent into mental illness. *The Wrong Man* also lacks "romance" in the sense that the couple is already formed as happily, if ordinarily, married and the story is a muted family melodrama of how external events beyond their control disrupt their life.[6]

The significance of *The Wrong Man* in Hitchcock's oeuvre thus lies in the fact that it is, in this way, both different from and like his other works. It shares both structure and theme with other "wrong man" films, but unlike them it presents the implications of misrecognition with utmost seriousness. Misrecognition has profound consequences for the lives of the protagonists, even when the criminal is finally apprehended. If one reads Hitchcock for his plots rather than only for the manner in which he narrates them, the study of the nature of knowledge, misrecognition, and its ambivalent consequences for the couple that forms the subject matter of *The Wrong Man* emerges as the abiding concern of all Hitchcock's work. Hitchcock's films are about the search for truth as the revelation of virtue and villainy, and the impact of that search for truth and its failure for the formation of the couple.

The logic of romantic irony in Hitchcock's work thus involves not simply the playful orchestration of a contradictory and ambivalent stance toward the narrative world of the film through strategies of doubling that subvert our customary moral responses. It also dramatizes the contradictory and ambivalent role that the search for knowledge plays in establishing or undermining the ideal of romance. This chapter explores the role of epistemology within the characteristic forms of Hitchcock's romantic irony. It identifies the way in which the nature of knowledge is at once based upon and helps to define distinctions between gender and sexuality in Hitchcock's work and the different kinds of recognition narratives that both invoke and arise from these distinctions.

Gender, Sexuality, and Plots of Recognition

In the *Poetics*, Aristotle defines recognition (*anagnorisis*) as "a change from ignorance to knowledge, producing either love or hate between the persons destined by the poet for good or bad fortune," and he conceived it to be at the heart of the tragic plot.[7] Recognition, both in Aristotle and Hitchcock's plots, consists in a change in the nature of what we know, usually knowledge about a character's identity that results in the establishment or breakdown of friendship or kinship ties and the reversal of fortune for a character or characters. Recognition is essential not only to establishing individual virtue but also, by vindicating the exemplary individual, to affirming the integrity and legitimacy of the social order itself. In a classic recognition plot, like the narrative of Odysseus, the accurate identification of the protagonist involves recognizing that he is a rightful member of the family and the society he claims to be a part of. In a fairy-tale romance such as "Cinderella," recognition ensures redemption of virtue, acknowledgement of kinship, and the restoration of the social order through marriage.

As Terence Cave emphasizes, all recognition narratives involve a form of knowledge that is based upon inference that turns upon the discovery and understanding of a tell-tale piece of visual or aural information (Odysseus's scar, the foot that fits the glass slipper, etc.). He proposes that the form of knowledge involved in recognition narratives is "the same mode of knowledge as the signature, the clue, the fingerprint or footprint and all the other tracks and traces that enable an individual to be identified, a criminal to be caught, a hidden event or state of affairs to be reconstructed."[8] Following Carlo Ginzburg's suggestion that the ancestral model of this form of knowledge lies in the practices of hunting, Cave calls this model of knowledge the "cynegetic model" by analogy with the French word cynégétique, after the Greek word for hunting. The analeptic or retrospective reconstruction of events that characterizes tracking finds modern equivalents in the arts of connoisseurship, detection (as least as it is practiced by Sherlock Holmes), and psychoanalysis. This kind of knowledge contrasts with the abstract, theoretical knowledge prized by Galilean science that is concerned with identifying general principles that underlie and unify discreet particulars, for it is a knowledge that is pragmatic, concerned with the particular, and one that depends on the kind of intuition that "make[s] capital out of chance occurrences: the talent sometimes known as serendipity."[9]

Hitchcock's plots are contrived from modern archetypes of the recognition narrative where the process of tracking and detection implicit in myth and romance are conventionalized in detective fiction and the spy story that self-consciously plot the establishment of law and order against those forces that seek to undermine it. They, too, typically feature a telling piece of visual information, such as an inscription on a ring (*Shadow of a Doubt*), a necklace (*Vertigo*), a missing finger (*The 39 Steps*), or twitching eyes (*Young and Innocent*, 1937), that discriminates the villain—Hitchcock's penchant for visual storytelling is deeply embedded in narrative archetypes. Occasionally the nature of the evidence is aural, like the high-pitched voice of the villain, Handel Fane (Esme Percy), in *Murder!*, that a witness confuses for a woman's voice. At the same time, Hitchcock's plots invoke another modern form of recognition narrative that links the discrimination of virtue from villainy to the investigation, diagnosis, or description of a psychological profile, whose model is provided by Freudian psychoanalysis. Hitchcock's plots typically involve identifying, tracking down, and neutralizing the threat posed to social propriety, procreative sexuality, and the future of the race by a figure of criminal perversity. Characteristically, this figure is a dandy whose concern with self-deportment and surface appearance harbors a perverse core of incipiently murderous sexuality, such as the character of Handel Fane in *Murder!*, Uncle Charlie in *Shadow of a Doubt*, or Bruno Anthony in *Strangers on a Train*.[10]

As Cave points out, the kind of knowledge involved in narratives of recognition may be subject to doubt. If knowledge of who a character is turns wholly on a tell-tale piece of visual evidence, such as Odysseus's scar, deception or false identification is always on the cards. As we saw in chapter 1, the orchestration of doubt or uncertainty about the nature of appearances that leads to mistaken inferences about guilt or innocence is a central way in which romantic irony is articulated in Hitchcock films. Hitchcock's films are peopled with heroes (male or female) who may be false heroes, and heroes who are wrongly accused—the figure of the wrong or wronged man (or woman). Indeed, the specter of wrongful incarceration haunts Hitchcock's films with such insistence that critics invariably refer to the apocryphal story that Hitchcock himself invoked to explain the pervasiveness of this theme—of his boyhood incarceration in a local police station arranged by his father.[11]

It is tempting to read into Hitchcock's dramatization of the instability of recognition claims the idea that his films tell us something essential about the nature of knowledge, or about the kind of knowledge claims that can be made in narratives. For example, Hitchcock's orchestration of uncertainty may seem to provide support for Cave's own "deconstructive" claim that narrative truth is inherently provisional or unstable, and that Hitchcock's work therefore dramatizes an underlying skepticism toward knowledge claims that depend on inference. Hitchcock's meditations on the idea of the MacGuffin as a plot pretext have inevitably furthered this kind of speculation. Hitchcock, borrowed the parable of the MacGuffin from sometime screenwriter Angus MacPhail: "What's a MacGuffin?" "It's an apparatus for trapping lions in the Scottish highlands." "But there are no lions in the Scottish Highlands." "Then that is no MacGuffin."[12] He used it to describe the way that the object of the quest in his films is arbitrary: the MacGuffin exists just as a something to provide a telos or goal for the plot and the actions of the characters, like the missing raincoat that motivates the plot of *Young and Innocent*, the uranium bottle in *Notorious*, or the microfilm that structures the quest of *North by Northwest*. However, to "deconstructive" critics of Hitchcock like Christopher Morris, the MacGuffin is much more than a plot pretext. The MacGuffin is the paradigm of the sign without a referent, or a sign whose referent is nothing, and hence essentially or "always already" undecidable. Hitchcock's films do not simply contain such "signs" as their plot pretext, they are constituted out of these signs.[13]

However, recognition in Hitchcock's films is not *in general* undecidable. In his "wrong man" narratives of the 1930s such as *Young and Innocent* and *The 39 Steps*, and his "wrong man" stories of the 1950s such as *To Catch a Thief* and *North by Northwest*, the innocence of the "wrong man" hero is never in doubt, at least for the audience. Conversely, in Hitchcock's narratives of ironic inversion like *Psycho* and *Vertigo*, while both protagonists and audience members are duped by an extreme and incipiently deadly form of deception, both in the end come to an understanding about the true nature of the deception. Hitchcock reveals to us Gavin Elster's diabolical plot even before Scottie Ferguson grasps its significance, and in *Psycho*, eventually, the true identity of Norman Bates as the killer is revealed. Even in narratives of ironic ambivalence, the audience is, in many cases, left in no doubt as to who the villain is. For example, while early in the narrative *Rear Window* temporarily dramatizes uncertainty as to whether or not Lars Thorwald killed his wife—by showing the audience Thorwald leaving the apartment with a woman who looks like his wife, while Jefferies sleeps—it progressively confirms the suspicions of the protagonists and the audience as to who the villain is rather than prolonging uncertainty. What we continue to doubt is whether the couple is really compatible. In *Shadow of a Doubt*, the audience is never significantly in doubt that Uncle Charlie is the Merry Widow Murderer, and when the police claim that they have apprehended the true criminal, we conclude that, ironically, they have got the wrong man. Instead, the drama turns on when the young protagonist, Charlie Newton (Teresa Wright), will discover the truth about him, and she finds out two-thirds of the way through the film.

To the extent that Hitchcock is a "skeptic," his skepticism lies not in doubts about the attainability of knowledge, but in doubts about the reliability of appearances. The unreliability of appearances is dramatized, as we shall see in chapter 5, by Hitchcock's use of expressionist mise-en-scène. Truth in Hitchcock is often, even characteristically, confounded by what we initially see, because the capacity for clear-headed understanding is often tainted by the emotions and interests that inform our perception. Thus in *The Wrong Man*, Manny is fingered by the female clerk as the man responsible for robbing the insurance office because his clothing and manner of deportment resemble those of the criminal; and once the idea has been planted in her mind, all his actions, like the action of innocently reaching into his coat for his wallet, conspire to confirm her initial perception. It is a perception that is then supported by her colleagues in a manner that resembles an emotional contagion. Yet, as we have seen, in *The Wrong Man* Manny is clearly innocent, an innocence that is never doubted by the audience and unambiguously affirmed at the end of the film.

The idea of the MacGuffin, while important, is salient only to some of Hitchcock's films, that is, to Hitchcock narratives of romantic renewal like *The 39 Steps* or *North by Northwest*, which are based upon the form of the quest thriller. The presence of the MacGuffin in these stories indicates that the pursuit of knowledge is essentially a pretext for bringing about the formation of the couple. The random nature of the object pursuit is an index of the self-consciously arbitrary and fictive character of the narrative worlds of these films. The MacGuffin does not have intrinsic significance like the pot of gold at the end of the rainbow; its role is purely functional. The pursuit of the MacGuffin gives the hero stature, possession of it discriminates hero from villain, and its discovery allows the wronged name of the hero to be restored and the couple to be formed. The MacGuffin, in fact, corresponds to our sense that the misrecognition that initially frames the hero of these films as the wrong man is something that we should enjoy rather than take seriously. Indeed, in this sense the "wrong man" idea in Hitchcock's narratives of romantic renewal is itself the real MacGuffin. Hitchcock and Ernest Lehman acknowledged this when they made the hero of *North by Northwest* one Roger O. Thornhill, whose central initial stands, he tells us, for nothing, and who is mistaken for and then assumes the identity of a nonexistent double agent, one George Kaplan.[14]

However, in Hitchcock's narratives of ironic ambivalence and inversion as varied as *Blackmail*, *Rebecca*, *Marnie*, or *Vertigo*, the quest is not to find the MacGuffin and unmask the criminal or secret agent who has committed the crime for which the hero is accused. Rather, what is fundamentally at stake is the question of believing that one knows and can influence, getting to know or failing to know, the mind of another person. The pursuit of knowledge is imbricated in interpersonal relationships and implicated in structures of social hierarchy and power that are internal to those relationships. This yields, at best, Hitchcock's characteristically ambivalent stance toward romantic renewal and, at worst, undermines romantic renewal entirely.

In one kind of story, usually but not necessarily focalized from the standpoint of the male protagonist, the male lead takes on the role of a detective who investigates the wrong woman (as in *Blackmail*, *Murder!*, *The Paradine Case* [1947], *Under Capricorn* (1949), *Marnie*, or *Vertigo*). Whereas the "wrong man" hero is a victim of impersonal forces of social authority (and in the process of clearing his name, the incompetence or uncaring nature of these authorities may be exposed), the detective-hero is a figure of authority who is in a position to mobilize the full force of the law to secure the romantic resolution that suits him. His pursuit of knowledge is a self-interested one that is intrinsically linked to winning the woman he loves. Stories in which the hero is a detective typically involve both the elimination of the figure of the criminal-dandy and the investigation and "containment" of wrong women whose actual or latent promiscuity must be reconciled to the social order. This "containment" involves a level of coercion, even though the alternative is even more unpalatable. For if the criminal figure fails to be eliminated, he preys on the heroine and undercuts the possibility of romantic renewal entirely, as in *Rope*, *Psycho*, and *Frenzy*.

A second kind of narrative is derived from the "gothic melodrama," in which a female protagonist on the cusp of womanhood falls in love with a handsome yet brooding man of the world. However, when they live together, he begins to pose a threat to her and she is forced by circumstances to investigate the secret that he harbors. The man is conventionally an authority figure who is old enough to be the heroine's father, as in *Rebecca* and *Shadow of a Doubt*, but in Hitchcock's *Suspicion* he is the same age as the heroine. All three films are focalized through the point of view of the heroine, who is forced to recognize the fact that the man she is in thrall to is latently murderous or perverse. In each case, the heroine must detach herself from this figure and assume agency in order to discover the true nature of this secret. In some of Hitchcock's most fully realized works, the detective plot combines with the elements of the female-centered domestic melodrama, as in *Sabotage*, *Shadow of a Doubt*, and *Notorious*, where the hero-detective rescues the woman from the murderous older man she is living with.

Structuring both the jointly focalized narratives of romantic renewal and the male and female narratives of detection and ironic ambivalence is a fundamental distinction that can be drawn in Hitchcock's work between male and female forms of knowing and being, even as that distinction is called into question. The female mode of interacting and relating to the world is rooted in bonds of emotional attachment or empathy with others, and more abstractly in a sense of attunement with their environment. This way of relating is not primarily based upon reason, yet it can afford knowledge of another in a manner that straightforward inference does not. In Hitchcock's films women "solve" crimes not so much by a process of ratiocination but through their emotional openness, which allows them to enter into the confidence of others, and by their overall adaptability and attunement to different environments in which they find themselves, which may, as in *Stage Fright*, involve the capacity to act and to wear a disguise. At the very least, Hitchcock's heroines have the ability to enter into alien environments and "provoke" something into taking place, like the intrepid heroine of *Young and Innocent*. In addition, of course, women possess an intuitive, immediately available knowledge of other women that is flaunted by Lisa Fremont, the heroine of *Rear Window*, when she claims a knowledge that L. B. Jefferies could not possibly possess: a woman would never leave her wedding ring behind when she goes for a trip! Reasoning may certainly be involved in female deliberation—indeed women are men's equal in reasoning; nonetheless, reasoning is something that men do (unless they are mentally impaired in their "wrong man" situation, as is John Ballantine, played by Gregory Peck, in *Spellbound*), whereas women's intuition sets them apart from men; it is a value added.

Female attachment or solicitousness not only helps them to solve crimes, their motivation to solve crimes itself invariably stems from their capacity for attachment or attunement with the other—from their capacity for love—as in, for example, *Rebecca*, *Suspicion*, *Spellbound*, or *Rear Window*. Love in Hitchcock embodies a secularized version of faith that is the residue of Hitchcock's Catholicism.[15] Women are the bearers of this faith, and their quest for knowledge arises out of the effort to vindicate their faith, especially where that faith is challenged or called into question. Faith is based upon commitment that is sustained in the face of all the evidence that points to the contrary. It involves a willingness to abandon the interests of the self, or self-preservation, for the interests of the other. But faith may also be blind because it issues from a romantic attachment that has been entered into naively. In female-focalized melodramas such as *Suspicion*, faith may block the process of discovery and supports wish-fulfilling delusion that is antithetical to the attainment of knowledge. Furthermore, reliance on faith may yield to self-doubt, in the face of overwhelming forces that undermine it. This receives its most extreme dramatization in Rose Balestrero's precipitous loss of reason in *The Wrong Man*. Yet faith may also support the intuition that is necessary to the clear-headed attainment of a knowledge that is all the more credible because it is achieved in the absence of self-interest, as in *Shadow of a Doubt*.

Male knowledge, embodied in the figure of the male "detective" in films like *Murder!*, *Blackmail*, and *Rear Window*, is more detached, and ostensibly neutral. It depends on powers of observation and deduction, and its strength lies in rationality and emotional detachment. But therein also lies the weakness of male reason, for it is susceptible to the dictates of self-interest and therefore to missing the point, and the emotional distance of Hitchcock's male characters can become coercive. Men also have the ability to back their reasoning skills with force. This distinction between male and female knowledge may be cast in the vocabulary that psychoanalytic critics have used to characterize gender difference—namely, the clichéd contrast between masculine agency and (voyeuristic) detachment from the other, and feminine passivity and overidentification with the other. Masculine agency and detachment lead to recognition based in large part upon reasoning by evidence and induction, whose strength lies in its rationality and whose weakness resides in its rigid application and coercive effects. Feminine passivity and identification lead to recognition arrived at, in part, through intuition, which remains steadfast in the face of contradictory evidence but may be contaminated by self-doubt or self-deception.

Hitchcock's narratives of romantic renewal, perfected in the 1930s in films such as *The 39 Steps, Young and Innocent* and *The Lady Vanishes* (1938), are characterized, unsurprisingly, by the complementarity between male and female modes of knowledge or being. This is achieved not simply by according a role to female intuition but by presenting women as self-sufficient and self-defined agents. Traditional femininity is revised through the assumption of agency in the public sphere. Hitchcock's narratives of ironic ambivalence expose a more problematic relationship between the genders. Where the male character is a detective, the male agency that is deployed to rescue or redeem the woman who has "fallen" outside the moral order is incipiently coercive, for it rides roughshod over feeling. Hitchcock's female-focalized melodramas, by contrast, center upon the articulation of feeling, where women's capacity for attachment becomes damaging to their well-being and it is something they must overcome in order to achieve knowledge. In Hitchcock's films of the 1940s and 1950s, masculinity, unexamined in works of the thirties, is subject to self-conscious revision, most notably in the films starring James Stewart, but also in Hitchcock's underrated work with Gregory Peck, *Spellbound* and *The Paradine Case*. In the case of Peck, the overly autonomous detached male shows signs of vulnerability and weakness. In the case of Stewart, he is possessed with feminine traits of attachment, in a manner that may complement a more assertive femininity (as in *Rear Window*), or may jeopardize masculinity altogether (as in *Vertigo*). This is one of the clearest ways in which one can trace a trajectory of "development" in Hitchcock's work in the traditional sense that implies an evolution to a greater depth or complexity of insight.

I have discussed the misrecognized wrong man who emerges as a partner to the heroine, but his antagonist and double is often a criminal-dandy or, as William Rothman labels him, a "gamesman aesthete," who is misrecognized as the "right" man. The "dandy," as we shall see in chapter 4, is a figure with a complex provenance. Often incipiently homosexual, though never explicitly so, the dandy displays an "excessive" concern with his clothing and appearance.[16] While the dandy may be a flamboyant figure, such as Bruno Anthony in *Strangers on a Train*, dandyism can also be associated, and commonly is in Hitchcock, with sobriety and decorum, but of a distinctly leisured upper-class kind, as personified by the suave master criminal

Tobin (Otto Kruger) in *Saboteur*, or Vandamm in *North by Northwest*. Furthermore, there is only a thin line between the dandy, whose fastidious-ness suggests an underlying perversity, and the brooding Jekyll/Hyde figure who harbors a secret beneath his thoroughly conventional semblance of propriety, like Maxim de Winter in *Rebecca*. The dandy is a figure Hitchcock derived in part from the novels of John Buchan in the person of the suavely attractive archvillains, Moxon Ivery (in *Mr. Standfast*) and Dominic Medina (in *The Three Hostages*). The dandy's orchestration of his own appearance and the perception of others is often an expression of his ability to seam-lessly inhabit and at times to personify social authority in a manner that allows him to act completely outside the rules of social morality.

Considered as a figure who is incipiently homosexual, though not explic-itly so, the dandy can also be defined by the way that he combines feminine and masculine traits in accordance with the theories of gender that circu-lated in Hitchcock's youth, where homosexuality was conceived in terms of male femininity—a feminine soul in a man's body. The "perversity" of the figure of the dandy then issues in part from the resulting fusion of mascu-line and feminine traits that bestow upon him a kind of hyperbolic, almost demonic knowledge of and power over another. This preternatural knowl-edge may be frightening, yet it issues from a hypersensitivity that renders the dandy someone who is unusually attuned to others and hence poten-tially vulnerable when his energies are not simply directed toward the exer-cise of social power. For this reason, the dandy in Hitchcock is not just a threatening figure but one who commands audience allegiance that may enter into conflict with the wish for romantic resolution, as if to expose the identity of the dandy as a criminal is, in a sense, to forcibly "out" him in a manner where his hidden criminal identity takes the place of or stands in for a hidden, essentially unnameable sexual identity. I shall explore the sig-nificance of this figure in Hitchcock's recognition plots at the end of this chapter, but first I want to discuss in detail the different gender-bound forms taken by these plots in Hitchcock's work.

The Joint Quest Narrative

Hitchcock's joint quest narratives form a distinctive kind of recognition narrative in which masculine reason and female intuition combine to yield knowledge of the criminal. Where the hero is a wrong man, identification of the criminal results in his exoneration. The object of knowledge in the joint quest narrative is characteristically a MacGuffin in the sense that it functions as a device designed solely to put into motion the process that will culminate in the realization of the romance. The presence of the MacGuffin essentially means that recognition of the hero's (and occasionally the heroine's) innocence is never in doubt. However, as Hitchcock's career developed, the joint quest narrative evolves into a more complex drama where, rather than the couple being formed in the process of the quest, they are re-formed in a manner that may involve the realignment of traditional gendered epistemologies, and sometimes issues in an ambiguous stance toward the romantic resolution that is ostensibly affirmed.

Hitchcock's paradigm for gender complementarity is also partly derived from the works of Buchan. Although a heroine is conspicuously absent from the first Richard Hannay novel, *The Thirty-nine Steps*, Buchan's subsequent novels, like *Greenmantle* and *Mr. Standfast*, feature a heroine, Mary Lamington, who, while she embodies all the grace and moral virtues of traditional womanhood, is also a New Woman whose identity has been forged from the experience of war.[17] She has a sharp mind, steely determination, and strength of character that is every bit the equal of Buchan's hero, but her femininity also allows her to operate in ways that the hero cannot. In *Mr. Standfast*, Mary works not with but in parallel to Hannay. Having won the heart of Moxon Ivery, the suave villain, Mary exploits the connection in order to stay close to him. Indeed, it is Moxon's softness for her that proves his undoing, since his delayed exit from the country allows the hero to catch up with him before his departure. Buchan's Mary Lamington remains a character who is strictly subordinated to the hero in importance—his trusty right hand. However, in Hitchcock's "wrong man" thrillers the hero is often much weaker: the wronged man needs the heroine's help, her active agency, in order to clear his name and restore his identity (as in *Young and Innocent*). Masculinity is not fundamentally criticized, but the woman's role is sharply revised, for her agency is required to redeem the man.

This modern female heroic ideal (and it surely remains a modern ideal) was undoubtedly appealing to Hitchcock in courting the all-important female audience, but it is plausible to speculate that the central role of the "female hero" in Hitchcock's work was also derived from Hitchcock's lifelong creative and collaborative partnership with his wife Alma Reville. It is noteworthy that in three of his scripts that we know she had a major hand in writing—*Young and Innocent, Jamaica Inn* (1939), and *Stage Fright*—a plucky detective heroine supports a weak hero and plays a pivotal role in the plot. In spite of the plethora of feminist criticism of Hitchcock, the importance of this picture of feminine agency in Hitchcock's work has been rather overlooked, not to mention the career of Alma Reville, who is scarcely mentioned. Commentary on women in Hitchcock's work has focused largely on his American films, where he develops a complex exploration of female psychology that paves the way for his later exploration of masculinity. But something is lost in Hitchcock's American films by the insistent sexualization of the female persona demanded by the star system where feminine agency is reduced to an expression either of sexuality or of motherhood. And feminist criticism of the 1970s and 1980s, while it sought to resist male definitions of female sexuality, remained fixated upon defining female agency through sexuality.[18] But women in Hitchcock's English thrillers are defined more by their agency than by their sexual identity, and this idea is carried over into some of the "transitional" films of the 1940s and the 1950s such as *Lifeboat* and *Stage Fright*, until Hitchcock's portrayal of femininity, in the context of his overall approach to storytelling and style, is completely Americanized.

Young and Innocent epitomizes the formula of the joint quest narrative with the "female hero." It opens with the murder of a movie star, revealing the eyes of the murderer to have a twitch (the visible "scar" of villainy). Young Robert Tisdall (Derrick de Marney) is wrongly incriminated in her murder. It appears they were lovers, and he cannot prove that his belt was not the murder weapon because he has lost his coat. He first sees the young heroine Erica Burgoyne (Nova Pilbeam), able daughter of a police inspector, when she resourcefully comes to his aid after he has fainted. Next time he sees her she is cranking the engine of her car! Thus her combined virtues of nurture, resourcefulness, and physical courage are elegantly summarized in the opening scenes. They meet up again after he has escaped and she has run out of gas. Because he is on the run, she hides him—although at first conflicted she quickly develops the faith in his innocence that arises from love—and then she proceeds to act as the hero.

Erica begins her heroic questing role by entering the raucous working-class roadside café Tom's Hat—the place where Robert lost his coat (if they can find his coat belt he can supposedly prove that his was not the belt used to strangle the murder victim). She gains crucial information about the coat by chatting with the patrons and extricates herself when a fight ensues. Here, female sensitivity and openness combine with pluck and resourcefulness. Realizing her father will be worried, she keeps up appearances by attending a party at her aunt's house, but her aunt suspects, and now she is on the run too. Robert tracks down the raincoat to Old Will (Edward Rigby), but it lacks the crucial belt. However, subsequently he realizes that the coat contains a crucial clue: a box of matches from the Grand Hotel, where he has never been.

In desperation, the couple repairs to the hotel with Old Will, hoping he will spot the man with the twitch who gave him the coat. While Robert lurks helplessly in the foyer, Erica and Old Will enter the ballroom where a band is playing, and Hitchcock's swooping camera reveals that the man with the twitch is none other than the drummer. When the drummer spots Old Will, his twitching becomes ferocious, his drumming incoherent, and after taking a sedative he collapses. Erica, about to be taken away by the police, rushes through the crowd to give first aid to the man, recapitulating the solicitous agency that initially defined her. Her intuitive response leads her finally to recognize the twitch that Hitchcock's camera has already revealed.

Young and Innocent exemplifies the manner in which the narrative of romantic renewal is structured around the MacGuffin. The literal MacGuffin is the stolen raincoat, but in a broader sense the MacGuffin is the "wrong man" device itself, for at no point do we believe that the boyish hero is possibly guilty of the crime. Rather, this device is one that throws the hero and his heroine helper together in the countryside or nature world, outside the boundaries of social authority, to begin the quest to clear his name. But their success is ultimately ensured by Hitchcock's benign hand-of-God narration. For example, at one point, as Erica drives Robert in the car, they reach a fork in the road. One way leads back to the police, the other leads to Tom's Hat. Erica hesitates which way to go until she sees that the road back to the police is blocked. Robert is delighted, and Erica claims that she was going to take the road to Tom's Hat anyway. But moments after they pass the fork, the sign is removed and the workmen disperse, as if they had been placed there by Hitchcock the narrator all along, to ensure that the story reaches its right conclusion.

The Lady Vanishes, made the year after, lacks the "wrong man" theme and thus possesses a more resourceful hero, but it also elaborates more fully on the role of female intuition in the quest for knowledge. Iris Henderson (Margaret Lockwood) begins her quest not through her desire to help an innocent man whom she loves, but through the relationship she has forged with an older woman, Miss Froy (Dame May Whitty), who suddenly disappears. No one who saw Miss Froy is prepared to testify. None of them, for various reasons, want to be involved. Prompted by the "suggestion" of a skeptical "doctor" who turns out to be responsible for the abduction, together with the aftereffects of a knock on the head that blurs her vision, the aptly named "Iris" herself begins to doubt what she saw, until she perceives Froy's name in the condensation on the window where she had etched it, moments before it disappears for good. Gilbert Redman (Michael Redgrave), the hero, continues to doubt her though he is supportive. Indeed, he provides an early, unassuming exemplar in Hitchcock of "revised" masculinity; he is a man of action possessed with intelligence and sensitivity—he is a musicologist on the continent recording disappearing folk culture—and he is the women's helper rather than the other way round (we may assume that he is a striking contrast to the man that Iris is set to marry). Nonetheless, it is only concrete visual evidence—a bag of Miss Froy's Harriman's herbal tea that appears stuck to the window for a moment before flying away with the rubbish—that persuades him.

The couple then forms a team, jointly negotiating the snares and delusions of a topsy-turvy world, in their quest for Miss Froy. They find Miss Froy's spectacles in the baggage car, and Iris notices that the Nun (Catherine Lacey) who attends a prone, bandaged patient, supervised by the sinister Dr. Hartz (Paul Lukas), is wearing high-heeled shoes. They are a recognition marker like the twitching eyes of the drummer in *Young and Innocent*, but this recognition is one that only a woman would be presumed to make! The patient is Miss Froy, who turns out to be an English spy. Eventually they manage to substitute Dr. Hartz's accomplice, Madame Kummer (Josephine Wilson), who has been posing as a decoy Miss Froy, for Miss Froy herself, appropriating the villains' own mastery of duplicity and deception, until Dr. Hartz finds out and alerts the authorities. A gun battle follows in which Miss Froy escapes and Gilbert saves the day through conventional, and rather unlikely, heroism.

The MacGuffin in *The Lady Vanishes* is the secret message coded in a tune memorized by Miss Froy; however, the figure of Miss Froy herself strikingly anticipates the overtly self-conscious invocation of the MacGuffin in *North by Northwest*'s nonexistent secret agent George Kaplan. The villains joke that she does not exist, and the hero and heroine join in a quest to discover her. Miss Froy is as much an elaborate narrative conceit as a flesh-and-blood character. However, Miss Froy is also much more than a MacGuffin, in the sense that she is a symbolic mother figure for Iris.[19] The restoration of Miss Froy prompts Iris to make the right choice of romantic partner at the conclusion of the film. In a corresponding way, Iris Henderson is the wrong woman. A single woman traveling with her companions, she is cast as an object of allure for Hitchcock's camera by being introduced standing on a table in a low-angle shot wearing her knickers. At one point, she declares: "I've done everything," which suggests her promiscuity. Furthermore, she is placed in the position of the wrong woman when her story about Miss Froy is not believed, and she must, in effect, clear her name. In a sense, the role of male and female are reversed in *The Lady Vanishes*; the hero functions as the initially skeptical helper of the wrong woman who, like the customary wrong man, is a victim turned agent.

Female agency in the public sphere that embodies resourcefulness and intuition remains a distinctive feature of Hitchcock's American films. *Stage Fright*, as Michael Walker has noted, reworks the plot structure of *Young and Innocent* with a female hero, though her faith in the male "hero" is undercut by the ironic discovery that, against all expectations, which Hitchcock himself fosters with a false flashback, the apparent wrong man really is the criminal after all.[20] And *Lifeboat* features the remarkable role of Constance "Connie" Porter, played by Tallulah Bankhead, who is one of the strongest women in all of Hitchcock's work. She exhorts the other characters in the boat not to give up hope, she detects the duplicity of Willie (Walter Slezak), the Nazi, picked up by the lifeboat crew, though like the others she was initially taken in by him, and she realizes that her diamond bracelet can be used as bait to catch fish when they are all starving near the end of the film.[21] But as Hitchcock inhabits the American idiom more completely, the idea of female agency is increasingly bound to female sexuality.

Like the "wrong woman" heroine of Hitchcock's early English film *Easy Virtue*, whose only recourse is to flaunt her femininity as a masquerade—to throw it in the face of her accusers—Hitchcock's American women, defined as "notorious" in virtue of their sexuality, turn that sexuality into a form of agency. The paradigm cases are the female double agents of *Notorious* and *North by Northwest*, played by Ingrid Bergman and Eva Marie Saint, respectively, who sleep with the enemy in order to derive from that proximity the knowledge that will undermine him. This kind of female agency is the logical extension of the traits of female knowledge and intuition in the joint quest narratives of the thirties—solicitousness, openness, and the capacity to adapt to alien environments. However, it also manifests a reductive conception of femininity that limits the scope of female agency and sets up, in both *Notorious* and *North by Northwest*, the conventional, concluding, fairy-tale rescue that Hitchcock's English films by and large avoid.

However, if Hitchcock's thrillers of the 1940s and 1950s are, in certain ways, more conventional in their portrayal of femininity, they provide a critical portrait of the masculinity that is taken for granted in his thirties thrillers. The key vehicle for Hitchcock's revisionist portrait of masculinity is James Stewart, who returned from his wartime experience with a profoundly different star persona than the fresh-faced "evangelical" do-gooder created in the works of Frank Capra.[22] Stewart's portrayal of "troubled" masculinity is manifest in *Rope*, but it is crystallized in two joint quest films of this period—*The Man Who Knew Too Much* (1956) and *Rear Window* (as well as in *Vertigo*, which I shall discuss in a later section). In *The Man Who Knew Too Much* and *Rear Window*, the couple already exists, but its status is in jeopardy due to the troubled nature of the man. The joint quest serves to revive the couple, and, in the case of *Rear Window*, it does so by realigning gendered epistemologies.

In *The Man Who Knew Too Much*, a self-conscious return to the works of the thirties that remakes Hitchcock's own 1934 film, James Stewart's character, Ben McKenna, is no longer youthful and inexperienced like the hero of *Young and Innocent*; he is an older, established professional who is rather rigid and inflexible, narrow and controlling. On vacation in Morocco with his wife Jo and son, he is unable to modulate his behavior to the alien environment in which he finds himself. He chats garrulously with a Frenchman—Louis Bernard (Daniel Gelin)—who they meet on a bus (as Jo observes, "You know nothing about him, but he knows everything about you"), and he fails to notice that an odd couple—Mr. Drayton (Bernard Miles) and Mrs. Drayton (Brenda De Banzie)—are watching them at their hotel. When they sit down to eat dinner, Ben cannot adjust to sitting on the floor and eating his food with his fingers. Not to mention the difficulty he experiences trying to have a conversation with the Draytons, sitting behind them. Stewart's brilliantly awkward performance illustrates the extent to which he is a fish out of water, ill-attuned to his environment and unable to see, to anticipate what is about to happen. Louis Bernard is killed—he dies in Ben's arms while passing him a message of an impending assassination: "Tell police to try Ambrose Chapel." Witnessing the scene, the Draytons, who are in league with the assassins, kidnap their son. Out of control of the situation, it is then as if Ben imposes control on his wife in compensation (although he is clearly also concerned about her well-being). He bribes her into taking pills before he tells her what is going on and, as she beats his chest in helplessness at the news and in anger at him, he forces her to lie down on the bed. They fly to London where Ben, thinking "Ambrose Chapell" is a person, is literally led up the garden path to the wrong address—Ambrose Chappell the taxidermist—where upon entering he provokes pandemonium and ends up catching his hand in the mouth of a tiger and being threatened with a stuffed swordfish! I shall examine the imagery of this sequence in more detail in chapter 4.

At this juncture, Jo McKenna, who is a professional singer, effectively takes control of the narrative: she both finds and uses her voice. In Morocco she has been consistently more attuned to the threat posed by their environment, and while Ben is away she realizes Ambrose Chapel is a place. Ben meets her there, only to be knocked out and left behind locked doors. Again Jo takes the initiative and rushes to Albert Hall, figures out that an assassination is about to take place, and tells Ben. Ben rushes from box to box while Jo scours the theater for the assassin. Just before he shoots, Jo lets out a guttural scream, as if intuitively responding to the situation. The assassin's bullet misses and Ben arrives (rather belatedly) at the box to grapple with the assassin who fired the shot. They go to a foreign embassy where the Draytons still have their boy, and Jo sings "Que Sera Sera?" in a manner that her voice carries all the way to her son, who responds in kind. Ben again acts as her accomplice, rushing up the stairs to where his son has been held hostage, and manages to foil Mr. Drayton as he seeks to make an escape with their son.

Although Day projects a very maternal conception of femininity that's more in keeping with Buchan's Mary Lamington than Hitchcock's heroines of the thirties, here, in this 1950s version of gender complementarity, female agency nonetheless takes a leadership role in the public arena and works to prop up an evidently damaged male character. By the end of the film, male agency is restored by working in tandem with a strong woman.

Rear Window, from the same period, not only criticizes but self-consciously "revises" masculinity in the context of establishing gender complementarity. As we saw in chapter 1, critics have been quick to point out that the wife murder that L. B. Jefferies seems to witness might be a wish-fulfilling fantasy on his part, but they have failed to recognize the extent to which Jefferies develops sympathy both for the victim of the murder and his own girlfriend as the narrative progresses. In other words, Jefferies develops a "feminine" sensitivity to the other. At the same time, inspired by her own attachment to L. B. Jefferies, by her faith in him, Lisa Fremont moves from a state of disbelief to belief about the wife's murder. Ultimately, the murderer is foiled by the felicitous conjunction of masculine logic and facility with technology, motivated by concern for the other, combined with female intuition and physical courage or pluck.[23] Jefferies demonstrates with "before and after" slides that the rose bed has been disturbed; Lisa opines that Jefferies' wife could not possibly have left without her wedding ring if she were alive, because wives never part with their wedding rings, and hence Thorwald is the murderer. (This is rather comparable to the deduction about the Nun's shoes made by Iris in *The Lady Vanishes*, to which *Rear Window* in its narrative of the vanishing lady bears more than passing resemblance.) Jefferies' success stems from the fact that he is passively stuck in his wheelchair, hence able to capture the before-and-after photographs. Lisa retrieves the evidence that clinches her argument by climbing in a window to Thorwald's apartment.

Both these narratives invoke but go beyond the logic of the MacGuffin. Like the earlier joint quest narratives, in each case the couple is brought together in a quest that is precipitated by an external event. The protagonists of *The Man Who Knew Too Much* are innocently caught up in a kidnap-espionage plot, and the protagonists of *Rear Window* are accidentally caught up in a murder plot. But the object of quest in neither case is simply arbitrary, for in *The Man Who Knew Too Much* it is the traumatic loss of their child that at once precipitates and symbolically registers the subtle tension in the surface calm of their marriage, while in *Rear Window* the investigation of the potential killing of a nagging wife by her abusive husband provides a grotesquely negative symbol of the protagonist's relationship. The plot of *The Wrong Man* has affinity with these films from the same period. The film is nascently a joint quest narrative, since it is Rose who initially contacts a lawyer and begins the quest to redeem Manny's name—the difference is that the quest fails, save for the hand of Hitchcock. Clearly, also, the "wrong man" motif is not a MacGuffin in *The Wrong Man*. The intrinsic significance bestowed on the importance of recognition in these plots points to the very different role that recognition plays in those films, that turns upon knowing the mind of another, which I shall now discuss.

Femininity, Faith, and Self-doubt

In Hitchcock's female-focalized narratives derived from the tradition of the gothic melodrama, represented in such works as *Suspicion*, *Rebecca*, and *Shadow of a Doubt*, the search for knowledge is no longer a joint quest with an "external" goal that bears an arbitrary or symbolic relationship to the couple's situation. Rather, the quest involves the investigation by a woman of a man to whom she is romantically attached in order to discover the secret he harbors and make legible his true intentions. In these stories belief is so entwined with desire and supported by faith that knowledge is hard to attain and is threatened by both self-deception and self-doubt. When recognition is achieved it exposes a profound, even unbridgeable, gap between the world as it is and the world as we would wish it to be, in a manner that punctures the romantic ideal.

The role of the heroine's faith in supporting belief in the hero's innocence is a central motif of Hitchcock's narratives of romantic renewal. This formula is established as early as Hitchcock's third film, *The Lodger*, where Daisy, the heroine, is convinced in the hero's innocence in spite of all the evidence that points to him being a Jack the Ripper figure, and she runs to him in his hour of need. In *Young and Innocent*, as we have seen, Erica's faith in the hero's innocence drives her to protect the "wrong man" hero even against the wishes of a well-meaning father whom she loves. But it is perhaps Hitchcock's 1945 film *Spellbound* that offers the deepest articulation of the redemptive powers of faith in Hitchcock's work because of the conviction with which that faith is held and expressed by the heroine, Constance, played by Ingrid Bergman.

For all its complex and rather silly psychoanalytic plot, *Spellbound* is essentially a love story that works according to the "wrong man" formula of romantic renewal where a thoroughly impotent wrong man is rescued by a female helper. The hero of the film, John Ballantine, has, without consciously realizing it, assumed the identity of a dead man, Dr. Anthony Edwardes, whose death he witnessed but felt responsible for due to a "guilt complex" originating in his youth—he was responsible for the death of his brother. By assuming the identity of the dead man, he can pretend that this man is still alive. He arrives in the person of Dr. Anthony Edwardes to take over a psychiatric institution, Green Manors, and immediately shows symptoms of his condition, and soon confesses to the murder of Edwardes, a confession that Dr. Murchison (Leo G. Carroll), head of the asylum, suspiciously endorses. Ballantine is thereby cast in the position of the wrong man. Pursued now by the police, he must clear his name. But in the meantime the dry but brilliant psychiatrist Dr. Constance Petersen has fallen head over heels in love with him. She remains steadfast in her faith that he is innocent and finally fingers the real culprit, Dr Murchison, in an intellectually astute and remarkably intuitive dream interpretation. As Lesley Brill writes:

> She maintains her belief [in the hero] in the face of assurances to the contrary from all her colleagues, the police, the courts, and even her old teacher and emotional father Brulov. Love, as usual in Hitchcock movies, sees deeper than the most brilliant empiricism. . . . Constance's first name underlines the importance of her unflagging faith in her lover's innocence; her second name, Peterson [sic], may contain a faint biblical allusion with similar reference to faith and grace.[24]

Ballantine reciprocates her love with a passion and vulnerability that anticipates the later role of James Stewart in *Vertigo* and the earlier intensity of *The Lodger*. Indeed, the shot/reverse-shot of their first kiss precisely replicates the staging of the kiss in Hitchcock's third film, though stripped of its ambiguity.

In Hitchcock's stories derived from the "gothic melodrama," faith is put to the test in a more profound way, for the hero is no longer simply the wrong man who turns out to be right; rather, initially appearing, at least to the heroine, as the right man, he turns out to be what Rothman calls a "wrong-one": a dandy or a Jekyll/Hyde whose true identity is concealed.[25] In the "gothic melodrama," epitomized by Charlotte Brontë's *Jane Eyre*, a young heroine marries into the house of an older man whose brooding behavior is a source of attraction—because he is someone ripe for emotional rescue, if only his secret could be understood—but also an incipient threat to the heroine. In Hitchcock's films that draw upon this tradition, the man of the world is sometimes an older figure of social authority, but he is sometimes a man of, more or less, the heroine's age (as in *Suspicion*), and while the heroine does not always marry into the house of the hero, they nonetheless live in the same house and enter into both physical and emotional proximity (as in *Shadow of a Doubt*). Moreover, Hitchcock's works in this tradition make manifest the incipient perversity in romantic attraction of the male, where the threat posed by the hero is a source of allure in a way that is no longer contained by the conventions of the "wrong man" narrative of romantic renewal.

The Lodger again provides a narrative template through the relationship Hitchcock establishes between the girl, her mother, and the Lodger. Daisy's blind faith in the Lodger is counterposed to the perspective of her mother, who increasingly suspects that he harbors murderous intentions toward her daughter. In later films, faith and doubt are combined in the person of the ingenuous newlywed, epitomized by Joan Fontaine in *Rebecca* and *Suspicion*, or the young woman on the cusp of maturity, Young Charlie in *Shadow of a Doubt*. *Shadow of a Doubt* effectively inverts the stance of the mother and daughter in *The Lodger*. Young Charlie's mother has blind faith in her brother, but Young Charlie learns to doubt. The threatening yet alluring figure of the Lodger is reproduced in *Suspicion* in the guise of a young rogue—the duplicitous playboy Johnnie Aysgarth. In *Rebecca* (which reworks *Jane Eyre*) and in *Shadow of a Doubt*, the man the heroine loves is an older man with the threatening, brooding presence of a Jekyll/Hyde— the emotionally remote patriarch Maxim de Winter in *Rebecca*, and the more dandyish Uncle Charlie in *Shadow of a Doubt*.[26]

The heroine of these films is motivated by a romantic desire to transcend the boundaries of isolation, social naïvité, and spinsterhood, or simply the monotonous routines of everyday life, in a relationship with a confident, debonair man of the world. This relationship of faith and trust is entered into naively, as if, as in a fairy tale, the heroine is granted the fulfillment of a wish only to find that the wish turns into a nightmare. In this context, the female-centered recognition plot begins from a place where the heroine has already been deceived, or rather, being young and innocent, she has not yet been tutored in the ways of the world and in the knowledge of good and evil. As the heroine begins to perceive a gap between the hero as she imagines him to be and the hero as he really is, this gap may be imputed to self-doubt or self-deception, which precipitates foolish anxieties, or it may represent rational doubt. Genuine knowledge rather than false recognition may be achieved, but given a context in which it is the romantic ideal that has lifted the heroine from isolation and monotony in the first place, the price of recognition is to be forced to acknowledge the fallen condition of the world and to experience the profound disenchantment truth reveals.

Rebecca, *Suspicion*, and *Shadow of a Doubt* each give a different inflection to this recognition narrative. In *Rebecca*, adapted from Daphne du Maurier's novel, the unnamed heroine is whisked Cinderella-like to the castle, Manderley, of the prince Maxim de Winter, only to discover that she has stepped into a different kind of fairy tale in which her husband and his castle are haunted by the spirit of his former wife, personified in the deathly presence of Mrs. Danvers or "Danny," the guardian of the house. The second Mrs. de Winter is consumed by self-doubt, believing that she can never live up in her husband's eyes to the "beauty, breeding, and brains" that characterized Rebecca, and this is certainly the opinion of Danvers, who does everything to confirm the heroine in her doubt. The attitude of her husband, who at once broods over his former wife and is profoundly unsympathetic to the anxiety felt by his new one, only serves to fuel her sense of inadequacy. At the same time, Rebecca has an allure, fostered by Danny, that is independent of Maxim and, as we have seen, an eroticized suspense surrounds the heroine's encounters with the talismans and traces of Rebecca. The moment of recognition liberates the heroine from her anxious state, for she realizes that her husband despised Rebecca. However, her freedom comes at the price of discovering, in the novel, that her husband is a cold-blooded murderer, and in the film, that her husband has accidentally killed Rebecca and covered up his actions. Knowledge thus brings with it disenchantment. Mrs. de Winter can now mother her husband (like Jane Eyre), who is a shell of his former self, and while the relationship is restored on the basis of a shared secret, the romance has lost its original sheen (again here the novel is darker than the film).

Given that the curiosity of the heroine in this kind of story is motivated by a desire to preserve her relationship, the question always arises as to whether she will read correctly the signs that are presented to her. Is her interpretation of the threat posed by her husband a product of self-doubt, or would she delude herself rather than believe that he is a murderer? The novel from which *Suspicion* is adapted, *Before the Fact* by Frances Iles, is a reductio ad absurdum of the idea that marriage must be preserved at all costs. At the end of the book the heroine, Lina, proves willing to die rather than to acknowledge her husband's murderous intentions, which have become transparent to the reader. In his adaptation, as we have already seen, Hitchcock played for ambiguity; however, the heroine is plainly blinded to the faults of the hero by her infatuation. His final confession of innocence is wholly unpersuasive, especially as delivered by Grant, and Lina's acknowledgment of his innocence has an air of desperation, as if she wants him to be innocent rather than believes that he is. In this sense, the film is a critique of naive melodramatic narratives of recognition, just as it is, as Mark Crispin Miller shows, a critique of naive spectatorship.[27] If recognition falls short, here, and the character is in error, it is because the female character reads her environment as she wants to read it. She molds her beliefs in conformity to her wishes, and she is deluded.

The knowledge achieved by the heroines of *Rebecca* and *Suspicion* is hard to win because of the degree of self-confidence that it is necessary for the heroine to attain in order to detach knowledge from love. In Hitchcock's *Shadow of a Doubt*, the heroine, Charlie, is infatuated by the figure of her older uncle (also named Charlie), who is at once her mother's childhood favorite and Young Charlie's double. Uncle Charlie is the vehicle of Young Charlie's yearnings to transcend the dull world of small-town Santa Rosa. Yet he turns out to represent everything that is opposed to Young Charlie's aspirations for freedom and self-determination. While Uncle Charlie ostensibly murders merry widows for their money, he actually cares little for it. He murders these women on account of their autonomy from men, for he loathes women who step outside the boundaries of family responsibilities.

The audience knows right away that Uncle Charlie is the antithesis of the right man he appears to be. He is the archetypal dandy, with the brooding persona of a Jekyll/Hyde, who ranges entirely outside the boundaries of middle-class morality and is associated by Hitchcock with the figure of a vampire. The film traces how Young Charlie progresses from blind faith in her uncle's virtue, which is bolstered by her mother's own naive and idealized image of him, to a dawning sense of his guilt. Young Charlie's emotional proximity to her uncle, of the kind that characterizes the relationship between identical twins, seems to yield a telepathic connection between them that affords her insight into his guilt, while all those around him believe that he is an absolutely wonderful man. Furthermore, it is her dawning sense of his guilt that moves her to act with the very independence she craves and looked to him to deliver. Young Charlie investigates her uncle alone and discovers that the ring he has given her to wear bears the initials of a murdered woman.

The knowledge she comes to possess of her uncle emboldens Young Charlie to fight and finally defeat him in a life-and-death struggle. But this knowledge also brings with it a radical disenchantment with the world. Her sense of self has been achieved only at the price of the destruction of the ideals of freedom and transcendence that are embodied, however naively, in her infatuation with her uncle. At the end of the film she faces the prospect of ordinary life in small-town America in a conventional marriage, like her mother's, with the stable but ordinary detective Jack Graham (MacDonald Carey). Although it may now seem a comforting antidote to her uncle's murderous nihilism, it also suggests conformity and a dispiriting containment of the sense of possibility expressed in her youthful ideals. Even more than *Rebecca*, and less ambiguously than in *Suspicion*, the knowledge achieved by the heroine of *Shadow of a Doubt*, arising out of an initial condition of blind faith, has as its consequence the loss of innocence and a sense of disenchantment that results from this loss. It is one of Hitchcock's most profound works.

Masculine Knowledge, Detection, and Coercion

Hitchcock's narratives of male detection offer a radical contrast to the female-focalized melodrama in the way knowledge is pursued and in the consequences of recognition. In a significant number of Hitchcock plots, the heroic agent is not a wronged man but a detective, or an ordinary individual with social status who assumes the role of the detective. His quest is to rescue a "notorious," "fallen," or wronged woman. The heroine may be redeemed as in *Murder!*, or partially redeemed, as in *Marnie*, but redemption only comes at a cost. The hero of these films, like the heroines of Hitchcock's female-centered melodramas, is motivated into action by his relationship to another; but unlike Hitchcock's heroines, the hero's actions proceed not from an already realized attachment but from the desire to conquer and win the woman's allegiance. Thus, the hero's quest often appears self-serving and betrays a fundamental ignorance of the motivations of the other. Moreover, since the male detective is a figure of authority, the pursuit of knowledge involves the exercise and deployment of power in a manner that strikingly contrasts with the impotence of the wrong man. This kind of exercise of power and reason may indeed be necessary to reestablishing the social order, but it comes at a price: it rides roughshod over human feelings.

Frequently, the guilty party turns out to be a dandy-criminal figure with whom the wrong woman is aligned in the story (as in *Blackmail*, *Murder!*, and *Vertigo*), and the detective offers an alternative, more stable romantic partner. The criminal-dandy is thus the double of both the detective and the wrong woman. The detective's attempt to redeem the wrong woman not only occurs against her will (as in *The Paradine Case* and *Marnie*), but it often comes at the cost of the dandy, who becomes partially aligned with her as a victim and a figure of sympathy (as in *Murder!* and *The Paradine Case*). The coercive effect of male knowledge in these stories is registered by actually focalizing the narrative in part, sometimes in large part, through the point of view of the female or the dandy-victim with whom she is aligned.

Notorious elegantly dramatizes the price that is to be paid for the formation of the couple even in a narrative that attains romantic resolution. The nominal hero of *Notorious*, Devlin, is singled out in Hitchcock's work by the fact that, though not a wrong man, he is a victim of the forces of social authority in the form of his employers, the U.S. intelligence service (OSS), as much as the heroine, Alicia Huberman, is a victim. This sets the stage for the narrative of romantic renewal. Yet, at the same time, Devlin is an agent of the law himself. While it is the OSS that instructs Alicia Huberman, daughter of a German war criminal, to demonstrate her loyalty to the country by essentially prostituting herself, Devlin himself is implicated in the action of the organization through his passivity, and also, it seems, through a residual suspicion of Alicia's promiscuity. He initially meets her at a wild party after her father's sentencing and in the nick of time stops her from going to live as a kept woman on the yacht of a rich man (who looks suspiciously like Hitchcock). The German spy whom Alicia is invited to court, Alex Sebastian, is, in contrast to Devlin, loving and generous to a fault.

The patriarchal order, embodied in Devlin's boss Paul Prescott (Louis Calhern), the leader of the OSS, exploits everyone in the pursuit of knowledge.

Devlin is abused and exploited, he in turn abuses and exploits Alicia, who in turn exploits Alex Sebastian. When the mission is accomplished and the proof of the Nazi plot is obtained, Alex, realizing that he has been set up, is ordered by his mother to poison Alicia. Devlin, who has been brooding with sour grapes over Alicia's behavior, turns into her redeemer, entering the Sebastian castle and rescuing "the princess." But he does so at the cost of exposing Sebastian, who has been the victim of love, to certain death at the hands of his colleagues. They leave the house together, but as Sebastian ushers Devlin and Alicia into the waiting car, Devlin cruelly locks the door on him, and he turns in long shot back to the house to await his fate. The achievement of Hitchcock and screenwriter Ben Hecht in *Notorious* is thus to combine the joint quest narrative with *both* kinds of gendered-plot structure: the narrative of the male investigation of a woman (Devlin and Alicia) *and* the narrative of the "gothic melodrama" involving the woman's investigation of a persecuting older man (Alicia and Alex). It is a tour de force of plot construction and illustrates the way in which the ambiguity and irony in Hitchcock's plots are sustained by the hybrid combination of these different plot archetypes.

Where the figure of the woman is counterposed to a more authoritative, less victimized male hero, masculine knowledge appears both deceptive and coercive. The hero may manipulate, even falsify, the truth in order to save the woman, regardless of whether she wishes to be saved, and what counts as the truth may reflect the limited point of view of the male protagonist. In *Blackmail*, adapted from Charles Bennett's stage play, the female protagonist, Alice White (Anny Ondra), fed up with her policeman boyfriend Frank Webber (John Longden), is lured by dandy-artist Crewe (Cyril Ritchard) to his attic and, as he attempts to rape her, she kills him. A blackmailer, who is tailing the dandy, witnesses the comings and goings from the attic and now threatens to blackmail Alice. In the meantime, Frank has concealed the evidence and the police suspect the blackmailer himself, who is hunted down in Alice's place. The "innocence" of the wrong woman is thereby preserved by the coercive force of masculine authority. Her voice is literally suppressed by Frank together with the truth, and the wrong man, or at least a man who is innocent of the crime of murder, is hunted down in her place. This is vividly described by Hitchcock's visual narration as he intercuts the inexorable pursuit and entrapment of the blackmailer with shots of a pensive Alice in a closed frame, emotionally boxed in by circumstances she is powerless to control. At the conclusion of Bennett's play both Alice and the falsely accused blackmailer are exonerated by a coroner's report that reveals Crewe to have died not of a stab wound but of a heart attack, but Hitchcock's film pulls no such punches. The possibility of the romance, although it is preserved by the death of the blackmailer, is undercut by the lie that serves to sustain it.

In *Murder!*, the detective-figure Sir John Menier is a theatrical actor, an impresario, who pursues dandy-villain Handel Fane in order to clear the name of a wrong woman, Diana Baring (Norah Baring), from the taint both of promiscuity and murder and from the specter of the gallows. Sir John, who is in love with Diana, sets out to rewrite the history of the Baring case by applying the technique of art to the technique of life and to use his command of disguise to decipher appearances in order to reveal the truth. Having uncovered the identity of the murderer when he realizes that the voice that a witness heard as a woman's voice was the voice of a man, he confronts Diana with the fact that she appears to be hiding something. Diana's secret is that she knows Fane's secret, and it is one that victimizes them both: Fane is a "half-caste." Sir John tries to trap Fane into a confession, but he resists and instead stages his own glorious death in the circus ring in a scene of drag performance that suggests something that Sir John fails to recognize—namely, that his half-caste identity refers not, or at least not primarily, to Fane's race but to his sexuality.

The authority of the white, aristocratic, procreative couple is thus restored in the film by exposing the body of the deviant, yet in a manner that at once registers the coercive force of that authority and the sense in which the body of the deviant resists being pinned down or named. His final striptease reveals an effeminate yet definitely masculine body swathed in a leotard of peacock's eyes that look defiantly back upon the prurient gaze of both the spectators in the film and of the film. Furthermore, while Sir John has successfully rewritten the inner history of the Baring case to its romantic conclusion, the final kiss between Sir John and the rescued heroine takes place within the proscenium arch of a stage in a manner that declares its own fictiveness. Some critics have interpreted the fictiveness of this ending as the apotheosis of romance; others argue that it is an ending that demonstrates Hitchcock's disavowal of the romance, after the hounding of Fane to his death.[28] It seems to me that, once again, both meanings are registered here: romance is at once triumphant and yet, at the same time, the impossibility or vacuity of romance is revealed.

The story of Hitchcock's *Marnie* is cast in terms of the hunt in a manner that explicitly connects this primitive archetype of the recognition narrative—of hunting and tracking—to a story of sexual pursuit and conquest. Hitchcock mobilizes the archetypal male hunter of women, Sean Connery—who had been, since 1962, the personification of James Bond on the silver screen—in the role of the bored, wealthy son of Maryland "aristocracy," Mark Rutland, who hunts down and captures Marnie. Marnie loathes men and manifests radical antisocial tendencies. She is a serial robber, a kleptomaniac, who, by inhabiting false identities, steals from her male employers. She also suffers panic attacks whenever she is confronted with the color red or the sound of a storm. Mark explicitly conceives Marnie as a wild animal—a jaguarundi—whose task it is his to tame and, tracking down her trail of crimes, he literally traps her into marrying him in return for his silence. This coerced union precipitates a suicide attempt by Marnie on their honeymoon, after an excruciating scene in which Mark, acting with what he believes are good intentions, forcibly disrobes and rapes her. The idea of detection and the psychoanalytic investigation into Marnie's social and sexual dysfunction are linked together in the plot, which culminates in a final recognition scene in which Marnie, escorted by Mark to her mother's home in the Baltimore docks, finally "remembers" the trauma that causes her panic attacks and her hatred of men. Yet when the man finally breaks the dam of female subjectivity, there is a sense in which the ensuing recognition explains nothing. The memory of sexual violence and murder that has been forced out of Marnie, from Mark's persistence, conceals as much as it reveals. Why?

What we see and hear at the end of the film in flashback is a scene from Marnie's childhood in which her mother is entertaining a sailor client during a thunderstorm. Already displaced from her bed, Marnie is afraid of the thunder and the sailor goes to comfort her. Her mother, distraught by the sailor's attentiveness toward her daughter, attacks him with a poker. He "defends" himself by turning on her and traps her leg in what now looks to the child like an assault upon her mother. At this point, Marnie's mother calls for help and Marnie hits him over the head with a poker, killing him. Blood flows from his head onto his white shirt and Marnie reacts with horror.

What she "remembers" is surely that her mother was a prostitute who entertained a sailor whom Marnie then killed in order to protect her mother.

What Marnie, and certainly Mark, cannot grasp from this scene, however, is the way in which her mother was responsible for the fact that Marnie kills the sailor. Her mother interprets the sailor's actions toward Marnie as hostile, perhaps on account of her own hostility to men, but also because she clearly feels guilty about her emotional abandonment of the child—it is the sailor and not Marnie's mother who offers comfort to Marnie during the storm. In this sense, Marnie's memory of the trauma cures nothing. For the origins of Marnie's trauma lie not, or not simply, in the buried secret she remembers—killing a man in response to a sexual assault—and the hatred of men and fear of her own sexuality that issues from it, but in her mother's guilt about the fact that she emotionally abandoned Marnie. Her mother has passed this guilt onto Marnie through her silence and evasion, reproducing within Marnie her own emotional deadness and strangling her capacity for affection. This is a secret that this male detective-analyst cannot cognitively penetrate, a problem that his caresses cannot possibly cure.[29] Marnie thus exposes the limits of its own psychoanalytic narrative, which focuses upon diagnosing the origins of sexual trauma. While Mark rescues Marnie for romance, the love he offers cannot compensate for the loss of a mother's love, and the effect of his actions upon Marnie remains coercive. At the end of the film, Marnie expresses her preference to be with Mark rather than to go to prison and thereby redeems the romance; but one is simultaneously left with the thought that it is marriage that for Marnie remains a form of prison.

The heroes of Murder! and Marnie appear invulnerable. However, two Hitchcock films, The Paradine Case and Vertigo, give a complex twist to the narrative of male detection by making the apparently wrong woman or wronged woman turn out, in part, to be the guilty woman. In other words, in The Paradine Case and Vertigo, the male detective, in a self-serving, and at times coercive, pursuit of knowledge to rescue a woman with whom he is obsessed, is undermined and rendered vulnerable by his encounter with this woman, who turns out to be a femme fatale. They are the works in which Hitchcock's recognition narratives approach the idiom of film noir, where the hero is trapped by a spider woman, yet in both cases the entrapment is caused as much by the hero's own self-deception as by anything that is done by the heroine. The hero is blinded by infatuation or love, like the heroine of the gothic melodrama. Furthermore, as in Blackmail, Murder!, and Marnie, neither film lets the male detective off the hook. If in both The

Paradine Case and *Vertigo* the male hero is victimized by the wrong woman qua femme fatale, he is also equally her tormentor.

The Paradine Case is perhaps the most dramatic example in Hitchcock's work of the manipulative self-serving pursuit of knowledge, by a powerful man in love with a woman, who seeks to establish the truth as he wishes it to be. Married lawyer Anthony "Tony" Keane (Gregory Peck) is hired to defend a beautiful, dark-haired woman, Mrs. Paradine (Alida Valli), accused of murdering her older blind husband. Tony, immediately attracted, seeks to tutor her in a story of her innocent life of wifely devotion, which she resists with an account of her earlier promiscuous, adventurous life. Tony insists that her husband's valet, the mysterious, obsessively devoted, and seemingly perverse André Latour (Louis Jourdan), is involved in the murder (he is, in certain respects, a male version of Mrs. Danvers in *Rebecca*) and starts seeking to pin the crime on him. At first, he chooses to ignore the ominous fact that Mrs. Paradine knows the valet by his first name, but when Latour says he hates Mrs. Paradine, he begins to suspect they had an affair. This then becomes his line of attack in the courtroom: the jealous Latour poisoned Mr. Paradine. But Keane's insistence upon defending his client radically backfires. Latour was seduced against his will by Mrs. Paradine and, harassed to the breaking point by Keane, he commits suicide. Like the figure of Handel Fane in *Murder!*, the "deviant" Latour is sacrificed by the hero, who wants to redeem the woman and win her admiration. But in *The Paradine Case*, the man's pursuit of knowledge is governed by self-deception, and Gregory Peck presents a hero with some of the vulnerability possessed by the heroines of Hitchcock's female-centered melodramas, although Tony seems blinded by infatuation rather than love. At the end of the trial, Mrs. Paradine confesses to her love for Latour and her responsibility for the crime and promises to Tony that the only comfort she has is the hatred and contempt she feels for him.

Peck is presented as a loving husband possessed by an infatuation for the enigmatic Mrs. Paradine, who never really exhibits the slightest hint of reciprocating that desire. Why would his character behave this way? His motivation is simply irrational. In *Vertigo*, however, Scottie's obsession with Judy as Madeleine is rendered convincing for two reasons. First, Scottie is assigned by Elster to rescue her from her irrational state of possession; it is his very belief in the power of reason to undo enchantment that becomes the vehicle of his own enchantment. Like the second Mrs. de Winter in

Rebecca, seduced by Rebecca's incipiently deadly world of dazzling surfaces, Scottie is lured by a masquerade of refinement and beauty that is a mask for moral corruption. Second, the twist in *Vertigo* is that Judy Barton, while Elster's mistress and therefore a "notorious" or "fallen" woman, is also, like other Hitchcock heroines, a wronged woman, for like Scottie, she too is instrumentalized by Elster. Judy falls in love with Scottie because she herself seeks to be rescued as he attempts to rescue Madeleine.

In the second half of *Vertigo*, Scottie's re-creation of Madeleine in the figure of a woman whom he discovers on the streets of San Francisco is a pathological rendition of masculine self-interest. But by revealing to the audience what really happened at the Mission San Juan Bautista and by making explicit the love that Judy Barton feels for Scottie, Hitchcock creates an excruciating pathos from the gap between the person whom she wishes to be, Judy Barton from Salina, Kansas, yet a Judy Barton somehow untainted by the backstory of her life, and the person that Scottie insists on her becoming, who is at once the imposter self that Judy despises, perhaps because it reminds her of her "fallen" state, and yet also the fiction that ignited their love and might reignite it again.

When Judy, exuding the newfound confidence she has discovered in the renewal of love, puts on a ruby necklace that is worn by Carlotta Valdes in a painting at the museum visited by "Madeline," Scottie, like the heroines of *Rebecca* and *Shadow of a Doubt*, recognizes the truth about the person with whom he is blindly in love. In a context where it is the fictitious identity of Judy that enables Scottie to love her, like a fetish that supports desire, the revelation of Judy's identity has a shattering effect.[30] The disenchantment and spiritual malaise that, in a film like *Shadow of a Doubt*, is attached to the female point of view becomes in *Vertigo* the property of the male subject, whose drive to author the world as he wishes it to be in the face of loss yields both the destruction of the other and destruction of the self.

In these films the gap between what the male character understands and does and what the wrong woman experiences (or, in the case of *Murder!*, the sympathetic dandy-villain) is registered through a division in focalization in the narrative, and in particular through the opposition between what is told or narrated and what is shown. In *The Paradine Case*, the heroine's point of view is afforded through the narrative device of a courtroom confrontation, but most of all, through Hitchcock's frequent recourse to shots of Valli's inscrutable impassive face, as Tony seeks to impose upon her his self-interested conception of her history. *Murder!* is largely focalized through the point of view of the male detective, though at crucial moments it diverges from that point of view, as for example in the scene where Fane stages his own suicide as Sir John looks on as a distant observer. *Vertigo* is largely focalized through the hero, but departs from that point of view in Judy's flashback to show what happened at the Mission San Juan Bautista in a manner that underscores our sympathy with the heroine. As Scottie drives Judy one final time to the mission, Hitchcock cuts to Judy's point-of-view shots of the trees overhead, which recalls an earlier drive to the mission, as he evokes the agonizing pathos of this woman, in part trapped by her own devices, but most of all coerced by the man she loves.[31] What the camera reveals to us in these scenes and others, such as the crosscutting of the final chase in *Blackmail* and in the revelatory flashback that concludes *Marnie*, is an emotional truth that is beyond the capacity of self-interested male rationality (embodied in the authority of the word) to grasp.

"Call it my female intuition": Knowledge and Gender "Inversion"

Thus far in this chapter, I have discriminated different kinds of plots according to the kind of gendered form of knowledge they enact and the nature and implications of recognition that each kind of plot entails. As we have seen, knowledge in Hitchcock has a different relationship to the human interests that inform it according to a logic governed by the gendered distinction between reason and intuition that shapes different forms of plots, even as the opposition is revised and complicated within them. Recognition turns on establishing the virtue of a wrong man or woman, or the vice of an ostensibly right man or woman. But the nature and consequences of this discovery are different according to the kind of gendered knowledge and plot forms that lead to recognition: the joint quest narrative; narratives of male detection; and narratives of female detection.

However, there is a further question to consider in Hitchcock's recognition narratives that complicates our understanding of their gendered forms. The criminal-dandy in Hitchcock is often implicitly though covertly homosexual, and, more generally, of an uncertain identity that in contemporary parlance would be labeled as queer. Hitchcock's criminal-dandies are the antagonists of his "wrong man" or detective heroes, but they are also, as I emphasize in different ways throughout this book, the doubles of Hitchcock's heroes, demarcated from them by their queer sexuality, which excludes them from entering into a normative heterosexual relationship. The dandy is also typically demarcated from the "wrong man" hero by the fact that he is a class apart. As we shall see in chapter 4, the dandy in Hitchcock is a residue of Hitchcock's English, Edwardian sensibility, which seeps through into his American films.

Hitchcock's dandy is defined by his combination of masculine and feminine traits. He is possessed with the sensitivity and capacity for attachment that is implicitly feminine in accordance with the logic of gender that Hitchcock inherited from his Edwardian upbringing. This makes him prone to the same kind of overidentification with the other that afflicts the characters played by Joan Fontaine in *Rebecca* and *Suspicion*. Indeed, because the dandy seems to possess a woman's soul in a man's body, his blind faith appears excessive, even pitiful. At the same time, however, this sensitivity transforms the masculine trait of instrumental reason into a form of hyper-intuition that takes on an almost supernatural aspect and translates, in its perverse form, into a paranoid, sadistic, defensive assertion of power and control. The qualities of omniscience and intuition that characterize this figure are often themselves divided or doubled—the double of the double—between the dandy-figure who exercises superhuman control and authority and the sensitive, intuitive, feminine ally or partner, who may be identified or involved with the female protagonist and who is rendered vulnerable and a source of audience sympathy.

The extent to which Hitchcock conceives this outsider to be a sympathetic figure is underscored by the fact that the dandy in Hitchcock's early work, such as *The Lodger* and *Murder!*, is not necessarily a demonic character but one whose intensified powers of observation and intuition are harnessed to the social good, even as they seem to exist outside ordinary structures of social authority. In his American films such as *Shadow of a Doubt*, *Rope*, *Strangers on a Train*, and *Vertigo*, the powers of the dandy are unambiguously demonic in contrast to a detective figure or "wrong man" hero, according to the formula first manifest in *Blackmail*. Nonetheless, even as a criminal, the dandy is often rendered sympathetic in Hitchcock's work precisely because he exhibits traits of vulnerability and empathy that the hero lacks, and, as we saw in chapter 2, Hitchcock further aligns us with his situation through the manipulation of narrative point of view. While the dandy-criminal is a figure whose true identity must be exposed, he often gets his own recognition scenes, which help align us to him. For example, in *Shadow of a Doubt*, after Uncle Charlie and Young Charlie have both overheard the news that the Merry Widow Murderer has apparently been caught, Uncle Charlie leaps up to the stairs to get ready for dinner. Hitchcock cuts from the face of a puzzled Young Charlie in close-up to Uncle Charlie and tracks him from behind as he briskly mounts the stairs. Suddenly, halfway up, he pauses, turns, and looks down from the stairs at the frowning Young Charlie, framed in the open doorway below, as if he has felt her accusatory gaze and recognizes that she knows the truth about him. At the denouement of *North by Northwest*, Leonard (Martin Landau) realizes that Eve is a double agent because she shot Roger Thornhill with a blank gun and communicates this knowledge to Vandamm by shooting him with the same gun.

The Lodger, whose dandy-hero is only ambiguously criminal and perverse, is a pivotal work in establishing the dandy as a sympathetic figure. In *Murder!*, Hitchcock's third sound film, he pries apart the two aspects of the dandy persona of *The Lodger* into Sir John Menier, debonair detective and romantic lead, and Handel Fane, the dandy-criminal. The Lodger, considered as a hero, and Sir John in *Murder!*, echo the sober, conservative, aristocratic, English tradition of the gentleman-detective of Sir Arthur Conan Doyle, G. K. Chesterton, and Dorothy L. Sayers. In a universe where appearances and identities are deceptive, the innocent are wrongly accused, and the guilty go free, these dandies are aristocratic amateur sleuths whose powers of observation extend beyond conclusions based upon unreflective conformist social behavior and judgments to truths that are obscured by social prejudice. They exist above or beyond the law and transgress the social norms and class boundaries that the law helps to sustain and reinforce. The ability of the dandy to penetrate the veil of appearances allows him to restore balance to the social order, a balance that is symbolized by the rescue and redemption of the fallen woman (the wrong or wronged woman) like some latter-day Arthurian knight.

In his persona as the aristocratic amateur detective, the Lodger is extremely sympathetic to the situation of women in the modern urban environment. He is motivated to hunt down the killer because of the death of his sister and promises his mother on her deathbed that he will not rest until the villain is caught. He thereby provides a benign archetype of the dandy as a "neurasthenically" sensitive man who is emotionally attached to women, not in the culturally stereotypical sense of a desire to possess them as an object, but in the sense of identifying with them or sharing their emotional space in a manner that is derived from a "romantic" sense of romantic love as sibling kinship. Thus in *The Lodger*, the figure of the Lodger-hero contrasts favorably with Daisy's dull lower-middle-class policeman boyfriend, whose emotions are rather rough-hewn and whose romantic advances are lugubrious and gauche. The Lodger's superior sensitivity, in this respect, also coincides with his better skills of detection. If we are to believe, at the end, in his innocence, Joe has fingered him as the wrong man, while the Lodger has single-handedly achieved almost the same authority over the case as the entire London police force. Sir John, in *Murder!*, is equally sensitive to the plight of the heroine, Diana Baring, the wrongly imprisoned heroine. His dawning sense of love for her is orchestrated by Hitchcock to the strains of Wagner's *Tristan and Isolde*, and it motivates him to overturn the superficial judgment of the jury that delivered the original guilty verdict.

While the dandy in *The Lodger* can be considered a romantic hero, the very ambiguity of his persona also makes him a template for the sympathetic figure of deviance in Hitchcock, and in *Murder!* Hitchcock goes to unusual lengths to portray the victimized status of the criminal, who in certain respects, as I have already argued, compares favorably with the aloof and rather ruthless Sir John. His crime is not the expression of a "perverse" impulse; rather, it is a spontaneous response to vicious ridicule.[32] Perhaps the closest equivalent to this character in the rest of Hitchcock's work is Alex Sebastian in *Notorious*, so brilliantly realized by Claude Rains. Rains, the dandy-deviant, compares sympathetically to the jealous, possessive hero Devlin (Cary Grant), who is in love with the same woman and who sends Alex to his death at the end of the film with cold-hearted indifference. He is further structurally aligned with the position of the heroine in the way that the central recognition scenes in the film are played out. The turning point of the film occurs when Alex notices that Alicia has used the keys to the cellar. His adored Alicia is thus not in love with him but is, in fact, a government spy who is simply using him. This moment of recognition exposes his own vulnerability in the manner of the virtuous heroines of Hitchcock's female-centered melodramas and renders him a figure of pity as he pathetically confesses his mistake to his mother (who suspected Alicia all along). However, unlike Hitchcock's virtuous heroines, goaded by his mother he takes action to redress the situation by eliminating Alicia—the tables are turned, and Alicia is now the victim.

Psycho's Norman Bates is the heir to both the Lodger and Handel Fane. Norman Bates is not a dandy in dress because, by the time of *Psycho* and partly as a result of working in television, Hitchcock resolutely inhabits an American idiom where the connotations of "deviance" have been stripped of all class dimensions. Yet, Norman *is* decidedly queer in his fastidious gestures, speech, and body language, and in this he is the heir to Hitchcock's dandies. As we saw in chapter 2, Hitchcock renders Norman a profoundly sympathetic figure. In part this is achieved by concealing his identity as the murderer, and in part by emphasizing those qualities of vulnerability and empathy that align him with the heroine and create a positive contrast to the one-dimensional hero, Sam Loomis (John Gavin). When, at the denouement of the film, Norman Bates is cornered by the self-righteous, patronizing, and physically intimidating Loomis while Lila Crane sneaks up to the mother's house, Norman becomes a sympathetic victim like Handel Fane. Furthermore, like Alex, he has his own moment of recognition. As Sam Loomis insists that his mother will tell them the truth about what Norman did to Marion Crane and why he stole her money, chivalrous Norman, ever protective of mother, suddenly reacts in panic—"Where's that girl you came here with, where is she?"—deftly knocks the hectoring Sam over the head, and rushes up to the house to save mother. Even here, at the film's climax, we are invited to sympathize with Norman, as much as with the ostensible hero of the film and his helper Lila, and this, of course, is what makes *Psycho* such a profoundly transgressive and disturbing work.

However, the feminine sensitivity of the dandy that aligns him with the heroine is precisely the quality whose characteristically incestuous origins render him criminally perverse, as Norman's fabled relationship to his mother in *Psycho* makes clear. This pattern of incestuous motivation can be traced all the way back to *The Lodger*. Considered as Jack the Ripper or the Avenger, the Lodger in fact must be the person responsible for the death of his own sister, the Avenger's first victim, at no less than her "coming out" ball. His motivation then might be explained by a kind of overidentification with his sister that renders the efflorescence of her (hetero)sexuality at her coming out ball something that is intolerable to him and results in her murder by his hand. His attachment to her is of an incestuous nature (the perverse corollary of the romantic sibling ideal), and he must then go on murdering golden-curled women again and again (insofar as all such women are incipiently fallen) lest their own (hetero)sexuality might emerge and expose his own (hetero)sexual impotence.

This hidden incestuous wish often seems to inform the criminal-dandy's particular relationship to knowledge. The incestuous violation of nature at once manifests a form of "supernatural" thinking that involves the effort to reorganize the world, magically and murderously, in accordance with one's wishes, and consolidates magical thinking as a trait of the "perverse" mind. *Strangers on a Train* makes this connection between incestuous desire and magical thinking explicit. Bruno, the dandy-criminal, is motivated by the incestuous oedipal wish to effortlessly or magically install himself in his father's place by arranging for him to "disappear." His plot is ingenious: he will murder Guy Haines's estranged wife if Guy agrees in turn to murder Bruno's father—"criss-cross." But Bruno also seems in general to be possessed with telepathic powers. He strangles Guy's estranged wife when Guy has admitted wanting to strangle her, and he constantly pops up within Guy's field of vision when he least expects it, once it begins to seem that Guy may not deliver his side of the bargain that Bruno believes he has struck. For example, he distractingly appears within Guy's field of vision in a tennis crowd, looking straight at Guy while the rest of the spectators follow the ball. Or he appears as an isolated black figure standing out against the white of the Jefferson Memorial. Bruno's "attachment" to Guy involves a demonic omniscience in which he somehow shadows and knows in advance Guy's every move.

In a similar way, in *Shadow of a Doubt*, the figure of the dandy, Uncle Charlie, demonstrates preternatural tendencies informed by incestuous desires. Disguised as the alluring, larger-than-life uncle, he harbors incestuous impulses toward both his sister—with whom he shares an illegible joke about his "loaded cade" at the dinner table—and to his niece to whom he gives the wedding ring he has culled from a murdered widow. These incestuous desires both inform and are informed by the telepathic affinity between the two Charlies. Hitchcock makes a rather Victorian "joke" by linking the mundane powers of telegraphy—Young Charlie goes to send a telegram requesting him to come only to receive a telegram that says he is already coming—with the magical powers of telepathy. In broader terms,

Uncle Charlie's supernatural powers are linked, via the visual rhetoric of expressionism, to the figure of the vampire, as we shall see in chapter 5. Just as the Lodger ranges over the streets of London, in and out of the London fog, always one step ahead of the police, apparently a force for good but possibly a force of evil, Uncle Charlie, who appears and disappears at will, seems to all, and especially to the women-folk, a larger-than-life pillar of the community, but turns out to be a serial killer.

As we have seen, *Murder!* divides the dandy between the dandy-hero, who is a figure of omniscient knowledge, and the dandy-villain, a figure of hyperintuition and sensitivity. Elsewhere, the villains themselves are often divided between a hyperbolic rational controlling figure and a more sensitive, feminine, partner or accomplice. This is, as it were, the perverse analogue of the structures of gender complementarity I have already explored (a homosexual variant of the perverse family that threatens the nuclear family in *The Man Who Knew Too Much*). In *Notorious*, the suave, sensitive Alex Sebastian is contrasted with the ruthless, sinister, and deadly Eric Mathis, who ends up victimizing Alex himself. This formula is repeated in *North by Northwest* through the opposition between the suave and sensitive Phillip Vandamm, who is blinded by love for the heroine, and the sinister, perverse, and murderous Leonard. However, *North by Northwest* also complicates the opposition. It is Leonard's "women's intuition," with Vandamm's interest at heart, that tells him that the gun that Eve used to shoot Roger Thornhill was filled with blanks, and that therefore she is a double agent. Furthermore, Vandamm proves as ruthless as Leonard is in his decision to unceremoniously "dump" his partner Eve from a great height. By endowing one (or more) of the protagonists of the criminal gang with sensitivity, these films suggest that the perverse family formed by the ostensible villains may ironically be bound by greater feelings of warmth and humanity than the "family" of American spies who ostensibly uphold social and moral order.

Hitchcock's most articulate dramatization of the doubled dandy-villain is *Rope*, whose protagonists Brandon and Phillip form an implicitly homosexual couple. Brandon conspires with Phillip to murder David Kentley, places his body in a chest in the center of the room, and contrives to orchestrate a party to demonstrate his superhuman powers of emotional control. Like Sir John, Brandon is a dandy who is seeking to author and organize the social world; but whereas Sir John, on the surface at least, acts morally,

Brandon, like Bruno in *Strangers on a Train*, seeks to disclaim or transcend the constraints of good and evil. He is paired with Phillip, a sensitive concert pianist who plays Poulenc and visibly suffers from the torment of exposure, for he is as much the subject of Brandon's manipulating, controlling personality as the rest of the party guests. Phillip is an hysteric, and as Brandon's double he provides an index of the emotional sensitivity that lurks within Brandon himself. The dandy in Hitchcock, as Rothman suggests, is a figure who is unable to satisfactorily love.[33] He is divided between the self-effacing and ultimately self-destructive attachment to the other (a hyperbolic manifestation of the self-doubt that afflicts the gothic heroine) or through a hyperintellectual form of control in which the other is bound to the self through a sadistic and paranoid possession (a distorted expression of the general male tendency in Hitchcock's films to use knowledge as a source of control). However, while Rothman sees the dandy's dilemma as a dramatic expression of a general human predicament, which of course it is, it is also much more specifically a product of a culture of compulsory heterosexuality where the idea of homosexual love is an impossible one.

The focus of this chapter has been on the different shape of Hitchcock's recognition plots according to the gendered forms of knowledge they inscribe. These forms of knowledge yield fundamentally different narrative patterns according to whether the romantic couple jointly investigate or investigate one another. It is where one member of a couple investigates the other that gender asymmetries and inequalities emerge most sharply in relation to positions of social power and authority. This gendered system of knowledge is revised in Hitchcock's works as orthodox gender identities are criticized and realigned in the reworking of archetypal plot forms. Furthermore, it is complicated through the projection of gender difference onto the figure of the dandy, who combines, hyperbolically and perversely, male and female forms of knowing, and who while criminal is often a figure of sympathy in the narrative.

I began the chapter by discussing *The Wrong Man* and noting how this film, while singular in his canon, points to the way in which Hitchcock's films are complex mediations on recognition and misrecognition and their consequences. Supporting this argument has involved taking the content of Hitchcock's work seriously or reading his films for their central themes as social parables. But what also emerges from this discussion is that this group of films constitutes a remarkable set of variations on a finite set of doubled roles—wrong man, wrong woman, cop, and dandy—and characteristic plot structures—joint quest, female detection, male detection—all of which can be discerned in his third film, *The Lodger*, and which are combined and reworked throughout his career. In other words, the content of Hitchcock plots issues from the orchestration of a set of formal choices that arise from the principles of doubling and parallelism between gender roles, or between the moral hero or heroine and the criminal or perverse antagonist, even as these roles are mapped onto the linear structure and moral telos of the recognition narrative. Content is always a matter of form in Hitchcock, and he is thus, in the final analysis, an aesthete, as I shall explore in the next chapter.

II
Visual Style

4

Sexuality and Style

The specific form taken by romantic irony in Hitchcock is, in large part, a response to the understanding of human sexuality and its relationship to art that develops in the nineteenth century and is distilled in the discourse of aestheticism, dandyism, and decadence embodied in the legend of Oscar Wilde, and articulated more systematically, if indirectly, by Freudian psychoanalysis. As I suggested in chapter 1, romantic irony essentially turns on the ambiguous logic of affirmation and negation that is staged by a self-conscious narrator, in particular the affirmation and negation of the ideal embodied in romance. The discourse of late-nineteenth-century aestheticism explores this dialectic of simultaneous affirmation and negation as a function of the activity of representation itself, wherein artistic representation, especially the artistic representation of the human form, at once embodies an uncorrupted ideal of a complete and timeless beauty, and yet also, through its very surface perfection, intimates the underlying decadence and corruption of human mortality. As a medium of surfaces, the visual rhetoric of cinema is used by Hitchcock to convey the sense that conventional forms of plotting and characterization embodied in the romance narrative are, in one sense, only skin deep. The performance of gentlemanliness and the masquerade of femininity, the romantic pursuit that is realized in the supreme, explosive moment of the kiss, may begin to seem like a pretext for the staging of a shadow world of perversity that is secreted beneath the veneer of orthodox values.

The subject of this chapter is the relationship that the aesthetic ideal bears to human perversity in Hitchcock's films. Since the model of human perversity within aestheticism and Hitchcock's films is a homosexuality that is deemed perverse and that threatens the heterosexual romance, I will be focusing more on the manner in which aestheticism in Hitchcock functions to undercut rather than affirm that romance. However, I do not wish to imply that Hitchcock's concern is simply to undermine the values of romantic love. As I have argued in earlier chapters, for Hitchcock all sexuality is incipiently perverse, including heterosexuality. In Hitchcock's romances like *The 39 Steps*, *To Catch a Thief*, and *North by Northwest*, artifice, masquerade, and the fictiveness of the narrative world serve to sustain rather than sabotage the romance. The opposition between the couple in the romance, their mutual misunderstanding, is an occasion not for the dissolution of romance, but the condition under which it flourishes, giving expression to the anarchic impulses of human sexuality. However, insofar as the forces of human perversity cannot be contained within the telos of heterosexual desire, Hitchcock's orchestration of artifice registers the lure of human perversity as a force that threatens the establishment of romance and moral conventions it reaffirms.

Consider the example of *Vertigo*. *Vertigo*, I shall argue, is the supreme illustration of Hitchcock's aestheticism. The romantic ideal embodied in the heroine, "Madeleine," is an idealization, and the pursuit of this fiction by the hero, Scottie Ferguson, can be construed as perverse. Not only is Scottie's desire socially transgressive in that "Madeleine" is another man's wife, it is perverse in the sense that "Madeleine," through her apparent possession, exudes an aura of death. Judy's attraction to Scottie is also perverse, in that it arises out of a duplicitous charade of seduction that manipulates and ensnares Scottie. Yet the fiction of Madeleine also represents an opportunity for two emotional drifters—the chaste, late-middle-aged John Ferguson and the promiscuous Judy Barton—to find redemption through love. Is *Vertigo* a film about a love that is cruelly lost or a film about the essential perversity of human desire? Does human perversity as it is orchestrated through artifice make romance possible, or does it expose romance as an impossible fiction or an illusion? This is a paradox that informs much of Hitchcock's work.

Sexuality and Style

Aestheticism and Perversity

Aestheticism emerges in the late-nineteenth-century cult of beauty and "art for art's sake" associated with the revival of Hellenism in the writing and teaching of Oscar Wilde's mentor, Walter Pater. Pater in his studies of the Renaissance valorizes the Greek influence upon the Renaissance with its pagan origins over the Christian spiritual tradition in which the sensuous representation of the human form exists to represent something nonsensuous or spiritual. In Greek art, Pater admires the Apollonian perfection of the youthful human form as the object of sensuous contemplation and self-consciously identifies this form with a male beauty without sexual content: "The beauty of the Greek statues was a sexless beauty: the statues of the gods had the least traces of sex. Here there is a moral sexlessness, a kind of ineffectual wholeness of nature, yet with a true beauty and significance of its own."[1] Furthermore, it is a form of beauty that is essentially timeless: "Greek sculpture deals almost exclusively with youth, where the molding of the bodily organs is still as if suspended between growth and completion."[2] This idealized masculine aesthetic form is implicitly contrasted by Pater with feminine Christian art, considered moral, sentimental, and mortal: "There is no Greek Madonna; the goddesses are always childless."[3] At the same time, the reverence accorded to the content of sacred art is transposed, as it were, to aesthetic form, to the worship of form as the transcendent value. Pater was attracted to High Anglicanism, not on the grounds of religion but rather of ritual form. In the words of Kenneth Clarke, "he was a professed pagan, but inhaled with voluptuous pleasure, the incense of the High Anglican ceremonial."[4]

Aestheticism thus exalts the perfection of form, as it is manifest in the appreciation of the artwork and the appearance of the gentleman-aesthete. This worship of form has an indirect relationship to same-sex passion that is expressed through the appreciation of male beauty, but same-sex passion is disguised as it were in the appreciation of the subtleties of form, as if the appreciation of form were a surrogate for that passion, which is itself without content in the sense that it is sexless. The aesthete is defined by his appreciation of form, a refined understanding which is a displaced or surrogate expression of same-sex passion or homosocial love, which itself has no sexual content. In this way Pater's idea of aestheticism seems to anticipate Freud's theory of sublimation. The displacement of sexuality within aestheticism is so complete that all references to human sexuality are lost. Pater writes, "In its primary aspect, a great picture has no more definite message for us than an accidental play of sunlight and shadow for a few moments on the wall or floor: is itself, in truth, a space of such fallen light, caught as the colors are in an Eastern carpet, but refined upon, and dealt with more subtly and exquisitely than by nature itself."[5] Aestheticism as a species of pure formalism detaches the cult of art for art's sake from any reference to human sexuality.

The distinction between aestheticism conceived as pure formal design and aestheticism considered as a displaced articulation of sexual content is central to considering the role of aestheticism in Hitchcock's work. Hitchcock is a second-generation aesthete in the sense that, as we shall see, he knowingly uses form as a displaced expression of sexual content. And yet, especially late in his career, the orchestration of elaborate design for design's sake is evident. The savoring of the moment of suspense, which postpones narrative resolution rather than propels it forward, may be linked to the allegiance Hitchcock invites to the forces of human perversity that undercut the romance, such as Bruno Anthony's agency in *Strangers on a Train* that I shall describe in detail later in this chapter. However, insofar as the orchestration of suspense is linked to the performance of what Hitchcock liked to call "pure cinema"—that is, cinematic narration without dialogue—it seems to exceed the perverse allegiances that motivate it and exist as a manifestation of Hitchcock's artistry for its own sake.[6]

Pater was a professor and an ascetic. His elevation of the aesthetic is humorless and lacks irony. Oscar Wilde's innovation, as Alan Sinfield suggests, was to link the discourse of aestheticism to dandyism, thereby wittily and ironically renewing the connection between dandyism and art forged by the Byronic legend earlier in the century.[7] Although the original Regency dandy, Beau Brummell, reformed male aristocratic dress codes into a more modern, masculine tailored attire, dandyism became associated in the eyes of the emerging, newly enfranchised middle classes of the 1830s with the effeminate manners of feckless aristocrats devoted to perfecting their own self-presentation and deportment in a life of leisured indolence.[8] Furthermore, through the life and legend of Byron, who self-consciously courted the reputation of a Don Juan, identified with "oriental" decadence, both in his life and through his art, the image of the dandy was at once amplified and embodied in the person of the "romantic" author. Subsequent

"Byronic" author-dandies Edward Bulwer-Lytton and Benjamin Disraeli consolidated the link between the writer and the dandy in the public imagination. In the eyes of the middle classes, the idea of male authorship was thus tainted with effeminacy and decadence, especially in a context where the profession of writing itself was already associated with the feminine sphere of sentiment as opposed to the male sphere of industry and action. But by the end of the century the Irish, Catholic, aristocratic Wilde turned the image of the dandy against the values of English middle-class morality by self-consciously cultivating and celebrating the image of the aesthete as an effeminate and morally decadent member of the upper classes.

Wilde's potboiler, *The Picture of Dorian Gray*, first published in 1890, dramatizes the relationship between dandyism, aestheticism, and decadence in a manner that makes explicit the relationship between aestheticism and sexual "depravity" or "perversity." In *Dorian Gray*, the persona of the gentleman-dandy is divided among three characters: an earnest gentleman-artist, Basil Hallward, who is in love with Dorian in a morally idealistic, Paterian way; a decadent idle aristocrat, Lord Henry Wooten, who is a corrupter of youth; and Dorian Gray himself, a beautiful young man who disintegrates into a guilt-ridden debauchee. Dorian Gray is afforded eternal youth by assuming the identity bequeathed upon him in an idealized portrait painted by Basil Hallward. Under the influence of the dandy, Lord Henry, this immunity to physical decay allows him to freely indulge his desires. However, the portrait unflinchingly registers the accelerated aging process yielded by his Dionysian depravity. The Apollonian image of a pure and uncorrupted beauty progressively degenerates into a physiognomy of unimaginable ugliness and horror.[9]

Wilde's visual pun conceives art not simply as an ideal but as an idealization, and therefore as an index of the very forces of chaos and corruption that it seems so completely to conceal. The ideal surface of the artwork "dissolves" into an image of the accelerated aging process that is the opposite of timeless perfection. In this way, the artwork becomes an index of the very imperfection, decay, and death that it is designed to conceal. Furthermore, by making the aging process itself signify moral degeneration, Wilde makes Pater's timeless beauty, as it is figured in the looks of the young Adonis, the criterion of moral value. Art, in Wilde's pun, takes the place of life. Not only is art valued above life as it is embodied in human maturation, it replaces life, "killing" the thing that it represents in a manner that echoes or reprises the death of the subject of a painting as the artist completes her portrait in Edgar Allan Poe's short story, "The Oval Portrait."[10] The corollary of this inversion of moral hierarchy between artistic perfection and biological life is Wilde's celebration of murder as a fine art after Thomas de Quincey in his essay "Pencil, Pen and Poison," whose subject is the artist/murderer Thomas Wainwright and whose title, as Peter Conrad points out, playfully alliterates upon the connection between art and murder.[11]

Hitchcock, like Wilde, has deep sympathy with the figure of the murderer, portrayed not as a mindless villain but as a dandy-aesthete who in seeking to preserve the illusion of self-perfection in his own self-comportment cannot bear the mortal "contamination" suggested by the presence of sexual desire.[12] As we have seen, most of Hitchcock's murderers are dandies in their self-deportment, and they are typically endowed with an aesthetic sensibility. For example, Handel Fane in *Murder!* is an actor and Wildean dandy; the flamboyant Bruno Anthony in *Strangers on a Train* has the hands of a strangler, which are carefully manicured, maintained, and preserved by his mother, as if they are the hands of an artist. Norman Bates in *Psycho*, while less obviously a dandy, is a consummate murderer-as-artist, killing then embalming his mother. But perhaps the ideal exemplar of the murderer-artist in Hitchcock is Brandon in *Rope*, who seems to murder purely for the pleasure of orchestrating the concealment of this act. Hitchcock's own identification with these figures is manifest in the way that the realization of the murderer's art becomes an occasion for Hitchcock to display his own directorial brilliance: for example, the tour-de-force fairground sequence in *Strangers on a Train* where Bruno Anthony stalks his female victim (analyzed in chapter 5); the shower scene montage in *Psycho* where Norman Bates kills Marion Crane; or Hitchcock's elaborate choreography of the moving camera and long take in *Rope*, whose game of revelation and concealment seems to mimic the game of his protagonist.

The Picture of Dorian Gray seems to entertain the possibility of homosexual desire in the triangular relationship between its male protagonists, only to deny it. It is as if, within a culture of compulsory heterosexuality, the possibility of that desire can be articulated only through aestheticization—in particular the idealization of the young male body of Dorian—which has as its corollary a sense of depravity and nihilism. Although Wilde's novel refers to Joris Karl Huysman's decadent novel, *Against Nature* (*À rebours*, 1884), where homosexuality is explicitly nominated as one of the many indulgences of its debauched aristocratic hero, Des Esseintes, homo-sexuality gets no mention in Wilde's novel among the myriad of Dorian's vices. However, the pressure of a sexual path that is sought but cannot be acknowledged is negatively registered through Wilde's portrayal of the romantic ideal in the relationship between Dorian Gray and the lower-class actress Sybil Vane.

The brief romance developed between Dorian and Sybil Vane is predi-cated upon Sybil mirroring, in her endless stage roles as lover, the idealized detemporalized identity of Dorian himself. The moment that Sybil resolves to step outside her roles as a lover, assume her real-life identity as a woman, and "fall" in love with Dorian, Dorian's desire is quenched and Sybil, rejected, precipitously dies by her own hand. Once the idealized imaginary space of pure semblance is abandoned, romantic love disintegrates. Romantic love is thus realizable only in terms of the ideal semblance of fic-tion, and the corollary of that ideal is nihilism. Again, the copresence of the ideal and nihilism in the portrayal of romantic love derives from the impact of a culture of compulsory heterosexuality upon Wilde. For from within a culture of compulsory heterosexuality, while heterosexual object-choice is the only way male sexuality can be expressed for the artist who is inchoately seeking an alternative to it—indeed, it embodies the ideal of love—it is also perceived as an illusory fiction and is therefore treated with nihilism.

This romance is a passing episode in Wilde's novel. Compared with Hitchcock's films, Wilde's treatment of the romance is perfunctory, lacks conviction, and is laced with misogyny. Nonetheless, the romantic ideal in Hitchcock's work, whether it is exuberantly affirmed or whether it is under-cut, is linked, in this way, to aestheticism. As we saw in chapter 1, in Hitchcock's narratives of romantic renewal like *To Catch a Thief* and *North by Northwest*, romance is affirmed through the delirious embrace of artifice. The key to romance lies in the mutual affirmation of belief in the masquer-ade. But this romantic façade harbors the threat of nihilism within it, as demonstrated in the seemingly vampiric kiss that unites the Lodger with Daisy in *The Lodger*, but also threatens to annihilate her. The surface appear-ance of the dandy-gentleman appears as a snare, the ideal of romance as a delusion. At this point, Hitchcock's narration begins to take a "perverse" turn, embracing artifice as a vehicle of nihilism and human perversity, cul-minating, perhaps, in Norman Bates's frenzied attack on Marion Crane in the shower in *Psycho*. In its utterly perverse way this attack is an act of love (he can preserve Marion's virtue only by killing her), and it is filmed with all the cinematic virtuosity that Hitchcock has at his disposal.

Only five years after Wilde published *Dorian Gray*, his homosexuality became public knowledge, and *Dorian Gray* was cited by the defense as evidence for his homosexual "depravity" in a manner that made explicit, in the public mind, the connection between aestheticism and homosexuality, homophobically conceived as a perversion. Shortly afterward, the nature of "perversion" and its relationship to the making of art began to be theorized by Freud. In Freud's explicit theory of creativity—the theory of sublimation—perversion and sublimation are contrasting outcomes of the sexual instinct in human development. "Perversions," Freud writes, "are the development of germs, all of which are contained in the undifferentiated sexual dispositions of the child, and which, by being suppressed or being diverted to higher, asexual aims—by being sublimated—are destined to provide the energy for a great number of our cultural achievements."[13] Yet the concept of sublimation is not quite adequate to Wilde's vision of art, for it suggests only the Paterian sense of the artwork as the object of self-contained "sexless" perfection (whose relationship to human perversity is displaced), rather than Wilde's sense of artwork as a sublime object, which in its very perfection intimates a core of corruption or decadence.

However, as Freudian theorist Janine Chasseguet-Smirgel has argued, Freud's concept of idealization suggests a different account of the relation of perversion to creativity in which the sexual instinct is directly implicated in aesthetic activity, and where aesthetic activity is not a displacement of "perversion" but an enactment or realization of it.[14] Freud suggests in his essay "On Narcissism" that "idealization" involves not a deflection of sexual instinct from sexual satisfaction, but an investment of the sexual instinct in the aggrandizement of self in an objectified "idealized" form, that seems very like the body of the dandy as it is conceived by Wilde.[15] The "pervert's" self-objectification is motivated by an impulse to sustain the illusion that undifferentiated "polymorphous" sexual impulses that appear abject in relation to socially sanctioned forms of normative heterosexual masculinity are, in fact, adequate to the normative expression of masculinity embodied in the Victorian father, indeed, better than them. The incipient "pervert" believes that his pregenital sexuality is equal, if not superior, to the sexuality of the father, and in this way idealizes his abject, fragmented, infantile state with respect to heterosexual genital sexuality, as if it is whole and perfect, as if it were adequate to or even better than the phallic sexuality of the father, adequate, in particular, to meeting the needs of the mother. However, the illusion of the narcissist is a fragile one; the surface of the narcissistic body is one whose idealized perfection intimates an abject core that lies beneath. For Freud, narcissistic illusion is sustained by fetishistic props other than the body of the self. These props often have the qualities at once of something unbroken and smooth and yet also something whose surface appearance conceals dirtiness, like a patent leather shoe. The fetish is an object that through the idealization of surface at once reveals and conceals a core of abjection.

In the context of narcissistic perversion, "aestheticism" can be understood both in relation to the idealized self-objectification of "the aesthete"— that is, through the presentation of his own dandified body—and in relation to the artwork considered as a fetish object that involves the fabrication of perfect, more-than-real surfaces, that at once conceal and reveal a "perverse" or abject core. It is the artwork conceived in this way as a fetish that is joked upon in Wilde's parable of *Dorian Gray*, where the idealized surface of the painting takes the form of a corrupted body, while the corrupted body of the dandy takes on the form of an idealized surface. Furthermore, Freud's account of narcissistic perversion, as interpreted by Chasseguet-Smirgel, makes explicit the temporal logic that underlies Wilde's parable. The elevation of the artwork and the narcissist's body as a fetish is undertaken in defiance of the temporal logic of human maturation and mortality and therefore also in defiance of the procreative heterosexuality that the fact of human maturation presupposes. Freud's theory, as interpreted by Chasseguet-Smirgel, attempts to provide a systematic explanation of the relationship between aestheticism and sexuality that is explored by Wilde in *Dorian Gray*. Thus Freudian psychoanalysis also presupposes the Victorian culture of compulsory heterosexuality in which normative sexuality is linked to the act of procreation and nonprocreative sexuality represents a perverse deviation from the developmental norm that leads to aestheticization.

The Dandy in Hitchcock

According to Hitchcock's biographer Patrick McGilligan, Hitchcock read Freud in the 1920s when his influence on the intellectual circles within which

Hitchcock moved was pervasive. He was certainly familiar with Wilde's *Dorian Gray*. Furthermore, his formation as an artist took place within a postwar culture where aestheticism and dandyism was in the air, as Thomas Elsaesser notes in his suggestive essay "The Dandy in Hitchcock."[16] World War I did not simply kill a lot of British young men; it challenged Edwardian complacency and self-righteous masculinity. A central manifestation of this reaction to Edwardian, masculine values of sport, spartanism, service, and self-denial was an efflorescence of Wildean dandyism that germinated in the corridors of Eton and Oxford. This was epitomized by such figures as Harold Acton and Brian Howard, who, as Martin Green writes, "saw themselves as originators of a new 'aesthetic' phase in English high culture, to be characterized by ornament, brilliancy, playfulness, and youthfulness, and by a turning of the back on the old forms of seriousness and power."[17] In Green's account, the more rambunctious rogue type is allied with the dandy in this act of rebellion: "The rogue," he writes, "is often coarse, rough, brutal, and careless. He is like the Dandy, however, in his conscious enjoyment of his own style and in his rebellion against mature and responsible morality. Sexually he is as much the narcissist as the dandy is, but 'typically' the rogue is heterosexual, the dandy homosexual."[18] The Byronic legend provided a model for both types. The rampant rebellious heterosexual rogue was based on the official legend. The dandy-aesthete modeled himself on Byron, who was rumored to be homosexual or bisexual, via the figure of Oscar Wilde himself, who appropriated the Byronic manner with full consciousness of its range of associations.[19] Yet while these rogues and dandies were rebels, they were also sons of the establishment, and they adopted establishment conventions and inhabited positions of authority. In this sense, the persona of both dandy and rogue presupposed an upper- and upper-middle-class conformity and gentlemanly civility that provided the veneer and pretext for a form of rebellion that did nothing politically to disturb the social class order.

As a middle-class Cockney Catholic, Hitchcock was a class apart from these sons of the establishment. However, Hitchcock was an inveterate theatergoer with his mother in the late 'teens and early twenties, where he absorbed this new sensibility of revolt through style. The figure of the rogue and the dandy were personified in the London stage of the early twenties by Gerald du Maurier (Daphne's father) and Noël Coward, respectively. In a post-Wildean culture, Coward was careful to conceal the homosexual dimension of his dandy persona beneath a veneer of debonair gentlemanliness.

While Coward was not one of the upper middle class, he aspired to acceptance. The milieu of the London stage of the 1920s represented by Coward and his circle was essentially conservative in the manner it nostalgically celebrated the manners and mores of an urban drawing-room elite. Coward's queerness was contained within but also expressed through the wry, witty, portrayal of the romantic yearnings and sexual peccadilloes of the idle, leisured classes, where the personas of the rogue and dandy become virtually indistinguishable. In this he was not very different from Wilde before him, whose plays inhabited a similar aristocratic and upper-middle-class milieu and where a dandy temperament was less an index of the homosexual "pervert" than the lounge lizard or womanizer, as in the character of Lord Illingworth in *A Woman of No Importance* (1893), or the characters of Jack and Algernon in *The Importance of Being Earnest* (1895). It must be remembered that Wilde's trial for "sodomy" was precipitated by Wilde's own libel suit seeking to defend himself from the scurrilous accusations made by Lord Alfred Douglas in order to preserve his public image. In the postwar twenties little had changed.

Hitchcock soon encountered the men and women of the London stage in a professional capacity. He collaborated with the matinee idol Ivor Novello, who, like Coward, was homosexual, on two films—*The Lodger* (1926) and *Downhill* (1927), the latter based on a Novello play in which it is possible to discern a homosexual subtext. With scenario writer Eliot Stannard, Hitchcock adapted Noël Coward's 1925 play *Easy Virtue* for the screen in 1927 and, in 1930, he adopted *Murder!* from a novel that was coauthored by conservative lesbian playwright Clemance Dane and Helen Simpson. Intriguingly, Hitchcock invited Dane to write the original scenario of his film version of du Maurier's *Jamaica Inn*. In the early 1930s, Hitchcock produced *Lord Camber's Ladies* (1932), starring Gerald du Maurier, who Hitchcock said was "the leading actor in London at the time, and, in my opinion, the best actor anywhere."[20] Later he was to adapt three of the novels of Daphne du Maurier, who grew up within the same theatrical milieu, and, as we shall see, Hitchcock's adaptation of Daphne's novel *Rebecca* had a decisive influence on his career. Daphne du Maurier developed as a writer by more or less self-consciously channeling her nascent lesbian identification into a "masculine" identification as a writer in a manner that can be defined as a form of female dandyism, which often took the form of "cross-writing" or identifying with a male hero endowed with certain feminine characteristics.[21]

The self-conscious performance of identity that is inscribed in the figure of the rogue and the dandy is central to the portrayal of masculinity in Hitchcock's work. The rogue persona provides the linchpin of Hitchcock's narratives of romantic renewal, for it attaches the incipiently threatening allure of human sexuality to the male hero, bestowing upon him an "outlaw" status. At the same time, it affords the promise of containing that sexuality within the boundaries of heterosexual desire, a containment that is necessary for romantic renewal, though ambiguity about the rogue persona may remain. Cary Grant in *To Catch a Thief* and *North by Northwest* provides the archetypal rogue persona in Hitchcock's work. On the other hand, the dandy persona in Hitchcock conforms to the homophobic stereotype of what Robin Wood has called the "murderous gay," the homosexual as perverted psychopath.[22] He is embodied in Handel Fane in *Murder!*, Bruno Anthony in *Strangers on a Train*, and most of all in Charles Laughton's puffed-up, perverted, Byron-quoting Regency dandy in *Jamaica Inn*, Sir Humphrey Pengallan, who parades his favorite white horse through the dining room like the Emperor Caligula. Yet it seems to me to be mistaken to conceive Hitchcock's dandies simply as a manifestation of post-Wildean homophobia.[23] Hitchcock is not concerned to demonize homosexuality. His interest in these characters lies in staging the performance of a gentlemanliness beneath which the darkest secrets are harbored in a manner that renders them alluring and often sympathetic. In this sense, Hitchcock's dandies are no different from his murderous, or seemingly murderous, rogues like Johnnie Aysgarth in *Suspicion*, or Arthur Adamson (William Devane) in *Family Plot* (1976). Indeed the rogue is hard to distinguish from the dandy. Is Jack Favell (George Sanders) in *Rebecca*, who dresses like a dandy, sleeps with Rebecca, and blackmails de Winter, a dandy or a rogue? Uncle Charlie in *Shadow of a Doubt* dresses like a dandy and is a psychopathic criminal who hates women, but unacknowledged homosexuality could only be inferred on the slim grounds of his bachelor status, unless we assume that Hitchcock equates unacknowledged homosexuality with misogyny. Both Hitchcock's rogues and dandies, as we have seen, are invariably attractive on account of their wit and style. Their alluring presence poses a radical threat to the romance, and their eradication casts ambivalence upon its completion. It is significant, in this context, that Hitchcock often employed actors who were known or rumored to be homosexual, since he presumably believed that homosexual actors have the capacity to bring to their acting a self-conscious sense of performativity and to project their masculinity as a mask.[24]

The presence and importance of female rogues and dandies has been overlooked in Hitchcock's work. The trial of Radclyffe Hall's lesbian novel, *The Well of Loneliness*, for obscenity in 1928, had a somewhat comparable role to the impact of Wilde's trials for the social construction of lesbian sexuality. Lesbianism was not outlawed, but it remained unacknowledged and invisible as the response to Hall's book attested. Just as dandy "effeminacy" at once concealed and suggested homosexuality, masculine drag suggests a female form of dandyism. The masculine lesbian is easily an object of caricature in the hands of a male director, as is arguably the case in the portrayal of one of the three women whom the hero of Hitchcock's silent film *The Farmer's Wife* (1928) pursues, or the female jurors in *Murder!*, or the sinister, humorless Danvers in *Rebecca*, but elsewhere the masculine woman is bestowed the subversive allure of the male dandy, even though she must be neutralized. The role Hitchcock accords to the lesbian actress Marlene Dietrich in *Stage Fright*, who turns out to be a femme fatale, responsible for goading the murderer into his crime, is comparable to the presence accorded to Charles Laughton in *Jamaica Inn*.[25] In Hitchcock's late film *Marnie*, the problem that seems to beset the character of Marnie is that on account of a childhood sexual trauma she "denies" her (hetero)sexual femininity and assumes an imposter status in the male world, disguising her identity in order to rob the safes of her employers. Yet, at the same time, her female dandyism is a source of empowerment that defies the attempts of Mark to restore her "natural" femininity. Indeed, the striking opening shot of the film brilliantly defies the ascription of a "natural" feminine identity. We see the character walking away from the camera with a handbag of stolen money under her arm, and "she" looks, to my eyes at least, like a man in drag (plate 4). Since she appears to be a woman who is dressed as a man dressed as a woman, she is represented as a woman whose real identity is that of a man.

The equivalent to the male rogue in Hitchcock's film is the female lead who masquerades or performs her feminine grace and charm to disguise a "promiscuous" core in the manner that the rogue disguises sexual predation and womanizing beneath the veneer of gentlemanly civility. The actress who epitomizes this figure in Hitchcock is Grace Kelly, whose rumored sexual license underlies Hitchcock's mobilization of her conservative New Look femininity, just as knowledge of Grant's serial marriages and possible homosexuality underlies Hitchcock's use of his star persona. Indeed, as male and female rogues, Grant and Kelly are ideally matched in *To Catch a Thief*. In *North by Northwest*, Eva Marie Saint brilliantly steps into the Kelly role. But again, the boundaries between the female rogue and the dandy, between the feminine, heterosexual masquerade and the masculine, queer masquerade are not so easy to draw. In *Vertigo*, Judy Barton's masquerade as Madeleine, ostensibly an idealization of femininity in the eyes of Scottie Ferguson, wears a gray suit and a severe "lifted" hairdo twist that resembles the suits and look of Tippi Hedren in *Marnie*. I think that this can be understood in terms of the overall aestheticizing impulse of *Vertigo* that I explore below, where Madeleine approximates the sexless beauty ascribed to the male in aestheticism. Rebecca, the absent antiheroine of Hitchcock's film *Rebecca* (and du Maurier's novel), is also an ambiguous figure, in part for the reason that she is so much a projection of different characters' imaginations. In both the novel and the film she is portrayed as heterosexually promiscuous, but both also hint at homosexual "perversity." She is described as being very beautiful, yet she is associated with a masculine power and authority. In Hitchcock's film, the idea of the masculine woman is suggested in the character of de Winter's sister, who is clearly portrayed as the woman who "wears the trousers." She sports the costume of Boadicea (or Boudicca) to the Manderley ball in a parody of masculine femininity, while her husband wears a leotard and a pair of dumbbells (or balls) that a fey male servant drops in a manner that jokingly suggests the husband's sexual impotence. This is one rare moment of Hitchcockian humor that survived Selznick's censorious oversight.

Yet what are we to make of Hitchcock's own persona? Raymond Durgnat speculates: "Isn't Hitchcock's sphingine, sinister pose a spiritual successor to a dandyism which, be it remembered, also aimed, blandly, to inculcate a certain disquiet?"[26] Hitchcock presented himself as a corpulent, sedentary, Edwardian gentleman, in a dark blue suit, which is always the same suit, even in sunny southern California. If a dandy, his was, as Elsaesser suggests a "dandyism of sobriety."[27]

For the ascetic Walter Pater, gentlemanliness was a mask of reserve that, as a mask, exerts the fascination for something unreserved, that is hidden from view.[28] But it is crucial to the command or self-possession of the gentleman that passion be clothed within a veil of indifference. Hitchcock adopted a Paterian restraint rather than Oscar Wilde's flamboyant theatricalization of gentlemanliness, but he did follow the example of Wilde, who realized that the artist-dandy could succeed in a modern consumer culture by wittily self-conscious management of his corpulent persona in the public eye. Hitchcock's wit is more middle class, more Freudian, and he possessed the prankster sensibility of the rogue. Hitchcock's persona is thus a self-conscious, ludic performance of Victorian English gentlemanliness that combines the austerity of Pater, the self-publicity of Wilde, and the roguish wit of a cultured Cockney. The lure of the Hitchcock persona was at once intensified and consolidated by its transposition in time (second half of the twentieth century) and place (England to America), and the scope of his appeal was incrementally enhanced through Hitchcock's canny manipulation of the mass media, most notably the carefully crafted personal appearances in his television shows.[29]

If we wish, we can suspect along with Donald Spoto that beneath Hitchcock's "dandyism of sobriety" lurks a sexual secret. John Russell Taylor, Hitchcock's first biographer, reports that gay actor and screenwriter Rodney Ackland, star of *Number Seventeen* (1932), confided that Hitchcock had told him: "You know, if I hadn't met Alma at the right time, I could have become a poof."[30] There is also some reason to think that Hitchcock was celibate and, perhaps, impotent for the latter half of his life.[31] However, it is not necessary to literalize the secret; indeed, it is necessary *not* to literalize the secret, in order to recognize that Hitchcock's self-stylization was contrived to solicit an uncanny fascination on the part of the audience.

Hitchcock's Pictures Are Like Dorian Gray's

Hitchcock's films are not only informed by a dandyism that performs the representation of a gendered self through costume and deportment, they also occasionally provide a self-conscious commentary on the relationship between representation and the thing represented—the artwork in the manner of Wilde's *Dorian Gray*. Just as the figure of the dandy within Hitchcock's films is intimately related to the presentation of Hitchcock's own authorial persona, Hitchcock's self-conscious meditations upon the relationship between the artwork and what it represents within his work provide us with a key to understanding the role of Hitchcock's "visual style" in relation to what is represented by it.

The first film I wish to consider in this context, *The Blackguard* (1925), is not strictly speaking a Hitchcock film, since it was directed by Graham Cutts. However, Hitchcock worked as both scriptwriter and art director for Cutts, and it seems likely that he directed a number of scenes in the film himself.[32] The story tells of a boy, Michael (Walter Rilla—young Michael; Martin Herzberg—adult Michael), abused by his grandmother, who is befriended by an artist. In return for painting his portrait, the artist supports his aspirations to be a concert violinist. He falls in love with a princess, Maria (Jane Novak), whom he saves from a revolution that is led by his former music teacher (Bernhard Goetzke). When the angelic boy first encounters his would-be patron, the boy is praying in church to the "mother of God" for a violin. A hand reaches gently onto his shoulders from off-screen, revealing an older man who has been eavesdropping. He approaches the boy, takes hold of his cheek, strokes his hair, and offers to buy the boy a violin in exchange for "posing" for him. The artist's intervention and gestures could be read as a combination of paternal solicitation and an "aesthetic" appreciation of male beauty, and yet the nature of his approach—in particular the way he invades the boy's personal space and touches him—carries the suggestion of a sexual offer or trade whose content is displaced into the "spiritual" realm of art. In the next scene, the boy poses nude while the artist paints his portrait—a Paterian figure of a young male body on the cusp of puberty. This portrait can be interpreted at once as a displaced, idealized expression of the love felt by the artist toward the boy, but also as prefiguring the self-identity of the boy as one who perfects himself and forges his identity through art.

In the same scene at the artist's studio, the girl princess, Maria, first meets Michael in a manner that coyly introduces the future romance between the two. But the encounter is also a troubling one, for the arousal of desire engenders a self-conscious sense of exposure in the boy that has a contradictory relationship to the idea of self-perfection in art. The gaze of the little girl at the boy perched high on his pedestal causes him to shrink at his nakedness, as if her gaze undermines the narcissistic self-perfection embodied in the portrait. When they next encounter each other as adults at the house of an art dealer who possesses Michael's portrait, Maria approaches Michael but again he shrinks from her and cowers in the corner of the room like a frightened boy. "Why are you running away?" she asks him. "Your eyes frighten me," he replies. Later in the film, the perfection of Michael's violin playing is explicitly imputed to the inspiration of love, but it is a love that is essentially unavailable to him since Maria is not from his class and is betrothed to a count. Maria subsequently leaves her husband to be with Michael, but his capacity to achieve perfection in his art is undermined by her presence. So Maria returns to her husband, sacrificing the fulfillment of her love for Michael in order that he may devote himself to his art. The couple is ultimately formed in the final part of the film only by arbitrarily turning Michael into the swashbuckling hero of a rescue fantasy who saves the heroine at once from the now villainous count and from the revolutionary mob, implausibly led by his former violin teacher who has now become a radical. Though seriously wounded, Michael survives to be reunited with Maria, who arrives, in fulfillment of his prayers, in the same church where he first encountered the artist. The goal of self-perfection through art—surely irretrievably undermined by his wound—has given way to marriage.

The Blackguard articulates only one side of the Wildean parable, where human sexuality is displaced into an idealization of form. The artwork in *The Blackguard* does not look back at a character in the film and/or spectator in a manner that self-consciously undermines their sense of equanimity, even though the threatening gaze—notably, a *female* gaze—is thematized in the film. In Hitchcock's third film, *The Lodger*, the capacity of the artwork to return the gaze of the observer and undermine his self-assurance is registered in the response of the Lodger to the portraits of young women on the walls of his lodging house. As I noted in chapter 3, *The Lodger* is the first fully realized figure of the dandy in Hitchcock's work, and while he is not himself an artist, he pays an artist's attention to his own appearance as well as to the harmony of his surroundings. When the Lodger first enters his bedroom he recoils in horror to the pictures of pre-Raphaelite beauties on his walls and demands that they be removed, either because they are too painful reminders of his beloved sister who died, or else, if we take the Lodger to be a serial killer of women, because these pictures evoke the same anxieties that caused him to murder in the first place. Either way, in their beauty and perfection they evoke a sense of insecurity and loss in the Lodger. Furthermore, the sense of lack they evoke is only underscored once they are removed from the room, for the faded patches on the walls serve to register their absence, and hence to remind the spectator of the anxiety they evoked in the character.

In both *The Blackguard*, and *The Lodger*, the theme of aestheticism is treated with utmost seriousness, but Hitchcock's characteristic tone is, like Wilde, to turn the threat of self-exposure posed by the artwork into a species of comedy, albeit black comedy. In Hitchcock's *Blackmail*, the young virginal heroine, Alice, bored with her policeman boyfriend, is lured to the upstairs attic of a gentleman-dandy, at once tempted by the transgression of entering the house of an enticing stranger, but still essentially innocent and unprepared to acknowledge what could transpire there. We see her standing nervously isolated in a single shot as she looks outside to see a policeman walking by, a sight that is at once reassuring to her and yet also a reminder of her potential vulnerability. At this moment she notices the pointing finger of a jester. He is a robust masculine figure, but he wears the full costume of the harlequin or jester that looks out of the painting, pointing and laughing.

The jester is traditionally one who is laughed at, but he is also a figure of pathos who reminds audiences of their own vulnerabilities in a manner that turns their laughter back upon themselves. Here, the double aspect of the jester is explicitly related to the representation of human sexuality in the sense that the jester's wide open mouth, with large front teeth, and his physical body posture (with phallic pointing finger projecting from the canvas) suggests an aggressive, voracious, obscene presence beneath the harlequin masquerade of fun. Alice laughs in a manner that initially suggests that she is laughing at the jester, at his peculiarity or strangeness. But it is also clear that she is laughing at the jester because the jester is laughing and pointing at her and making her feel uncomfortable. The jester makes Alice aware of her own vulnerability, her lack of sexual and self-identity. Her discomfort is brilliantly registered in the movement of Hitchcock's camera. Beginning on a close-up point-of-view shot of the jester's face and pointing finger, the camera pulls back along the axis of her look in a manner that suggests violence and disorientation both through the speed of the movement, the manner in which the camera weaves slightly from side to side, and by the way in which the face itself moves in and out of focus.[33] Alice's confrontation with the artwork provides a complex expression of her own (sexual) anxiety.

A second artwork continues the complex play between representation and self-identity in the scene. Alice picks up the dandy-artist's palette like a child playing with her father's tools. In the sound version of the film, Crewe is whistling a tune that he later plays on the piano called "Miss Up-to-date" while he pours himself a drink. Clearly, the tune pictures Alice as he wishes her to be. Alice asks him how to hold the palette and he steps over to show her. Alice paints, at his urging, a self-portrait. It is the smiley face of a girl-child that is childlike in its execution. Crewe responds that it is "rotten," braces her arm, and suggests that they "complete" the picture together. He guides her hand to produce a "kittenish" feminine profile that emphasizes curved hips and breasts. The gesture of joint authorship creates a condition where Alice appears to produce an image of herself that is congruent with the image that Crewe wishes to see—a sexual young woman, that is, a modern young woman who is "open" about her sexuality. She responds to the picture with a knowing "oh, you are awful" and proceeds to sign her own name to the portrait, thereby authorizing his version of her portrait as her own. Of course, she is able to do so because she takes the picture, the activity of making the picture, as a shared joke, as harmless fun. The joke is evident in the incongruity between her face and her body. However, their authorship is not really a joint one; rather, the dandy subordinates her authorship to his. A male-authored sexual body is imposed on the childlike face in a manner that prematurely brings into being a distorted parody of a female sexuality available for the male gaze. Joint authorship is a ruse or disguise for his exercise of control, and in this context the juxtaposition of the childlike head and sexualized body is not a joke, but an ugly, darkly comic reminder of male control and fashioning of the female body. As Tania Modleski writes, "The sexual woman is a product of male desire and male artistic practice."[34]

After the dandy attempts to rape her and she responds by killing him, Alice again encounters the look of the jester as she pulls away her black dress, which covers his face. The jester's pointing finger and laughing face, disclosed beneath her dress, seems to mock her for her foolish naïveté and lost innocence. She reaches out and slashes the portrait with the hand that she had used to slash Crewe, in a gesture of symbolic castration that echoes Dorian's final destruction of the portrait, which reminds him of his guilt. As Alice turns to leave the apartment, she erases the signature she appended to her portrait, as if to cover up evidence that implicates her in the situation. The gesture of erasing the words "Alice White" with the black paint also signals the loss of the innocence that still existed when she signed the portrait. Both gestures of erasure fail. When the policeman boyfriend arrives to investigate the crime scene, he discovers, just beside the erased signature, a glove that incriminates Alice. Having already looked at the image of the mocking jester, he visualizes the pointing mocking finger as he holds the glove that implicates Alice in the crime. The jester's figure mocks Alice again at the close of the film when a blackmailer has been fingered for a crime he has not committed. Alice, guilt-ridden, goes to confess to the police. But while she confesses to her boyfriend, she lacks the opportunity to tell her story to his supervisors. As they leave, he jokes with the doorman, "Did she tell you who did it? ... You want to look out or you'll be losing your job. I say, I suppose we shall soon have lady detectives in the yard ... and I should be alright on the door, won't I!" They laugh, but the laughter turns into the brittle laughter of a black comedy. Alice is certainly not laughing, and, at the same moment, she spots the picture of the jester, laughing back at her, as it's being carried into the police station.

Hitchcock's *Strangers on a Train* is concerned with the commission of a perfect crime that is linked indirectly to the making of art in a scene that takes place in Bruno Anthony's parents' mansion. Hitchcock dissolves from Guy Haines on the phone to his fiancée saying that he could strangle his estranged wife, who will not give him a divorce, to a close-up of Bruno Anthony's hands in strangling position as if he is practicing his art, and as if these hands are the agents of Guy's wish. A dolly back reveals Bruno dressed in a Cowardian-style smoking jacket and sitting opposite his mother, who is doing his nails. "I do wish you'd keep your hands quiet," she declares. "They are so restless lately." "I like them to look just right," he replies, like a craftsman admiring his tools. She worries about his health and teases him, though indulgently, about his foolish plan to blow up the White House: "You're a naughty boy, Bruno, but you can always make me laugh." Then, after Bruno expresses angry hostility to his father—"I am sick and tired of bowing and scraping to the king"—she invites him to look at her painting. She commends painting as "a soothing pastime," a way of staying in control. Bruno assumes the painting is of his father and bursts into excessive hysterical laughter: "That's the old boy alright, that's father." In Hitchcock's alarming expressionist maelstrom of the portrait, two beady eyes stare from a skull-like head that appears severed from its body as if on a platter. The subject of the painting appears to hold a third eye in the form of a glass sphere or ring in its hand. At the same time, this death's head also has attributes of the clown or harlequin costume. The mother replies in shock to

Bruno's comment about the portrait being of father: "Is it? ... I was trying to paint St. Francis." Nonetheless, we are invited to infer that, unconsciously, the portrait of the father is indeed what she intends to paint.

Hitchcock and his screenwriters suggest a complex chain of associations that condense a whole set of Wildean-Freudian themes. Bruno's emotionally invasive mother has clearly elevated her son to be his father's equal by pampering him, and he parades around as master of the house. Bruno does no work, his hands are the finely manicured hands of a narcissist and a dandy, and it is his mother who has cultivated them. The incestuous perversion of the social order is expressed in Bruno's fantasy of usurping the throne of the father by the commission of a grandiose scheme to blow up the White House or murdering his father undetected. Bruno achieves a symbolic "superiority" over his father by assuming his place in fantasy and imagining that he is not bound by the rules of the social order that require him first to "grow up" in order to assume that place. His grandiose narcissistic ego and precocious fantasy-driven intellect take the place of a position of sexual "normalization." Bruno's hands, by which he commissions an act of murder, seem (rather like—and in place of—a sexual organ) to have a will of their own as, for example, when Bruno later demonstrates strangling to a female admirer at a party and cannot let go of her neck.[35] They at once focalize his restless chaotic energy, which is presumably a displaced expression of an impotent sexuality, and they are fetishized as beautiful objects. This sense of focused energy is displayed by his performance with the sledge-hammer on the strength-testing machine at the fairground under the admiring gaze of Guy's estranged wife, whom he intends to murder, as well as in his acts of strangulation. But these hands are equally, like his mother's hands, the hands of an artist. The painting parodies the mother's belief in art as a soothing pastime linked to the crafting of a beatific object— St. Frances. Instead, she paints a death's head that looks back at the painter and spectator with a darkly humorous grimace. Bruno's reaction to this portrait as that of his father is a further "joke," as if his mother has painted the picture of the father just as the parricidal son imagines him to be.

In both *Rebecca* and *Vertigo*, the idealization embodied in pictorial representation is equated with the larger-than-life portrait of a lady who is brought to life in a real-life model. Since, in both cases, the woman is long deceased, the paintings are endowed with the Dorian Gray-like perfection of perpetual youth sublimely preserved in the artwork. But when this ideal of aesthetic semblance is brought to life, it serves at once to mask and to expose the vulnerable, mortal body it conceals. In *Rebecca*, the unwitting second Mrs. de Winter, in ignorance of the perverse character of her predecessor, Rebecca, and her husband's hatred of his first wife, seeks to emulate the position of apparent esteem held by Rebecca by holding a costume ball. Mrs. Danvers, the sinister guardian of Rebecca's legacy, encourages her to wear the white floral dress that appears in a portrait of Lady Caroline de Winter that occupies a position of prominence on the landing of the grand staircase. It was Maxim's favorite, she insists. Unbeknownst to the second Mrs. de Winter, Rebecca herself had worn the costume to the many balls she hosted at the house. The hidden connection between Rebecca and the portrait is tellingly suggested by Hitchcock's camera which, after the second Mrs. de Winter has departed, approaches closer, as it had earlier approached the doors of Rebecca's bedroom. We might imagine that when Rebecca wore this dress, connoting femininity and purity, she must have worn it in the spirit of a triumphant masquerade, in full knowledge that she was merely acting the part of the woman that she knew Maxim wished her to be. In disguising her "perverse" identity through a masquerade of feminine passivity and purity, she would have been, like a dandy, simultaneously asserting it.

However, the second Mrs. de Winter believes that by wearing the dress, and in comporting herself in a manner that befits it, she will become the woman that she believes Maxim wishes her to be and earnestly desires to be herself. But she can only be an imposter, although in this case an unwitting one. As she sweeps down the stairs she is met by Maxim's humiliating public reprimand, and she stands exposed, without an identity. Rushing back up the staircase, she pauses at the painting, looking up at it (offscreen), then along the hall to where Danvers, dressed in black, disappears through the white doors of Rebecca's bedroom. The ugly, black, witchlike Danvers is an objective correlative of the corrupt deadly core of Rebecca that is concealed beneath a façade of timeless beauty. When she first introduces the second Mrs. de Winter to the painting, Danvers casts a black shadow upon the white image as she crosses its path. Here, it is the second Mrs. de Winter's connective gaze that suggests the sense in which it is Danvers's dark presence that stares back at her from the painting.

Vertigo also makes implicit reference to the picture of Dorian Gray. Judy Barton, posing as Gavin Elster's wife Madeleine, seemingly possessed by the spirit of the dead Carlotta Valdes, models herself, in part, on the picture of the young Hispanic beauty and passionate lover in the San Francisco art museum. She borrows her hairstyle, though not the color of hair, the color of her dress, but not her dress. She also carries Carlotta's bouquet and "poses" in front of the portrait in a manner that confirms to Scottie Ferguson that she is obsessed with this woman. But the resemblance of the image to the woman who makes herself over in its likeness cuts both ways, for it suggests that the woman who masquerades as the figure in the painting is herself a semblance, an image or an illusion. Like Dorian Gray, who borrows the eternally youthful properties of his image, Judy Barton dons the masquerade of Madeleine possessed, the ghostlike quality of Madeleine's apparent possession bestowing a sense of timelessness, or masklike immortality. Furthermore, as I have already noted, the manner in which Judy as Madeleine differs from Carlotta in her austere gray suit and flat, smooth, expressionless face actually strips her of her overt sexuality and disguises it with an androgynous aestheticism not unlike the sexless beauty celebrated by Pater.

Scottie's friend Midge projects a very different conception of femininity. Her approach to the woman's body reflects a thoroughly down-to-earth, demystifying attitude to female sexuality. She admires the design of a brassiere displayed in her studio that works on the principle of the cantilever bridge, although one cannot actually imagine *her* wearing this contraption. Her own attire is thoroughly practical: cotton tops and woolen skirts. Midge is the voice of reason and sobriety, who seeks to challenge Scottie's willingness to go along with the idea that Madeleine believes she is possessed with the thought that it is in fact Scottie who is possessed ... by love. To this end, she seeks to puncture Scottie's fantasy by painting the portrait of Carlotta with her own alert, intelligent, bespectacled face and wry smile juxtaposed with curvaceous breasts and a plunging cleavage that emphasize, though not obscenely, the fact of female sexuality. It is a juxtaposition that is reminiscent of the childish face on the woman's body that Alice paints in *Blackmail*, except that now the juxtaposition asserts female authority and parodic control over the creation of her self-image (fig. 28).

Midge's gesture is one that asserts female authorship of the image of femininity—one that is no longer idealized. Her gesture is intended as a joke, but Scottie Ferguson cannot see the joke. He has just realized his fantasy in a passionate embrace with Elster's wife "Madeleine" against the crashing ocean breakers, and to one so invested in the idealization of

Madeleine, Midge's image appears offensive or even obscene. Scottie in *Vertigo*, like Dorian, pursues an aestheticized or idealized image of desire, and Midge's all-too-human face inscribed upon the idealized portrait of femininity punctures the illusion. When Scottie leaves, abandoning their proposed movie date, Midge defaces the image, for now the picture looks back at her just as the portrait looked back at Alice in *Blackmail*, reminding her of her own sense of inadequacy.

These Dorian Gray-like picture parables scattered through Hitchcock's oeuvre provide a key to the role of visual style in Hitchcock's works and his particular approach to the medium of film. The underlying relationship between the artwork and what it represents in these parables is one in which the visual representation is imagined as an ideal, sublimated image free of sexual content, of pure Apollonian form, only to be contaminated with the Dionysian element that had been thought to be erased, as if the ideal or sublimated image contained this content all along. The visual representation in this way looks back at the viewer, undermining the sense of reassurance and security and engendering a sense of chaos or the shattering of identity that the reassuring ideal surface representation serves to occlude. This double aspect of visual representation in Hitchcock's works is inscribed in what Slavoj Žižek has called the "Hitchcockian Blot"—an element in Hitchcock's visual field, usually centered upon the vanishing point, which looks back at the onlooker within the film or the onlooker of the film.[36] The blot indicates the presence of the chaos world or shadow world lurking beneath the ideal surface of appearances, like Marnie's yellow handbag which occupies the vanishing point of the colorless, gray image at the beginning of *Marnie* (plate 4).[37]

Hitchcock's Masculine Aesthetic

As I suggested in chapter 2, Hitchcock's dominant form of aestheticism, derived from his own well-documented prankster sensibility and fondness for obscene jokes, is a playful one in which Hitchcock's dramaturgy and visual style functions as punning displacement of sadistic sexual content that is at once asserted and denied. I called this aesthetic a "masculine aesthetic" with reference to the way Hitchcock understood his own sense of humor and because of its characteristic relationship to male sexual aggression.

This aesthetic, I suggested, is linked to the subversion of morality in classical suspense, where Hitchcock invites us to perversely relish the expression of the murderous impulses manifested by his male villains. In the context of this chapter, I want to now make explicit the relationship between this aesthetic and the inscription of a homosexuality that is deemed perverse.

Rope was the first of two films that he made with Transatlantic Pictures, the company he formed after he had finally escaped contractual obligations with Selznick. *Rope* was adapted from Patrick Hamilton's stage play of 1929 and represents one of the many instances in Hitchcock's oeuvre when English source material is transposed into the American context. Brandon, who incites his companion Phillip to murder David Kentley (Dick Hogan) at the film's opening, is a dandy-aesthete who seeks to make his life into a work of art. As Durgnat wryly observes, "The two boys owe a great deal to dear Oscar."[38] Everything Brandon does is a measured, self-conscious performance calculated to control his emotions and his emotional interactions with the other human beings he comes into contact with. He is the consummate narcissist. For Brandon, the crime asserts his capacity to transcend constraints of human mortality, which means, at once, to render the fact of killing insignificant but also to render insignificant the human bonds of love, dependency, vulnerability that human mortality gives rise to, and that are traditionally embodied in the figure of the woman. Indeed, it could be argued that the killing of Kentley is a substitute for the killing of Janet Walker, Kentley's girlfriend, whom Brandon himself once dated, and whom he will try later to palm off on her former beau, Kenneth (Douglas Dick).

The connection between the act of murder and the making of the beautiful semblance of art is expressed in the creation of the dinner party and the ritualistic sharing of food over the body of the corpse. By inviting Kentley's significant others to dine on top of his concealed corpse, Brandon manufactures a social façade that allows him to revel in his superior knowledge and capacity for self-control. All the social interactions portrayed in the film gain their significance from Kentley's death (known only to the perpetrators and the audience). The universe of *Rope* is an artificially constructed social environment contrived to reflect the genius of its creator who, in seeking to deny the salience of death to life, has rendered death omnipresent, at once concealed and revealed by the glittering surface of his own artwork, the elaborately contrived dinner party.

The meal that is laid out on the caisson in the center of the living room in *Rope* takes on the appearance of a sacramental ritual. When asked to move the meal from the dining table to the chest, Mrs. Wilson declares that "it looks downright peculiar," especially the candlesticks. "On the contrary," Brandon replies, "I think they suggest a ceremonial altar, which you can heap with the foods for our sacrificial feast." If the caisson is an altar, Brandon and Phillip function as "altar boys," and Rupert Cadell is the figure that Brandon wishes to cast as the high priest. But this is a ritual whose meaning lies not in the spiritual value it holds for its participants; instead, its meaning inheres in its sensuous form, in its being staged and being observed. Furthermore, the body and blood of Christ are replaced with the body and blood of David Kentley, and the meaning of the sacrament is, almost satanically, inverted. Not only do the guests dine on top of the corpse, but by eating "chicken" they dine in displaced fashion *on* the body of Kentley,[39] especially given the associations that, as we shall see, the term "chicken" accrues in the film. The Christian sacrament celebrates the triumph of life over death for the participants as the water and the wine turn into the body and blood of Christ. This ritual expresses not the triumph of life (shared in community) over mortal death, but the triumph of death over life.

Phillip and Brandon in *Rope* are knowingly portrayed by Hitchcock and his screenwriter as a homosexual couple whose "perversity" cannot be named. Indeed, Arthur Laurents discusses the fact that during the preparation of the script Hitchcock never mentioned homosexuality even as it was constantly alluded to.[40] The killing of Kentley has all the connotations of a sexual act. Phillip (the "female" partner) pants over the caisson and urges his partner in crime, Brandon, to "stay this way for a minute," while Brandon (the "male" partner) lights up a "postcoital" cigarette. Later, the connection between strangling and perverse sexuality is made through double entendres that center upon strangling and eating chickens. As the chicken is being eaten over the corpse, Phillip claims he doesn't eat chicken. Janet Walker responds, "How queer ... Freud says there is a reason for everything." At this point Brandon tells the following story about an incident that occurred at his mother's house in Connecticut.

> We were going to have chicken so we walked over to the farm. It was a lovely Sunday morning in late spring. Across the valley the church bells were ringing. And in the yard Phillip was doing likewise to the necks of two or three

chickens. It was a task that he usually performed very competently. But on this particular morning his touch was perhaps a trifle too delicate, because one of the subjects for our dinner table suddenly rebelled. Like Lazarus, he 'rose ...

There are a wealth of buried connotations, here, which are usually not spelled out but point to the Dionysian perversity concealed beneath the controlled Apollonian surface of the work. "Chicken Hawk" is Regency slang for men who like boys. "Choking the chicken" is slang for masturbation and implicitly links the activity of strangling to sex. Furthermore, it is rumored that in rural communities boys will strangle the heads of chickens in order to use the twitching, dying corpse to achieve orgasm.[41] In this way the chicken discourse harbors a wealth of perverse connotations—linking masturbation, homosexuality, and death—that center on the obscene image of the rising chicken neck/phallus ("like Lazarus he 'rose") that is actually given life by having its neck wrung. As D. A. Miller has pointed out, this is surely also the secret of the strangled corpse of David Kentley, whose lower body, cut off at the bottom of the screen in the moment of strangling "a tergo," contains the obscene image of the phallus frozen in erection at the moment of death.[42] This image is also implicit in the public death by hanging that ends *Murder!* and is alluded to in Hitchcock's Regency gothic drama *Jamaica Inn*.[43] The secret that is both revealed and concealed in *Rope* is not simply the corpse in the caisson, but the idea of "buggery," in which the secret of the corpse itself serves to conceal, that is embodied in the unseen image of Kentley's erect penis. The caisson with the corpse thus becomes a knowing, that is post-Wildean, embodiment of the homosexual closet.[44]

In *Rope*, Hitchcock, the director of the film, is in one sense like Brandon, the orchestrator of the party, and we the audience are witness to his virtuoso work of cinematic storytelling. The film is famously composed of eleven shots in takes that are up to ten minutes long, and only five of the cuts are obviously visible. The aesthetic of the long take is one that allows the representation of space and time by means of space and time: it seems to epitomize full disclosure or visibility. The camera is an all-seeing eye and ear that is eavesdropping in "real time" on the behavior of a particular urban elite of society homosexuals. But the fact that Hitchcock cannot actually depict the protagonists as homosexuals, and more specifically, cannot actually depict the activity that defines them as homosexuals, leaves us seeking evidence of something we cannot prove. This evidence is suggested, but simultaneously concealed, in the way in which the male couple comport themselves, interact, and inhabit each other's personal space. In this sense, the elaborate camera movements of Hitchcock's film itself are a "joke." *Rope* shows the audience everything there is to see, including the murder of Kentley, except the corpse in the caisson that harbors the "dirty secret." Furthermore, it is also a joke whose meaning is further disguised, as Hitchcock's intentions often are in his official pronouncements, as simply the undertaking of a technical exercise that, it seems, has nothing to do with the content of the work.

But if Hitchcock orchestrates the film as Brandon orchestrates the party, in search of the knowing audience member he can count on as his equal, his searching camera is also one that allows us to side with the victims of Brandon's machinations. It lingers with the party guests while Brandon is absent and registers their increasing concern about David's absence; it dwells on Phillip's progressive emotional breakdown, which affords us a critical perspective on Brandon's behavior; and, most of all, it situates us in Rupert's point of view as he begins to piece together the evidence that will lead him to the conclusion that a crime has been committed. Rupert is aligned with the moral sensibilities of an audience that experiences discomfort in its complicity with Brandon. Rupert's final speech in which he berates Brandon for distorting the meaning of his words, in his actions, has been criticized for its moralizing tone, but it does serve to restore the crucial distinction between the murderer (who acts on his impulses) and the aesthete in whom "perversity" is contained, and hence it is surely a speech that commands the allegiance of Hitchcock himself. It is one thing to make a joke out of the idea of murder; it is quite another altogether to treat the act of murder as a joke. Rupert, too, is an authorial surrogate. If there is a problem with Stewart's Rupert, it lies not in his final speech but in the fact that, as Arthur Laurents points out, Stewart is totally unpersuasive as the mentor of Brandon and Phillip.[45] For Stewart's character to be convincing he must himself be a dandy, but Stewart seems incapable of playing such a role. Stewart himself reportedly said: "*Rope* wasn't my favorite picture. I think I was miscast, though not terribly so. So many people could have played that part, probably better."[46] Laurents, like Hitchcock, wanted Cary Grant, but surely the suave James Mason would have been ideal, though he may not have wanted the role.

Sexuality and Style

The possibility of a conventional romance is nipped in the bud at the very beginning of *Rope* with the death of Kentley. More commonly in Hitchcock, the displaced expression of male "perversity" is articulated through the presence of forces that threaten to derail the hero from the path of the straight and narrow. *Strangers on a Train* provides a privileged example of this kind of story because it gives equal weight to the romance and its subversion. As we have seen, in one sense *Strangers on a Train* is a conventional romance. Guy Haines is the innocent tennis star hero threatened by a perverse and psychotic villain, Bruno Anthony, whose bizarre proposal, subsequently carried out, to murder Guy's estranged wife in return for Guy killing his father, wrongly implicates him in a crime from which he must clear his name in order to marry the senator's daughter. But although Bruno commits the murder and Guy does not, morally speaking the line between the wrong man and the villain, between Guy and Bruno, is blurred by the fact Bruno is the agent of Guy's unconscious wish to get rid of Miriam. Furthermore, Bruno's actions actually make it possible for Guy to achieve the upwardly mobile social goals that he couldn't otherwise achieve, because the pregnant Miriam refuses to divorce him. Bruno is thus the perverse double of Guy, able to think and act in ways that Guy would if he could but cannot.

Bruno's "perversity" goes beyond the act of murder. For as in *Rope*, *Strangers on a Train* suggests that Bruno's proposal to murder, and the bond of complicity that this "unnatural" act creates between the protagonists, is a displaced expression of a different kind of "unnatural" relationship. Bruno meets Guy and makes his "proposal" to him at the very beginning of the film on a train, which is the archetypal space of romantic encounter in Hitchcock due to the way that the space of the railway carriage is at once a public space of random meeting and at the same time intimate and enclosed.[47] Bruno has clearly admired Guy from afar for his masculine sporting achievements (as a male pinup). Killing Miriam for Guy is a perverse expression of a love that, while it clears the path for Guy to marry the senator's daughter, also creates a bond of intimacy between the two men. For Guy to murder Bruno's father as Bruno wishes would symbolically reciprocate this expression of love, fulfilling Bruno's desire to be "magically" installed in his father's place, with Guy, as it were, at his side. In this sense, the proposal that Bruno makes to Guy on the train is a displaced form of romantic proposal. Furthermore, the situation of complicity Bruno creates in carrying out the murder and placing Guy at his mercy creates a scenario that mimics homosexual blackmail, even if it does not actually embody it.

Guy is an oddly square, cold, and unattractive character. Finely played by the homosexual actor Farley Granger, he appears emotionally "closeted," especially in the context of the contrast with Bruno, who is intelligent, witty, flamboyant, gregarious, and carries himself with an "aristocratic" sense of his own superiority and a freedom, it seems, to do anything he wishes. Farley Granger reported to Charlotte Chandler:

> We never discussed any homoerotic attraction Walker's character had for me, but I think Hitch did that with Walker, and he just wanted me to act kind of normal and not be aware of too much undercurrent. Of course, Hitch understood all of this, and he knew what he could do, and what we could do.[48]

If Bruno envies the aptly named Guy his masculine vitality—"I certainly admire people who do things"—Bruno, in Guy's eyes, has an enviable class status that allows him freedom from personal ties and moral scruples. This is a source of attraction and allure to Guy that he unconsciously articulates by "accidentally" leaving the lighter and love token behind on the train and that is inscribed with "From A to G [Anne to Guy]" with crisscrossed tennis rackets.[49] Bruno earlier describes his murder plan as "crisscross." Guy's unconscious gift links shared murder to shared love.

However, as in *Rope*, the core of Hitchcock's interest in the film lies in its visual arabesque of patterned doubling through which the affinity between the characters is stated, like the opening sequence I discuss in detail in chapter 5. These patterns often involve sequences of pure cinema, as if it is Hitchcock's bravura style itself that expresses in purely formal, geometric terms the love that otherwise dare not speak its name. As the narrative moves toward its climax, Hitchcock's increasingly elaborate pattern of doubling itself seems to be the force that derails the romance. Guy has failed to reciprocate Bruno's crime by killing Bruno's father, and he now wants his lighter back. Bruno refuses and seeks to incriminate Guy in the murder of his wife by seeking to plant the lighter at the scene of the crime. Bruno is in danger of losing Guy, and in this sense his plan to discard the gift, though ostensibly a way for him to pin the murder on Guy, is also a way for him to get Guy to chase him. While Bruno is seeking to implicate Guy in the crime of murder, he is also still trying to "seduce" Guy. Guy's chase to clear his name and realize his goal to marry the senator's daughter continues to be derailed into the "relationship" with Bruno.

As we saw in chapter 2, in the final act of the film Hitchcock divides our allegiance. While we root for Guy to win his tennis match so that he can foil the plan, we also root for Bruno to retrieve the lighter he drops down the drain, in a manner that interferes with our ostensible allegiance to Guy. At this juncture a kind of narrative implosion takes place that involves a nesting or *mise-en-abyme* of doubling structures. For although Guy is ostensibly trying to beat his opponent in the service of his larger quest to foil Bruno, the repetitive to and fro of the tennis ball in the sequence, and the sound it makes, transposes an opposition between the tennis players into a parallelism that itself doubles or echoes the parallelism created in the larger structure of the sequence between Bruno and Guy.

When Guy arrives at the fairground he is filmed from a low angle in pursuit of Bruno in a manner that Bruno earlier was seen pursuing Miriam. Their relationship achieves, as it were, its consummation in a fight to the death upon the merry-go-round at the fairground, which was, in an earlier sequence, a space of sexual contagion, and that now spins furiously out of control. First, they writhe beneath the relentless, mechanical, phallic pounding hoofs of the merry-go-round horses, and then Bruno sadistically kicks down on Guy's hands in time with the rhythm of the hoofs, as Guy clings on for dear life, flailing over the abyss. Yet it is notable that even in this frenzied climax Hitchcock has recourse to humor. An old man, his ass sticking prominently into the air, crawls under the spinning machine and shuts it off. The fight ends not with Guy's triumph but in an explosion as the merry-go-round loses its moorings and Bruno lays broken, still clutching Guy's love token in his hands.

The pattern articulated, in the large, in *Strangers on a Train*, in which romance is derailed by a disguised homoerotic encounter articulated in a tour de force of dramaturgy and visual design that ends in a sexualized assault or in murder, is evident, on a smaller scale, in more films than may be imagined. In the opening sequence of Matthias Müller's and Christoph Girardet's fascinating Hitchcock installation, *The Phoenix Tapes* (1999), entitled "Rutland," three sequences of suspenseful mystery from Hitchcock are complexly intercut: the encounter between Roger Thornhill and the man he thinks might be George Kaplan at the deserted prairie bus stop in *North by Northwest*; the encounter between Ben McKenna and the man he thinks might be "Ambrose Chapell" on the London streets in *The Man Who Knew Too Much* (1956); and the pursuit by Hermann Gromek (Wolfgang Kieling) of Michael Armstrong (Paul Newman)in the Berlin Museum in *Torn Curtain* (1966).[50] "Rutland" is the phallic name of Sean Connery in *Marnie*, and the out-of-context intercutting of these scenes, accompanied by the echoing footsteps from *The Man Who Knew Too Much* (1956) and *Torn Curtain*, cannot but evoke a sense not simply of suspense but also the erotic atmosphere of a homosexual encounter or "cruising."

When considered in context, the "interpretation" of these sequences by Müller and Girardet proves surprisingly robust. All three sequences have important similarities. In each case, the hero has been forced, for different reasons, to temporarily leave his female partner, and once outside her feminine orbit he is rendered potentially vulnerable. In each case the hero meets a strange man in a deserted public space whom he is seeking out, and the sequence concludes in an assault. Finally, all three sequences are examples of "pure cinema," and each of the scenes does very little to further the narrative. The crop-dusting sequence simply serves to stage a failed attempt on Thornhill's life; the scene from *The Man Who Knew Too Much* is literally a diversion, since in it Ben follows a mistaken lead to the whereabouts of his son; and while the scene in which Gromek pursues Armstrong into the Berlin Museum is designed to throw Gromek off the scent, it does nothing of the kind. All three scenes thus have a gratuitous quality, as if they are occasions for Hitchcock to flaunt his mastery of pure cinema in the context of suspense.

In *Torn Curtain*, just before the scene in which he encounters Gromek, Armstrong has ostensibly left his wife to defect. However, as Theodore Price points out, Hitchcock intended this film not simply to be about a man's suspected defection to the Communist bloc, but also about his suspected homosexuality.[51] Hitchcock says to Truffaut: "I got the idea from the disappearance of the two British diplomats, Burgess and MacLean, who deserted their country and went to Russia. I said to myself, 'What did Mrs. Mclean think of the whole thing?'"[52] Donald Spoto reports that Universal insisted that Hitchcock drop the homosexual subtheme.[53] But Hitchcock had his way of getting by censorship. What makes the pursuit in the museum the analogue of a sexual encounter is the nature of the pursuit and the manner in which it is orchestrated.

Armstrong is not only being followed, he desires to be pursued. This is ostensibly in order to lead Gromek off his tail, but Hitchcock lingers on the details of the "seduction" and pursuit itself in a manner that far exceeds its narrative significance. The museum has a muscular beige façade that is symmetrically profiled in the establishing shot through a veil of thick classical columns. Armstrong enters into the museum and turns back toward Gromek (who is clad in a black leather coat), just before he enters the pitch-black portal of the museum into an empty and cavernous, symmetrically designed, hall. Armstrong repeatedly disappears past monumental gray columns and erotic classical statues, across the gray and white tiles of the floor, into the cavernous deep spaces of the museum, and pauses to listen to the echoing footsteps that envelope the space with Gromek's presence. Gromek's *visual* presence is registered only once, in an elongated phallic shadow that appears in the lower left-hand corner of the image. If the museum is a tomblike space, the eroticism that is registered in the sequence is not the vaginal or womblike imagery of *Rebecca*, but the anal-phallic imagery of homosexual seduction writ large in the monumentalism and deadened, cavernous interiors of the museum, which begins to approach what might be termed a "homoerotic sublime," that is, a form of Hitchcock's feminine aesthetic that idealizes through form the allure of homoeroticism. Unlike the concluding sequence from *Strangers on a Train* or the pursuit in *The Man who Knew Too Much* (1956) that I shall discuss shortly, this allure is not diffused or displaced into humor.

This sequence from *Torn Curtain* in many ways recalls a sequence from a much earlier Hitchcock film, *Blackmail*. At the conclusion of the film, the shifty blackmailer who is wrongly accused of a murder that he did not commit is pursued by the police. Closed in on all sides, he enters the gigantic neoclassical façade of the British Museum. Inside, he is dwarfed by the gigantic columns. As in *Torn Curtain*, Hitchcock shoots this figure in long shot moving away from the camera into the labyrinthine bowels of the museum. Eventually, pursued by the police, he climbs a ladder out onto the phallic-shaped dome of the museum, where he slips and plunges through the glass roof to his death. While the imagery does not really connect with the kind of suspense that is evoked in the sequence—it is a pure chase without erotic charge—one can better understand Hitchcock's conception. For it seems that Hitchcock may have thought of the fear of the police as well as the chase and capture in terms of homosexual rape, and this informs his pictorial imagination in the sequence. The blackmailer has been "shafted" by the system.

Visual Style

After the museum scene in *Torn Curtain*, Armstrong fails to lose Gromek, who follows him to the farm where Armstrong meets a female accomplice, the farmer's wife (Carolyn Conwell), whom he introduces to Gromek as being "related to his mother." Together, they manage to kill him. The killing is filmed as a prolonged sequence of sexualized suspense (how will they be able to kill him?) which, as Price points out, suggests a homosexual rape, in this case enabled by the "mother" figure. Armstrong grabs Gromek from behind, having taken his gun, and they struggle breathing heavily, but Armstrong cannot "kill" him. The farmer's wife, having rejected shooting (which will alert Gromek's accomplice), grabs a large carving knife. As she approaches, Gromek says to Armstrong, "She should put that down, she is going to cut your fingers off," but she plunges it into his breast, and it is the knife that (implausibly) breaks off—she has appropriated the phallus in place of Armstrong and "stabbed" Gromek for him. But Armstrong still cannot take him down, so the farmer's wife breaks his legs. Yet Gromek rises again (like Lazarus 'rose) and grabs Armstrong around the neck. Finally, Armstrong falls on top of him as Gromek continues to squeeze. The wife pulls and Armstrong somehow pushes the prone Gromek toward the black hole of the gas oven she has turned on—a gigantic mechanical asshole that emits noxious, deadly fumes. The sequence intercuts a forward tracking shot toward the approaching oven, a reverse tracking shot of his body being pulled, a close-up of her straining to pull him and a close-up of Armstrong, while being strangled, straining to push, as if engaged in a strenuous sex act. When his head is in the oven Gromek releases his hold and Armstrong quivers as if he has, finally, managed to complete the act of sex/murder. The sequence, largely of pure cinema, is 208 seconds and contains a remarkable 88 shots, but the final shot is held for 39 seconds as, like the murderers in *Rope*, they recover from the experience.

The Man Who Knew Too Much (1956) explicitly evokes an aura of "perversity" through the contrast made between the normative family of the McKennas and the perverse family that kidnaps their son, but it does nothing to motivate the sense that this perversity might be alluring. However, the scene quoted in *The Phoenix Tapes* follows a similar trajectory to the later scene from *Torn Curtain*. Temporarily apart from his wife, Ben walks along a deserted London street and begins to hear footsteps echoing behind him. He walks on warily then turns. No one is there. Again, he walks on and turns: a man approaches him. He stops and looks at his watch as if he is not looking at the man. The man passes him, and then, arriving at a sign reading "Ambrose Chappell, Taxidermist," he stops and turns to look back at Ben. Ben is now the pursuer. At this point Hitchcock invokes his signature technique of a forward-tracking point-of-view shot and backward-tracking reaction shot to register the sense in which Ben at once advances toward and is lured into the dark back alley toward the taxidermist shop that is located behind forbidding garage doors. It is a scene that in its dramaturgy and visual rhetoric suggests a pick-up and the anticipation of consummation.

However, when Ben arrives at the taxidermist, the incipiently sublime turns ridiculous and Hitchcock stages a carefully crafted parody of homosexual sex. The shop turns out to be a dark, sterile masculine space filled with dead stuffed animals and bald old men. While Ambrose Chappell himself seems sinister and deviant, he is an essentially comic figure. The scene quickly degenerates into farce as McKenna realizes he has come to the wrong place in search of his son. Ben is then attacked by the bald old men (one of whom gleefully holds on to him from behind), who wield various kinds of phallic-shaped stuffed animals, including a swordfish, in a parody of a gang rape. He is "bitten" by the stuffed head of a tiger and beats a hasty retreat. Retrospectively, we understand that Ben and the spectator have been "led up the garden path," as Hitchcock's characteristic mode of deflationary humor takes over, though not, in my view, altogether successfully.

North by Northwest, like *The Man Who Knew Too Much* (1956), is structured by the contrast between an apparently upright world, represented by the U.S. secret service led by the Professor (Leo G. Carroll), and the perverse family formed by the villains. In seeking out George Kaplan, the nonexistent double agent, in the desolate prairie landscape, Thornhill unwittingly exposes himself to the forces of his enemy. However, unlike the previous sequences there is little sense of seduction in the encounter, for the man who stands opposite is both an anonymous and a passive player in the drama. To emphasize this, the backward-tracking camera movement that accompanies Thornhill's forward movement is not shot from the stranger's point of view. Thornhill, on his part, merely wishes to know whether the man is George Kaplan. However, when the crop-dusting plane attacks, it *can* plausibly be conceived in phallic terms (a steel bird/phallus) as it swoops down upon Thornhill, who first runs with his back to it and is then forced headlong onto the dry ground. The imagery here is quite specific: running with his back to the approaching plane, on its third pass, Thornhill falls in close-up, his back half-turned to the camera, and his left leg swings up high into the air exposing his backside in a manner that exceeds any plausible motivation for his fall (Hitchcock must have instructed Grant to fall this way). Thornhill then seeks refuge among the gigantic dried-up corn husks where he is "dusted" by the plane. *North by Northwest* shares with *The Man Who Knew Too Much* (1956) and *Torn Curtain* the evocation of a monumental sterility, and it shares with *Torn Curtain* the evocation of phallic assault writ large, as it were, in the imagery of the film. But as in *Blackmail*, if this sequence contains phallic imagery, it conspicuously lacks an erotic charge. It is as if in the crop-dusting sequence in *North by Northwest*, the homoerotic content has emptied itself out into the monumental formalism of cinematic montage and visual design, taking nine minutes and 133 shots.

In all these examples, Hitchcock's aestheticism, his displacement of human perversity into form, inscribes the competing attraction of a homosexuality deemed perverse in relation to the dominant heterosexual romantic trajectory of the work. Perversity informs the imagery of the scene like a picture puzzle, which can be seen only if one looks at it with the right mind. These cases are a more generalized expression of the situation described in chapter 2, wherein the spectator imputes a "perverse" content to the look of a character even where it is not plausible to ascribe to the character a consciously held motivation that is perverse. I have already noted how this works in the case of *Rear Window*, where L. B. Jefferies observes Lisa under assault. But if we are invited to think that L. B. Jefferies might, unconsciously as it were, take pleasure in watching Lisa under assault from Thorwald, this places him in the position of Guy in *Strangers on a Train*, who unconsciously desires to have Miriam removed by Bruno. We then begin to see Jefferies' rear-window voyeurism in a different light. As his nurse Stella observes, "You have a hormone deficiency. Those bathing beauties you've been watching haven't raised your temperature one degree in a month," and he utterly ignores the flattering attention of the radiant and available Lisa Fremont. Is Jefferies' voyeurism—entirely "unconsciously" of course—really directed through his gigantic phallic lens upon the hairy-chested Lars Thorwald, who enacts the murderous thoughts that Jefferies himself harbors toward his own wife. If so, then Lisa helps establish a connection between the two men by breaking and entering Thorwald's "rear window" on Jefferies' behalf and provoking the returned gaze. This creates a panic in Jefferies that culminates in the deadly assault upon the prone Jefferies by

Thorwald at the denouement of the film. This logic of sexual alterity, or what Robert Samuels calls "bi-textuality," is thoroughly buried in *Rear Window* and becomes convincing only if the film is understood in the context of the entire pattern of Hitchcock's work.[54]

An exchange between Truffaut and Hitchcock that Lee Edelman has drawn attention to is relevant in this context because it suggests the way in which a homoerotic gaze is concealed or veiled, in Hitchcock's mind, within a heterosexual gaze.[55] Hitchcock is describing, with reference to the kissing scene in *Notorious*, how he liked to create a kind of ménage à trois between the camera (and hence the spectator) and the protagonists (referred to in chapter 1). He says the idea of "not breaking up the romantic moment" was inspired by a very cinematic memory of something he witnessed in France:

> I was on the train going from Boulogne to Paris and we were moving slowly through the small town of Etaples. It was on a Sunday afternoon. As we were passing a large, red brick factory, I saw a young couple against the wall. The boy was urinating against the wall and the girl never let go of his arm. She'd look down at what he was doing, then look at the scenery around them, then back again at the boy. I felt this was true love at work.[56]

Truffaut responds that, "Ideally, two lovers should never separate," as if this is the moral of the story. But his response ignores the fact that when Hitchcock referred to "not breaking up the romantic moment," he was speaking not simply of the length of the kiss but also of the *ménage à trois*. Furthermore, Hitchcock's picture of the "romantic moment" here is of a girl looking at her boyfriend's micturating penis. But what is Hitchcock actually looking at here? First, he is looking at the girl looking at the boy's micturating penis and hence imagining her look.[57] Second, he is looking at the boy's behind as he pees. And note the reference to a "Sunday afternoon," which recalls the chicken anecdote from *Rope*. *This* is the extraordinary analogue Hitchcock suggests for the spectator's *ménage à trois* with Cary Grant and Ingrid Bergman in *Notorious*!

Hitchcock is a director who is interested in drawing on the particular capacity of cinema to evoke connotations that exceed any immediate narrative context or meaning. In the sequences I have examined, the possibility for "excess" meaning is enhanced by the place they occupy as detours from the main story, which of course is one that establishes the hetero-sexual couple. I am not claiming Hitchcock intended these meanings to be perceived by the spontaneous spectator; rather, his aestheticism is designed, successfully, I think, to put that spectator off kilter, to contribute to one's sense of unease. Whatever the claims that have been made for the radical nature of Hitchcock's cinema, it is ultimately, like the work of most aesthetes, *both* radical *and* conservative (the logic of romantic irony again). One cannot but return to Hitchcock's celebration of the technical achievements of his film *Rope*, which he famously discusses in preference to its homosexual subtext, or to his comment to Truffaut apropos *Strangers on a Train*: "Isn't it a fascinating design? One could study it forever?"[58] For Hitchcock, one feels, the purpose behind these sequences of pure cinema is not that they exist to stage "perverse" sexual content, but rather that the "perverse" sexual content is the alibi upon which Hitchcock can construct his pure cinema. He is, first and last, an aesthete.

Hitchcock's Feminine Aesthetic

Hitchcock's masculine aesthetic employs structures of suspense, visual nar-ration, and visual metaphor in a manner that at once invokes human per-versity and holds that perversity, at arm's length, through elaborate, playful, aestheticized double entendres, until it erupts in horror late in Hitchcock's career. In what I call Hitchcock's feminine aesthetic, on the other hand, while structures of suspense and forms of visual narration continue to func-tion as a displaced expression of human sexuality, camera movement and mise-en-scène now serve to register, through the richness and intensity of the visual design of the image and the manner in which the spectator is drawn to perceive it, the full intoxicating allure of human sexuality. In Hitchcock's feminine aesthetic, idealization through style serves, as it were, to ennoble desire. The beautiful surface of representation creates a sense of reverence, rapture, and awe.

Rebecca, like *Strangers on a Train*, is structured upon competing alle-giances. On the one hand, the second Mrs. de Winter seeks knowledge of Rebecca because she wishes to be the wife that her husband desires, and the arc of the story is to gradually reveal the true nature of Rebecca and thereby remove the barrier she poses to the realization of the romance between the second Mrs. de Winter and Maxim. On the other hand, the second Mrs. de Winter's encounter with Rebecca is mediated by the sinister yet fascinating housekeeper, Mrs. Danvers, who keeps Manderley as a temple of devotion to Rebecca in a manner realized in the lush visual design of Hitchcock's film. If, in *Rope*, Brandon functions as authorial surrogate, in *Rebecca* it is Danvers who is Hitchcock's surrogate. The mise-en-scène of the film is a realization of her own unrepresented eroticized look, transferred onto the gaze of the second Mrs. de Winter and displaced into aesthetic forms, into the textures of fabrics and the play of line and light.

The representation of corrosive and deadly nature within the walls of Manderley at once suggests Rebecca's corrupting influence but also her sublime power, which is embodied in the beautiful shimmering light created by the rain reflected on the white plaster walls through the mullioned windows of the house. Giant floral arrangements of orchids and gladioli suggest the imposing grandeur and authority of her "artificial" nature, and the fabrics, often inscribed with Rebecca's monogram, fill the gargantuan rooms with a sense of Rebecca's imposing elegance. The sense of submissive awe inspired by this environment is emphasized by the manner in which Hitchcock in *Rebecca* consistently focalizes audience response through the point of view of the earnest, vulnerable second Mrs. de Winter as played by Joan Fontaine, who is seeking to discover the secret of Rebecca. Hitchcock's orchestration of suspenseful mystery endows the mise-en-scène with an aura of fascination as if the secret of Rebecca is literally contained within the house.

Rebecca's affective mise-en-scène, and the mediation of character in the audience's experience of it, is illustrated in the scene where the second Mrs. de Winter finally enters Rebecca's bedroom, the "forbidden room." Maxim has left Manderley, and the second Mrs. de Winter is distraught and at a loss. We hear a clock ticking and violins begin a crescendo as Fontaine pauses on the landing, bathed in the light of a giant cathedral-like window, and turns to Rebecca's door. Hitchcock films her approach using a backward-tracking reaction shot and a forward-tracking point-of-view shot, to evoke the mysterious lure of Rebecca's room and its compulsive grip upon the second Mrs. de Winter's imagination. As she enters, a flute plays Rebecca's eerie theme, and Fontaine's character is framed against a gigantic Gothic arch draped with luminous white muslin against which the shadows of "dead nature" are projected. These shadows are in fact cast in part by a gigantic formal flower arrangement in the foreground of the image.

As the second Mrs. de Winter passes through the gap in another curtain of white muslin (entering a dark womblike space), a theremin augments the *Rebecca* theme, and she is transported, awestruck, into the feminine space of Rebecca's inner room shrouded in darkness. She opens a giant curtain that casts a pool of light in the room, and then the window itself, which allows the wind to enter. Fontaine's character moves to pick up Rebecca's brush on her nightstand but, surprised by seeing a picture of Maxim that seems incongruous in these surroundings, she withdraws her hand guiltily. This is a moment in the film where it is quite clear that Fontaine, the actress, is being directed to perform an action whose significance she does not understand. That is, Fontaine does not understand why she withdraws her hand; she just withdraws it in a mechanical gesture. As script supervisor Lydia Schiller reported, "She was practically a puppet."[59] However, by directing her in this way Hitchcock effectively conveys the sense that she is being impelled by forces that are beyond her control. Suddenly, the second Mrs. de Winter is cold and disconcerted as she passes in front of a large splay of roses. The shutter bangs, and Danvers materializes through the muslin gauze. She dramatically opens a second curtain, and the camera pulls back to reveal a room bathed in light—"the loveliest room you have ever seen"—framed by roses on the left and orchids on the right, a temple to Rebecca, whose nightstand appears as an alter against the far window.

Danvers approaches Rebecca's closet. Framed by the dark fur on one side and a white dress on the other, Danvers pivots to face Rebecca with a kind of animal-like intensity: "This is where I keep all her clothes. You'd like to see them, wouldn't you?" When they share in caressing her furs in tight close-up, it is as if by touching them they are engaged in a shared experience of touching Rebecca's skin. Danvers shows the second Mrs. de Winter Rebecca's underwear, whispering that they were "made specially for her by the nuns of the convent of Saint Clair," enacts combing Rebecca's hair by pretending to comb the hair of the second Mrs. de Winter, then finally, as the culmination of the second Mrs. de Winter's initiation rite into lesbian desire, takes her over to Rebecca's bed to show her the exquisite silk case with its splendiferous "R" monogram embroidered by Danvers that contains Rebecca's see-through negligee. At first, Fontaine's character stands to the left of the two-shot, shadowed by dead nature; she had previously lingered over the photograph of Maxim de Winter, and she is now intensely trying to resist the lure of Rebecca, as her fascination is aroused.

Then, as she is irresistibly drawn toward Danvers after the latter picks up Rebecca's negligee—"Did you ever see anything so delicate?"—Hitchcock reframes the second Mrs. de Winter alongside Danvers within the confines of the bedposts and, as Rhona Berenstein writes, "she is locked into the space that most explicitly signifies Rebecca's sexual activities."[60] "Look, you can see my hand," Danvers softly murmurs as she places her hand inside Rebecca's negligee, as if touching Rebecca's skin. Here Danvers takes on the function of director, orchestrating the scene—that is, the queer Danvers is Hitchcock's authorial surrogate in the fiction. Fontaine's character stands so close to Danvers that she almost touches the untouchable Danvers as her gesture reciprocates and mimics Danvers' gesture of caressing Rebecca's negligee from within, from without. Then she recoils in horror, flees from the room, and enjoins Danvers "to forget everything that happened this afternoon."

Vertigo, like *Rebecca*, is a film about the allure of the dead upon the living, but in *Vertigo* the deathly object of desire is fully incarnated in the figure of Judy Barton, who dons the masquerade of Madeleine possessed. The ghostlike quality of Madeleine's apparent possession bestows a sense of timelessness, or masklike immortality. As legions of critics have pointed out, Madeleine is a fetish object for Scottie Ferguson in a manner that is made explicit by the way in which, when he loses her, he reconstructs her image by using the body of one Judy Barton from Salina, Kansas, who, of course, turns out to have been Madeleine after all. But, as in *Rebecca*, Hitchcock fully implicates the spectator in the deathly allure of Judy, not simply through character identification and point of view, but through the orchestration of camera movement, color, graphic design, mise-en-scène, and performance in a manner that makes the world of the film itself an extension and amplification of the aestheticized object, Madeleine, within it. The result is a film of aching beauty, the fullest realization of what I have called Hitchcock's feminine aesthetic, and a supreme achievement in the history of cinema.

This achievement is impossible to summarize within a brief compass, but it is exemplified in three set-piece camera movements that are profoundly interrelated in their structure and meaning: the scene at Ernie's restaurant that initiates Scottie's pursuit of Madeleine; the famous stairwell "vertigo" shot; and the equally celebrated 360-degree pan that encircles Scottie's embrace of Judy Barton, retransformed into Madeleine.

The scene at Ernie's and indeed the entire sequence of pure cinema that follows it is thoroughly pictorialized and aestheticized. It begins with a camera movement into a doorway of radiant red glass that has the force at once of a barrier and a lure. The next shot consists of a languid, fluid camera movement that tracks back from Scottie at the bar as he glances right, to the back of the restaurant, taking in a full view of the restaurant bedecked with its glorious, deeply saturated red "tapestry" walls and white formal floral arrangements. The camera pauses to take in the whole scene, opposite a floral picture that is itself framed by flowers, and evokes, in its symmetrical position at the vanishing point of the image, the sense of the film image itself as a picture.

The camera then begins to move forward toward the object that Scottie seeks out, Judy Barton playing Madeleine Elster dressed in black and swathed in a deep jade shawl. The camera movement here suggests the point-of-view structure that Hitchcock subsequently develops in the film. The backward-tracking movement evokes the backward-tracking move-ment reaction shot that draws Scottie toward his object of desire. The forward-tracking movement suggests the forward-tracking point-of-view shot that brings him toward her. However, here the backward track and the forward track do not simply articulate a point-of-view structure; rather, Hitchcock self-consciously stages the terms of the relationship. Scottie does not actually see Madeleine; instead, it is the camera itself that traces the con-nection between Scottie and his object of allure, while simultaneously dis-playing that relationship, as if on a stage. The shimmering allure of Madeleine is equated with the allure of the film world as a whole. Ernie's restaurant is a microcosm within which the ideal surface of appearance is identified with the world itself. In this way, Hitchcock's aestheticism becomes surreal; the landscape of fantasy becomes coextensive with reality.

Of course, at the other side of this beautiful illusion lies the fact of human sexuality and human mortality that the beautiful illusion conceals even as it intimates its presence. This sense of human mortality is revealed by the famous "vertigo" shot itself, where Hitchcock finds a way of embodying the visceral experience of Scottie's acrophobia for the spectator in the combina-tion zoom in–track out point-of-view shot on the stairwell and elsewhere. Again this shot combines two opposing movements within a single shot, but the effect of the shot is, at once, to close the gap or the distance between the self and the world that must be maintained to sustain Scottie's beautiful illusion of Madeleine and his own sense of self, and to disrupt the spectator's absorption in the world of the film. Thus the shot has a significance that is precisely the opposite of the act of creation in Ernie's, which had at once established Scottie's beautiful illusion of Madeleine and the beautiful illusion of the film itself.

While Scottie follows Judy as Madeleine, in the graveyard sequence (and elsewhere), the forward movement of the point-of-view shot and the backward-tracking or the reaction shot sustain the distance or boundaries between self and other, even as they assert the allure of immersing self in the other. However, in the vertigo shot the relationship between self and other implodes. Scottie is at once pulled out of and seems to fall into the spatial field, collapsing the distance between subject and object that is sustained by the cut between forward and backward motions of the camera. Scottie confronts an implosion of space in a colorless spiraling void in a manner that is akin to madness. The destruction of Scottie's subjectivity corresponds with the loss of Madeleine, for Madeline perishes moments afterward. But equally, in the vertigo shot, the beautiful illusion of the film itself is destroyed, for the contemplative experience of beauty is transformed into the sensation of shock and overt manipulation. The vertigo shot, in effect, represents Hitchcock's inscription of Dorian's defacement of the painting in the body of the film.

The 360-degree camera that occurs after Scottie has succeeded in reconstructing Judy as Madeleine re-creates this beautiful illusion as a microcosm that transcends the drab colorless environment of the everyday represented by Judy's aging hotel room. But here, the illusion that is created is no longer one of which Scottie is primarily an observer. Rather, it is a world of illusory perfection that somehow contains the observer within it. Brilliantly, Hitchcock contrives the movement of the camera as a spiral with Judy and Scottie together within its eye, as if the gap between self and other has been transcended, in contrast to the implosion of self and other created by the vertigo shot itself.[61] We should note that in the shot/reverse-shot that precedes this cameral movement, Scottie looks at Madeleine bathed in ghostly jade light, and we see that light reflected back in the look of his eyes, as if the eye of the beholder has become or merged with the object of his gaze.

As Scottie kisses Judy as Madeleine in close-up, the camera tracks around them to the right but pans left as if being drawn into them. Then it continues to track right and is again drawn in. Suddenly, the background of the shot begins to transform into the environment of the Mission San Juan Bautista stable, the historical place of Scottie's last encounter with "Madeleine" and the place associated with Carlotta Valdes. As Scottie senses the background changing, as if triggering his historical memory, the camera slows its movement and begins to pull back to medium shot. Simultaneously, the background itself begins to move from left to right, creating a sense that the spiral is being opened out by centrifugal forces. Then, as the hint of a memory recedes, the camera begins tracking and panning again to conclude the shot in the tightest close-up of the whole camera movement, against a background of ethereal timeless jade green light (nominally motivated by the presence of the neon sign outside the hotel room). It is an idealized image of romantic embrace, as if the contradiction between present and past has been "dialectically" overcome in a moment of sublime transcendence.

However, Bernard Herrmann's liebestod-inspired Wagnerian theme, together with Hitchcock's ghostly light, reveals that this ideal is one that cannot be reconciled with living historical reality, and Hitchcock's camera movement reveals the conditions under which this microcosm will unravel in the very act of being created. For if the circling movement overcomes the contradiction between past and present in a moment of sublime transcendence, it also suggests, by bringing the past back into the present, the illusory nature of that transcendence. Judy participates in Scottie's fantasy because she is in love with him and wants their love to be realized, but the terms upon which their love is realized can only bring about its destruction. For at the moment their past embrace at the mission is replicated exactly, Scottie, the literal-minded dreamer, is reminded, as it were, by Hitchcock the narrator, that if the beautiful illusion that is Madeleine has now been completely re-created, then it must have always already been an illusion, a fraud, though at this moment he is not yet ready to fully comprehend the implications of this intuition.

The Aesthetics of Horror

I have distinguished between Hitchcock's masculine or ludic-sadistic aesthetic which is predominantly linked to the displaced expression of an incipiently deadly, predatory masculinity, often homoerotic in character, and a feminine or masochistic aesthetic that is primarily expressed through the idealization of an incipiently self-annihilating femininity. However, in Hitchcock's imagination of horror, these two forms of aestheticization converge. The form of horror combines Hitchcock's ludic-sadistic aesthetic and the darkest form of his black comedy with the "idealization" of perversity in aesthetic form, not as something beautiful but as something overpoweringly frightening.

The imagery of horror takes Hitchcock beyond a simple opposition between the heterosexual romance and the allure of homoeroticism deemed perverse, for it defies the distinction between male and female upon which that opposition is founded. If romantic renewal is based on a union of opposites, male and female, and narratives of ironic ambivalence compete with the narrative of romantic renewal through the allure of homosexuality deemed perverse, the aesthetics of horror in *Psycho* and *The Birds* threaten the very distinction between male and female itself. Rather than a union of opposites, horror in *Psycho* and *The Birds* signifies the implosion of opposites—both male and female, and neither male nor female, and therefore both heterosexual and homosexual, and neither heterosexual and homosexual. In the sense that the adjective "queer" signifies ambiguous sexual identity, the aestheticization of horror in Hitchcock forms a "queer aesthetic" whose sexual content is indeterminate.

I will discuss the imagery of horror more fully in the next chapter; suffice it to say here that Norman Bates in *Psycho* represents a perverse and deadly psychic fusion of himself and his mother that is embodied in the figuration of Norman at once as a "stuffed bird" and as someone who stuffs birds. We must remember that "bird" in Cockney slang is a "sexually desirable woman," and it is in relation to this metaphor of woman as bird that Norman's agency takes on its full perverse connotations. For stuffing a bird condenses the rapacious imagery of heterosexual intercourse with the imagery of phallic-anal aggression that, as we have seen, recurs in Hitchcock's films. Norman's original "stuffed bird," which is his supreme artistic creation, is the one he keeps in his attic, his "mummy" (or "mommy"—the pun does not work so well in American English). This "stuffed bird" was created by the act of "stuffing a bird" in the sense that it combines both a sexual act—the implied incest between Norman and his mother—and the act of killing. The monstrous figure of Norman/mother, which arises like a phoenix from the ashes, is condemned endlessly to repeat this act. Animated by Norman, Norman's mother swoops down from the gigantic gothic bird-house, endowed with a predatory phallic agency. Accompanied by the piercing birdlike screech of Bernard Herrmann's violins, Norman/mother devours Marion Crane in an act of sexual frenzy that is visually inscribed in the beaklike stabbing of the kitchen knife, but largely expressed through Hitchcock's tour de force of "pure cinema," which was in fact storyboarded by Saul Bass. Depending on how the scene is measured, it consists of 49 shots in 109 seconds (beginning with Marion stepping into the shower and ending with her death) or 34 shots in just 40 seconds of screen time (beginning with the camera placed inside the bathtub just before the murder itself).[62]

In *The Birds*, for no apparent reason (though a number are suggested in the film), birds gather en masse to attack the human inhabitants of Bodega Bay. Hitchcock's film focuses on the isolated Brenner homestead, inhabited by Lydia Brenner (Jessica Tandy), her son Mitch (Rod Taylor), and her daughter Cathy (Veronica Cartwright), while they are visited by Melanie Daniels, a young socialite from the city who is courting Mitch and seems to provoke the birds to attack. As is *Psycho*, while phallic in their attack, the birds seem to express possessive maternal rage in a context where Lydia Brenner is intensely jealous of her son's courtship of Melanie. But the birds are indiscriminate in their attacks, and they especially attack the children. Ultimately, they seem to represent an attack on the very idea of making of meaning out of human experience through the story of boy meets girl.[63] For while *The Birds* is a melodrama of family division and reconciliation forged in the face of adversity, it is boringly mundane. The center of the film resides not in the drama of the human protagonists, but rather, as Slavoj Žižek points out, this drama forms a generic background against which the bird attacks, the locus of all Hitchcock's creative energy, stand out.[64] The birds are a relentlessly negative destructive force, and yet it is as if Hitchcock invites us to anticipate not simply with fear but with fascination the sublime apocalypse as it is represented in the sequences of pure cinema that orchestrate their attacks.

I have introduced the idiom of horror as one more strategy of aestheticism in Hitchcock's work. However, the aesthetics of horror have more immediate and direct provenance that comes from Hitchcock's exposure to the work of German filmmakers in the 1920s. German expressionism may be considered, if not a species of aestheticism, a cousin of aestheticism in the manner that it was influenced at once by romanticism and by Freud, and more specifically in the way it evokes unconscious human motivation and extreme emotional states through visual style. Expressionism offered the aspiring professional filmmaker a very precise repertoire of visual strategies, themes, and iconography associated with the representation of unacknowledged human motivation, upon which he could draw. Much of Hitchcock's success and influence as a filmmaker, especially in the United States, resided in his ability to integrate expressionist imagery and techniques into mainstream filmmaking practice that led, finally, to *Psycho*, his greatest achievement in black-and-white film.

$$5$$

Expressionism

Ever since Lotte Eisner penned her famous remark—"It is reasonable to argue that German cinema is a development of German Romanticism and that modern technique merely lends a visible form to romantic fancies"[1]—it has become a cliché to speak of the way in which the dark and brooding quality of German romanticism is reenacted in certain films of Weimar cinema. In films such as Robert Wiene's *Cabinet of Dr. Caligari* (1919), F. W. Murnau's *Nosferatu* (1921), and Fritz Lang's *Destiny* (1921), the uncanny forces of darkness and chaos, personified in the figure of the double, exert a deadly influence upon the living. As we have seen in earlier chapters, Hitchcock's tone is far from brooding and portentous. It is essentially comic even where his themes are very dark, and where the portrayal of love is imbricated with death in a manner that evokes the liebestod, this is often the source of a joke or a pun. Nonetheless, if Hitchcock's tone is character- istically English, he nonetheless borrows from German romanticism the themes of the shadow world and the doppelgänger through the visual rhet- oric and narrative forms of German expressionist cinema that he absorbed in his formative years as a filmmaker. Hitchcock worked at UFA in Berlin in 1924 while he was set designer and sometime director on Graham Cutts's *The Blackguard*, and he observed F. W. Murnau at work on *The Last Laugh* (1924): "My models were forever the German film-makers of 1924 and

1925," he later recalled, for they were "trying very hard to express ideas in purely visual terms."[2]

As a movement in the visual and dramatic arts, expressionism in Germany flourished in the first decades of the twentieth century before its appropriation by the renascent German film industry in the postwar period, eager to capitalize on its talented practitioners. German expressionism can be defined in terms of an aesthetic and a moral psychology that motivates it.

The moral psychology of expressionism articulates the theme of the double, which posits the existence of an occult or shadow world that exists beyond the domain of the ordinary and that is often linked in a very Freudian way to the articulation of unacknowledged sexual motives or impulses. This moral psychology is, in part, expressed through the rhetorical stylization of the opposition between light and dark that is linked in the expressionist aesthetic to the angular distortion of sets, highly stylized costume design, and non-naturalistic acting styles. The canonical example in films of this aesthetic is *The Cabinet of Dr. Caligari,* whose sets are self-consciously angular, contrived, and studio-bound, with shadows painted on the wall. While *Caligari* is typical in its use of unrealistic settings, even films shot on location, like Murnau's *Nosferatu,* or those with more realistic studio sets, like the "Kammerspiel" films, are characterized by the visual rhetoric of light and darkness, and often contain elements of expressionist performance.

The moral psychology of expressionist film is also articulated through a distinctive approach to visual design and narration that emphasizes patterns of doubling or parallelism. In Murnau's *Nosferatu,* Ellen, the virginal heroine, on the cusp of marriage to Thomas Hutter, waits at home for the hero's return from his visit to Nosferatu. When Hutter returns home, Nosferatu begins his own separate journey to Bremen. As Murnau cuts from Hutter's journey, to the voyage of Nosferatu and to the awaiting Ellen, it becomes ambiguous whether she is waiting for Hutter or summoning the vampire. *The Cabinet of Dr. Caligari* is narrated in an elliptical fashion that allows the murderous agency of the sinister somnambulist Cesare to be interpreted from the perspective of a number of characters in the film: Caligari the showman, who dispatches him to kill a town clerk who grants a license for the show; the hero, Frances, whose rival in love is killed; and the heroine, Jane, for whom Cesare's black rigid torso is a source of phallic allure.[3]

The Lodger manifests the overall expressionist visual design, elliptical narrative, and psychological ambiguity of *The Cabinet of Dr. Caligari.*

In both films we remain uncertain of the moral status of the central protagonist. The character of the Lodger condenses the doubled figure of Caligari (is he good or bad?) and the doubled figure of Caligari and Cesare into one person.[4] Furthermore, as in *Nosferatu*, the male protagonist is himself doubled between the potentially sinister black-caped figure of the Lodger himself, who holds such an allure for the heroine, and the figure of the ordinary policeman, Joe, who initially tries to win her hand. Hitchcock also experiments in the film with a non-naturalistic acting style in the performance of Ivor Novello, which draws from both *Caligari* and *Nosferatu* and lends the Lodger an unsettling, uncanny presence in the film. The Lodger is also linked to Nosferatu through other iconographic allusions such as his pallid fingers, his rigid phallic form, and the way he hovers in front of the window of his room and the door to the bathroom where Daisy bathes.

However, *The Lodger* is clearly the work of a director who is utilizing the rhetoric of expressionism for his own purposes and self-consciously adapting expressionist tropes as part of his authorial style. In a sense, expressionism in film was always a second-generation movement, self-consciously invoked as a "style" by the small group of talents responsible for the German art film. This self-consciousness is evident in a film like Arthur Robison's *Warning Shadows* (1923). Various figurations of the shadow-play in the film invoke the idea of cinema itself as a "shadow play," a world of the double. This is announced in the opening credits, where the shadows of the main protagonists—a duke, a duchess, and her lover—split off from their characters and occupy the white space of a film screen that doubles as the space of the film itself. Shadows are used to dramatize the ambiguity between appearance and reality through the inability of the protagonist to discern whether or not his wife is sexually involved with her admirers. For example, shadows created by the folds of a curtain lend the appearance of physical contact until, behind the curtain, the camera reveals that this is not the case. Furthermore, the doubled world of the shadow play, which is used in the film to dramatize a story of infidelity, literally becomes the world of the film itself, when, mesmerized by the shadow-player, the protagonists of the film act on their anarchic impulses. The duchess runs off with her lover, and the duke forces her suitors to put her to the sword after she has been tied to the dining table. Finally, we return to the world of normality. Domestic order is apparently restored after transgressive impulses have been cathartically enacted and released.

Expressionism

The Lodger casts doubt on the motivation of the protagonist, by the use of shadows and expressionist performance, and also, as we have seen, through elliptical editing. Is the Lodger picking up the poker to stoke the fire or to hit the heroine over the head? Is he going to the bathroom to talk to her or to murder her? Hitchcock's narration certainly bears close affinity with the motivational ambiguities that characterize *Warning Shadows*. However, by comparison, the melodrama of *Warning Shadows* is moralistic, and the authorial conceit heavy-handed and intrusive. In Hitchcock's work, visual expressionism becomes a self-conscious mark of the author, as punning wit, as the transcendental buffoon of romantic irony discussed in chapter 1. His narration casts the shadow of expressionism as a mark of authorial virtuosity that the audience is invited to enjoy. Hitchcock's expressionism is also a form of aestheticism where visual style evokes or contains a sexual payoff. Hitchcock teases us with the thought of human perversity as if he is, as Bettina Rosenblatt suggests, an authorial Caligari. Like Caligari, who exhibits the phallic Cesare to onlookers, Hitchcock invites us to imagine the sexual content beneath the official moral surface of his narrative.[5]

Hitchcock's punning expressionism often utilizes visual symbols and metaphors—often visual translations of verbal phrases or puns—to comment upon the position of his characters in a manner that suggests the intimate connection between Freudian wordplay and Hitchcock's approach to visual style. An excellent example is provided by a sequence of nominal suspense in his second sound film, *Murder!*, when the hero, Sir John, hunts down the criminal-dandy Fane, whose precise sexual identity is ambiguous, while the heroine, Diana, faces the hangman's noose. A conventional suspense situation is established that poses the question: will Fane be exposed before Diana hangs or will Sir John rescue her? Hitchcock cuts with increasing intensity between Diana pacing her cell, shots of a weathervane that puns both on "Whether Fane?" and "Whither Fane?" as we hear voices searching for Fane, and shots of a hangman's noose on the prison wall. But as William Rothman points out, the noose is visually configured in such a way as to suggest the symbol of both male and female.[6] Hitchcock leaves the audience in doubt as to whether the person who will occupy the hangman's noose will be Diana or Fane. But what is also invoked in order to be denied in this complex "gallows humor" is the idea of imagining something hanging that is neither man nor woman, or both man and woman, that is, imagining seeing the perverse secret about Fane displayed.

Although there are many reference to theater in Hitchcock, he explicitly enacts the kind of self-referential allusion to cinema suggested by *Warning Shadows* only twice in his career—again, inflected by his distinctive comic tone.[7] *Sabotage* is set in a cinema, in a manner that links the saboteur, Verloc, who is responsible for the death of the innocent child, Stevie, to Hitchcock the director of the film we are watching. Shortly after Stevie's death, the innocent heroine, Mrs. Verloc (Sylvia Sidney), watches the Disney cartoon, *Who Killed Cock Robin?*, which functions as a direct commentary on the events of the film and provokes a similar tone of uneasy laughter that the death of Stevie provokes.[8] A comparable scene unfolds in *Saboteur* when the villain, Fry, is cornered by the police in front of a giant film screen, where a melodramatic shoot-out unfolds. The dialogue of the film-within-the-film acts as a commentary on what is about to happen to the villain and to the onscreen audience: "He threatened to kill you on sight . . . You must go before he shoots you to death"—as Fry is trapped by the police. "So you are trying to tell me old Henry has got a real gun"—as the audience is not yet awakened to the real-life drama that is being played out. And finally: "Get out of here, he has gone mad . . . murder . . . run for your life," as real life intrudes into the experience of fiction and an audience member is shot. The key moment of transfer between fiction and reality occurs through a visual and aural pun (noted in chapter 1) where a man in the auditorium wrongly appears to be shot by a character in the film-within-the-film when he is really laughing, only to be shot in the real shoot-out that Fry is involved in, at a moment when Fry himself seems to inhabit the film-within-the-film and the sound of his gun seems to issue from within it.

Expressionism and Modernity

In addition to Hitchcock's highly self-conscious, commentative deployment of the rhetoric of doubling, a second dimension to Hitchcock's status as a second-generation expressionist is the manner in which these tropes are integrated in his work into a recognizably modern, verisimilar narrative world. Again, Hitchcock is anticipated in this by Weimar directors themselves in the so-called Kammerspiel film. The idea of the Kammerspiel, or "chamber theater," was invented by Max Reinhardt, who conceived that a theatrical space of a small size would provide the audience with intimate access to the feelings and emotions of characters.[9] The Kammerspiel film was a logical extension of this approach. Often set in a contemporary urban setting, many Kammerspiel melodramas expressed their themes of adultery, deception, or jealousy through the rhetoric of expressionism. Particularly significant, in this context, is the manner in which expressionist imagery provides a figuration of the modern urban environment itself.

Frances Guerin has argued in her study of Weimar cinema that the representation of light in Weimar film is closely connected to the representation of urban modernity, embodied in spaces of nighttime illumination, such as the fairground or the street. The visual rhetoric of light evokes the transgressive allure and danger of public spaces that are sharply demarcated from the private space of domesticity and propriety. This aesthetic is exemplified in Karl Grune's "street film," *The Street* (1923). Grune's middle-class protagonist, apparently trapped in domesticity, is enticed by the siren call of the street. The lure of the street is initially figured as a shadow play perceived through the skylight in his room in which a stranger approaches a prostitute, evoking at once the Platonic world of illusion and Descartes' conceit in the *Second Meditation* that the passersby that we believe to be real might merely be automata.[10] Furthermore, it is not clear whether what the protagonist sees are actual shadows through the window or the shadows of his imagination, as the "window" in a subsequent shot looms larger than life, projected on his ceiling.

By leaving the safety of his home and entering into the street, the protagonist thus enters into a world of illusion. As the male protagonist begins to follow the prostitute, he is drawn into an intoxicating world of light: "Car headlights weave their way over the façade of a sparklingly clean shop window, window dressings are luminous with lights displaying their wares, neon advertisements decorate walls, and the brilliant glow of fairground attractions form a kaleidoscopic background to the events in the street."[11] In *The Street*, the moral psychology of expressionism, the dramatization of the shadow world of anarchic impulses, is transposed into a melodrama of modern urban life where an aesthetically dull, sexless, but reassuring domesticity is contrasted with the visually and sexually intoxicating, but potentially life-threatening, anonymity of urban space, which offers the alluring pleasures of class and sexual transgression.

The use of visual expressionism to register, in this way, the ambivalent allure of modernity is a feature of Hitchcock's work. *The Lodger* is about the dangerous thrill of sexual desire as it arises in modern urban space, where the alluring and incipiently deadly quality of sexual desire is embodied in the flashing lights of a neon sign: "Tonight Golden Curls." Hitchcock combines the connotations of vampirism—the Lodger as *Nosferatu*, coming not from the Carpathian Mountains but out of the London fog—with the allure of modern love, as it is figured in the persona of the matinee idol, who emerges out of and is at home in the anonymous, nocturnal, but light-filled world of the city. When the Lodger first knocks on the door of the family home of the Buntings in *The Lodger*, the lights in the house dim as his silhouette approaches the front door. But when Mrs. Bunting (Marie Ault) opens the door, he stands in black against the background of the white fog illuminated by streetlights. As he enters the hall the gas light flares, and when he goes upstairs to his bedroom, light plays across the room, connoting perhaps the phantom carriage of Nosferatu, but also evoking, more immediately, the sweep of car headlights and the intrusion of this sexually alluring figure from "the street" into the home.

While the setting of Hitchcock's second film with Novello, *Downhill*, is very different from the spaces of German modernity—it begins in an English public school and follows the downward trajectory of the protagonist to the French Riviera—the film shares the themes of *The Street*. In both films, a passive protagonist is seduced by a woman who makes a cuckold of him by flirting with a "rival" in whom she has no interest, and then, when things go wrong, falsely accuses him of a crime he did not commit. In both films, the protagonist becomes unthinkingly attached to a woman, who, together with an accomplice, fleeces him of his money. In *Downhill*, the nocturnal allure of the street is replaced by the decidedly English setting of Ye Olde Bunne Shoppe, which is a place of sexual encounter for the public school boys who visit illicitly, after hours, the shop girl who works there. The scene of seduction is veiled through an expressionist play of light and shadow that helps to cast ambiguity upon our perception and understanding of what exactly takes place. In both films, the protagonist, upon leaving home, enters into a world of illusion. In *Downhill*, a title card announces "The World of Make Believe" as we see the hero serving, as a waiter, the woman who will subsequently deceive him. It is soon revealed to the spectator that what appears to be real is on stage. But if this resolves the status of what we see, it also dramatizes the difficulty of making the distinction between fiction and reality in the first place.

Expressionism

Blackmail, like *The Lodger*, explicitly links transgressive desire to the opportunity that modern urban life affords for meeting strangers. Again, sexual allure is embodied in the figure of a dandy (who is the double of the heroine's detective boyfriend). But in *Blackmail*, Hitchcock dwells on the enticements of the nighttime street, filled with light, sound, and movement, only after the heroine has suffered the terrible consequences of forming a liaison with the enticing stranger. They thus form an ironic counterpoint to the heroine's distraught mental state. Again, in *Blackmail*, the nocturnal world of the street is figured as a world of illusions. The passersby appear, through superimpositions, as phantom presences to whom the heroine is oblivious, or is it the heroine herself who has become a phantom presence?

In *Blackmail* the nature of the heroine's response to the environment is often rendered through point-of-view structures that register the threatening landscape through a distorted point of view. This constitutes a third characteristic of Hitchcock's expressionism also adapted from Weimar directors.

Subjective Expressionism

Some directors of the Kammerspiel also developed strategies for evoking extreme psychological states such as fear, anxiety, and desire by using a combination of point-of-view shots, superimpositions, camera movement, and visual distortion, in a manner that renders certain objects in the environment pregnant with meaning and blurs the boundary between what is visually perceived and what is visually imagined. However, the representation of extreme mental states is characteristically anchored in the narrative world by a state of intoxication or madness in a character, or else by supervening upon naturally occurring movement, such as a swish pan that may register, at once, the movement of a character through space and acute mental anxiety. I call this way of representing mental states through distorted or displaced point of view "subjective expressionism." Visual expressionism is already "subjective" in the way it can be interpreted as a displaced expression of mental states; however, it is "objective" in the sense that these mental states are only indirectly inscribed through the configuration of mise-en-scène. In contrast, "subjective" expressionism makes explicit that mental displacement, directly registering its mental component.

F. W. Murnau's Kammerspiel film, *The Last Laugh*, which narrates the response of the doorman of a downtown hotel to the loss of his job and the sense of status and dignity that is attached to it, is replete with representations of the mental state of the character that are registered through perceptual distortion. Having lost his job, the doorman steals back his precious uniform and rushes guiltily from the hotel. Lying breathless across the street, he turns back. The hotel seems to loom over him accusingly and he puts his arm up as if to protect himself. Later, having become intoxicated at a wedding, his vision blurs in a manner that is registered through the combination of point-of-view, haphazard camera movement and loss of focus. As he finally falls into a stupor, eyes closed, he imagines himself a doorman alongside a giant (massively elongated) revolving hotel door. A car arrives and, acting as the protagonist in his own grandiose fantasy, he lifts up a giant bag in one hand. As the camera tracks into the hotel, we see through a fractured and blurred image that the doorman is triumphantly throwing the bag up in the air and catching it. The camera continues to track in a circle around the protagonist, registering the enthusiastic applause of his younger colleagues now turned into spectators. Then the dreamer awakes.

Early in *The Street*, before the protagonist leaves his apartment, he imagines, as he looks in a point-of-view long shot upon the street, in successive superimpositions, a clown's face at a fun fair, the face of a woman, and then, as though through a glass darkly, an image of dancers that spin in an abstract ball of light that renders him nearly delirious. He sees again a woman's face, then, finally, fireworks and sparklers. In *Variety* (1925), E. A. Dupont pictures the chaos of the fairground through the use of psychological point-of-view shots from the position of a character in a swinging boat. When the three participants in the love triangle that forms the story of the film all perform on the flying trapeze, we view the swirling lights of the auditorium from the point of view of the cuckolded husband on the trapeze, in a manner that registers his psychological dislocation. As he sits framed in medium shot on the moving trapeze, the camera moves with him against the background of spotlights, as if he is cut adrift from the space of the auditorium. He looks down to see, in a subjective image, a cluster of moving eyes staring up at him that is intercut with an image that suggests swirling shards of light.

Hitchcock uses expressionist camera techniques throughout his career. Often, they are realistically motivated by fainting or by a state of intoxication.

For example, in *The Lady Vanishes*, Iris Henderson has been hit over the head by a flowerpot and she faints as she says goodbye to a friend. Hitchcock cuts to a shot which would have been her optical point of view. The image blurs and dissolves into the superimposed images of a whirlpool and multiple shots of her friend saying goodbye that combine with images of a train conductor waving and the spinning wheel of the train, whose rhythmic sound accompanies the montage. It is not simply a physical state of fainting that is represented here but, as in the examples from German expressionist cinema, a sense of mental dislocation that is both cognitive and emotional. Significantly, too, this montage registers a subjective sense of time, or of time lost. When the montage concludes on the spinning wheels of the train in "objective" time, Iris awakens in the compartment of the rail carriage to hear the kindly voice of Miss Froy.

In *Notorious*, an intoxicated Alicia Huberman, languishing in bed, views Devlin in a canted angled shot. As he walks around the bed, in a point-of-view shot the camera tilts to a position where he is now upside-down. The shot is partially motivated by her prone state but also serves to register her awakening into a hangover and the sense of disorientation it produces, as well as the disruptive intrusion of Grant's character into her world. In a later scene, Alicia looks at Alex Sebastian and his mother, who are poisoning her, and their shapes dissolve into shadows that begin to blur into one, as if to form the composite mother-son monster that Hitchcock was to fully realize in *Psycho*. In *Downhill*, having reached the depths of narcosis in the Paris docks, the hero walks throught the streets of London, disoriented, trying to reach home, in a manner that recalls the subjective expressionism of *The Last Laugh*. The camera moves about haphazardly, evoking perceptual and psychological disorientation, and successive superimpositions suggest a subjective sense of time passing. Psychological breakdown is registered in a different way by Hitchcock in *The Wrong Man*. Manny Balestrero, locked in his cell, closes his eyes and throws his head back (half in shadow) as the camera begins to circle around with increasing intensity, as if registering the confusion and disorientation of Manny's mind.

Elsewhere in Hitchcock, as in *Variety*, subjective expressionist techniques are supported by camera movements that register the physical location of character. On a carousel in *Strangers on a Train* and on a moving train in *Shadow of a Doubt*, Hitchcock uses swish pan point-of-view shots to register the anxiety of the protagonist in the face of imminent death. In *Murder!*, as

Sidney Gottlieb points out, the denouement of the film is drawn directly from the scene of psychological collapse on the trapeze in *Variety*.[12] The dandy Fane, who has been identified by the hero who has hunted him down as a murderer, performs on the flying trapeze. As Fane takes off on the trapeze, he is freed from the constraints of bodily space by the manner in which Hitchcock's camera depicts the background moving in a blur behind him, as if, as Rothman observes, he has become detached from a world that has cast him out and has entered into a trancelike state of sexual ecstasy or delirium that renders him momentarily omnipotent. As he swings to and fro in this womblike space, he sees before him in a subjective point-of-view shot the still, silent faces of the hero, who is his persecutor, and the woman they both love. Appearing against the moving background, these faces are possessed with a hallucinatory intensity. They are bisected by a pattern of lights that reflect from behind his trapeze and evoke the jaws of death that surround him.

In her booklength study of sound in Hitchcock's films, Elizabeth Weis explores in detail the way in which Hitchcock uses sound in film in a manner that develops from these strategies of subjective expressionism. In aural expressionism, sound that emanates from objective sources in the environment is used to articulate and represent the feelings of the person who hears that sound, in such a way that the representation of sound is "colored" by the emotional responses of the listener. An ideal illustration of this expressionist use of sound is a sequence in *Blackmail* where the heroine, riddled with guilt over the killing of her attacker, listens to a gossip talking about the murder. She repeatedly uses the word "knife," which Hitchcock underscores with reaction shots of Alice. The words become increasingly abstracted from the flow of the dialogue and the volume is intensified as Alice reaches down to pick up a bread knife that her father has asked for and which looks like the murder weapon. When Alice finally screams, the bread knife seems to leap out of his hand by its own volition, as if the sense of repulsion that Alice feels toward the object through her subjective association has actually become, through projection, a property of the object itself. As Weis points out, the subjective use of sound in this sequence involves a combination of selective hearing and distortion through volume.[13]

A sequence of approximately three minutes' duration without dialogue from Hitchcock's first sound film *Blackmail* provides an elegant summation of the way in which Hitchcock integrates subjective expressionist techniques with "objective" expressionist techniques that evoke the "shadow world" of the modern street, creating a highly commentative visual narration that works though visual/verbal punning. It is an example of Hitchcock's expressionist aesthetic in what might be called its high phase, where it is yet to be tamed within the linear protocols of classical narration. Here, Hitchcock wears his expressionist tricks upon his sleeve and self-consciously displays his bravura style. While, as Charles Barr has shown, *Blackmail*, the film, cleaves closely to Charles Bennett's play from which it was adapted, this sequence of pure cinema has no precedent in the play, which does not dwell on the psychology of Alice after she kills the man who has attempted to rape her.[14]

In a tracking shot the heroine, Alice, walks screen left to right, in medium shot, dressed in a black coat edged in white fur trim. She has just left the atelier where she has killed her assailant. She is thoroughly traumatized, and in a state of shock and dissociation. As a figure who drifts, lifeless and alone, through the nighttime streets, she has become a fallen woman. Clad in black with a trim of white that suggests the residual innocence of her former identity, she has become her own black phantom double of the bright, ebullient Alice White. Alice has walked through the looking glass into the shadow world, or the world of illusion. A low-pitched pizzicato string with strummed chord sets an ominous tone that is picked up by an ironic melancholic reprise of the "Miss Up-to-date" theme that was played by her assailant earlier in the evening in a manner that had suggested his vision of her as a modern woman, not hidebound by restrictive moral codes. Now it provides a poignant, ironic characterization of her emotional state. A horn and claxon sound in the background continues to punctuate the rest of the sequence. While they are, in one sense, realistically motivated as a part of Alice's environment, the sounds are amplified in a manner that suggests the acute sensitivity of the heroine, whose nerves are on edge. We hear the sound of these horns and claxons as the heroine hears them. Furthermore, these aural intrusions are individuated against a background of unrealistic silence.

The silence is especially eerie because the heroine is oblivious to her environment, and thus we see, yet do not hear, the crowds of people passing her by. The crowds are mostly moving in the opposite direction to her, evoking the sense in which she is isolated and "swimming against the tide of humanity." Furthermore, their image is superimposed on hers in a manner that suggests that they are to her like phantoms or ghosts in a world in which, subjectively, she is completely isolated. But if the crowds appear as ghosts to her, she is equally invisible to them; if they are silent, she too is silent. If the crowds are real, it is Alice who is a phantom passing unaware through this mass of people. Alice walks in front of a wall of black and white checkered tiles, and then a sign that reads "Crossword puzzles" can be seen, which picks up the idea of the black and white checkered pattern and puns ironically and commentatively on crosswords, cross words, and crossed words or voices that are at loggerheads with one another. The background continues to dramatize black versus white as she passes a black doorway illuminated by a white light through the curtains. Next to this is a radio shop, which again provides an ironic comment upon communication and miscommunication within the wider social context. It is by using their radio that the police capture a villain in the opening sequence of the film.

A new sequence is initiated as Alice stops to cross the road. In long shot, people walk past her to cross the road and rush behind her on the sidewalk, creating a moving grid within which she remains silent and rooted to the spot, inhabiting her own universe as life goes on around her, like a lost soul. Hitchcock cuts to a medium reaction shot as if, from the perspective of her own isolated space, Alice responds to something we see in the next shot, a policeman's arm, detached, as it were, from the policeman himself. A second reaction shot follows and Hitchcock cuts back, not to the policeman's arm but to an arm intended to evoke the arm of the man she has killed, thereby making explicit the way in which, within Alice's point of view, the policeman's arm is psychologically laden with the thought that it is the arm of the dead man she is seeing. The audience first perceives the arm of the man she has killed as it falls from behind a bed curtain, rigid and lifeless, an uncanny reminder of his once living body. Metonymically, the arm and hand stand in for the now rigid lifeless body of the dead man; metaphorically, it suggests a rigid, detached castrated phallus, one that accuses Alice like the jester's pointing finger discussed in discussed in chapter 4. Alice's state of dissociation is prompted not simply by guilt about having killed, but the guilt that is precipitated by her confrontation with the fact of human sexuality, and her own sexual desire, projected and objectified in the phallus.

A third transition punctuated by a claxon takes us to the canopy of a theater announcing again, ironically, "A New Comedy." From a high-angle shot, Alice moves against the crowds of eager theatergoers toward the camera, under the brightly lit canopy of the theater. She appears lost, their laughter sounding brittle and darkly ironic. Isolated in the frame, she looks up at a neon sign for Britannia matches in which it is as if "Britannia is going up in flames." In a second point-of-view shot she looks at an advertisement for Gordon's gin where a moving drink's shaker turns into the stabbing motions of a knife, again making explicit the subjective valence of point of view through montage. We are invited to think that the protagonist actually hallucinates the dagger. Beneath the stabbing knife we read "Good cocktail," which we may assume, if we wish, to be a darkly comic, obscene joke on Hitchcock's part, the good "cock-tail" being the murdered man's severed/castrated arm/phallus. Here, as elsewhere, Hitchcock's imagery has a self-consciously commentative character that is rendered overt by making a joke to the audience that is unavailable to the character.

In the final segment in this sequence, Alice finds herself in the morning mist of Trafalgar Square, having walked around all night. Then a tracking shot begins, which parallels the tracking shot that had initiated the sequence in the opposite direction. If, in the first part of the sequence, she was running away from the scene of the crime in a state of dissociation, in this final part of the segment she begins the path toward recognition or rebirth from her phantom-like state, though still somewhat traumatized. She sees the hand of the murdered man, which Hitchcock shows the audience as an insert shot, and reacts to it as if in flight, as she walks along the edge of a fence which creates a background of horizontal parallel lines (a recurring visual motif in Hitchcock's work). A sign behind her reads ironically "fortifies against." She passes another sign ("is prayer answered") and "sees" the hand again. She passes another fence that creates a background of vertical parallel lines with a sign on it saying "ideas." She looks down at the hand of a tramp in a point-of-view shot, and then pulls away in long shot and opens her mouth to scream. We do not exactly hear her scream because, instead, Hitchcock creates an immediate sound bridge to the scream of recognition made by a landlady as she discovers the murdered man by perceiving his dead outstretched arm. As she stiffens with fear, her own arm mimics the position that his occupies. The scream marks, as it were, the return to life of Alice. It marks her liberation from the deathly nighttime phantom world, into the world of daytime reality. But it is not a transition that she fully makes on her own; it is a transition that Hitchcock the narrator anticipates for her.

The landlady is Alice's double in the land of the living to which Hitchcock, the narrator, brings her and the audience back with a "magical" cut.

The Role of Nature

I have suggested thus far that in Hitchcock's expressionist films, like those of the German expressionist filmmakers, the double or the shadow world can be interpreted as a figuration, in a Freudian way, of unacknowledged human impulses. As I have already discussed in earlier chapters, Uncle Charlie and Young Charlie in *Shadow of a Doubt* are doubles of one another in a manner that evokes the unconscious connection between the heroine and the vampire of *Nosferatu*, as if the arrival of Uncle Charlie in Young Charlie's hometown is the fulfillment of a wish. Bruno, in *Strangers on a Train*, can be interpreted as a projection of Guy's paranoid imagination, a figuration of his own unacknowledged impulses, not simply to get rid of his annoying wife but also to be bonded to another man. Norman Bates's divided self in *Psycho* is a grotesque expression of his Oedipal conflict/relationship with his mother. The agency of the birds in Hitchcock's film *The Birds* can be readily understood, expressionistically, as an articulation of the negative emotions of one or more of the characters in the film: they function as doubles of the human characters, who are in turn given avian or birdlike attributes. In each case, the aesthetics and rhetoric of doubling articulate an unacknowledged or barely acknowledged psychological motivation.

However, there is another rationale for expressionist themes and style that is to be found both in the works of German filmmakers and in the films of Hitchcock, which exposes the superficiality of an interpretation that is simply *psychological*. In this rationale the double or the shadow world takes on a metaphysical dimension, articulating the power of archaic and potentially anarchic forces of nature that render human beings powerless against their force. This romantic conception of nature, which ascribes to human actions a causality that is essentially inexplicable from the standpoint of human psychology, is deeply embedded within the idioms of expressionism that inform Hitchcock's work. It is important for the argument of this book to acknowledge the role of nature in Hitchcock's films, for it suggests the way that Hitchcock's romantic irony aspires to a "philosophy" or worldview.

The logic of the double in Hitchcock's expressionist works suggests that the human being is essentially divided, his or her very agency subtended and informed by an alien, inhuman, anarchic force.

In the stories of Ludwig Tieck, such as "Blonde Eckbert" (1797) and "The Rune Mountain" (1802), nature is portrayed as a place that threatens psychic disintegration by confronting the individual with a sense of otherness. The alien-ness of nature is often embodied in the uncanny figure of a stranger who inhabits the nether regions. Tieck's imagination of an uncanny, threatening nature enters Hitchcock's cinema through the influence of Murnau's *Nosferatu* and Fritz Lang's *Destiny*.[15] In the framing story of *Destiny*, the figure of Death appears in the natural environment, which is portrayed in the opening shots of the film as short, rather stunted, black trees and bushes moving in the wind against the white background of the sky. The white curtains that cover the open windows of a carriage in which a young couple drive are whipped by an ominous wind. The figure of Death then enters the vehicle, which thereby doubles as a hearse. In *Nosferatu*, nature is portrayed as a place, at once, of great beauty possessed with restorative powers, and incipiently deadly, the universe from which Nosferatu's corrosive powers emanate.

The redemptive beauty of nature in *Nosferatu* is associated with the heroine, Ellen Hutter (Greta Schröder), who is framed by flowers and floral-designed wall coverings, and is suggested by the waves of the sea crashing on the seashore in the sunlight that functions as a romantic harbinger of Hutter's return to Wisborg. But nature also harbors predatory beasts, disease, corruption, and death. When Hutter, en route to Nosferatu, awakens from his night's sleep, the foothills of the Carpathian Mountains are depicted as a place of great beauty. Later, the same mountains appear as stark, blackened mounds of twisted rock against the white sky; they seem cold and lifeless in a sense that evokes the deathly presence of Nosferatu. When a coffin-like carriage arrives to meet Hutter, tall dark conifers cast jagged shadows across its path. When Hutter wakes up, the morning after his possession, and gazes horrified at Nosferatu sleeping in the coffin, Murnau cuts to an image of dawn breaking against dark clouds and the black Carpathians with spindly stunted black trees denuded of vegetation in the foreground. While the sea's waves in the sunlight have a redemptive aura as Ellen awaits Hutter's return, she is also situated in a graveyard that overlooks the sea. Is it Nosferatu, the figure of death, that she awaits? It is

Nosferatu, not Hutter, who travels by water, first by river then by sea, and when Nosferatu appears to Ellen at the denouement, Murnau intercuts speeded-up shots of the motion of the sea in the moonlight, in a manner that combines wind and water as the elements through which Nosferatu works his corrosive influence. Nosferatu himself is compared to forms of predatory nature—a carnivorous plant, "a polyp with tentacles, transparent, almost ethereal . . . a phantom almost," and to a spider that is observed by the deranged Knock. Nosferatu appears as the living dead, whose visage is a cross between a bat's head and a skull, and whose fingers are like the talons of a fantastic bird of prey.

Although *The Cabinet of Dr. Caligari* is set far from the world of nature—indeed, nature in *Caligari* appears as artifice—the world of the fairground in the film itself functions as a correlative of the nature world in *Nosferatu*. That is, like the elemental landscapes of *Nosferatu*, the fairground world is the "source" of an essentially alien, inhuman agency of death that stalks the city of Holstenwall. The contrived fairground landscape of *Caligari*, which stylistically is an extension of the city of Holstenwall itself, functions as "second nature." It is a thoroughly urban, modern landscape that is now the source of the irrational and inchoate forces of nature, which in *Nosferatu* is associated with "first nature." *Caligari* thus sets the stage for understanding the role of expressionism in the Kammerspiel film, both those of Weimar cinema and Alfred Hitchcock. The significance of transplanting the aesthetics and moral psychology of expressionism into the spaces of urban modernity is that the world of the modern itself is rendered uncanny. It becomes, at once, a place for staging the drama of the division of the self and the ambivalent allure of human sexuality, but also a place that seems to frame and even determine that drama.

The idea of nature as a blind force that works beyond the control of the protagonists does not, of course, preclude a psychosexual understanding of the figure of the double as an externalized, objective projection of unacknowledged human desires. But it transforms the way we understand such an "explanation." For, by conceiving the double or the shadow world as the objectification of a split-off aspect of the self, the psychological explanation of expressionism still thereby domesticates what is alien or other by making it relative to human psychology in the way that Freudian psychology itself tends to domesticate or rationalize the role of blind nature in romanticism. But the affinity of the figure of the double with blind nature in expressionism shows the fundamentally antipsychological nature of the double: it demonstrates the core of irrationality or blind instinct that is lodged within the human, that romantic philosopher Arthur Schopenhauer refers to as "The Will."[16]

In Hitchcock's films, likewise, the theme and stylistics of doubling that are omnipresent in his work are not reducible to a psychological under-standing, but function as a metaphysical force of blind nature, of pure drive or energy, inexplicable from the standpoint of human psychology and totally alien to the human, though it may appear, as it were, in the guise of a human form. This inhuman force or agency is linked to the hand of the director himself, who seems to authorize this force and identify himself with its agents. For example, the figure of the double in *Strangers on a Train*, Bruno Anthony, seems to be a character that is inexplicably driven by a kind of life force or energy. He intrudes into Guy's world in a wholly arbitrary way and has an element of the demonic in his ability to enter into Guy's field of vision, apparently at will. Furthermore, his disruptive energy is deeply connected with the playful hand of Hitchcock, the narrator himself as he, alongside Bruno, self-consciously toys with the fate of his hero.

Uncle Charlie in *Shadow of a Doubt* is implicitly equated with a vam-pire.[17] He appears in Santa Rosa as if magically summoned by his niece; he has a gap at the center of his top front teeth; he blows cigar smoke like a vampire's breath; he lodges in a house numbered 13; he lies on a bed with a headboard of devil's horns; he lies on another bed with a headboard that forms black devil's wings (the angel of death) that are also formed by the shadows from a lamp at the meal table; he rises from his bed phallically rigid as if from a coffin; he does not like to be photographed; and he seems to appear and disappear at will. His presence is also linked to the influence of corrosive nature. The urban landscape he comes from is associated with rusting cars by the side of a river in the panning shot which opens the film (the corrupted world of "second nature"), and his presence inside his niece's house is accompanied by the play of light and shadow on the wall (as a breeze blows through the curtained window), which subtly invokes the invasion of a corrupting natural force. Later, the deadly threat he poses to Charlie is registered by the projection of the black leafy shadow of "dead nature" onto the clapboard walls and garage door of the family house.

In *Rebecca*, the presence of the dead Rebecca in the house of Manderley is evoked not simply through her witchlike double, Mrs. Danvers, but also through the invasion of deathly and corrosive nature: dead, blackened floral arrangements against whitewashed walls create stark contrasts of black and white; rain shimmers on the whitewashed surfaces of the walls; and wind enters through the mullioned windows, sustaining a play of light and shadow. Rebecca's body has been deposited in the sea, and it is as if the watery play of light and shadow acts as an uncanny emanation of her spirit.

At the end of *Psycho*, a psychologist explains that Norman Bates murdered his mother on account of his jealousy of her taking a lover. Then, feeling unbearably guilty, he kept her body intact and finally incorporated her own personality into his. The mother part of Norman committed the murder of Marion Crane to protect the Norman part, because Norman assumed his mother was as jealous of him as he was of her. The psychologist's interpretation actually spells out the kind of psychological explanations routinely made by those who interpret expressionist doubling in psychological terms. It is as if Hitchcock invokes this explanation in order to make clear its limitations. The figure of Norman/mother is a deadly force of nature, a monster whose actions defy any psychological explanation.

The masculine dimension of this force of nature is embodied in the imagery of the phallic bird of prey, which Norman/mother embodies as he swoops down upon his victims. Here the avian imagery anticipates Hitchcock's depiction of the birds in *The Birds*, which I shall discuss in the next section. The feminine dimension of nature as a corrosive force, as in *Rebecca*, is suggested by the water imagery of the film. The black swamp located on the grounds of Norman Bates's motel complex where the corpse of Marion Crane is deposited, and from which her car is retrieved at the end, forms the primal landscape of *Psycho* from which the sources of corruption in the film emanate. Norman keeps his mother's corpse in a fruit cellar, and the bodies of two other young women are buried in the swamp. As she drives toward the Bates motel to her death, Marion Crane is blinded not simply by the beating rain but by the headlights of the oncoming cars that shine through it, creating a shimmering environment of light, as if Marion, sealed within her car, is pressing into a void where forms dissolve in a play of aqueous light. When she arrives at the motel she sees "mother" in a window framed by the driving rain.

Although the causal intervention of nature in human affairs in Hitchcock's work tends to be depicted as a corrosive one, there are important exceptions to this rule. Even in Hitchcock's *The Birds*, the death birds are countered by the force of the lovebirds, which represent a kind of natural mating instinct. But it is in *The Trouble with Harry* that Hitchcock most fully explores the benign, redemptive dimensions of nature. In this light black comedy, set in a leafy autumnal New England town, the corpse of a man—a city gent and, judging by his tie, something of a dandy—turns up in the leafy woods. Various townspeople encounter the corpse: a young boy, who returns to his mother Jennifer Rogers (Shirley MacLaine); a retired "sea captain," Captain Wiles (Edmund Gwenn), who is out poaching rabbit; a spinster, Miss Ivy Gravely (Mildred Natwick), out walking; and a young, unsuccessful artist, Sam Marlowe (John Forsythe). In encountering the body, these human beings encounter one another and conversation ensues. Who killed Harry? And more importantly, what should be done with the corpse? Did Captain Wiles shoot him as he initially believes? Did he die from being hit over the head by Mrs. Rogers, who turns out to be his wife, though long estranged? Did Miss Gravely kill him with a knock on the head as he began to assault her in the woods, thinking she was Mrs. Rogers? Every time one of the protagonists, thinking themselves responsible, seeks to bury him, a new reason emerges to dig him up. They spend a lot of time digging, but they are unable to bury the corpse. This only stimulates further sociability. Soon romance is budding between individuals who were previously isolated—Captain Wiles and Miss Gravely, Sam and Mrs. Rogers—and the community renews itself.

The Trouble with Harry belongs to the least expressionist group of films within Hitchcock's corpus, not simply because it is in color (the significance of which I shall explore in the next chapter), but because it is a narrative of romantic renewal that orchestrates oppositions into unity rather than dramatizes division. The difference here is that it is not a young couple that is playfully placed outside the law and brought together, come what may, but the whole aging community that is cast as a rogue, seeking to collectively outwit the local deputy sheriff, and it is the whole community that is thereby rejuvenated. Like other narratives of romantic renewal, and benign irony, the film is governed by playful artifice. Although set in nature, the space of the clearing in which the body is discovered is shot by Hitchcock frontally, as if the nature world is a stage upon which characters enter and leave, and the ways the characters stumble over the body and each other are hilariously contrived. Furthermore, characters dissemble. For example, Captain Wiles is not a sea captain, and Miss Gravely conceals her role in the crime and buys a cup to serve Captain Wiles tea while pretending it belonged to her father. But these masquerades only serve to fuel the romance.

By failing to bury the corpse, by feeling its weight and yielding to the fact of its existence, the corrosive forces of nature, of death and decay, that are so visible in Hitchcock's expressionist works, are turned in *The Trouble with Harry* into something that is life-affirming. Nature is cyclical and human life is part of that cycle.[18] Like the fall season that recycles nature for the summer to come, the corpse provides compost for the soul of the community. Indeed, in one carefully crafted shot at the beginning of the film, the little boy, the promise of the future, is perceived to sprout from the head of the corpse. At one point, Mrs. Rogers (still Harry's wife), when asked what to do with Sam, says, "You should stuff him for all I care, stuff him and put him in a glass case." Of course, this is exactly what Norman Bates does to his mother (if we consider the glass case to be the windowed bedroom). But the life-giving corpse in *The Trouble with Harry* is the precise antithesis to the death-dealing corpse of *Psycho*. In *The Trouble with Harry*, the human being is not irreducibly divided from itself and from the other according to the logic of the double, but in harmony both with community and the cosmos.

Analytic Expressionism

John Orr is right to observe that, "It was not until he had left Europe that Hitchcock really honed his European influences to perfection."[19] Hitchcock's high expressionist style undergoes a final decisive development when the overtly self-conscious stylistics and thematics of high expressionism are seamlessly integrated into the "invisible" narration of classical style. It should be noted, however, that such integration is already anticipated and fully realized in his fine late silent film, *The Manxman* (1928). Here, the stylistic and rhetorical strategies of expressionism are consistently employed by Hitchcock to suggest the doubling between the two male leads, Pete Quilliam (Carl Brisson), a lowly sailor, and Philip Christian (Malcolm Keen), a lawyer, and the dramatic irony of the triangular relationship they form with Kate Cregeen (Anny Ondra); yet they are unobtrusively integrated into the "analytical editing" techniques of classical narration, in particular the rhetoric of shot/reverse-shot editing.

Expressionism

Hitchcock achieves the synthesis of expressionist technique with classical style by restricting his use of the overt distortions of representational space that characterize subjective expressionism to isolated and realistically motivated instances, and embedding his commentative expressionist narration within the "invisible" techniques of classical narration. Hitchcock "contains" both the overt registration of mental states and the pointedly commentative authorial interpolations that mark the use of expressionist iconography within the techniques and strategies of classical cinema.

The subjective aspects of perception in films such as *Rear Window* and *Vertigo* are conveyed through and within objective point-of-view shot structures, in part through intense restriction to and repetition of character point of view that conveys the interest, attention, and desire of a character, and in part through the strategies of framing and camera movement discussed in chapter 4. These various techniques serve to "psychologize" the gaze, conveying through the look of a character various mental attributes. However, in *Rear Window*, *Vertigo*, and elsewhere, we can only understand the nature of the character's emotional state through the reaction shot that objectively registers the character's emotional response to what it is that he or she sees. The psychological state of a character is no longer, or only very rarely, directly registered through the distortion of representational space.

I have noted the association in subjective expressionism with an object in the environment that is rendered pregnant with significance, like the trunk in *The Last Laugh*, or the severed arm in *Blackmail*. In Hitchcock's mature expressionist style, the significance of objects is characteristically detached from their embeddedness in point of view. Hitchcock's cinema is littered with objects that are at once part of the environment yet uncannily larger than life: the illuminated glass of milk that Johnnie Aysgarth carries up to Lina in *Suspicion* (fig. 21); the lighter that Bruno drops down the drain in *Strangers on a Train*; the coffee cup filled with poison that looms ominously in the right foreground while Alicia Huberman suffers from her poisoning in the winged-back chair that looks like a coffin in *Notorious* (fig. 22); the giant undrunk bottle of champagne left behind in Prescott's office in *Notorious*; the close-up of the giant telephone dial in *Dial M for Murder* (1954). These are objects endowed with a psychological weight, both for the characters in the fiction and for the spectator. Yet by simply enlarging size, often by placing the object in the foreground of a fuller deep-space composition (though sometimes, as in the telephone dial, through a close-up), and by avoiding the distorting point-of-view techniques of subjective expressionism, Hitchcock also maintains naturalistic representation. The rather grotesque exception to this rule is the gigantic handgun in *Spellbound* that rotates from pointing at Constance Petersen and toward the character who holds it, Dr. Murchison, and the spectator herself.[20]

The rhetoric of the double is integrated into classical Hollywood technique by unobtrusively embedding patterns of doubling within the protocols of classical narration through graphic design and mise-en-scène. As we have seen, expressionist mise-en-scène that involves the inscription of natural elements such as wind and rain through the play of light and shadow is a ubiquitous feature of Hitchcock's films. But these expressionist elements unobtrusively supervene upon the "realistic" milieu that defines the space of the story, such as the house of Manderley in *Rebecca*. Similarly, graphic design serves to register the double while utilizing the conventions of classical narrative style: the single-shot profile suggests the idea of the Janus face; the standard two-shot suggests the divided screen of the double; and the shot/reverse-shot registers through symmetrical or complementary graphic design that characters are doubles of one another. This pattern of doubling is sustained and reinforced by rigorous and repetitive patterns of alternation in Hitchcock's work that go well beyond the pragmatic norms of alternation in classical cinema.

Hitchcock's doubling technique is evident in *The Manxman*. For example, when Pete tells Philip that it is time for him to ask for Kate's hand in marriage, the shot/reverse-shot point-of-view structure articulates at once their identification and their opposition. William Rothman points out the same process of doubling that occurs in the scene from *Murder!* where the hero Sir John visits the heroine Diana in prison and assumes a position at the opposite end of a long table.[21] The shot/reverse-shot point-of-view structure frames them symmetrically and suggests the extent to which he is assuming her position. But it is only in Hitchcock's Hollywood films where this pattern of alternation across graphically complementary images becomes a sustained technique.[22]

The parlor sequence in *Psycho*, which Rothman calls "the most extraordinary of all Hitchcock's shot/reverse-shot sequences,"[23] provides an ideal exemplification of this technique. Marion Crane has arrived at the Bates Motel in pouring rain and, having been berated by "mother" for inviting strange women to dinner, Norman Bates comes down with milk and sandwiches and invites her to join him in the parlor, as if entertaining her on a chaste Victorian "date." Once they are seated, in a medium two-shot, the scene breaks into a pattern of shot/reverse-shot alternations. Each of these at once moves us closer to the scene in the manner of classical scene dissection, and punctuates a shift in the relationship between the characters. Prior to the two-shot in which they sit down, Marion, standing, her reflection doubled in the windowpane of the door, looks at the stuffed owl on Norman's wall. As she does so there is a squeak on the sound track almost subliminally suggesting the animation of the bird. Then she looks at a stuffed raven that casts a shadow over the oval painting of an angel. Norman rises to partly obliterate the oval in such a way that, as Rothman points out, turns into an eye that stares back at her from the image. After the shot of the raven, Hitchcock cuts to Norman framed by the owl on the wall and then to Marion in the doorway as he invites her to sit down. This announces the pattern (from Norman to Marion) that will be maintained until the end when Marion initiates the shot/reverse-shot sequence. The two-shot establishes the scene. It is a divided two-shot, literally bisected by a line on the rear wall. On the right side sits Norman, framed by what will become clear later in the sequence is his "bird altar" in the background and the milk jug in the foreground, which covers his hands and his crotch. On the left side sits Marion, framed by a parakeet, plausibly a lovebird, the painting of a nude, and a picture that is surely Norman's mother. A Victorian lampshade adjacent to the picture links this parlor in the modern anonymous motel with the mother's house (fig. 23). In the subsequent shot/countershot sequence, the elements in the mise-en-scène are retained, but Hitchcock reconfigures their position in a "cheat cut" in order to maximize their expressive potential within the subsequent frames. The following shot breakdown is adapted from Sam Ishii-Gonzales.[24]

Series 1: 40 Shots

It begins on Norman's comment: "You eat like a bird."

> Dark-haired, dark-jacketed, Norman sits in three-quarter shot slightly off-center to the right of the frame with a stuffed wild bird looking at him from the left (fig. 2).

Visual Style

Fair-headed, light-dressed, Marion sits in three-quarter shot off-center to the left with what appear to be lovebirds and a parakeet to her right, the oval picture of the angels visible above her head, and a milk jug to the left (fig. 1).

Norman talks to her about his hobby of stuffing birds and how isolated he is. She sympathizes and he responds, "You know what I think … we are all in our private traps." Marion and Norman are both doubled with birds within their respective frames, and they are doubles of one another: they are both birds in their private traps. At the same time, they are opposed— Norman as bird of prey and Marion as lovebird, male and female.

Series 2: 28 Shots

It begins on Marion's comment: "You know, if anyone ever talked to me the way I heard, the way she spoke to you … " and shifts on her words to a new framing of Norman.

Norman sits in low-angle medium profile shot, at first leaning forward then leaning back. He is now doubled in all four corners of the frame by birds. And his profile, illuminated by backlighting, suggests a Janus face (as if it were half human, half avian). Next to the bird's shadow, bottom right, is the picture of a naked woman, doubling the relationship between Norman and Marion within his frame. When he leans back he reveals a picture of the "Rape of the Sabine Women," foreshadowing the future (fig. 4).

Marion sits in medium shot, now in an uncluttered frame (the milk jug is visible on the left), still "eating like a bird." The base of the oval picture of angels frames her head. She is bisected by side lighting into light and shadow (but not in as exaggerated a fashion as Norman) (fig. 3).

Marion, with her opening remark that draws attention to Norman's treatment by his mother, establishes the difference between them which is emphasized by the framing, even as there remains a complementarity between the characters.

Series 3: 19 Shots

It begins on Marion's comment: "Wouldn't it be better if you put her ... someplace?"

> Norman is now in medium close-up profile shot, again doubled by the bird in the left-hand side of the frame. (This is actually a mismatched cheat cut from the previous shot because the stuffed bird was behind Norman's head. Now he is leaning forward and it is on the left of the frame. But this way Hitchcock preserves the doubling imagery.) The stuffed bird faces Norman, its beak toward his eye, in a manner that suggests Norman's self-division (fig. 6).

> Marion in medium close-up in an empty frame. The back of her seat bisects the image into black and white across the back of her neck in a manner that anticipates her broken neck (fig. 5).

> Norman is now on the defensive, and hence on the attack: "People mean well, they cluck their thick tongues and shake their heads and suggest oh so delicately."

Series 4: 12 Shots

Marion says thank you. Norman replies, "Thank you, *Norman*," wanting to extend the conversation. "Norman," Marion says, and stands up.

> Marion is now framed in low angle with a stuffed raven to the right of her face (fig. 7).

> Norman in low-angle medium shot, no longer doubled into his avian profile. The chest behind him has a bird book open on top of it. It now looks rather like an altar table with Norman's bird bible (fig. 8).

> Marion looks powerful and maternal, and Norman looks like a boy. The stuffed bird from the beginning of the sequence (Norman's double) has now entered into Marion's space. She has already, as it were, become

one of Norman's stuffed birds, and Norman is momentarily free of his deadness.

The opening sequence from *Strangers on a Train* provides another ideal example of Hitchcock's technique. It is particularly revealing, for here Hitchcock's reverse field cutting actually emerges out of a didactic pattern of graphically matched alternations. The film begins with a rigorous series of mirrored alternations between the two protagonists, with Guy always in the dominant or first position. However, when we are initially introduced we do not see their faces, merely their feet and clothing, in a manner that indicates through graphic matching their doubled status. Hitchcock articulates their relationship in a tour-de-force sequence of expressionist montage in the following sequence of shots. All transitions are cuts unless otherwise stated, and here I adapt a shot breakdown by Sabrina Barton.[25]

1. Bruno Anthony, wearing pin-striped trousers and ostentatious saddle shoes in medium close-up, exits a black-and-white diamond cab, turns, and walks to screen left, tracked by a left pan.

2. Guy Haines, wearing wool slacks and tan brogues in medium close-up, exits a black-and-white diamond cab, turns, and walks to screen right, tracked by a right pan.

3. In medium close-up of feet, Bruno walks screen right to left from top to bottom in right-to-left tracking shot, across a white-tiled floor with black diamonds (fig. 10).

4. In medium close-up of feet, Guy walks screen left to right from top to bottom in left-to-right tracking shot across the same floor (fig. 9).

5. Medium close-up of Bruno's feet tracked right to left.

6. Medium close-up of Guy's feet walking across the same floor, tracked left to right.

7. Bruno enters platform in low-angle full shot along floor, creating parallel tracks. Guy follows Bruno, paralleling action but now in the same shot. Dissolve to ...

8. Shot from the train of crossing motif, which combines parallel lines and the diamond motif, but now the diamond is bisected. The pointed ends of the resultant triangles now touch to form a cross, announcing the "crisscross" motif that recurs in the film (fig. 11) The railway tracks create the motif of barred parallel lines and the crisscrossing multiplies (fig. 12). Dissolve to ...

9. Medium close-up of Bruno's shoes; Bruno walks right to left in railway carriage in right-to-left tracking shot, sits down, and crosses his legs (fig. 14).

10. Medium close-up of Guy's shoes. Guy walks left to right in railway carriage in left-to-right tracking shot. He sits down, begins to cross his legs (fig. 13). Match on action to …

11. Medium close-up two-shot looking down the carriage at ground level. Guy nudges Bruno's shoe as he crosses his legs (fig. 15).

12. Full shot two-shot looking down the carriage. Guy is left of screen in dark suit, Bruno is right of screen in light pin-striped suit. Panes of transparent glass with wavy parallel lines frame them both. White parallel lines traverse the roof of the carriage, creating a dramatic black-and-white striped effect (fig. 16).

At this point the symmetrical alternation (punctuated by three shots in which the two characters are combined in the image, if we include the abstraction of shot 8) resolves into a shot/reverse-shot point-of-view structure. But this classical editing structure retains the commentative, doubled, montage structure of the opening sequence. Seven rapid alternations oppose Bruno in his light pin-stripes in medium shot, sitting slightly off-center right, framed by window on left with horizontal bars of window blinds (fig. 18), and Guy in his dark jacket in medium shot sitting slightly off-center left, framed by window on left (and partly on right) (fig. 17). The framing of these shots makes them, in part, mirror shots. Then, after a transitional two-shot in which Bruno steps into Guy's space to introduce himself, a further 13-shot alternation commences, again of symmetrically complementary and contrasted shots. Bruno, in medium two-shot, is framed over the shoulder of Guy in profile (fig. 20). The image is replete with parallel lines that frame Bruno vertically and horizontally and cast shadows across his face. Guy in medium two-shot is framed over the shoulder of Bruno in profile. In contrast, Guy, in medium two-shot, is framed by the blinds of the window, but the image is much cleaner and the character stands out from the background (fig. 19). The over-the-shoulder two-shot squeezes the two characters into the frame in a manner that expressively configures the invasion of Guy's life by Bruno as an invasion of his personal space.

After sharing drinks ("a pair," says Bruno, "the only kind of doubles I know"), the "couple" retires to Bruno's private quarters to dine, and the pattern of shot alternation resumes. As Sabrina Barton notes, out of the 67 shots that take place on the train, "fifty-eight (roughly 86%) are paired into twenty-nine sets of reverse-angles."[26] In this canonical example of Hitchcock's analytic expressionism, the narration is at once linear and doubling. As in the sequence from *Psycho*, we are at once inside and outside the point of view of the character. In the later part of the movie, as I described in chapter 4, the parallel construction of the opening is once again resumed, but now in the large, as it were.

In Hitchcock's mature style, editing serves as an authorial commentary on narrative events whose connection and causality is psychologically articulated through character. It is a technique that at once retains the relative "invisibility" of classical editing, where changes in what is taking place in the story are cued in a linear way through a character-focused narrative, yet articulates a commentative, doubled perspective upon character through the orchestration of graphic matches embedded in patterns of alternation. In this way Hitchcock, the narrator, sustains a pervasive presence in the text, offering a "vertical" commentary on the narrative world and at the same time orchestrating at the "horizontal" level of the text the both/ and logic of the double. All the while, the narrator remains unobtrusive and invisible, rather in the manner of the "objective" romantic ironist discussed in chapter 1, and in conformity with the narrative idioms of classical cinema.

Expressionist Iconography

Hitchcock culled from expressionist films a distinctive iconography of visual motifs and objects recurrently deployed in his films. Visual motifs include figurations of the double, such as the Janus face, the divided screen, and mirror images. Objects include the merry-go-round, the vertical staircase, the rectangular staircase, and the mullioned window. But these objects also become elements of Hitchcock's visual design, in the sense that Hitchcock abstracts the visual design of objects from any single concrete occasion of their use. For example, the precipitous staircase, shot frontally and given hard lighting, such as the staircase in the Balestrero home in *The Wrong Man*, creates a black-and-white barred design in the image. However, the black-and-white barred or parallel line is an autonomous and ubiquitous design motif in Hitchcock's works. The overhead shot of a rectangular staircase that creates the sense of a vortex in the image, first used in *Black-mail*, recurs in his work, but the spiral motif that can be derived from it takes on an independent significance in *Vertigo*, even as the square staircase remains a prominent motif of that film.

Furthermore, it is inadequate to think of Hitchcock's expressionist ico-nography and visual design as static elements. First, movement is essential to the portrayal of light and shadow in his expressionist aesthetic, especially where Hitchcock seeks to evoke the force of nature. Second, expressionist iconography and visual design motivate the large-scale structure of his work. The visual motif of doubling is not simply inscribed in a mirror shot or a divided screen; it is evoked, as we have seen, in Hitchcock's rendition of shot/reverse-shot structures and parallel editing. Similarly, specific visual motifs may inform the design structure of an entire work, such as the ring motif that informs the mise-en-scène and structure of Hitchcock's silent film, *The Ring*, or the spiral motif that informs the camera movements in *Vertigo*.

Far from being a species of mere formalism, these design elements form the substance of Hitchcock's work, sowing ambiguity into the structure of the image and the texture of his stories. In the remainder of this chapter, I will suggest the origins of specific elements of Hitchcock's expressionist iconography, and trace the relationship between these elements and larger narrative patterns.

The Profile Shot /The Janus Face

The iconography of the Janus face is a recurring feature of Hitchcock's work. He may have been inspired by F. W. Murnau's film *Janus-Faced* (*Der Janus-kopff*), now unfortunately lost. *Janus-Faced* is an uncredited adaptation of Robert Louis Stevenson's novella *Dr. Jekyll and Mr. Hyde*, the archetypal narrative of the double, which features a marble bust with two faces, "one godlike, one diabolical," that comes to haunt the protagonist.[27] The Janus face in Hitchcock's films is suggested in one of two ways: either through a lighting design which divides the face of a character in two, or through the emphatic use of the profile shot whose one-sidedness suggests a hidden, dark side beneath. In *The Lodger*, the Lodger is shown bisected by the light reflected through a mullioned window. Divided in half, his face expresses the ambiguous aspects of his personality. I have already suggested how light is used to divide Norman's face into two aspects in *Psycho*. This is particularly apparent when, confronted by Detective Arbogast, he leans over the motel register (fig. 24).

The profile shot evokes a similar ambiguity. In *Rope*, the murderers, Brandon and Phillip, confronted with their crime by their teacher Rupert Cadell, are framed in profile in a two-shot against the jade light of a flashing neon sign, which illuminates, as it were, their deadly, dark side. I have noted Norman Bates's Janus face in *Psycho*, which is half human, half avian. In a similar way, in *The Birds* the human characters are consistently shown looking in profile shot, their chins jutting forward. Not only does their off-screen gaze connect them with the birds, who seem to respond to their look with an attack, their profiles also suggest the Janus face of the human being: half human, half bird (fig. 25). Again, the bird profile represents the hidden aspects of the human. When Scottie Ferguson first encounters the woman who masquerades as Madeleine in *Vertigo*, she appears in a close-up profile shot. Scottie's gaze fails to quite connect with Madeleine's profile shot in a way that suggests that this image of Madeleine is a subjective image (an illusion) made real, as it were, by Hitchcock's camera.[28] Furthermore, the rigorous profile of the face made radiant through a momentary heightening of light suggests an ideal image that conceals or hides a dark side. Judy as Madeleine is profiled yet again in the graveyard (plate 9). Later, in the second half of the film, after Judy Barton has been discovered by Scottie, she is seen in close-up profile. Finally, in her hotel room, as the reincarnation of Madeleine, she appears in profile shot again, now framed against a jade neon light (plate 12).

The Mirror Shot

The mirror shot in Hitchcock is an extension of the motif of the Janus face, displaying the hidden aspect of the character and functioning, like the shadow, to convey a doubling effect. A signal instance of the mirror shot occurs in *The Wrong Man*, when Rose Balestrero, at the point of breakdown, hits Manny on the forehead with her hairbrush that breaks in two the bedroom mirror. Manny stares in horror, and in the reverse-shot, mirror image, his face is horrendously split in two combining the Janus face with the mirror image, and suggesting how the false accusation and its effect on Rose has brought into being the self-division of his character.

It is no surprise that in *Psycho*, which is a tour de force of doubling strategies, mirrors should play a prominent role. For example, the character of Marion Crane is doubled in a mirror in her bedroom, after having stolen the money; in the restroom at the car dealership when she exchanges the money for the car; as she arrives at the Bates Motel where she is reflected in the window; when she registers in the motel's guest book; in her room (number 1) at the motel where Norman Bates has escorted her; and in the doorway to the parlor when she sits down with Norman. Notably, a mirror shot is absent when she has decided to return the money she has stolen. Later, Sam and Lila are doubled in a mirror as they register at the motel masquerading as husband and wife, Sam again is mirrored as he hectors Norman about stealing Marion's money, and, near the film's denouement, Lila is startled by her mirror reflection as she nervously explores the bedroom of Mrs. Bates.

Mirror shots are equally central to the visual design of *Vertigo*. When Judy masquerading as Madeleine Elster leaves Ernie's with Gavin Elster, posing as the worried husband, they are framed in a mirror in the point of view of Scottie Ferguson. In the flower shop, Judy as Madeleine is framed in a mirror that is positioned alongside a doorway. In two-shot, we see both Scottie (who looks in on her at the door) and Judy as Madeleine (the object of his look), in a manner that suggests at once the doubling of Judy as Madeleine and a parallelism or doubling of identification between Scottie and Madeleine through the split-screen effect (cover photo). Later, Judy Barton is framed in a mirror in her shabby hotel room when Scottie first visits her, and again at Ransohoff's, the clothing store, alongside Scottie, as she is being forced by him to be remade in the image of Madeleine (fig. 26). The final image suggests, at once, the double that is Judy being re-created as Madeleine and the perverse double of himself that Scottie has become in attempting to bring back to life his lost love through the vehicle of Judy. Furthermore, it conveys the sense that Scottie and Judy are in fact doubles of one another. This shot echoes the doubling effect created by the mirrored profiles of Gavin Elster and Judy playing Madeleine in Ernie's restaurant. Then, Judy was Elster's puppet; now she is Scottie's puppet. Furthermore, again, as in Ernie's, both characters are framed in profile in such a way as to underscore the doubling effect with the evocation of a Janus face.

Visual Style

The Divided Two-shot

Hitchcock portrays doubling between individuals through the formal symmetry of the two-shot, which places characters in mirrored opposition within the frame. This form of shot construction allows Hitchcock to embed expressionist style (the opposition between black and white) and themes (the double) within the conventional two-shot of classical narration. Eloquent examples of two-shot doubling occur in virtually every Hitchcock film, often repeatedly, and I have already noted complex instances of this in *Psycho*, *Strangers on a Train*, and *Vertigo*.

A striking example occurs in Hitchcock's early film *The Manxman*. When the two friends and rivals introduced at the film's inception go to meet the heroine at the bar where she works, they approach her in a two-shot point-of-view shot as if squeezed into the frame. In her reaction shot, she divides her attention between them, and the viewer, like her, is unable to settle her gaze on one or the other of this doubled character. In the scene in *Shadow of a Doubt* where Uncle Charlie first arrives and places the present of a ring on Young Charlie's finger, Uncle Charlie stands in a gray suit on the left of the frame, symmetrically divided by the door jamb, while Young Charlie stands on the right in a white dress in front of the door, whose panel bears the sign of the cross. In *Rebecca*, when the second Mrs. de Winter first talks to Danvers about Rebecca after her arrival at Manderley, Hitchcock frames the second Mrs. de Winter and Danvers in a two-shot. The second Mrs. De Winter, attired in pale floral dress, occupies the left-hand side of the screen, framed by the floral drapery on the window, whose edge splits the screen in two. Danvers, dressed in black, is framed on the right by the black mullions of the rain-swept window.

In my analysis of *Psycho*, I have shown how birds can function as the double of characters in the two-shot. But human beings are doubled with many other kinds of objects in Hitchcock's work. For example, in *Notorious*, Devlin, suffering from a headache from knowing that he has to send Alicia on a dodgy mission, is expressionistically doubled by a "knotted" abstract sculpture (fig. 27); and Midge, in *Vertigo*, is doubled by the painting of herself as Carlotta discussed in chapter 4 (fig. 28).

In *Marnie* (a film where the divided two-shot plays a significant expressive role), suspense is created by dividing the shot. In a low-angle long shot, we watch as Marnie robs cash from the office safe of Strutt's (Martin Gabel), while on the other side of the translucent glass of the office wall, we watch as a cleaning lady scrubs the floor, gradually moving in the direction of Marnie's escape route (fig. 29). We fear vicariously on Marnie's behalf. Spotting the woman, Marnie puts her shoes in her pockets and tries to tiptoe out. Then suddenly the shoe drops ... but Marnie is okay—the woman turns out to be deaf. The scene might appear to be just a brilliant though gratuitous exercise in suspense, until we realize that the cleaning woman bears an uncanny resemblance to Marnie's mother. Marnie's mother is a "psychic" cleaning lady who is always trying to erase the guilt of her past and transferring that guilt to Marnie. Marnie's response, the way she asserts her identity, is to steal back from men in authority, from the patriarchal social order that has left her mother bereft, while keeping up appearances as her mother's daughter. The shoe drops (perhaps unconsciously Marnie wishes to be caught), but the cleaning lady is deaf to her presence. The split screen thus sets up this little drama of symbolic doubles: Marnie and the cleaning lady.

The Mullioned Window and Double

In Murnau's Nosferatu, the figure of Nosferatu hovers behind the blackened windowpane crossed with white mullions, as he seems to communicate telepathically with the heroine, who looks across at him from the house opposite. The windowpane is a transparent or translucent conduit between inside and outside, and suggests more metaphorically the figuration of the idea of a "medium" of communication between the inner and the outer that carries hidden or dangerous knowledge. It is as if the window is a portal to the shadow world, at once conceived either in psychological terms as the world of the unconscious or in literal terms as the place of danger. The window affords access to the other, but it also suggests that something is being hidden. In Murnau's film, Nosferatu stands behind the window, and it is as if the window enables the kind of secret communication that takes place between him and the character of Ellen, whose bedroom window lies opposite.

In Hitchcock's works, the figure behind the mullioned window is either watching (or listening) or being watched (or overheard), or both. The Manxman provides a "benign" example of this motif: the sailor, Pete, watches through the mullioned window as his jealous friend seeks, on his behalf, to persuade Kate's father to allow Pete to marry her. He looks on from the outside as his "secret communication" is passed to the father. The father then looks back enraged. The sailor is caught out, shamed, and the father comes round from behind the window to confront him.

In *Rear Window*, the motif of watching and being watched is played out through the entire film. The mullioned window is mostly replaced by the modern white steel-framed windows of an apartment building, and the black-and-white motif is replaced by the white-and-red color design of the white steel window frames and the red bricks. The rear window becomes a medium of secret communication between the inhabitants of the apartments across the courtyard and L. B. Jefferies—for example, when Jefferies returns the toast Miss Lonely Hearts gives to her phantom lover with a toast of his own. There is one mullioned window, noted in chapter 1, through which Jefferies looks upon the body of Miss Torso, fragmented by the cross-hatching, and imagines what it would be like to cut up a human body (fig. 30).

Lars Thorwald, the murderer, eventually looks back through a window, too, and then he comes round the window to confront Jefferies, the voyeur, in the space of his own apartment. While obviously not a vampire, Lars Thorwald is a nocturnal creature who has prominent teeth and preys on women (the wife he murders). Faced with Thorwald's attack, Jefferies attempts to blind him with flashing light bulbs, not only the tools of his trade but also a substitute for the sunlight that kills the vampire in *Nosferatu*. If we consider *Rear Window* as an allegory of film spectatorship, the allegory illuminates the function of the mullioned window in Hitchcock's work as a stand-in for the cinema screen itself, at once a window that reveals and a screen that conceals.

However, frequently in Hitchcock's films, characters stand in front of the blackened face of a mullioned window. Here, the connotation is less that of communication but opacity, as if the mullioned window is reflecting the opacity or the dark side of the Janus face. The Lodger hovers in front of a mullioned windowpane in the *The Lodger* when he first enters the upstairs lodging room of the household in which he is staying. Mrs. Danvers is framed in profile before a mullioned window in *Rebecca*, in a scene I have already discussed. In both cases it is raining outside, suggesting a secret communication between the figure before the window and the forces of nature beyond. In *Rebecca*, Hitchcock actually pulls focus in such a way that the corrosive forces of nature seem to enter in through the window as the raindrops become visible on the windowpane adjacent to the face of Danvers. Through the intermediary of Danvers' corrosive nature, the form of Rebecca has invaded or has taken over the house of Manderley. Uncle Charlie in *Shadow of a Doubt*, who is endowed, like the Lodger, with connotations of the vampire, stands before an opaque mullioned window.

For the opening of *North by Northwest*, Saul Bass created a moving abstract grid design that distills the gridlike matrix or web that defines the interlocking agencies of power in the Cold War world order, where friend or foe actually looks very much alike. This grid is then projected onto the surface of a modernist United Nations–style skyscraper, which functions as a giant reflective window or screen in which the world of everyday life (cars and traffic) is reflected, but reflected opaquely through the blue-green glass of the building. This surface of glass panes against pale crisscrossing lines is a mullioned window writ large, which literally occupies the space and frame of the film itself. Later in the film, the character of the Professor, played by Leo G. Carroll, stands in front of a mullioned window behind which we see the Capitol dome, situating him at once not only as the supreme figure of authority who draws upon and embodies symbolic power but also as a highly manipulating and controlling character beneath his benign, avuncular exterior. He is the phantom figure before the mullioned window, a figure of the living dead, a concrete embodiment of the deathly coldness of the Cold War world order (fig. 31). This order is portrayed as having, metaphorically, a vampiric relationship toward its ordinary subjects, embodied in the manipulated and exploited figure of Roger Thornhill, even as *North by Northwest* is essentially comic not horrific in tone.

A variation on the mullioned window is simply the upstairs window of a house, sometimes a Gothic mansion. Norman's mother seems to appear in the window of the Gothic house in *Psycho* illuminated by a bright light and obscured by the rain. Equally, in *Vertigo*, Judy as Madeleine appears in the upstairs window of the McKittrick hotel, but then mysteriously disappears. Once again, the sight afforded by the window conceals as much as it reveals. On the opposite side, characters will watch and eavesdrop from upstairs windows. Uncle Charlie lurks threateningly in his upstairs window as he watches Young Charlie dating the detective, as if his reach stretches beyond the confines of the room. Lil (Diane Baker), the jealous sister-in-law of the hero of *Marnie*, Mark Rutland, hovers in an upstairs window, eavesdropping on Mark and his new wife.

Visual Style

The Staircase, the Banister, and the //// Effect

In a pivotal scene in Fritz Lang's *Destiny*, the heroine visits Death with a request to retrieve from him her dead fiancé. They meet on a giant causeway that symbolically represents the path from life to death. But by the end of the film we realize that it also represents, in a sense, the path back to love since, unable to defeat Death, the heroine voluntarily dies to join her lover in the world of death. Lang shoots the scene in a manner such that the staircase looks less like steps, in depth, than a series of brightly illuminated horizontal parallel lines or bars running as a formal design across the background, creating a kind of flatness to the image which helps serve to articulate the imaginary space inhabited by the characters—Death and the maiden—who meet there.

However, Hitchcock also draws his staircase imagery and the parallel lines with which it is associated from Murnau's *Nosferatu*, where a domestic staircase is the site of Nosferatu's ascent to Ellen's bedroom at the climax of the film. In a remarkable silhouette dominated by the vertical parallel lines created by the banisters of the staircase, we perceive Nosferatu in medium shot slinking up to her room like a giant rodent. Then, from a panicked reaction shot of Ellen inside the room, Murnau cuts to a low-angled shot of Nosferatu at the top of the stairs, framed by the shadow of the banister, his hand elongated by shadow, poised to open the bedroom door.

Hitchcock domesticates Lang's image of the staircase from earth to heaven (or hell) and Murnau's supernatural expressionism to re-create the staircase as the key expressionist space of modernity that links the everyday public space of the street, the hall, and the downstairs to the private, sexual, deadly secrets contained in the upstairs room, a space that, in the words of Dennis Zirnite, "is incarnated by those who unleash the darkest human impulses."[29] As Zirnite points out, an archetypal image in Hitchcock is a low-angle shot, looking up, of a staircase framed by the vertical lines of the banister, which are often augmented by shadow, as in the shot from Alice's point of view of the dandy's room in *Blackmail* (fig. 32, and note the cross on the door), or from Arbogast's point of view in *Psycho*. Often the perverse figure who inhabits the upper space is perched Nosferatu-like at the top of the banister, as in a shot of Uncle Charlie at the top of the staircase in *Shadow of a Doubt* (fig. 33), which is an image that replicates a similar shot from *The Lodger*. In *Frenzy*, the trajectory between upstairs and

Figure 1

Figure 2

Figure 3

Figure 4

Figure 5

Figure 6

Figure 7

Figure 8

Figure 9

Figure 10

Figure 11

Figure 12

Figure 13

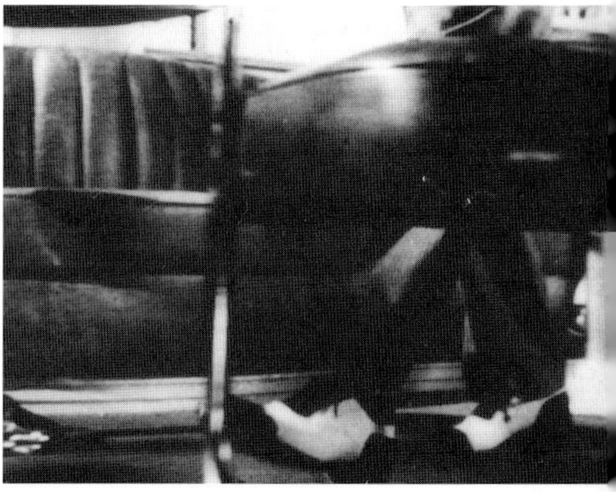

Figure 14

Figure 15

Figure 16

Figure 17

Figure 18

Figure 19

Figure 20

Figure 21

Figure 22

Figure 23

Figure 24

Figure 25

Figure 26

Figure 27

Figure 28

Figure 29

Figure 31

Figure 30

Figure 32

Figure 33

Figure 34

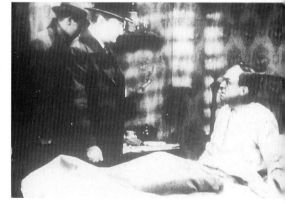

Figure 35

Figure 36

Figure 37

Figure 38

Figure 39

Figure 40

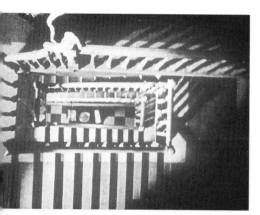

Figure 41

Figure 42

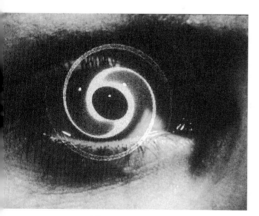

Figure 43

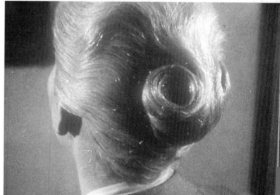

Figure 44

Figure 45

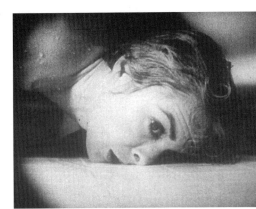

Figure 46

Figure 47

Figure 48

downstairs is actually traversed by the camera itself as it slowly withdraws from witnessing the sexual murder taking place in the killer's upstairs lodgings.

However, Hitchcock also shoots the staircase in a manner that exactly replicates the visual construction of Lang's image—the stairs creating rungs that orchestrate the opposition between black and white as a sharply defined linear design. Thus, when the Lodger enters the house of the Buntings for the first time, he is framed against the background of the staircase. When the heroine of Hitchcock's *Blackmail* is seduced by the dandy to go to visit his upstairs apartment, the dandy is, for the knowing spectator, framed in sinister fashion against the parallel lines formed by the staircase. The deadly staircase in *Psycho* is framed and lit in a similar way at the denouement of the film, where, with the sinister space of the stairs well established by now, Lila Crane enters the house, unaware of the danger that lurks there (fig. 34). In *Shadow of a Doubt*, the battle between Uncle Charlie and Young Charlie is in part a battle over control of the staircases in the house. The rungs of the wooden back staircase to Young Charlie's bedroom, which Uncle Charlie sabotages in order to cause Young Charlie to fall, create and accentuate the visual effect of barred or parallel lines. These staircases all lead to or constitute a threatening space, but the black-and-white parallel line design motif itself functions in these scenes as an index of the threatening shadow world that haunts both Hitchcock's protagonist and his viewers.

However, as William Rothman was the first to point out, this visual motif—which he refers to as "the //// effect"—becomes a general feature of Hitchcock's work.[30] More ubiquitous than the cross-hatched or grid motif that can be derived from the mullioned window, the //// effect can also be seen as a variation on the motif of the opaque window, since it is so often conveyed through the parallel lines of blinds against the background of a window frame that doubles the frame of the film or the shadows cast by those blinds on a wall. The figure can be placed alongside, in front of, or behind these lines. Though, of course, this design is a ubiquitous feature of film noir, Hitchcock used it early, and in a characteristically systematic way. The //// effect conveys the double aspect of Hitchcock's narrative universe and suggests, in the context of the pane of glass, both a sense of opacity yet also the possibility of revelation, of seeing through the window to the shadow world. The two possibilities coexist like the two sides of the Janus face. Again, there is a ready analogy between this figure and Hitchcock's cinema screen, which is at once a window that reveals and a screen that obscures, which is why Rothman identifies the //// effect with Hitchcock's authorial signature.

This visual motif is eloquently used by Hitchcock in *Shadow of a Doubt.* After the police detective, Jack Graham, has communicated to Young Charlie that he is conducting a murder inquiry in which her beloved uncle is the main suspect, her last words to the detective as they part in the front yard are, "It's going to be funny when you find out you were wrong." She then turns to the window to look upon what might seem to be a harmonious domestic scene (fig. 35). Her uncle paces up and down on the left-hand side of the window, earnestly engaged in a disquisition with his sister, who sits on the left left-hand side of the room in rapt attention. However, while on the left-hand side of the image lies a cross on the mantelpiece above Emma's head, on the right-hand side Charles exhales a profuse amount of smoke, and in the center hangs a ring on the window blinds, which in the context of the film connotes both the circle of marriage and life and the circle of incest and death. The whole scene is framed by a series of vertical parallel lines (the window blinds) that cut down across it and combine with vertical distortion to elongate Charles into the figure of Nosferatu. The blinds serve as Young Charlie's window into the shadow world, and the frame of the window doubles in the point-of-view shot as the frame of the film itself.

But this device is a general feature of Hitchcock's work throughout his career. The victim arrested at the beginning of *Blackmail* is framed this way (fig. 36), as is Diane in her prison cell in *Murder!* Alicia Huberman is cast in the shadow of the //// effect when we see that she is being poisoned in *Notorious* (fig. 37). In *Strangers on a Train,* as I have already described, the //// effect features prominently in the opening sequence (figs. 16, 17, 18, 19, 20). In *Rear Window,* when one of the characters, Miss Lonely Hearts, is about to commit suicide, she draws the blinds in such a way that both L. B. Jefferies and the film viewer look upon the character in a manner that is veiled by the //// effect (fig. 38). In *Psycho,* the parallel line effect, announced in Saul Bass's credit sequence of interlocking black and white parallel lines, defines the space of the hotel room in the opening scene in which Marion Crane and Sam Loomis (John Gavin) meet, through the omnipresent window blinds against which the characters are framed (fig. 39), and permeates the work as a whole through the slashing diagonal lines created by the motifs of the lashing rain and water from the shower in which Marion Crane is murdered (fig. 45).[31] In *The Birds*, the parallel line effect is created by the way in which the white clapboard siding of the buildings is lit to create shadows and thereby becomes a ubiquitous feature of the visual design of the environment of the film. It signals the manner in which the world of normality, signified by a realistic space, is doubled by the shadow world inhabited by the threatening birds. By the time of his late work *Topaz* (1969), the //// effect is effectively quoted by Hitchcock from his own work in a manner that exceeds any realistic motivation. A Russian spy is eluding his pursuers. He looks out of a window through Venetian blinds by opening the slats and peering through them. Instead of cutting to a point-of-view shot of what the character sees, Hitchcock cuts to a shot that portrays the slats of the window itself. They fill the frame of the film image with an abstract diagonal composition behind which, as it were, the general threat within the world of the film lurks (fig. 40).

The Square or Rectangular Staircase and the Spiral

In *Blackmail*, when the heroine leaves the attic of the dandy whom she has murdered, she is shot from above, walking slowly down a rectangular stair-case that is lit to highlight the //// effect, and at whose center lies a disk that contributes to the sense of a spiraling vortex created in the image (fig. 41). But the motif of the spiral takes on an independent significance in Hitch-cock's work. An overhead shot in *North by Northwest* from the top of the United Nations Building after Lester Townsend's murder creates a spiral vortex effect though the visual design created by the ground-level sculpture that occupies the vanishing point of the image, which is juxtaposed with the //// motif created by the lines of the building (fig. 42). In *Psycho*, after the death of Marion Crane, water "polluted" with blood spirals down the drain, followed by a shot in which Hitchcock's camera spirals out of her dead eye, mimicking the spiral movement of the water and linking the drain and the lifeless eye. The image of the drain and the lifeless eye in *Psycho* makes explicit the function of the spiral in Hitchcock's visual style. In the spiral motif the vanishing point of the image becomes a space of the Hitch-cockian Blot, a "dead" space at the center of the image that causes a kind of visual implosion (see below).

Vertigo is the film where the spiral motif receives its most elaborate development.[32] It defines the meaning of "vertigo" in the film and links the protagonist's acrophobia to the theme of sexual desire. In *Vertigo* again, Hitchcock literally stages an overhead shot of a square staircase spiraling downward, but here he evokes expressionistically the subjective effect of vertigo through the combination of a backward-tracking shot and a forward zoom. This special effect evokes the crisis of the character and creates for the spectator a sense of the implosion of visual space. In the opening credits of the film, Saul Bass's abstract spiral design with a flattened center slowly spins out of a women's eye bathed in a red filter in a manner that links the image of the vortex both to an impassive yet alluring eye that stares back at the onlooker, and to female sexuality (the spiral at once connoting vision, vagina, and vortex) (fig. 43). The image is picked up again in the spiral loop of Madeleine's hairdo, which is a focal point of her allure (fig. 44). But the spiral motif is also writ large in the film. By shooting Scottie's pursuit of Madeleine on the hills of San Francisco, Hitchcock builds a downward-spiraling motif into the overall structure of the chase. In this way, the spiral motif in *Vertigo* is no longer simply a spatial motif, but indicates the spiral of time down which the hero travels or is drawn as he is fascinated and lured by the object of desire.

In the pursuit through the streets of San Francisco, when Scottie does not directly connect with the object he pursues, the spiral of pursuit remains initially, nonetheless, in a state of unstable equilibrium. The slow languid movement of fascination and nascent desire evokes a "subjective" dreamlike experience of time. But in the combination backward track–forward zoom of the vertigo shot, the spiral structure, now embodied in the staircase of the Mission San Juan Bautista, suddenly stretches like a spring whose tension has collapsed. Scottie will never reach his destination. Scottie's vertigo stretches to the breaking point the thread linking his present desire to its future realization. In the spiraling 360-degree camera movement that culminates Scottie's re-creation of Madeleine (discussed in chapter 4), Hitchcock achieves the opposite, mirror effect of the vertigo shot. Instead of being pulled into the vanishing point in a manner that destroys the possibility of any relationship between self and other, Scottie now, as it were, is magically united with his object of desire, in a moment of suspended animation at the eye of a spiral where time is standing still. The camera movement now registers not a moment in time, nor a sense of the loss of time, or time receding, but the utopian sense of an infinite present, as if by achieving his object of desire, Scottie has momentarily transcended the limits of mortality. However, as we have seen, Hitchcock deftly reminds us that this is but an illusion by momentarily transforming the mise-en-scène of the present in Judy's hotel room to a scene from the past in the stable of Mission San Juan Bautista. Exposed to the doubt cast by memory, this imaginary temporal enclosure will inevitably unravel back into a sense of history, of the passing of time, of separation, and of mortality.

The "Hitchcockian Blot"

As I noted in chapter 4, the "Hitchcockian Blot" was named by the Lacanian cultural critic Slavoj Žižek, to describe a characteristic visual design of Hitchcock's films in which a place in the visual field, usually at the central, vanishing point of the image, contains a privileged "object" that functions as a kind of stain or blot that cues the spectator to the disruptive, threatening presence of the shadow or chaos world that subtends the everyday world of appearances and social respectability. The idea of the blot is literalized thematically (though not yet integrated graphically) in an extraordinary shot in *The Street*. The hero, beginning his furtive pursuit of the prostitute in the street, encounters an optician's sign consisting of a pair of spectacles with eyes. As he passes underneath the sign, the eyes of the spectacles open and look back at him and then, after he has passed, they look again at the spectator of the film. The effect of this device is to represent the character as a psychologically diminished, shamed object, the outer gaze of the world turned back upon him. Hitchcock uses a similar device in *Blackmail* as the blackmailer, wrongfully accused of murder, climbs down a rope in the British Museum past the gigantic face of an Egyptian sculpture that looks frontally out of the image. The returned gaze combines with the size of the sculpture to turn the character into a diminished figure whose life is now literally and visually "hanging by a thread."

The "Hitchcockian Blot" might be better termed the "Langian Blot" since it is a device Hitchcock surely learned from Lang. The eponymous Dr. Mabuse (Rudolf Klein-Rogge) in Lang's 1922 film, who has orchestrated a stock market crash, stands still at the center of the image amid a frenzied crowd of speculators. In a sequence from a later Lang film, *The Testament of Dr. Mabuse* (1933), the target of a murder (driving his car) is surrounded by automobiles at a stop sign. Drowned out by the noise of honking horns, he is shot. Lang cuts to an overhead shot as, when the lights turn green, all the automobiles drive on—all, that is, save for one, stationary when it should be moving forward.[33]

These examples illustrate the way that the "blot" involves at once the isolation of a privileged object (or person), and an element of visual design. Sometimes, however, as we shall see in the case of color, the element of visual design, such as a red "stain," may be completely abstracted from any specific "object" of significance. In both these examples from Lang, the blot is not simply discriminated by the vanishing point, but in the contrast between stillness and surrounding movement. Hitchcock seems to borrow the composition of the stock exchange scene in the sequence from *Blackmail* that I have already discussed, in which Alice is an isolated point of stillness at the center of the image as pedestrians move in all directions around her. An image from *Foreign Correspondent* (1940) recalls Lang's conceit from *The Testament of Dr. Mabuse*, where an American journalist pursuing an assassin in Holland notices that there is one windmill in a field of windmills that is moving in the opposite direction from the others, *against* the wind. In *Strangers on a Train*, Guy plays a tennis game watched by a large crowd. Hitchcock cuts to the crowd itself in long shot, as the heads turn back and forth in rhythm with the ball as it is played, and we immediately spot his nemesis, Bruno, sticking out like a sore thumb. Hitchcock's camera zooms in upon him as if to emphasize the extrusion he creates (a shot that can be considered experimental in the context of the period), and he sits at the center of the image, wearing a dark suit, stock still, looking dead ahead.

Lang's films contain a further important feature of the blot. The blot may cue the spectator to the threatening or controlling presence in the visual field, as in the examples above. However, in *Dr. Mabuse,* Lang uses the same kind of visual device to register this sense of threat or control by the external environment as an element of subjective projection or subjective expressionism. State Attorney von Wenk (Bernard Goetzke) plays cards with Dr. Mabuse; Mabuse, occupying the center of the image in a point-of-view long shot, begins to hypnotize him. As Wenk begins to feel the force of his controlling gaze, the image of Mabuse begins to enlarge to close-up in his visual field, occluding the presence of the other cardplayers that surround him. Mabuse here provides a literal embodiment of the idea of the blot as a gaze that is "returned" to the viewing subject from his own visual field in such a way as to undermine his sense of self, insofar as it is sustained by the idea of a physical boundary between the "inner" and "outer." The forward zoom and backward track of the vertigo shot is an exemplary illustration in Hitchcock's work of the subjective dimension of the Hitchcockian Blot that registers Scottie Ferguson's psychological breakdown as an implosion of the boundary between self and world. In *Marnie*, psychological breakdown is registered through the use of the color red, which first appears as a stain in the visual field of the character, and then subsequently suffuses the entire image (see chapter 6).

The attention that Hitchcock pays to this element of visual design is registered by the way in which he orchestrates elaborate camera movements to discriminate the blot, either by a movement toward the vanishing point and the telltale object it contains or a movement away from it. In *Young and Innocent*, a long crane shot takes us over the guests at a hotel dance until it begins to track toward the band at the far end of the dance hall and isolates the drummer whose blackface renders him obviously visible at the center of the image. It finally alights on the whites of his twitching eyes, which immediately reveals to the audience that he is the killer. In *Notorious*, a crane camera from high up on a staircase swoops slowly down on the glittering party held by the ostensibly ideal couple of Alex Sebastian and Alicia Huberman, only to end in tight close-up on the key to the cellar that Alicia clutches in her hand, indicating at once the duplicity that belies the perfect marriage, and the treason that literally lies beneath this glittering bourgeois display, in the stocks of uranium that are concealed there. They are hidden, it should be noted, in some of the very wine bottles that are lubricating the party. In *Rebecca*, when the second Mrs. de Winter dines with her new husband Maxim after she has first arrived at Manderley, Hitchcock begins the scene with a tight close-up of her napkin with the telltale inscription of Rebecca's monogram. The camera slowly pulls back and up, revealing the distance between the couple seated at either end of the long dining table, and the huge formal floral arrangements on the far walls, which signal Rebecca's continued presence in the house. The shot ends in a bird's-eye view that frames the scene with two large black funereal urns, which suggest how the deathly presence of Rebecca in the house bestows an aura of death upon their apparently perfect marriage. Finally, in the opening shot of *Psycho*, which Hitchcock had intended to be a continuous uninterrupted long take, the camera pans (through two dissolves) in a bird's-eye view of Phoenix, Arizona (at 2:43 in the afternoon), zooms in, and then glides down (across a cut) toward the partially opened window of a hotel room largely obscured by a closed blind, alights momentarily (like a bird) on the ledge, and then enters into the room where an "illicit" sexual liaison is taking place. Marion Crane lies prone in a white petticoat, her breasts prominent, looking up at the torso of a standing man whose face we do not see, but whose dark pants and midriff occupy the left-hand side of the frame. The bars of the bed for the //// effect against the wall behind her.

The Merry-go-round and the Circle of Life

The fairground in expressionist cinema is a symbol of chaos, a place where social and sexual boundaries break down. The fairground and the circus form the backdrop to the licentious behavior of the principal characters in E. A Dupont's *Variety*, which ends in tragedy. In *Variety*, the fairground and the circus, like forces of nature, seem to determine destiny. A circular, moving, circus attraction figures prominently in the opening of *The Street*. The specific image of the merry-go-round recurs in *Caligari*, where it occupies a prominent space in the highly expressionist establishing shot at the fairground—for example, in the scene where the heroine, Jane, visits Dr. Caligari in search of her father.

In the short modern story in Paul Leni's tripartite film *Waxworks* (1924), one Spring-Heeled Jack stalks the narrator and his fiancée through a fairground of merry-go-rounds and Ferris wheels.[34] The characters are superimposed on this background, which through the movements on either side of the image creates a kind of vortex into which they enter. In one scene, as Spring-Heeled Jack walks into the frame in pursuit of the protagonists, a Ferris wheel rotates on the left side of the screen as a merry-go-round superimposed on it moves clockwise, and on the right side of the screen another merry-go-round rotates in a counterclockwise direction. Spring-Heeled Jack is drawn into the space in-between. The merry-go-round stands in for the space of the fairground, a public space at once primitive and modern in which sexual and class transgressions occur. But it also functions graphically in perceptual space as an image of kinetic light energy and perpetual motion, a metaphorical figuration of fluidity and change. And in the scene from *Waxworks*, the kinetic movements of the merry-go-round are used to create a kind of perceptual vortex, even while, in the context of the super-imposition techniques used by Paul Leni, the space of the frame remains rather flat.

Hitchcock returns to the motif of the merry-go-round repeatedly in his work. Hitchcock's silent film *The Ring* is set in a fairground and obviously borrows its form and theme from *Variety*. Like *Variety* it tells the story of a love triangle between a girl and two men, one an interloping dandy, the other a more ordinary working-class type who is in love with her. The interloping dandy is a source of allure and the cause of intense jealously on the part of the man who loves her. *Variety* ends tragically—the ordinary man kills the dandy—but in *The Ring* the ordinary man wins the girl back and the dandy leaves. The destabilizing entry of the dandy into the story occurs just after an opening montage sequence, where the place of the fairground is depicted in a Chaplinesque and carnivalesque way as a place of contagion in which the official categories of morality are undercut.[35] The sequence elaborates, pictorially and verbally, on the idea of the merry-go-round and recapitulates both the form and the function of the disorienting fairground montage that opens Dupont's film, as well as the "subjective expressionist" montage from *The Street* I have already described.

The opening montage of *The Ring* depicts a "merry-go-round" of images that create a contagion of meaning. The idea of the merry-go-round is a cata-lyst for a series of visual metaphors that suggest the ideas of loss of control, abandonment, primitive aggression, reversibility, and the dissolution of boundaries evoked by anal-genital humor. The circular movement of the machine is linked to the orifice of the laughing mouth whose "teeth" are "punched" out (anticipating the boxing "ring" that plays a prominent part in the film), and suggests the reversibility of laughter and aggression. The round ass of the coconut man is linked to the mouth by association, and a montage sequence evokes the anal-sadism of being hammered in the ass. A laughing, falling black man picks up the mouth motif and provides a figure (undoubt-edly racist) of a more primitive body, which catalyzes the "primitive" laugh-ter of the audience in the film and of the film, who participate in a veritable merry, go-round of fun. The undermining of the social order implied by this contagion is embodied in the figure of a laughing policeman. It is into this context that the transgressive and incipiently threatening sexuality of the interloping dandy, the third figure in the love triangle of the film, enters.

Later in the film, when the dandy invites the girl for a nighttime assignation for the first time, we again see the merry-go-round as a point-of-view shot from her sight line. In this image, Hitchcock exactly replicates the shot from *Waxworks* that I have already discussed: a merry-go-round on the left of the screen moves in a clockwise direction while another merry-go-round on the right of the screen turns in a counterclockwise direction in a manner that evokes the sense of a vortex into which the gaze is being drawn. The scene then darkens in preparation for the nighttime assignation.

The image and metaphor of the merry-go-round is prominent in two later Hitchcock works that are heavily expressionist in tone—*Strangers on a Train* and *Shadow of a Doubt*. The denouement of *Strangers on a Train* takes place on a merry-go-round as the dandy Bruno fights the hero Guy in a chaotic life life-and-death struggle. But the sequence I want to describe in detail is the prior fairground sequence in which Bruno gratuitously murders Guy's estranged wife (previously discussed in chapter 2), which is largely a sequence of "pure cinema."

Bruno enters the fairground, whose entrance is lit and framed with parallel neon bars (the //// effect). He encounters Miriam and watches in shot/reverse-shot as she speaks of her craving for ice cream and wraps her tongue enticingly around an ice cream cone. "Let's go to the tunnel of love," she declares to her two male companions (suggesting her promiscuity, but also as an implicit "come-on" to Bruno). Bruno follows. We observe from his point of view as Miriam and her companions enter into the space of the fairground, framed on the left by the merry-go-round moving counterclockwise into the image, and on the right by a Ferris wheel moving toward the spectator. The position and movement of these objects—together with the forward momentum of Miriam into the image away from the camera in a point-of-view shot, and the forward momentum of Bruno toward the camera in reverse shot—create the sense of the characters plunging into a vortex. The "movement" into the vortex is interrupted when Miriam's friends try out the sledge-hammer test-of-strength machine. Miriam looks right over her shoulder, then left, suddenly to find that Bruno has magically appeared by her side (like Lang's figure of Death appears to the heroine in *Destiny*). The calliope plays, "Oh you beautiful doll, you great big beautiful doll." Bruno walks forward as the Ferris wheel rotates forward behind him. Miriam watches, entranced, as Bruno powerfully makes the bell ring with the sledge-hammer to win the "cupie" doll. Miriam and friends then mount the merry-go-round (adorned with a cupid) as it plays "The Band Played On" ("Casey would waltz with the strawberry blonde"). Bruno mounts his horse from behind, whose movements (when mounted by Bruno in a suit) suggest primitive, uncontrolled sexuality. Miriam looks back to meet his lascivious gaze, and then he joins them (in a *ménage à quatre*) in singing the song, whose lyrics link the merry-go-round to the waltz, and romance to violence.[36]

They proceed to the tunnel of love as the organ strikes up "Baby Face" ("You've got the cutest little baby face"). Bruno, staring at Miriam, is framed eating popcorn at the center (vortex) of the moving Ferris wheel. The Ferris wheel moves clockwise left to right and into the image, suggesting again forward propulsion, a movement that is picked up in the reverse shot by a similar mechanical motion where the waterwheel at the entrance of the tunnel of love propels Miriam and her friends into it. Bruno follows them into the tunnel, and Hitchcock uses their shadows on the wall to suggest that Bruno, Nosferatu-like, is "taking over" Miriam. Now, on an island isolated from the main grounds, Miriam runs freely across the face of the water, laughing with sexualized excitement, with the Ferris wheel on the left, the merry-go-round in the center, and a third merry-go-round on the right moving in the opposite direction (reworking a visual motif from *The Ring*). While the "Casey" tune plays in the background, Bruno suddenly "appears" again by her side. Using Guy's lighter, he lights up her face to identify her—"Is your name Miriam?"—against the rippling reflecting surface of water bathed in moonlight. She smiles: "Why, yes ... " Then he strangles her. Hitchcock films the strangulation as reflected in her glasses, which have dropped to the ground, and her glasses become the eyes of death, uncannily looking back at her. The strangulation is an embrace, a slow waltz or dance of death to the strains of "The Band Played On," and is framed by the ironic reflection of the nature world in Miriam's glasses. As her body "falls" into the foreground of the reflected image, it gradually becomes a shapeless blur, a nothing, without recognizable visual identity.

The doubling idea of the merry-go-round of life and the merry-go-round of death, or the merry-go-round as the compulsive machine of deathly repetition, and the merry-go-round as a revitalizing waltz of life, is eloquently inscribed in *Shadow of a Doubt*, where aristocratic couples waltz in the round to the "Merry Widow Waltz" in a manner that evokes a never-never land of aristocratic luxury and fulfilled desire (the civilized analogue of the promiscuous fairground). In his musical comedy *Waltzes from Vienna*

(1934), Hitchcock had explored the motif of the waltz, but mainly in terms of the progressive composition of a theme tune that anticipates the role of music in *Rear Window*, rather than in terms of the motif of the dance itself.[37] The specific representation of waltzing couples in *Shadow of a Doubt* is surely inspired by Ernst Lubitsch's representation of this waltz and others from Franz Lehár's operetta in the delirious embassy ball dance in *The Merry Widow* (1934), in which scores of couples whirl in symmetry around a giant ballroom and then advance down a hall of mirrors.[38]

The image of waltzing couples in *Shadow of a Doubt* occupies a surreal space in the world of the film, neither simply imagined nor part of a place where the characters live. It is an image of identical couples that replicates the figure of a circle both in their individual dances and their collective movements. It is a circle of life, romance, and merriment. Yet there is a profoundly mechanistic quality to their movement, as if the figures were puppets rather than people, their movements operating to a preordained scheme. The image seems to anticipate the merry-go-round of *Strangers on a Train* and its theme song (the "Casey" tune) that links that waltz with a mechanism. Again, it is as if the circle of life were a figure of deathly repetition: that life and romance are inhabited by death. Furthermore, the merriment carries with it an aura of nostalgia, as if it represents an imaginary utopia of romance and leisure—aristocratic and Viennese—before the fall. The "Merry Widow Waltz" is repeated four times in the film and becomes the site of the struggle over ownership and interpretation, like the ring that is exchanged between Uncle Charles and Young Charlie in the film. Who controls the image; is this waltz the circle of life or the circle of death?

The first time we see the image of the waltzing couples is in the credit sequence, where Dimitri Tiomkin's score introduces a modernist dissonance into the waltz, and the image of luxury dissolves into the scene of rotting cars by the river from where, as we have seen, Uncle Charlie seems to rise. The second time the waltz occurs is after Uncle Charlie gives his young niece the stolen wedding ring. Young Charlie discovers the initials on the back of the ring that will ultimately reveal its evil provenance, and Uncle Charlie follows Young Charlie back to the family meal with a blank ominous stare upon which the image of the waltz is superimposed. The dresses of the dancers are now visibly edged in black, as if marking the death of the widows and anticipating the resistance of Young Charlie to her uncle. This resistance begins a moment later when she begins to hum the tune and identifies it as the "Merry Widow Waltz." Uncle Charlie's reaction to this is to knock his glass over and break up the meal, as if through her uncanny closeness to his thoughts she has exposed him.

The third time we see and hear the waltz is when Young Charlie discovers the truth about Uncle Charlie from a newspaper article in the Public Library. As she (and the audience) reads the story, which fills the screen, Tiomkin's dissonant "Merry Widow Waltz" leaps suddenly to a thundering crescendo; then, as she gets up from her chair, Hitchcock's camera rises to a bird's-eye view as she walks across a big black shadow, cast by what appears to be a round table (out of view), which looks like a big circular black stain in the field of vision. In fact, she is trapped in an image that proliferates with circles: the library desk, the backs of the chairs, and the circular chandeliers. The image of the waltzing couples appears and connects her with her uncle, as it bleeds into a shot of him pacing the garden. But this time, a female chorus vocalizes the waltz tune. Young Charlie has managed to appropriate the meaning of the image. When her mother hums the "Merry Widow Waltz" the next morning, Young Charlie reprimands her: she has finally got the waltz out of her head.

The final occurrence of the waltz occurs in the denouement of the film. Charlie forces her uncle's hand by donning the ring he has given her and— with the ring prominently displayed on her finger—parading down the staircase in front of assorted luminaries from the parish, to whom Uncle Charlie has been "preaching." Charles, feeling "exposed," resolves to leave town. However, when Young Charlie escorts him to the train he refuses to let her get off. As the train starts to leave, he pulls her toward the open door and they engage in a life-and-death struggle that is, again, portrayed as a waltz or dance of death. Uncle Charlie holds her over the edge of the precipice and she stares into the abyss, but miraculously she pulls away, and somehow it is Uncle Charlie who slips and falls into the vortex created by the differential movements of the oncoming train and the train they are on. This image of the vortex is brilliantly completed by Hitchcock as he superimposes the image of the "Merry Widow Waltz" and its theme, now entirely appropriated by humming female voices. The visual effect here approximates the effect of plunging into a spiral, which anticipates the visual effects of *Vertigo* that Hitchcock achieved by combining a backward-moving camera with a zoom. But here, Young Charlie survives wrestling with the angel of death, and the incestuous circle of death is redefined as the circle of life, though the life that Young Charlie now faces is the dull everydayness of Santa Rosa.

Visual Style

Lovebirds and Death Birds

In the opening intertitle of *Nosferatu*, the title character is explicitly introduced at the beginning of the movie as a death bird: "Nosferatu: Does not this word sound like the call of the death bird at midnight?" The final intertitle concludes: "The shadow of the death bird lifted, as if blown away by the victorious rays of the living sun." *Nosferatu*, as I have noted previously, has a batlike face and avian claws and is compared to other predatory animals.

The "death bird" undoubtedly has a complex provenance that is not simply reducible to this one image. Nonetheless, the figure of Nosferatu conceived as the death bird provides a very direct way to understand the link between sexual predators in Hitchcock's work and the figure of the death bird, which receives its fullest realization in *Psycho* and *The Birds*. In *Psycho*, the main character, Norman Bates, a psychotic murderer, is not simply likened to birds of prey, but to stuffed birds of prey. In his unassuming way, he articulates the key significance of the death bird as the figuration of a nature that is emotionally dead—that is, inhuman, and destructive of the human. The idea of the stuffed bird suggests the absence of the "inner" and this mental opacity is a quality that even living birds suggest. Birds lack the expressive repertoire upon which we might base the ascription of feeling: their beady eyes stare blankly; they seem governed by pure instinct (as in the cliché "birdbrain"). Norman, the bird-philosopher, well understands this: "I don't really know anything about birds," he tells Marion Crane in the parlor scene. "My hobby is stuffing things. You know, taxidermy. I guess I'd just rather stuff birds because I hate the look of beasts when they're stuffed. You know, foxes and chimps. Some people even stuff dogs and cats but, oh, I can't do that. I think only birds look well stuffed, well, because they're *kind of passive* to begin with." If Norman is analogous to a stuffed bird, he is a stuffed bird brought to life, and hence like Nosferatu he is one of the "living dead" whose emotionally numb exterior harbors a blindly destructive impulse that has nothing recognizably human about it. As we have seen, Norman Bates is explicitly likened to birds of prey when he is juxtaposed with the stuffed birds on the walls of his parlor that function as his doubles. Later, when he swoops down on Marion Crane, the stabbing position of his raised knife and his dark costume against the white shower curtain suggest the beak of a gigantic bird of prey (fig. 45).

In *The Birds*, the idea of the death bird is no longer represented simply by analogy with the human, but is literally represented in the form of massing birds that seem to attack human beings for no reason. But the human beings in *The Birds* are also likened to birds. They are possessed with a beady-eyed avian-like stare which seems to provoke the birds to attack, and all the characters at various times seem to don the costume of the death birds, a black-and-white-speckled wool attire that evokes the commingling of black birds and seagulls which constitutes, in part, the horror of the death birds (figs. 25, 46). The force of this analogy of human with bird in both *Psycho* and *The Birds* is to provide a universal figuration of the double. As we have seen, while there is a psychological explanation for Norman Bates's actions, as a death bird, as a monstrous fusion of Norman and mother, he embodies a blindly annihilating and wholly arbitrary force of nature. Equally, while the death birds may represent the presence of alien nature *within* the human or a split-off aspect of human psychology, of unassimilated negative emotion, they also represent a randomly destructive emanation of a nature that is wholly alien to the human. Indeed, because of the way in which the sounds of the birds in the film are "orchestrated" by an electronic score, the birds take on an alien-ness that is beyond nature and evokes the relentless, mechanical energy of the machine.

In both *Destiny* and *Nosferatu*, the figure of Death intervenes in the relationship of a young couple portrayed in a way that might be described as like lovebirds. In *Destiny*, the couple rides in a carriage next to a goose in a basket, and the hero ties his scarf around the goose, presumably to stop it from jumping out, before turning to his fiancée and trying to kiss her, as if capturing his own lovebird. The goose and its owner, an old woman (Mother Goose?), step out of the carriage when Death steps in.

As in the image of the death bird, the idea of the lovebird, and of the birdcatcher, as a man who seeks his mate, has a long and complex provenance. It is canonically represented in Mozart's *The Magic Flute* (1791), whose birdcatching hero, Papageno, is in search of his mate, his Papagena. The metaphor also receives complex elaboration in von Sternberg's *The Blue Angel* (1930), where Papageno's aria "Ein Mädchen oder Weibchen" ("A Girl or Little Wife") is explicitly quoted. At the beginning of that film the Professor's bird is dead, evoking the absence of love; but in the morning after his first night with nightclub singer Lola Lola, her bird chirps merrily as they exchange looks of love. The Blue Angel nightclub is full of birds hanging from the ceiling. As Lola Lola sings "Falling in Love Again" in full shot to the Professor in the gallery, a bird's wing inclines toward her phallically in the foreground.[39]

In both *Psycho* and *The Birds*, Hitchcock makes the metaphor of the lovebirds more explicit, by posing Marion *Crane* and Sam *Loomis* (is a loom/loon) as lovebirds in a hotel room in *Phoenix*, Arizona (fig. 47), and by beginning *The Birds* in a bird shop where Melanie Daniels (the female protagonist), buys lovebirds as she banters with the hero Mitch Brenner. But, as we saw in the previous chapter, Hitchcock also adds a Cockney twist to the metaphor by linking the concept of "bird" to the notion of a sexually desirable female, suggesting that beneath the ostensible innocence of the lovebird lurks promiscuous sexuality.

In both films, the gender complementarity of the lovebirds is threatened by the obscene figure of the death bird, which both embodies and threatens the erasure of difference. In *Psycho*, the death bird is the "stuffed bird," the Norman/mother composite, both male and female, both alive and dead. Swooping down from the gigantic Gothic birdhouse, accompanied by the birdlike screech of Bernard Herrmann's violins, Norman/mother devours Marion Crane in an act of sexual frenzy that is visually inscribed in the beaklike stabbing of the kitchen knife. Marion Crane, the lovebird, ends her life slumped like a bird with a broken neck on the bathroom floor, with a blank, wide-eyed avian stare of death (fig. 48). Equally, the attack birds in *The Birds* are a gender composite, phallic harpies that single out not only the lovebird Melanie Daniels but also and especially the children, the promise of a future that issues from the mating instinct that she embodies. Crucially though, Melanie somehow survives the assault, and thereby represents a glimmer of hope for a procreative future, which the "couple" formed by Sam and Lila (Marion's sister) scarcely provide in their joint quest to discover what happened to Marion in *Psycho*.

The rhetoric of expressionism is as fundamental to Hitchcock's romantic irony as the discourse and rhetoric of aestheticism, to which it is closely allied in his work. However, as I have already suggested in discussing *The Trouble with Harry*, it proved to be an idiom more suited to the articulation of what I called (in chapter 1) narratives of ironic ambivalence, like *The Lodger*, *Suspicion*, *The Paradine Case*, or *Shadow of a Doubt*, or narratives of ironic inversion like *Downhill*, *Blackmail*, or *Psycho*, rather than the essentially comic narratives of romantic renewal such as *The 39 Steps*, *Young and Innocent*, and *North by Northwest*. For the rhetoric of expressionism dramatizes the identity of opposites by emphasizing and exaggerating difference, rather than through emphasizing complementarity and convergence. There is thus a dramatic difference between not only the tone but also the style of Hitchcock's more comic and more ironic works in his black-and-white period. This difference was to disappear once Hitchcock embraced the idiom of color. Color allowed Hitchcock to articulate all the logics that encompass romantic irony, and is thus, as we shall see in the next chapter, partly responsible for the remarkable stylistic unity attached to his later work.

6

Color Design

German expressionism, the defining influence on Hitchcock's style, is identified with the visual repertoire of black and white. Yet Hitchcock embraced color with enthusiasm. Fully half (fifteen) of his American films are completely in color, including both films he made in the 1940s with his independent production company—*Rope* and *Under Capricorn* (1949). *Under Capricorn*, as we shall see, is relatively conventional in its use of color; however, Hitchcock's carefully controlled use of color in *Rope* deserves to be considered experimental alongside the other elements of that film, and it created a precedent for his subsequent practice with color.

Hitchcock approaches color design with the same complexity as his orchestration of visual motifs in black and white. Hitchcock's use of color must be understood as an extension and transposition of his black-and-white expressionist aesthetic into the domain of color, in a manner consistent with his prior embrace of sound as an expressionist idiom. The term *expressionism* in the 'teens was used to describe the bold non-naturalistic, expressive use of color in the work of painters such as Wassily Kandinsky and Franz Marc, who moved increasingly from representation toward abstraction. However, Hitchcock's color expressionism is not expressionist in this sense, in part because by the time he incorporated color into his practice, he had already adapted expressionist rhetoric to the protocols of classical narration. Hitchcock's approach to color design is one that balances the expressive demands of color with the constraints of realism. Furthermore, Hitchcock's color design, like his black-and-white aesthetic, is always motivated by character and narrative events. Hitchcock's use of bold and contrastive color patterns that symbolically express character motivation and theme surely owes a great deal to the pre-Raphaelite colorists, in particular William Holman Hunt (1827–1910) and Dante Gabriel Rossetti (1828–1882), whose work was widely circulated in print form in Hitchcock's youth.

Color does not afford the direct and pervasive articulation of the opposition between light and dark that characterizes black-and-white expressionism and the moral psychology of the double that it articulates, save in the manner that Hitchcock retains the opposition between black and white as one important parameter of color expressionism. At the same time, color offered Hitchcock an expanded and nuanced vocabulary for articulating and commenting upon character and the narrative world of the film. Black-and-white expressionism does not readily allow the ambivalence between the ordinary world and the chaos world to be simultaneously maintained in the image (other than through the forms of visual metaphor and the //// effect explored in the previous chapter). The rhetoric of color allowed Hitchcock to articulate the doubled world of appearances—that is, the way in which the chaos world supervenes upon the world of the ordinary—in a manner that black-and-white expressionism did not allow.

In his use of the color red in films such as *Rear Window, Vertigo,* and *Marnie,* Hitchcock explores the edges of a surrealist aesthetic that he had earlier dipped into through his collaboration with Salvador Dali in *Spellbound,* and in the sequence of the waltzing couples in *Shadow of a Doubt.* Surrealism is the modernist heir to aestheticism in the sense that is it an aestheticism that has become fully conscious of itself. Representation can no longer be considered a displaced expression of the unacknowledged realm of sexuality; it embodies that realm. Surrealism has in common with expressionism the suggestion that a deeper reality lies behind the world of appearances, or the ordinary. However, surrealism displaces the hierarchy of surface reality and shadow world by rendering the unconscious or dream world coextensive or continuous with reality itself. Hitchcock's color aesthetic affords this world a sense of complete realization that is absent from the rhetoric of black and white, precisely because the colors that are indicative of this world can entirely supervene upon an everyday reality depicted on the screen.

In this way Hitchcock's surrealist color design is in some ways closer to the both/and logic of romantic irony than expressionism, where the polarities of identity and difference maintain their separation.

Hitchcock's color surrealism is evident in a film like *Rear Window*, where the everyday white-framed windows and red brick of the Greenwich Village apartments double as a surrealist world of danger and desire. However, it is perhaps most fully articulated in *Vertigo*, where, as we saw in chapter 4, the world of the ideal, or the more than real, becomes identified with reality itself; and in *Marnie*, where the scenes in which Marnie's fantasy erupts upon the world in the color red exceed the boundaries of subjective expressionism to denote a landscape of fantasy that is, for a moment, coextensive with the world. The scene in which Marnie returns to her mother's house in Baltimore, the site of the original trauma that precipitates her hysterical attacks, is marked by one of the most extraordinary compositions in all of Hitchcock's work. Marnie enters in a yellow taxi from the foreground of the image into a corridor of bright red brick houses that stretch back symmetrically toward the vanishing point of the image where the black prow of a ship looms over the lip of the dock (plate 1). This image of Marnie's place of origin doubles as an image of the primal scene, the bright red walls of the house forming a vaginal opening, the gigantic phallic ship looming obscenely in the background as if forced up onto dry land, and Marnie returning under its shadow as if she herself has taken the man's place. The scene suggests in the manner of surrealism that the true reality is a world of fantasy sustained by sexual desire that the world of surface appearances and decorum conceals. This scene is notable among other things for Hitchcock's use of a painted backdrop. This backdrop, like his use of back projection elsewhere in his work, demonstrates his readiness to sacrifice realism for the sake of control over image and overall design, and, in particular, the creation of the characteristic doubleness of the image that was first identified by André Bazin.[1]

I have emphasized the way that color allows Hitchcock to articulate the supervenient or coextensive character of opposites in a way that black-and-white expressionism cannot. But because color expressionism offers a more nuanced and varied vocabulary than the highly articulate but restricted palette of light and dark, it also allows the complementarity between opposites to be represented in a way that expressionism does not readily afford. This complementarity of opposites characterizes the narratives of romantic renewal discussed in chapters 1 and 2, whose form of romantic irony is resistant to the vocabulary and rhetoric of black-and-white expressionism, which drama-tizes division and difference. Thus in Hitchcock's hands, color can express, equally effectively, the logic of complementarity at work in a narrative of romantic renewal such as *To Catch a Thief* or *North by Northwest*, narratives of ironic ambivalence such as *Rear Window*, *Marnie*, or *The Birds*, and the qualities of a dark work of ironic inversion such as *Vertigo*. Indeed, the combination of color and expressionist iconography in Hitchcock's last phase of filmmaking gives that work a particular consistency, even as Hitchcock reprises and perfects all the forms of storytelling he has explored throughout his career.

As Ian Cameron points out, Hitchcock's approach to color, like the other elements of his style, draws upon received practice, in this case the practice of Hollywood colorists.[2] Natalie Kalmus, whose "authorship" of color as the Technicolor consultant on many Hollywood films directly influenced a whole generation of Hollywood practitioners, wrote in 1935 that "the designs and colors of sets, costumes, drapes, and furnishings must be planned and selected just as an artist would choose the colors from his palette and apply them to the proper portions of his painting."[3] She also recommends the "judicious use of neutrals," which "lends power and interest to the touches of color in a scene."[4] In an essay published in 1937, well before his first color film, Hitchcock echoes Kalmus:

> I should never want to fill the screen with color: it ought to be used economi-cally—to put new words into the screen's visual language when there's a need for them. You could start to color film with a boardroom scene: somber panelling and furniture, the directors all in dark clothes and white collars. Then the chairman's wife comes in wearing a red hat. She takes the attention of the audience at once, just because of that one note of color.[5]

In a later interview with Charles Thomas Samuels, Hitchcock makes a simi-lar point by drawing an analogy with his sound practice:

> Color should start with the nearest equivalent to black and white. This sounds like a most peculiar statement, but color should be no different from the voice which starts muted and finally arrives at a scream. In other words, the muted color is black and white, and the screams are every psychedelic color you can think of, starting, of course, with red.[6]

Hitchcock's practice also conforms to Hollywood norms in the way he puts color in his films to enhance our understanding of character and story. For example, Kalmus writes: "We plan the colors of the actor's costumes with especial care. Whenever possible, we prefer to clothe the actor in colors that build up his or her screen personality."[7] Hitchcock's attention to color in costume is borne out by the comments of his longtime collaborator and costume designer, Edith Head, who worked on his color films *Rear Window*, *To Catch a Thief*, *The Trouble with Harry*, *The Man Who Knew Too Much* (1956), *Vertigo*, *The Birds*, *Marnie*, *Torn Curtain*, *Topaz*, and *Family Plot*. Head wrote:

> Hitchcock thinks in terms of color; every costume is indicated when he sends me the script. . . . There is always a reason behind his thinking, an effort to characterize. He's absolutely definite in his visual approach and gives you an exciting concept of the importance of color.[8]

Hitchcock confirms this attention to costume detail in his own report of a shopping trip with Eva Marie Saint, the star of *North by Northwest*. He recommends she be dressed in "a basic black suit (with simple emerald pendant) to intimate her relationship with [James] Mason"; in "a heavy silk black cocktail dress subtly imprinted with wine red flowers, in scenes where she deceived Cary [Grant]"; and in "a charcoal brown, full skirted jersey and a burnt orange burlap outfit in the scenes of action."[9]

In comparison with black and white, color yields far more choice and hence far more elements to control, especially since after *To Catch a Thief* Hitchcock's color films were in the new industry standard widescreen aspect ratio of 1:1.84, as opposed to the old industry standard of 1:1.66. Hitchcock's approach to color design demands first imagining the location as a colorless as well as an objectless space and building up the elements of color design alongside the construction of the mise-en-scène. Within Hitchcock's practice of "coloring" the mise-en-scène, certain objects, like lampshades (plate 6) or flowers, within interiors become privileged bearers of color meaning in the sense that their color can be most readily calibrated without undermining the overall surface realism of the design. Costume in Hitchcock is perhaps the most privileged color index because it is at once attached to character and can be readily calibrated to changes and development in the story. Color in the design of costume extends beyond the clothing of the protagonists to the clothing of the extras who populate Hitchcock's mise-en-scène. By carefully controlling the color worn by his extras, Hitchcock is able to control the color design of public spaces. For example, plate 2 shows the opening shot of *North by Northwest*, in which the clothing of the extras "announces" the symbolic color scheme that pervades the film: red, white, and blue. The color of vehicles, too, becomes readily orchestrated, and Hitchcock obsessively exploits the color of taxis (plate 1), buses, and planes for expressive purposes.

Hitchcock's self-conscious use of flowers is evident in the jokes he makes about it. In his tongue-in-cheek *To Catch a Thief*, John Robie, the suspected "cat burglar," is pursued through a flower market and arrested by the police after having fallen headlong into large bunches of red, pink, and white chrysanthemums—a pointed joke on the use of flowers to convey the colors of warning (because there is really no danger here), and one of the many quips, through "feminine" pink, upon the foolishness attached to Grant's character, and possibly, like elsewhere in the film, upon his sexuality. At the costume ball finale, for example, he is a eunuch. In Hitchcock's late film *Topaz*, American agent Michael Nordstrom (John Forsythe) interrupts the family weekend of a French agent and friend, André Devereaux (Frederick Stafford), in order to get him to help: "Hello Nicole... André... I hope you don't mind me dropping in like this. I wanted to be sure that the flowers were in the room when you arrived," he declares, standing next to a large vase of yellow chrysanthemums that have just been installed in their room.

Yet Hitchcock's color design cannot be discriminated simply on the grounds of his rigor, which after all informs the work of other colorists like Vincente Minnelli. What distinguishes Hitchcock's work is the nature of the rationale that informs that rigor. Kalmus details many of the meanings that are attached to color, such as the opposition between warm and cold colors, which Hitchcock also deploys in his films. However, the emphasis of her thinking about color, an emphasis that informs the work of many Hollywood colorists, is on the emotion or mood that color conveys:

> By understanding the use of color we can subtly convey dramatic moods and impressions to the audience, making them more receptive to whatever emotional effect the scene's action and dialogue may convey. Just as every scene has some definite dramatic mood—some definite emotional response which it seeks to arouse within the minds of the audience—so too has each

scene, each type of action, its definitely indicated color which harmonizes with that emotion.[10]

This use of color predominantly to express emotion underlies the *generic* constraints dictating the use of color in genres such as the musical, the melodrama, and the costume picture through the 1940s and 1950s.

However, while conveying mood and emotion is central to Hitchcock's color practice, he is more interested, as we shall see, in using color to create a system of meaning or signification that supervenes upon the everyday world. This is why *Under Capricorn* is the exception in Hitchcock's work that proves the rule. Hitchcock worked with Michael Powell and Emeric Pressburger's cameraman Jack Cardiff and at least under the nominal direction of Technicolor consultant Kalmus to create what is at times a very luxuriant Technicolor feel in *Under Capricorn*. This is a look that is generically motivated by the costume melodrama but has little relationship to the realism of his other works. Saturated, but diffused colors create mood (plate 3), but lack the kind of organization and control that typically attends Hitchcock's color design. It is not that the colors in *Under Capricorn* lack meaning—pink is clearly attached to the feminine space of the house (though elsewhere it is a color Hitchcock seems to avoid)—but the nighttime blues, and the pink and blue together, convey above all a mood. However, typically Hitchcock will organize color into discrete and solid blocks (as a glance at the color plates will attest), and color will signify emotion rather than seeking to actually purvey or communicate emotion. In short, just as Hitchcock developed visual expressionism into a punning, commentative visual discourse that often involves visual/verbal play, color too, in Hitchcock's hands, is self-consciously deployed as a system of symbolism and meaning. Thus black, associated with night, may evoke negative emotions like fear, whereas white may uplift and ennoble; but in *The Birds*, the commingling of black and white *denotes* the subversion of moral boundaries that is signified by the opposition between black and white.

It is this dimension of Hitchcock's use of color that was to profoundly influence modernist Hitchcockians like the French director Jean-Luc Godard. However, as we shall see, while Hitchcock's approach to color is highly creative in its deployment of the full expressive repertoire that color affords, and even "experimental" in the way he organizes the elements of mise-en-scène to convey meaning, the function of color in his work remains strictly to augment, counterpoint, and clarify narrative meaning and expression. More specifically still, Hitchcock's use of color is calibrated in relation to the conventional moral coordinates of the romantic thriller or melodrama and the identification he invites with his protagonists. To be sure, Hitchcock subverts the conventional meanings of color and, in particular, the conventional ways in which color and color contrasts express gender difference, and in this respect his color design is congruent with his overall aesthetic where the tension between the norms of the romance and an ironic subversion of those norms is consistently maintained. However, whether Hitchcock is asserting conventions or subverting them—and often he is doing both at the same time—his deployment of color consistently serves the amplification of character and the elaboration of story.

The exception that proves the rule is an early scene in his late work *Torn Curtain*, which is particularly self-conscious in its use of color. Sarah Sherman (Julie Andrews) walks to Elmo's bookstore to pick up a book for her husband Professor Armstrong, without knowing that it contains a message about Pi, a spy organization. As she walks along the Copenhagen street, apparently carefree, with a man who unbeknownst to her is an East German agent, they are followed by a moving camera in medium close-up against a background of building walls that are, successively, a saturated solid red, a saturated solid blue (broken by solid yellow lines), and a dark green storefront. The colors in this sequence approach the limits of thematic motivation. To be sure, they suggest the colorfulness of life on the Western side of the Iron Curtain (see below), but it is also as if Hitchcock is simply displaying the color palette that will define the color schemes of the film, in the manner that a modernist filmmaker like Jean-Luc Godard will playfully deploy color in a work like *Pierrot le fou* (1965), where color is divorced from any thematic motivation. But the "autonomy" in color design Hitchcock displays here is the limit point of his approach to color, almost as if the filmmaker is purposely enlivening dull narrative material.

As color theorists, including Kalmus, have long recognized, while colors can be uniquely discriminated and can carry symbolic value by virtue of that discrimination—for example, red conventionally means warning—colors also gain significance by their association and contrast with other colors. It is thus helpful, as Edward Branigan points out, to approach the analysis of color in terms of groupings of systems of color, some of which conventionally have contrastive or opposed meanings and all of which may overlap with one another in different ways.[11] This approach, I believe, is particularly illuminating in relation to Hitchcock's work because Hitchcock himself employs color in such a rigorous, even didactic way. I will identify four main color groupings in Hitchcock's films and demonstrate some of the ways in which Hitchcock uses these groupings in the context of individual films, where color systems take distinctive meanings according to the context in which they occur. None of these color meanings originate with Hitchcock; what is distinctive is their use.

Color and Its Absence

The first contrastive grouping of colors to consider in the context of Hitchcock's work is the opposition between the presence of color, or *colorfulness*, and the absence of color, or *colorlessness*. Absence of color is, literally speaking, the use of black and white and the gradations between them as opposed to the primary colors red, blue, and yellow (and the blue-yellow combination, green) and their derivatives. However, if we take the absence of color less literally, it is also registered by the presence of muted colors, such as pale beige. Conversely, colorfulness as opposed to colorlessness is registered not simply by the use of color but by the deployment of a range of hues in discreet blocks of bright, saturated color. This contrast between colorfulness and colorlessness invokes the emotional resonance attached to the idea of color. Colorfulness evokes in Hitchcock's work gaiety or cheerfulness, warmth or love, depending on the context. Colorlessness, which is ubiquitous in Hitchcock's late works, evokes negative emotions such as anxiety or depression, a sense of emotional vacuity or emptiness, and the loss of identity.

The colors in the flower market scene in *To Catch a Thief*, such as the reds against white, carry particular meanings, but there is also an overall sense of colorfulness in the scene that contributes to the comic spirit of the film where artifice is celebrated and amorality indulged and enjoyed. It is as if in *To Catch a Thief* the idea of a "colorful" incident is rendered in a literal way that culminates in the costume ball at the end of the film which, in narrative terms, is highly gratuitous. *Topaz* is defined, in contrast, by an absence of color. In *Topaz* the international Cold War environment is one in which human beings and human relationships are instrumentalized by all sides of the conflict in the name of national interest. The world of *Topaz*, though it contains color, is essentially a colorless world of black and white, or beige. The conclusion of the film takes place in France where the main protagonist André Devereaux, a French agent, seeks to ferret out the French diplomats who are working for the Russians. The diplomats all wear dark suits and black ties, rendering them visually indistinguishable. In one scene, a culprit is confronted by Devereaux's son-in-law, posing as a journalist, in the belief that he will crack. The two men wear black suits and black ties (over white) and are tightly framed by the light from the three black lampshades in the room.

In another Cold War film, *Torn Curtain*, the opposition of colorfulness and colorlessness is orchestrated across the entire film in a manner that is carefully cued in the opening sequence. *Torn Curtain* begins with a group of international scientists meeting on a freezing-cold cruise ship off Copenhagen. The ship is white, the sea is gray, and an interior scene introducing the scientists dining in winter coats with their knives and forks clanking coldly on their plates is depicted in black, white, and grays. The overall effect of uniformity is underscored by close-ups of the scientists' name tags on nearly identical black-and-white check jackets. When an East German agent enters the dining room to look for the protagonists, Hitchcock shoots the reflection of the diners behind his head in black and white, emphasizing the dullness of the place. Hitchcock then cuts to a couple, the protagonists of the film, Sarah Sherman and Michael Armstrong, making love in bed. A red, yellow, blue, and green checkered blanket is thrown over a gray one, articulating the emotional warmth that is evident in the scene in a manner that temporarily blots out the surrounding coldness of the Cold War environment.

The loss of identity and emotional vacuity that is a generalized condition in the East Germany of *Torn Curtain* is evoked in precise moments in other Hitchcock films through the loss of color. In *Vertigo*, when Scottie Ferguson languishes in hospital in a state of melancholia, his room is an insipid gray that underscores his emotional state. The corridor into which Midge Wood walks when she leaves the doctor's office echoes the sense of emptiness and vacuity of Scottie's room. At the beginning of *Marnie*, the heroine, disguised in a dark gray suit and black wig, walks toward the vanishing point of a symmetrical, close-framed shot of a gray station with a gray gasholder in the background against a gray sky. Marnie seems almost to disappear into the urban gray, suggesting the disappearance of identity that is the subject matter of the film (plate 4).[12]

In *North by Northwest*, the colors in the room occupied by the nonexistent George Kaplan are the insipid and anonymous creams and beiges that may be standard fare in an American hotel suite both then and now but also serve to evoke the nonexistence of its inhabitant. When the hero of the film, Roger Thornhill, reaches the destination in the Midwest where he believes he will at last meet Kaplan (but almost meets his death instead), he is framed from above standing at a crossroads. Not only is the landscape denuded of signs of life (except for a field of dried-up corn), but also of color, save for the beiges and grays of a colorless, vacated wasteland, perhaps suggesting the wasteland that lies at the heart of America but certainly evoking expressionistically the degree zero reached by the character (plate 5). In *The Birds*, the Brenner household, in particular the family's living room, is a space denuded of color and lit by black lampshades (in a living room!), articulating the sense of emotional desiccation and emptiness that is attached to the character of Lydia Brenner after the death of her husband.

Cool Colors Versus Warm Colors or Earth Tones

The distinction between color and colorlessness is a general organizing principle of color design in Hitchcock's work. It intersects and overlaps with a second distinction between cool colors and warm colors or earth tones, and cool colors and hot colors or yellows, oranges, and reds. The distinction between cool colors and warm colors, again, draws upon the emotional valence that is attached to color. Cool colors are colors associated with the left-hand side of the visible spectrum and include most shades of blue but especially pale blue, sky blue, and aquamarine, and certain greens like lime green, and they include the grays if we consider gray a color. Cool colors evoke in Hitchcock's work a sense of emotional detachment or distance, of the domination of reason over emotion that is linked to the depiction both of masculinity and modernity. For example, the landscape of the film *North by Northwest* is dominated by blues and whites right down, as we have seen, to the character and organization of the clothing worn by the extras in the film. This color is embodied in the representation of the United Nations Building in the film, which is an image of the new world order, an order that is controlled by the impersonal and calculating machinations of mostly male agents in dark blue suits, and one in which it is impossible to visually distinguish friend from foe.

Color Design

The grays of *Torn Curtain* in this respect condense the cool colors of *North by Northwest* into the dull grayness of a colorless, fallen world. Sherman follows Armstrong to East Berlin, where she suspects him of being a defector until she discovers that he is working for the Americans. East Germany is portrayed as a colorless world of metallic grays associated with a coldly rational and emotionally deadening Communist regime and images of urban gray modernity are juxtaposed with the gray bombed-out corpses of buildings in a manner that evokes the wider connotations in the film which link the gray modernity behind the Iron Curtain to death or to a state of limbo between life and death. "When we did *Torn Curtain*," Hitchcock states, "we set up a rule: the moment we got into East Germany we'd go to gray and beige tones only." Hitchcock shot the scenes through a gray gauze in order to "reduce the risk of color taking over too much."[13] The colors of Sarah's clothes—green and brown—provide an oasis of warmth and security amidst this gray desert. When Michael finally communicates his true motives and erases Sarah's doubts about him, the couple retreats to a hilltop, a nature world of browns and leafy greens that is rendered artificial in the denatured environment behind the Iron Curtain. She turns to recognize him against an intensely romantic lavender sky, and they kiss amidst the leafy green of the woods.

In contrast to cool colors, warm colors or earth tones are colors such as tan, brown, and forest green that are widely associated with a sense of emotional warmth and the redemptive qualities of the nature world that is linked to the idea of femininity in Western culture through the figure of Persephone, goddess of spring, as well as of Eve in the Garden of Eden. Earth tones in Hitchcock's films signify both redemptive femininity and redemptive nature, which provides safe haven and emotional sustenance. Thus when Margot Wendice (Grace Kelly) in *Dial M for Murder* is exonerated from the false accusation of murder, she appears in a brown coat framed by trees outside the garden window. When Lisa Fremont transforms herself into the helper of L. B. Jefferies in *Rear Window* and goes over to retrieve the wedding ring from Lars Thorwald's apartment, she combines female agency with the reassuring traditional image of femininity embodied in the postwar new look. Her costume unites elegance and redemptive femininity embodied in an autumnal floral design on a white background (plate 6). When Judy Barton in *Vertigo* dates Scottie Ferguson, before her true identity is finally exposed, he first sees her wearing an olive green wool skirt and top, and she later sports a brown sweater and full green skirt. When Lydia Brenner finally reciprocates the affection of Melanie Daniels at the end of *The Birds*, she changes from the black-and-white wool coat and gray sweaters she has worn throughout the film and dons a coat of redemptive brown. Roger Thornhill's mother in *North by Northwest* also wears a brown coat, in keeping with the tone of a film which renders the kind of mother-son relationship that is elsewhere so oppressive in Hitchcock's films as a source of comedy. The redemptive role of Sarah Sherman in *Torn Curtain* is defined not simply by her association with color but by the fact that she wears earth tones, and her green dress is keyed to the one or two trees that grow in the desolate gray landscape of East Germany. The female contact Armstrong meets from the Pi spy organization lives in a rustic brown farmhouse and wears a floral dress of warm earth tones. The field behind the house where Armstrong meets an American agent appears in a long shot as a green oasis in a colorless, desolate landscape. The nature world where they reconcile is an oasis of earth tones within the urban gray. In the *Trouble with Harry* the redemptive earth tones of the nature world are writ large across a film that is set in a sleepy, leafy New England hamlet where the discovery of a corpse, and the relationship that each of the protagonists is revealed to have to it, serve as an occasion for romantic and social renewal.

As this discussion already suggests, the opposition between cool colors and earth tones often serves to dramatize sexual difference in Hitchcock's work: a cool, rational, but sometimes rather rigid masculinity versus a warmer, emotionally sensitive, intuitive femininity. Where the couple is introduced beneath a multicolored blanket in *Torn Curtain*, on top of the blanket underneath their heads (which are barely visible and cannot be individuated by gender), lie a blue (male) jacket and a brown (female) jacket. In *To Catch a Thief*, John Robie consistently wears blue, and in two key scenes where he flirts with the opposite sex, the color schemes oppose his blue to the pale pinks of his female companions. In the first scene he takes a spin with Danielle Foussard (Brigitte Auber) on a boat. She wears a pink top with a red dress. Her pink meshes with the rocky shoreline; his blue, in contrast, mirrors the sea and sky. As her costume suggests, pale pink mediates between warm colors or earth tones and the hot color red that poses danger, while both colors are linked to femininity. The red of her dress inflects the complementarity of blue and pale pink toward the starker, dramatic contrast of blue and red. In contrast, in a later scene with Francie

Stevens on the cliffs above the sea, Grant and Kelly share a chicken and double entendres: "Do you want a leg or a breast?" He is dressed in gray, complementing the blue sky and the metallic-colored sports car she is driving. She wears a pale pink top covered in a redemptive white leaf motif that complements both the cozy tan interior of the open car and, elsewhere, the surrounding landscape (plate 7). While the idea of sexual difference is articulated through this color scheme, this difference is by no means oppositional or clashing; rather, the cool colors and brown or tan tones are complementary as befits this narrative of romantic renewal.

Hitchcock explores the opposition between male blues and female earth tones again in *The Man Who Knew Too Much* (1956). The opening scene of the film contrasts a tan-colored outfit worn by Jo McKenna to the blue jacket of her husband Ben McKenna. The differences between these characters, who are American tourists in Morocco, are marked in the relationship they bear to their environment and the dangers it harbors for them. Ben is very trusting, freely sharing his background with the mysterious stranger, Louis Bernard, who rescues them from embarrassment when their son accidentally rips the veil from the face of a Muslim woman. Ben's willingness to talk about himself is less an index of an emotional sensitivity than the self-centeredness that, as I noted in chapter 2, renders him blind to his environment. Jo is more cautious, berating him for being too open, but her caution reflects the fact that she is more adaptable and hence more attuned to her environment and the threats it harbors, in contrast to Ben who is rather rigid and inflexible. The tan-versus-blue color scheme of the couple articulates the opposition between Jo's groundedness and Ben's lack of adaptability and awareness of his environment, in part, by being precisely calibrated to the environment that surrounds them. In plate 8 the color of the blue-gray suit worn by Ben is picked up in the road behind them, whereas Jo McKenna's tan outfit matches the sand of the desert and the Moroccan houses and the interior space of the cart. The opposition in color here is more dramatic than the scene I described from *To Catch a Thief*, since the patches of color are both darker and more saturated. There is perhaps a more emphatic sense of gender difference established here, even as the film will strive to achieve gender complementarity.

However, Hitchcock also complicates and inverts these color conventions. In *Under Capricorn*, he makes complex use of the opposition between warm and cool colors. As we have seen, the house that harbors the troubled marriage of stable boy Sam Flusky (Joseph Cotten) to aristocrat Henrietta Flusky (Ingrid Bergman) is bathed in a blue and pink glow (plate 3). The blues are associated with the hues of the night and the exterior of the house; the pinks emanate from within, especially from the large upstairs window that houses the heroine. This contrast is in keeping with a dramatization of the relationship of opposition and complementarity between male and female, between coldness and warmth, between exterior and interior, between the brooding, latently violent Sam Flusky and his wife Henrietta, physically and emotionally "imprisoned" inside Minyago Yugilla. When the dashing aristocrat Charles Adare (Michael Wilding) arrives at the house as a catalyst for change, he wears a blue jacket that also conforms to the conventional colors of masculinity, but these color schemes shift. While Henrietta wears pink elsewhere in the film—most notably, the pink heart-shaped bonnet she wears when she makes a public confession of her role in a killing that her husband took responsibility for—Sam also sports pink streaks on a black waistcoat, suggesting that in spite of his apparent darkness of character he harbors a strong identification with his wife. Adare changes from a blue jacket to a green one, as he takes on the role of redeeming Henrietta Flusky from her condition of mute inaction, and Sam's black and gray outfit alternates with earth tones, as it becomes apparent that he is not the monster he appears to be toward Henrietta but has her well-being at heart.

If men in Hitchcock may don redemptive earth tones, women wear cool colors, too. When, in *The Man Who Knew Too Much* (1956), the strange Mrs. Drayton befriends the McKenna's young son Hank just prior to kidnapping him, Jo McKenna wears a pale blue pantsuit when she, too, is afflicted with some of her husband's sense of blindness to his environment. In contrast to Jo, it is Mrs. Drayton who now wears a tan suit, appearing ironically in the false guise of the redemptive mother. However, when women wear blue in Hitchcock's films it usually signals something more powerful than Jo McKenna's moment of emotional detachment or blindness, for it is also linked to the representation of female sexuality. Hitchcock often dresses his female characters in close-fitting, cool-colored "masculine" suits, which suggests that the hypercoolness of this female persona is proportional to the dangerous sexuality that lies beneath her veneer of civilized deportment, a threat that, as we shall see, is associated with the color red. The gray tailored suit worn by the figure of Madeleine in *Vertigo* epito-mizes this persona. Grays in *Vertigo* connote more than a cool deportment that harbors a mystery beneath; they are also related to death in the form of the grays of the graveyard wandered by Madeleine, who is ostensibly pos-sessed by the ghost of Carlotta. Thus *Vertigo*'s grays help to cast the shadow of perversity upon the representation of sexual desire in the film: the repre-sentation of death and female sexuality as an object of desire are entwined (plate 9). In *The Birds*, the heroine of the film, Melanie Daniels, wears a tailored wool suit of cool lime green that echoes the coloration of the love-birds in the film. Her lime green suit combines with other features of her self-presentation—her lipstick, nail varnish, fur coat, and gestures—to evoke a sense both of urban sophistication (rather out of place in Bodega Bay), through a cool and hence provocative female sexuality, and an avian-like posture (plate 10). Female sexuality is also linked to death in *The Birds* through the doubling between Melanie Daniels, as a lovebird, and the death birds described in chapter 5. Indeed at the film's opening, when Melanie courts Mitch, Melanie wears the black-and-white speckled costume associ-ated with the death birds (see below).

Hitchcock's *Frenzy* subjects the association of earth tones with redemp-tive nature and redemptive femininity to a systematic ironic reversal. In the opening sequence of the film, a high-angled shot takes in the massive black-stained London embankment overlooking a filthy brown Thames where a crowd is gathered outside the imposing gray neoclassical façade of the Greater London Council (GLC) building. The crowd standing on the embankment is dressed in browns and blacks save for a few patches of red. A stentorian official intones:

"Bliss was it in that dawn to be alive," as Wordsworth has it. Brook lime and flag iris, plantain and marsh marigold rioted on the bank, and kingfish-ers darted about, their shadows racing over brown trout... Well, ladies and gentlemen, I am happy to say that these ravishing sights will be restored to us again in the future. Thanks to the diligence of your local authority, all the water above this point will be clear. Clear of industrial effluent, clear of detergents, clear of the waste products of society with which for so long we have poisoned our rivers and canals. Let us rejoice that pollution will soon be banished from the waters of this river and that there will soon be no foreign bodies...

At this point we are alerted to a woman's body that floats in the filthy brown water facedown by the embankment. In a closer shot, where the concrete embankment gives way to mud, we see she has been strangled with a distinctive brown-and-white necktie (plate 11). The government official exclaims, "I say, it's not my club tie, is it?" Moments later we see Richard Blaney putting on the same tie, falsely implicating him in the murder which has actually been committed by the psychopathic Bob Rusk, who happens to be a dead ringer for the politician.

Gorhem Kindem points out that the ubiquitous browns of *Frenzy*, to which we may add their association with black and whiteness, suggests the overwhelming presence of pollution.[14] The pompous and grandiose government official articulates the fantasy of a pollution-free environment, but the camera reveals that the pool of London presided over by the pompous official is like a cesspool. The corpse of a dead female prostitute floats in this cesspool with its ass exposed in a manner that links the theme of pollution to the body of the woman and to the anus. This imagery, reworking Hitchcock's rhetoric of horror I have described in earlier chapters, articulates a range of associations that precisely invert the redemptive connotations of earth tones in relation to female sexuality. Here Hitchcock draws a metaphorical equation between the pool of London as cesspool and the body of the prostitute as diseased or corrupted nature. The London revealed by Hitchcock's camera is metaphorically like a "dirty whore." This imagery may seem to implicate Hitchcock in misogyny. But if London is like a "dirty whore," the politician in pinstripes is the whore's pimp. The clean masculine façade of the GLC, echoed in the posture and pronouncements of the stentorian public official, which function (like the embankment) to keep the ostensibly feminine waters of pollution at bay, is merely a façade. The pollution comes not from a feminine other but from within. The equation between the politician and the murderous dandy, Rusk, makes clear that corrupted nature, embodied in the corpse of a prostitute, is a product of (male) civilization rather than being its antithesis. For it is (male) civilization's attempt to contain and control nature that pollutes or corrupts it; it is Rusk who turns women into corpses.

The meaning of earth tones is inverted in a different way in *Vertigo*. Judy Barton, playing Madeleine possessed by a ghost from the past, first appears to the eyes of Scottie Ferguson in a costume of black, swathed in a shawl of deep jade, edged with black, which stands out prominently against the deep red background of Ernie's restaurant. Much later in the film, when Scottie re-creates Judy as Madeleine, she is bathed in the pale jade light emanating from the neon sign outside her seedy hotel (plate 12). As Scottie embraces this reincarnation of Madeleine, the camera pans around them to silhouette their figures against this same jade light in a manner that wholly abstracts them from the hotel room they inhabit. Although green, jade is a "cool" green rendered decidedly unlike the earth tones that green customarily evokes. This jade green light was derived from the London stage of Hitchcock's youth: "I remember the green light—green for the appearances of ghosts and villains."[15] Perhaps pale jade is associated with ghostliness because it is close to the color of mold and hence evokes the presence of death. This color is used consistently throughout Hitchcock's work. In *Rope*: the jade color of a neon sign, alternating with red, bathes Phillip and Brandon's apartment when Rupert Cadell identifies them as killers at the denouement, and turns Phillip's face, in particular, into a pasty, deathly green. A jade-green light bathes the night sky of *To Catch a Thief* in a ghostly hue as the phantom-like cat burglar prowls. Milly (Margaret Leighton), the sinister housemaid in *Under Capricorn,* sports a face of pasty jade-green as she tries to poison Henrietta Flusky, and a very blue jade, perhaps better described as a turquoise, is also the color worn by Mark Rutland's sister-in-law Lil, another sinister "housemaid," in *Marnie.* Like Mrs. Danvers in *Rebecca*, Lil jealously guards the memory of her sister and fulfills household functions in her absence, and like Milly, she harbors designs on the man of the house and is jealous of his wife.

Hot Colors: The Warning Series

The "warning series" consists of bright, saturated, and solid yellow, orange, and red, either individually, in sequence, or combined in the same image to indicate progressively greater degrees of danger. Often Hitchcock's use of these colors, especially red, is highlighted in the image via a contrast with white and sometimes with blue. By using hot colors to convey caution or danger, Hitchcock is obviously drawing upon universal associations between red and blood, and yellow or red and fire. The basic significance of this color patterning is to warn of the danger posed within the world of the film to the central protagonist, and its use in this respect is a ubiquitous feature of Hitchcock's color design. The close of *Torn Curtain* makes a knowing reference to the colors of warning as Sarah and Michael, desperate to escape from East Germany, are trapped in an opera house. Michael looks at the yellow and red fire blazing at the center of the ballet set, which is an index of the danger they are in, and responds to this warning with the cry of "Fire!," thereby effecting a means of escape. The use of red against white (and the warning series as a whole) is an index of the shadow world in Hitchcock, the life-threatening world that subtends the apparently benign world of appearances, self-consciously and ironically contrived by Hitchcock as a species of theater. In this respect, red in Hitchcock's color films assumes the role of the //// effect discussed in chapter 5, and the warning colors often accompany it. For example, in the opera scene from *Torn Curtain*, the flames from the fire are abstractly rendered as a parallel series of red, pink, and white wavy lines against a red background.

The warning series relates to Hitchcock's protagonists in two distinct ways. Sometimes, where a protagonist is wearing the warning colors, it may represent the fact that they are a target of danger, as when Eve Kendall wears an orange dress in the final sequences of *North by Northwest*, or Babs Milligan (Anna Massey) wears an orange dress just before she is murdered by Rusk in *Frenzy*. Elsewhere, the red clothing worn by a protagonist or the presence of warning colors within the environment serves to signal the fact that the character or their environment is a threat. Thus when Jo McKenna first spots Mr. and Mrs. Drayton, who abduct her child, in *The Man Who Knew Too Much* (1956), Mrs. Drayton is wearing orange against the white suit of her husband, who stands behind her in the image. Usually the context is clear as to which of these functions the warning series is performing. A further distinction may be drawn between the objective and subjective functions of the warning colors. In these examples the warning color is objective, indexing something threatening or threatened, but a warning color may also indicate "expressionistically" the mental state of a character. *Frenzy* provides an extraordinary illustration of this when Richard Blaney loses a bet on a horse and, in a close-up, crushes the grapes he is eating beneath his foot (a literalization of the "sour grapes" that afflicts the character). This shot is followed by an "insert" shot of a red double-decker bus that looms in the image, moving in the same direction as the character. Obviously the bus could be realistically motivated by its proximity to the pavement, but the shot in fact exists purely to cue the color red and hence index Blaney's rage.

The colors of the warning series may pervade the image, but there is also a very specific way in which Hitchcock incorporates these colors into his overall visual design and that is in the form of the "Hitchcockian Blot" discussed in chapter 5. A signal illustration of the use of color to register the Hitchcockian Blot takes place in *Rear Window* where Lars Thorwald, the suspect in a murder, lights up his cigarette in an otherwise darkened room and thereby reveals to L. B. Jefferies and Lisa Freemont, who are tracking his actions, that he is purposely hiding from view. His menacing presence is signaled by the red glow of his cigarette in an otherwise empty image. In the opening shot of *Marnie*, the focus of our gaze as Marnie walks away from us toward the vanishing point of the frame is a yellow handbag that is tucked under her arm. We soon learn that it contains stolen money, and it resembles in its contours at once a fortune cookie and female genitalia. This yellow bag, a stain in the visual field, functions as the Hitchcockian Blot par excellence and we are led, as it were, to this vanishing point by a red platform line along which the protagonist walks (plate 4).

Two striking camera movements in *Frenzy* use a color field as their target. *Frenzy* opens with an aerial shot of London, in which the camera tracks down to the Thames River and along toward the pool of London. As the arches of Tower Bridge raise, allowing the camera to enter, a tugboat passes across the image belching black soot. This movement recurs as the camera swoops down on the stentorian official in front of the GLC, and is completed, in a sense, by the shot of the upturned corpse in the Thames. The whole movement is one of penetration into filth, into the black soot, and ultimately into the upturned female corpse, a pollution that ruptures the official façade to reveal the perversity or "chaos world" beneath. A later camera movement reverses this. The killer Rusk takes his second victim to his upstairs room where we know he will commit a sexual murder when he says to his victim, "You know, you are my kind of woman." But rather than entering the room, the camera slowly withdraws (in silence) down the red staircase (which also forms the //// effect) that stands in, as it were, for the unseeable and unrepresentable act occurring "beyond." A man carrying a sack of potatoes (and who is Rusk's ironic double, in the everyday world, since Rusk will place his victim in a potato sack) walks across our visual field. This movement allows Hitchcock to cut invisibly from inside the house to the outside world and continue the camera movement all the way across the street in a manner that takes in the everyday, anodyne world of gray colors and ambient sounds, of which the ordinary façade of Rusk's obscene lodging place forms a part.

Often Hitchcock will simply put an object of warning color at the vanishing point, or place an extra dressed in warning colors that foreshadow a threat to the protagonist in the future or beyond the frame of the visible world. For example, as Roger Thornhill approaches the United Nations Building, his yellow taxi pulls up into a frame that is entirely shot in the cool blue (and white) colors of the film. We see the imposing modernist façade of the UN building rising obliquely on the right of the image and the steps up to the plaza bisecting the image in the foreground in a manner that arguably evokes Hitchcock's parallel line motif. In the precise center of the shot, amidst all the people milling about on the plaza and dressed in cool colors, is a man exercising, dressed entirely in red. Similarly, in the shot where Melanie Daniels arrives at Bodega Bay, a cleaning man, clad in red, occupies the exact center of the image. Hitchcock's approach to visual design in shots such as these (and I want to emphasize that these are not isolated instances) suggests the extent to which Hitchcock approaches a "modernist" privilege of form over content—that is, the purpose of the man outside the United Nations or the man sweeping the stairs is purely to provide a splash of red.

Both *To Catch a Thief* and *The Birds* contain a shot where the entire image becomes a pretext for visual design. A robbery has just taken place in the hotel where John Robie, Francie Stevens, and her mother are staying, and Robie looks down on the plaza in an overhead point-of-view shot as a man leaves the image at the top of the frame. The spectator sees in this point-of-view shot a series of white tables and chairs geometrically organized against the background floor of the yellow brick plaza and, at the center of the image, a red chair cushion indicating the vanishing point of the image. The visual design of the image signals for the spectator who reads it the presence of the threat (plate 13).

When Melanie Daniels arrives at Bodega Bay to deliver lovebirds to Mitch Brenner and continue her courtship, she stops to ask directions to the Brenner household at a hardware store. The store is portentously decked out in Hitchcock's warning colors of yellow and red on white that are only intensified within the claustrophobic interior, which anticipates the many images of entrapment in the film. Melanie inquires about the name of the Brenner girl and, unsure, the owner of the store turns for confirmation to Harry, who is out back. From a shot of Melanie looking, Hitchcock cuts to a point-of-view shot of the back of the store: a graphic configuration of the colors of danger. Harry, offscreen, responds with the wrong name. In this strangely jarring moment, what Melanie sees, together with the spectator, is a visual array that seems to defiantly look back at her as if putting her own identity into question. The items cluttered within Melanie's visual field, filling every inch of space, provide a kind of visual correlative to the cluttered massing of the birds later in the film, in whom the returned gaze is given a deadly embodiment that literally causes her breakdown (plate 14).

The Birds provides a good example of the systematic way in which Hitchcock uses the warning series where its central use is keyed to the anticipation and arrival of the birds. When Melanie Daniels drives through the town of Bodega Bay, having been "sent off" by the intimidating figure of Annie Hayworth (Suzanne Pleshette), perched in red by her red mailbox, she is framed portentously by the yellow sign of Bodega Bay in the background and a red stop sign in the foreground. Other red signs adorn the colorless sidings of the stores, and the windows of Tides Restaurant, where Melanie repairs with Mitch after the first bird attack has caused her to bleed, are framed in red against the white siding. In the birds' first massed attack at Cathy Brenner's birthday party, red, orange, and yellow balloons festoon the house (together with white and blue), which the birds pop in their attacks. They stand out against the white siding, which also serves to register Hitchcock's //// motif. In the birds' second attack the school children are singled out as targets in their clothing of reds and yellows against blues and whites. In the third attack, at the Bodega Bay gas station, the gas station itself is arrayed in black and white and is then ignited by a yellow line of flame. From a literal bird's-eye view, the conflagration, framed by the red-tiled roofs against white buildings, suggests a target area.

Just as Hitchcock orchestrates the relationship between cool colors and earth tones, cool colors and the warning series are defined in relation to each other. In *North by Northwest*, the cool blues and whites of the Cold War landscape combine with the warning series, in particular red on white, to create an overall color scheme which in general terms evokes the danger that looms in this cool rationalized world for his protagonist, but also more immediately evokes the colors of the American flag prominently displayed at Grand Central Terminal and writ large on the landscape of the film in the manner that the faces of the American presidents are inscribed in the natural landscape of Mount Rushmore. The identification of the colors of the film with those of the American flag evokes the surface patriotism of *North by Northwest* that orchestrates the rescue of the heroine on the cliff of Mount Rushmore with the defeat of the villains, who seek to undermine American national security. At the same time, the color design of red, white, and blue is distributed equally between the representation of the "family" of spies that centers upon Vandamm and Leonard (shown in a high-angle interior shot pacing across a red, white, and blue carpet), and the officials of the CIA, headed by the Professor, who sit in their blue and gray suits and white shirts in an office of red leather chairs with an American flag in the corner. These respective groupings are visually interchangeable in the film, reflecting the way in which they both seek to destroy Roger Thornhill: Vandamm through actively wishing to kill him, thinking he is an American agent; the Professor by allowing Vandamm to continue to believe this fiction, which also has, as its consequence, the targeting of Roger Thornhill by the American police, who wrongly believe him to be a murderer. Indeed, given that Vandamm believes that Thornhill threatens his life, the Professor's cold indifference to his fate, later echoed in his treatment of Eve, seems to render him more culpable.

In a similar way, in *Topaz*, as Lesley Brill points out, Hitchcock manipulates national colors, in the context of his wider use of color symbolism, to articulate the ambiguity of Cold War politics and allegiances and the ironic way in which all sides instrumentalize human beings in the name of national interest.[16] Here the blues of *North by Northwest* and the emphatic grays that pervade *Torn Curtain* give way to an essentially colorless urban landscape of washed-out beiges and grays inhabited by men in dark suits and black ties who all look the same across the international arena. Blue and white is central to the color schemes of the flags of three of the central countries in the film—America and France, who are ostensibly allies, and Cuba, whose people struggle against their government. While red is associated most emphatically with the color of the Russian flag, linking red to the threat of Communism, the stars of the Russian flag are present in the colors of the Cuban flag, and the color red is echoed in the red hair of the bodyguard of the Cuban leader Rico Parra (John Vernon) and the briefcase containing the secrets of Russian nuclear weapons installation. Also, the French double agent Jacques Granville (Michel Piccoli) wears a burgundy red dressing gown in the scene before he is finally exposed.

At the same time, the color red carries the more general connotation of warning and danger that cuts across national distinctions. For example,

Parra's bodyguard is a figure who threatens Franco-American agent André Devereaux; the briefcase is clearly a "hot" item; and when Granville wears red he is about to send a fellow double agent to his death. While the French flag echoes the colors of the American and Cuban flag, the French, as Donald Spoto points out, are associated with yellow through topaz, both a yellow stone and the French-based spy organization.[17] Yellow links the French to the sickle and hammer of the Russian flag, and yellow flowers are to be found in Granville's room, but yellow is also associated with Philippe DuBois (Roscoe Lee Browne), a French agent who undertakes to steal the red briefcase from the Cuban delegation to the United Nations. The color scheme of *Topaz* not only exploits the relationship of identity and difference between the different national flags, it also exploits the ambiguity that characterizes Hitchcock's deployment of the warning series. For example, France, depending on the context, is both threatening and threatened.

Over and above the role that red, and in particular red against white, plays in signaling danger, red on white is a pervasive index of the threat posed by female sexuality in Hitchcock's films. Here, too, Hitchcock draws upon deep-rooted cultural associations and iconography that link whiteness to feminine purity and virginity, and red to menstrual blood and thence to the threatening dimension of female sexuality. Men in Hitchcock's films who appear threatening are occasionally associated with red, as in Granville's burgundy smoking jacket in *Topaz* or the red carpet that adorns Gavin Elster's office in *Vertigo* as he lords over Scottie Ferguson. However, where female characters are threatening they will invariably adopt a red costume, and their threat is tied to their fascination or allure.

In *North by Northwest* Eve Kendall wears a dark red dress that merges with the red carpet of the hotel lobby where Roger Thornhill finds her, having survived an almost certain death from the crop-dusting plane. In *Torn Curtain*, when Sarah Sherman, who elsewhere in the film wears redemptive earth tones, begins to threaten Armstrong's mission by her presence, she appears in a red robe, though it is worn over a white nightgown that demonstrates the underlying purity of her motive. In *Dial M for Murder*, Margot Wendice wears a full-length, bright red dress, with red lace top, as she conducts her affair with Mark Halliday (Robert Cummings) under the nose of her smooth husband Tony (Ray Milland). In *Marnie*, the character of Lil, who threatens the marriage between Marnie Edgar and Mark Rutland, wears yellow when she first appears in the film, red at the wedding of the protagonists, and orange when she brings to their dinner party a man who has the potential to expose the fact that Mark is harboring a thief. In *The Birds*, Annie Hayworth, a former girlfriend of Mitch Brenner, the hero, is portrayed as a threat to Melanie Daniels, who comes to court him: in a portentous shot, she follows with her glance the departing Melanie while wearing a red sweater, with her arm perched on a red mailbox in front of her white clapboard house. Later, when they are together and the threat she poses has abated, Annie wears a white bathrobe with a red trim—just the hint of danger.

In two of Hitchcock's films, *Vertigo* and *Marnie*, the colors of red and red on white take on a pervasive meaning in relation to female sexuality. I have already noted the manner in which cool colors in *Vertigo* convey a relationship between female sexuality and death. This association is further cemented through the role of the color red, which links female sexuality and danger. Scottie first sets eyes on Madeleine in her black dress and jade satin wrap in the glorious saturated red surroundings of Ernie's restaurant, bedecked with red and white flowers. The posy carried by Judy as Madeleine consists of red rosebuds against bluish greenery against the background of a white doily (plate 9). Scottie observes the same posy in the painting of Carlotta as it is looked at by Madeleine, where it clearly evokes female sexuality. Carlotta also wears a ruby necklace which, later in the film, Judy Barton will put on, unwittingly conveying to Scottie the fact that she was really acting the part of Madeleine possessed by Carlotta in order to trick him. In the context where blues and reds are combined in the film to evoke female sexuality in *Vertigo*, the color violet, as a cross between blue and red, is a variation on the theme. In the opening credit sequence, the spiral motif designed by Saul Bass that evokes at once the spiral of vertigo, the image of an eye, and an image of female sexuality begins in violet. Later in the film, when Judy Barton resolves not to tell Scottie who she really is (although the spectator now knows), Judy herself wears the color violet, which crudely clashes with the red background of Ernie's restaurant in a manner that underscores the difference between Judy Barton and Madeleine Elster.

Marnie, unlike *Vertigo*, is a story that is focalized throughout from the standpoint of the heroine. The suffusions of red in the film, which "flash" like a red light on the face of the heroine, present the most sustained use of subjective expressionism in Hitchcock's work. Hitchcock had earlier experimented with red suffusions in the sequence in *Rear Window* where L. B. Jefferies defends himself from Lars Thorwald with flashbulbs that cause Thorwald to "see" red. The red suffusions in *Marnie* are a symptom of Marnie's disturbed mental state, which is connected to a repressed childhood trauma that has caused her frigidity. Part of the difficulty audiences had and have with *Marnie* is due to Hitchcock's invocation, in this late classical Hollywood film, of an earlier aesthetic of high expressionism where the color effect intrudes non-naturalistically into the mise-en-scène. Each figuration of the trauma is constructed in terms of a shot/reverse-shot point of view. Marnie actually perceives the color red in a manner that, realistically motivated by an element in the mise-en-scène, also carries a symbolic value, by virtue either of the nature of the triggering object or the context in which it occurs. Then, in the reverse shot, this color is superimposed as a flash of red light upon her horrified reaction in a manner that violates spatial realism in order to give concrete embodiment to the character's psychological state. The flash of red light at once denotes the psychologically "inner," but also suggests a force that comes from without. It is a response of the character to her environment, but it is also an overtly commentative act of narration.

The link to Marnie's childhood is established in the first occurrence of the trauma when she visits her home in Baltimore and stiffens with horror at the sight of the phallic red gladioli arrayed against the white curtain (also the //// effect) in the front room of the house. Later, she "sees" colors again as, half asleep, she reacts to a nightmare provoked by the knocking of the shade pull on the rain-swept window of her room. This nightmare, which stages, in dissociated elements, the scene of her original trauma, is repeated much later, more vividly, in Mark's house. But Marnie's reactions first become visible to her obsessive suitor and self-appointed therapist, Mark Rutland, in his office, when she spills ink on her white sleeve as she is about to write. This shot is an abstract literalization of the blot of red on white in the center of the image, which also serves to register the way in which Marnie's hysteria places her outside the realm of language and the authority of the word, the mastery of which she otherwise "masquerades" with such aplomb. Later, Marnie reacts in horror to the thunder while working at Mark's office. The red suffusion is now projected onto the point-of-view shot of the white curtain behind Mark's desk (plate 15), which again evokes the //// motif, but the colors are wholly imagined: "Stop the colors, stop the colors!" Marnie whispers. "What colors?" Mark responds.

The irruption of Marnie's trauma in Mark's office is prompted by the lightning, to be sure, but it also is caused by being alone with Mark in Mark's office. The desk is arrayed with a superabundance of phallic symbols and, as lightning strikes, a phallic tree branch plunges through the window. Clearly Marnie fears phallic sexuality. Yet her fear strangely coexists with her own sense of phallic self-mastery. Marnie's horse, Forio, functions as a support for her self. Riding him not only allows her to relax, but Hitchcock invites us to surmise that it is her sole source of sexual pleasure (a phallic fetish). Marnie has appropriated phallic power and authority; she has no need of men. However, Mark, whose father owns a horse farm, seeks to cure her of this illness. His strategy, in part, is to authorize Marnie's interest in horses himself and thereby to redirect her phallic self-sufficiency into a desire for him. He kisses her in the horse barn on his father's estate and forces her to dismount from Forio then mounts the horse himself when he discovers she has stolen money from him. As Mark assumes male proprietorship over the horse, it is horses and their male riders that begin to trigger her psychological collapse.

Mark takes Marnie to the races, and she breaks down upon seeing the red spots on the white shirt of a jockey. Later, near the denouement of the film during the hunt on Mark's father's estate, Marnie watches the hounds savaging their prey as her companions, male and female, seem to her to laugh together at the sight, creating a moment of extreme cognitive dissonance. Looking first at the hounds, then at her companions, her gaze alights upon a red huntsman's jacket. Her traumatized response causes Forio to bolt and then fall, and she is forced to kill him in an act that eliminates the prop to her subjectivity and precipitates her final breakdown. Returning with Mark to the house in Baltimore, Marnie relives the original trauma (as discussed in chapter 2). The child Marnie looks on as her prostitute mother gets into a fight with one of her sailor clients, who has earlier tried to comfort Marnie during a storm. When her mother, who is all tangled up with him, cries for help, Marnie beats him over the head with a poker. The blood pouring out from his head over his white shirt forms the original trauma in which the child's horrified reaction to the sight of blood is marked as a red suffusion.

Marnie's aestheticism can be compared to the forms in which sexuality is displaced into style described in chapter 4. In the way that it tells the story of a woman's "madness," and a man's fascination with that "madness," from a woman's point of view, *Marnie* can be understood, in part, as a response to *Vertigo*. Critics usually focus upon the way in which Marnie resists the domination of the male that Judy, in the last part of *Vertigo*, is forced to succumb to. But here I want to draw attention to their complementary and contrasting aesthetics. If *Vertigo*, like *Rebecca*, registers the incipiently self-annihilating force of femininity, *Marnie* registers the fascination-repulsion of phallic masculinity. In the scene that takes place in Mark's office, Marnie realizes a "phallic sublime" in which it is male sexuality that is represented as a source of horrendous fascination, as both awe-inspiring and incipiently life-threatening.

I have suggested that both *Marnie* and *Vertigo* approach a surrealist aesthetic. For Scottie in *Vertigo*, the ghostlike incarnation of Madeleine that conforms to his fantasy is more real to him than the world of the ordinary represented by his friend Midge and their failed relationship, and in *Marnie* the everyday world is flat and colorless in comparison to those moments of "phallic sublime." Yet Hitchcock's surrealism in these works falls short of the surrealist aesthetic that is embodied in, say, Buñuel's *Belle de Jour* (1967), a film which has striking resemblances to *Marnie* in its imagery of female fantasy and desire, but where the experience of a world that conforms to fantasy is ultimately privileged as an antidote to the world of the everyday, rather than seen as a way of inhabiting the world from which the character must be rescued. In *Vertigo*, Scottie's fantasy is exposed with devastating consequences, and *Marnie*'s surrealism is staged within a therapeutic narrative that seeks to normalize Marnie's fantasy life and "straighten out" the relationship between self and world. But *Vertigo* is the more successful film because Scottie's delirium is made credible, made real, whereas Marnie's delirium is pathologized from the start.

Thus far I have considered hot colors in relation to the warning series, but hot colors may take on an altogether different connotation when they are combined with earth tones, as in *The Trouble with Harry*. The "Caravan Color Season in Red" reads a red sign in the emporium of Mrs. Wiggs (Mildred Dunnock), which is bedecked, like the store in Bodega Bay, with the speckled colors of the "warning series" against white, and with the large canvases of painter Sam Marlowe boldly cast in yellow and red. However, the presence of Sam's paintings is a key to the overall design of the scene because the colors in his paintings, like the colors of nature, lack solidity; they enter into one another in a fluid way. In short, they look natural rather than artificial. And the scene that takes place in Wiggs Emporium is quite the contrary of danger. The camera pans across the store, accompanied by Bernard Herrmann's haunting clarinet melody, to cue a magical moment of awakening and renewal for the spinster Miss Gravely (as she buys a large cup so that she can serve tea to Captain Wiles), as well as signaling the presence of the millionaire who will buy Sam's paintings and in turn make Sam's future with Mrs. Rogers secure. Yellows and reds thus function in *The Trouble with Harry* as redemptive colors, as an intensification of the colors of nature. The exception that proves the rule is the solid bright red blob of color that appears at the end of the blue socks of the corpse, when his shoes are taken off. This red blob functions in a very obvious and humorous way as the Hitchcockian Blot.

Black Versus White

I have already discussed the role played by black and white in Hitchcock's films in opposition to color. However, in the context of Hitchcock's color films the opposition and relationship between black and white takes on its own independent significance as an element of color design. Indeed, Hitchcock's use of black and white is arguably as central as the opposition between cool and warm colors and his use of the warning series in his overall approach to color.

Here Hitchcock draws on what I described in chapter 5 as the moral psychology of expressionism. The opposition between black and white signifies morality via its association between light and darkness. Obviously, villains appear in black, from Mr. Verloc in the black-and-white *Sabotage* to Gromek in *Torn Curtain*, or Arthur Adamson in *Family Plot*, but threatening women also wear black. When Judy Barton first appears as Madeleine she wears black, and when she stages Madeleine's death as a suicide, she wears a black dress that is initially concealed under a white coat, suggesting the manner in which her threat to Scottie is concealed beneath her apparent innocence. When she actually leads Scottie to the bell tower she wears a black-and-white speckled wool coat over her black dress as her dark motives come to the surface. Later, in the second half of the film, after she has made love to Scottie but has still not revealed her true identity to him, she wears a black dress at the moment she puts on the ruby necklace that gives the game away, shattering Scottie's fantasy once and for all. The purity of motive evoked by white tends to be attached to the figure of women. She may appear in the white of innocence that harbors black beneath, as in the *Vertigo* example, or the reverse. Eve Kendall in *North by Northwest* starts out wearing a black suit over a white blouse that is largely concealed when she first encounters Roger Thornhill on the Twentieth Century Limited. When she sends the police who are pursuing Thornhill off the scent, her jacket is open and her white top more exposed. By the time she kisses Thornhill, her black jacket has been taken off and her presence is defined in medium close-up. Once Eve has contacted Vandamm and his men and she sends Thornhill to his death, she is once again defined by her black suit. Finally redeemed by the end of the film, she climbs up into a bunk in the sleeping car of the train in white pajamas.

But men, too, can change their spots, though the change is not dramatized in quite the Manichean terms that characterize Hitchcock's aesthetic embodiment of female sexuality. When men reveal their underlying goodness it is normally by taking off their jackets and revealing a white shirt beneath. Mitch Brenner takes off his jacket in this way in *The Birds* after a gull hits Melanie Daniels. At the end of *Marnie*, Mark Rutland takes off his tanned jacket, revealing his white shirt, in order to protect and comfort Marnie. Roger Thornhill wears a suit throughout *North by Northwest* until the fake staging of his death and his subsequent hospitalization. He rises from his bed a new man, determined to take action to rescue Eve Kendall in spite of the wishes of her minder, the Professor. Thornhill's presence is now defined not by his cool blue suit but by a crisp white shirt as he saves the microfilm and rescues Eve, who is dressed in the warning color of orange, which further stands out against his white shirt on the cliffs of Mount Rushmore.

When Judy Barton as Madeleine wears her speckled black-and-white coat, the mingling of black and white suggests the blurring of moral boundaries, as in the expression that something is not black and white. In *Under Capricorn*, both Sam and Henrietta Flusky are morally culpable and both wear costumes that combine black and white, exemplified in the black and white stripes of Flusky's waistcoat and the dresses worn by Henrietta. However, aside from *The Birds*, perhaps the most sustained use of black-and-white color design is in *The Trouble with Harry*. The main conspirators all wear black (with some white). Captain Wiles wears a black-and-white checkered shirt, black cap, and speckled jacket; Sam Marlowe wears a black sweater over a white shirt; and Miss Gravely, perhaps the protagonist of the film who is most responsible for the death of Harry Warp, wears a costume of black with white spots, until she dates Captain Wiles and sports a satin dress of restful tone that is close to the cornflower blue worn by Mrs. Rogers. These colors, of course, signal the moral ambivalence of these characters, but insofar as black predominates, the film ironically inverts the significance of black. Just as hot colors signal redemption in the film, so in a sense, in this light black comedy, does black actually signify white.

In *The Birds*, the combination of black and white suggests not simply the breakdown of moral oppositions or the blurring of moral boundaries, but the breakdown of category distinctions altogether, which breeds chaos or monstrosity. The commingling of black and white is announced in the credit sequence as black birds (which peck away at the credits, including the director's name) flutter against a white background. This is echoed later when a flock of crows attacks the school children against the background of Annie's white-walled, black-roofed schoolhouse, which looms on the horizon like some gigantic gothic birdhouse. It is repeated again when black birds and white birds, crows and seagulls, combine in the final assault on the Brenner household and on Melanie, alone in the attic. We learn in the film from an ornithologist that different species never mix. When they do, a kind of collective monster is created that is represented in the film in part through the commingling of black and white birds. At the close of the film, when the birds' attacks have abated, the birds roughly sort themselves back into their respective species—seagull and crow, black bird and white bird—suggesting that the attacks on the human beings have at least temporarily abated (plate 16).

This black-and-white motif, which signals the monstrosity of the birds, is one of the central ways in which human beings are linked to the birds in the film, in a manner that indicates that, if the birds represent a rage against humans that comes from the humans themselves, their source neither arises from nor is ranged against a single individual. Lydia Brenner is especially associated by color with the birds. Her hair is black flecked with light gray, and she consistently dons a black-and-white speckled wool coat and a black-and-white speckled wool skirt (in the first scene she wears this costume over the maternal brown that is finally revealed at the end of the film). But Melanie Daniels wears a specked black-and-white wool suit in the opening scene of the film before changing into the lime green outfit of the lovebird; Mitch Brenner wears a black-and-white-flecked jacket in one scene and later sports a gray-and-white-flecked jacket; finally, the near-hysterical

Plate 1

Plate 2

Plate 3

Plate 4

Plate 5

Plate 6

Plate 7

Plate 8

Plate 9

Plate 10

Plate 11

Plate 12

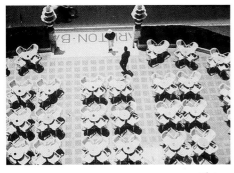

Plate 13

Plate 14

Plate 15

Plate 16

woman in the cafe, the "mother hen" who protects her offspring, wears a black-and-white-flecked wool dress.[18]

The signification of black and white also serves to designate gender difference as it is derived from the association of white with feminine purity and the clichéd wedding attire of white for women. Hitchcock's *Marnie* is, among other things, a complex investigation of gender difference and complementarity that invokes and inverts this convention. While the blonde-haired Marnie is at times virginal, with white connoting her innocence, she is also frigid and resists playing the gender role that Mark wishes to ascribe to her, where her white becomes merely a masquerade. Marnie wears white the only time she feels herself to be a sexual being, when riding her phallic black horse Forio. She wears white on her honeymoon cruise in the scene where she is assaulted by Mark Rutland after having been blackmailed into marriage; in the morning of their return, when she "sees Mark off to work"; when she pretends to be the perfect wife and hostess at a party at the Rutland estate; and in the scene where she lies prostrate in bed and Mark seeks to diagnose her condition. On the honeymoon cruise Mark Rutland wears yellow, but at the party, and the morning after, Mark wears black and dark checks, respectively, and in the diagnosis session Mark wears a black dressing gown.

The masquerade of conventional femininity is further subverted in the film by reversing the traditional ascription of white and black to gender. As we have seen, in the opening scenes of the film, Marnie, dressed in a dark gray woolen suit and a black wig, looks strikingly like a man in drag. The image seems to signal that there is an aspect of gender confusion or disguise that is attached to the false identities she assumes, which is linked to the "masculine" sense of autonomy and agency afforded to her by these roles. Indeed, rather than seeing the yellow handbag as the Hitchcockian Blot, in this remarkable image it is the "obscene" figure of Marnie herself who is the blot. The image in which Marnie arises from the sink, shaking her flowing blonde hair after having rinsed out the black dye, can be understood as the reassertion of a feminine identity, but this identity is unstable, one she wishes to escape from. In the montage sequence of the couple on their honeymoon, Mark and Marnie switch shades—he wears black, she wears white; he wears pale gray, she wears black—as if to index this "gender" instability. When Marnie visits Mark to work for him at his office, she wears a black coat over white, as opposed to his pale gray suit and white shirt, but then she takes off her black coat to reveal her white blouse and her vulnerability. Marnie wears a black coat (over brown) when she steals money from Strutt's office, and a black gown when she attempts suicide on the honeymoon. After the debacle of the party, she wears a black sweater and changes to black (over white) for the hunt and in her final attempt to steal money. When Marnie returns to the scene of the trauma at the end of the film, the source of her confusion is in part represented through an inverted color scheme. Mark wears a light tan (earth-toned) suit against Marnie's black and, as I have already mentioned, when they arrive at the house he takes off the suit and places it around her shoulders so that he is now wearing white. Marnie's mother is dressed in a white sweater over black, and she is also dressed in black in the flashback where she confronts the sailor, who wears white. The conventional gender alignment of black and white is thus shown be inverted in its origin.

In this chapter, I have described Hitchcock's approach to color design in considerable, and, no doubt, obsessive detail, in order to demonstrate just how intricate and precise Hitchcock's attention to style is in his work. In the introduction, I spoke of how his color design is indebted to surrealism as the heir to aestheticism. But I think his approach to color design suggests the way in which Hitchcock is also an aesthete in a different, more mundane way. Though Hitchcock's deployment of color is creative, there is also, perhaps, something pedantic or academic about it that is reflected in this chapter. It reveals the way in which Hitchcock as a visual stylist is something of a formalist. This tendency emerges especially in the late period of his work after *Marnie*, where Hitchcock lost control of his material at a moment when, after a string of acknowledged masterpieces, he perhaps felt most entitled to have it. By formalism I do not mean that Hitchcock's use of color lacks meaning and is purely decorative. On the contrary, it always has meaning. It is rather that Hitchcock's mastery of form becomes academic when it coincides with narrative material that fails to meet expectations of form, in the way it does in his supreme achievements in film such as *Rear Window*, *Psycho*, *Vertigo*, or *North by Northwest*. *Topaz* is a significant work of color design, but it is ultimately a mediocre film. *Torn Curtain* is a masterpiece of color design and pure cinema, yet the central relationship lacks conviction and it falls apart as a story once Sarah Sherman knows her husband is innocent. These are stories that ultimately fail to do justice to the unique cinematic intelligence they nonetheless manifest.

Conclusion

In the introduction I proposed this book as a study in poetics characterized as, first of all, a method that involves the formulation of descriptive generalizations about a narrative art form, and in this case more specifically about the work of a single film director: Hitchcock. If authorial studies such as this have validity it is because, as in the study of genre, it is possible to discern a unity beneath the diversity of the work of a single author, regardless of the merits of the individual works at hand. My aim in this book has been to derive principles of aesthetic organization that were sufficiently broad to encompass the diversity of Hitchcock's output while retaining the power to explain the detailed character of individual works.

The both/and logic of romantic irony that I have outlined in this book, which unites the romantic ideal with the lure of human perversity, is broad enough to encompass works as diverse as *The Trouble with Harry*, a narrative of romantic renewal, *Psycho*, a narrative of corrosive irony, and the many films like *Rear Window* or *Strangers on a Train* which lie in between. At the same time, the concept is flexible enough to account for the very different tone of these works. The different forms of Hitchcock's plots described in chapter 3 discriminate Hitchcock's narratives of romantic renewal from his plots of ironic ambivalence and inversion by the manner in which they portray the nature and consequences of recognition. Chapter 3 also demonstrates how Hitchcock's portrayal of the nature and consequences of knowledge is further differentiated according to gender and sexuality.

As we saw in chapter 2, Hitchcock's suspense (with an ironic edge that is closely related to black humor) defines a central rhetorical form taken by romantic irony in his work. Suspense in Hitchcock is the converse of recognition since it often involves the withholding of recognition either for the spectator or for a character, or for both. Suspense contributes to the sense of artifice that characterizes narratives of romantic renewal, but it also fosters ironic allegiance with forces that subvert the romance in Hitchcock's more ambivalent works. Furthermore, Hitchcock's narration manifests two distinct forms of suspense, and these are intimately tied to the major forms taken by Hitchcock's aesthetic, which I described in chapter 4: his masculine aesthetic, where Hitchcock alludes to homoerotic "perversity" through dramaturgy and a visual design that is predicated upon double entendres, and his aesthetic of the feminine sublime, where his visual style approaches its greatest formal beauty. The idea that Hitchcock is a second-generation aesthete, self-consciously mobilizing style as a displaced expression of sexual content, whether through punning (his "masculine" aesthetic), or through idealization (his "feminine" aesthetic), also bestows a unity upon his distinct modes of narration and stylization. Note that "masculine" and "feminine" here designate the form or the mode, "ludic-sadistic" and "sublime-masochistic," respectively. The content, however, may vary. As we saw in chapter 6, *Marnie* arguably exemplifies a phallic sublime, and as chapter 5 demonstrates, there are many places in Hitchcock's work where his phallic sublime takes on an anal-phallic or homoerotic character.

In the concluding chapters, I have argued that Hitchcock's aestheticism takes different forms not only in the ways in which sexuality is given displaced expression through style (via punning or idealization) but also by how the stylization of sexuality is expressed through the rhetoric of doubling. The black-and-white aesthetic of expressionism emphasizes the contrasts that define polar opposites in the both/and logic of romantic irony. In what is arguably a purer form of aestheticism inscribed in Hitchcock's color surrealism, the domain of the shadow world is not marked out as something distinct. The normal and the perverse are represented as coextensive, and difference is expressed through identity; identity through difference. An expressionist work might be informed by Hitchcock's ludic double entendres, as in the punning of *The Lodger*, or the more sophisticated but also, ultimately, comic treatment of homosexuality, as in the doubling of *Strangers on a Train*. At the same time, Hitchcock's visual expressionism may approach the sublime, as in the allure bestowed upon the aesthetic traces of Rebecca in Hitchcock's film. Hitchcock's surrealism may readily approach the sublime, as in *Vertigo*, but surrealism is equally amenable to comedy as, canonically, in the punning surrealist conclusion of *North by Northwest* when the train enters the tunnel. Perhaps the light black comedy about the corpse, *The Trouble with Harry*, could be considered surrealist humor, albeit of the most decorous kind. Sometimes the two modes are combined—even *Rebecca* has one or two moments of Hitchcockian comedy.

I have argued that aestheticism can be considered the stylistic expression of romantic irony by articulating the both/and rhetoric of romantic irony as a relationship between human perversity and its displaced expression, which is inscribed in the form taken by visual representation itself. The distinction between romantic irony as a narrative form and aestheticism as visual style is reflected in the two-part structure of the book. However, the arguments of parts 1 and 2 are closely entwined, as the relationship between the arguments of chapters 2 and 4 suggest. Furthermore, as we saw in chapter 1, the both/and logic of narration is dramatized in its three different modes by the way in which the relationship between the romantic ideal and the domain of human perversity is articulated through artifice and stylization. In Hitchcock's case, to say that he is a romantic ironist is also to say that he is an aesthete.

I have not discussed every one of Hitchcock's fifty-three feature films, and I have been repeatedly drawn to discuss films like *Strangers on a Train* or *Vertigo*, which any critic would place at the center of Hitchcock's canon. Some important films, like *Lifeboat*, have received less discussion than they deserve, and some films that are, arguably, less important, like *The Skin Game* (1931), have received no discussion at all. My criterion of selection has been governed by which films best illuminate the principles and norms under discussion, while giving reasonable space to discussion of exceptions that prove the rule, like *The Manxman*, with respect to Hitchcock's narrative technique; *The Wrong Man*, in the context of the thriller; and *The Trouble with Harry* in terms of Hitchcock's treatment of nature. Although some English films have received detailed discussion, like *The Lodger*, *Blackmail*, and *Sabotage*, I am undoubtedly guilty of bias toward Hitchcock's American works. But the nature of this bias is consistent with the importance of style to the argument of this book. For it was in America, with the remarkable technical resources, both human and mechanical, that were placed at his disposal, that Hitchcock was able to achieve the fullest realization of his style.

My understanding of Hitchcock's career overlaps in many respects with received wisdom. It has often been noted that *The Lodger* is a film that anticipates the contours of Hitchcock's development. However, I have tried to demonstrate exactly why this is so. *The Lodger* anticipates all the major forms taken by Hitchcock's recognition narratives as well as the major modes of Hitchcockian suspense, and it is the first full realization of his ludic, "masculine" aesthetic, although it also has touches of the sublime. The three types of romantic irony that I have discerned are all present in Hitchcock's English films, and I have discussed in detail representatives of each. However, stylistically speaking, his English films are not of a piece. Rather, they are broadly divided between melodramatic narratives in an ironic mode with expressionist touches, such as *Downhill, Easy Virtue, The Manxman,* and *Blackmail,* and his later consolidation of the picaresque thriller idiom in the 1930s in collaboration with Charles Bennett in works such as *The 39 Steps, The Man Who Knew Too Much* (1934), and *Young and Innocent*. In these narratives, rapid editing in high-key and open-air locales takes precedence over expressionist dramaturgy. This bifurcation continues in Hitchcock's early American period in the contrast between *Rebecca* and *Foreign Correspondent,* and between *Suspicion* and *Saboteur*.

However, Hitchcock's shift to America proved decisive for his artistic development in the way that the technical resources placed at his disposal allowed Hitchcock's stylistic vocabulary to be sharpened and expanded. Something was undoubtedly lost in the perfection of Hitchcock's technique from the rougher, faster, more spontaneous idioms of the English thriller and yet much was gained.

First, Hitchcock perfected the technique of analytical expressionism, whereby the doubling idioms and imagery of expressionism, and the visual/verbal play that characterizes the controlled and displaced eroticism of Hitchcock's ludic, masculine aesthetic, were seamlessly entwined within the tightly structured, character-driven narration that characterizes classical cinema. This aesthetic culminates in his horror masterpieces, *Psycho* and *The Birds*.

Second, beginning with *Rebecca,* Hitchcock developed a character-centered idiom that focused upon feeling rather than action, and combined

Conclusion

suspenseful mystery with what I have called Hitchcock's "feminine" aesthetic, an aestheticism of the sublime that yields Hitchcock's master-piece *Vertigo*. In terms of the portrayal of woman, something was gained in terms of the articulation of feeling or affect but something was also lost as female subjectivity became defined in terms of sexuality and desire, rather than in terms of an agency and pluck complementary to that of the male.

Third, this development paved the way for a complex examination of male subjectivity. Hitchcock's male characters, most notably in the roles accorded to Gregory Peck and James Stewart, increasingly manifested the vulnerability of Hitchcock's heroines. As a result, the narrative of gender complementarity in the 1930s became, in the 1950s, a drama of the revision and re-establishment of the couple.

Fourth, the introduction of color into Hitchcock's craft unified his aes-thetic in a way that was not possible in black and white. The aesthetic of expressionism marks out the domain of the shadow world, the domain of human perversity, from the world of the everyday. However, Hitchcock's surrealist color design allows the domain of the shadow world to be repre-sented as coextensive with the world of the everyday. Furthermore, Hitchcock's color design allows the articulation of complementary opposi-tions that characterize Hitchcock's narratives of romantic renewal, where the narrative world is not irretrievably divided. For this reason, in his color films Hitchcock achieves the fullest realization and integration of his aes-thetic, as a comparison between three very different works—*North by Northwest*, *Vertigo*, and *The Birds*—attests.

If Hitchcock's work (with the exception of *Frenzy*) goes into decline after *The Birds*, with *Marnie* poised oddly between being a work that could, in some ways, be considered his greatest achievement and the beginning of his decline, it is not because Hitchcock's visual style fails him but because of the absence of conviction in characterization and storytelling. This lends a work like *Topaz*, in which there is so much to admire in the intelligence of its design and realization, the appearance of being a rather arid exercise in form.

Earlier I asserted that Hitchcock's romantic irony is to be identified with aestheticism. However, there is an important historical rationale for keeping the concepts of romantic irony and aestheticism distinct and, in particular, for beginning this book with an account of romantic irony and then dis-cussing the influence of aestheticism and its modernist avatars on Hitchcock's work. The emphasis of this book has been upon poetics of form and style rather than upon a historical poetics; nonetheless, there has been an implicit historical argument that I shall now make explicit.

In his prolific and seminal writings on film, David Bordwell conceives historical poetics, in an admirably rigorous way, as a historical inquiry that seeks to describe the historical norms governing film style and the manner in which the practice of any filmmaker must be understood in terms of the choices made against the background of those norms.[1] The chapters in the later part of this book, especially chapter 5, begin to approach this kind of study, though in terms of Hitchcock's use of color more work needs to be done on Hollywood color aesthetics before an adequate understanding of Hitchcock's place within it can be attained. However, it is also my conviction that in the study of a director like Hitchcock, the concept of historical poetics must extend beyond the history of film style to comprehend broader aesthetic forms and trends of which the parameters of film style are themselves a manifestation.

There are undoubtedly pitfalls to such an approach. Too often broad aesthetic categories like "modernism" and "postmodernism" are wielded or invoked by film scholars and others in the humanities in a vague and ambiguous way that lacks explanatory value. Skeptics might feel that the concept of "romantic irony" is a late entry (in the study of film) to a dubious list. However, the value of any aesthetic concept lies ultimately in how precisely it is defined and how successfully—that is, how clearly and completely—it illuminates the phenomena it seeks to describe. I have argued that the value of the concept of romantic irony lies not only in that it allows for a clear and comprehensive understanding of Hitchcock's aesthetic, but it also allows us to understand why Hitchcock's work has yielded, and will no doubt continue to yield, such a diverse array of interpretations, as critics emphasize now one, now another aspect of his films. However, here I want to consider the significance of placing Hitchcock's oeuvre, through the concept of romantic irony, within the historical context of late romanticism.

I am not, of course, claiming that Hitchcock was exposed to Schlegel when he was a schoolboy or that he was an avid reader of romantic literature, although one can discover fertile correspondences between Hitchcock's films and works of English romanticism in the romantic-ironic vein, such as Keats's "Eve of St. Agnes" and *The Lodger*, Keats's "Lamia" and *Vertigo*, and Coleridge's "Rime of the Ancient Mariner" and *The Birds*.[2] Rather, my claim is that Hitchcock inherited the idiom of romantic irony through his exposure to the cultural influences of the fin de siècle, in particular Wilde's manual of aestheticism, *The Picture of Dorian Gray*, the writings of Edgar Allen Poe, Robert Louis Stevenson's *Dr. Jekyll and Mr. Hyde*, and the ideas of Sigmund Freud. *Dorian Gray* is a crucial text because, as we have seen, it forges a connection between literary romanticism as it is manifest in the fin de siècle and aestheticism as a visual style. The European fin de siècle is generally considered the last gasp of romanticism before it was transformed into modernism, where, in visual modernism at least, romantic irony is transformed into a reflection upon the identity of the artwork itself as at once a representation of something and as an artifact that ultimately "represents" itself. Even the more properly modernist avatars of aestheticism that influenced Hitchcock—German expressionism and surrealism—are both heavily tinged with a romantic rhetoric of transcendence and melancholia, of the ideal and the perverse.

Yet if Hitchcock inherits romantic irony in an increasingly modernist, that is, self-referential guise, through the legacy of aestheticism, expressionism, and surrealism, his work also moves, as it were, in the opposite direction from the self-referentiality of modernism. For Hitchcock's cinema, as I have emphasized throughout this book, is a popular cinema, popular, above all, in the manner in which it embraces the melodramatic idioms of the suspense thriller and romantic comedy, from John Buchan, D. W. Griffith, and American cinema of the 1930s. Unlike modernist writers and artists who embraced popular idioms and its icons in order to rework them on their own terms, Hitchcock is an artist who thoroughly inhabits the conventions of popular storytelling and has adapted the idioms of aestheticism, expressionism, and surrealism to it. In this way, Hitchcock's syncretic practice becomes the source of his originality. By combining the romantic ideal of the popular thriller with a self-reflexive, aesthete's sense of the relationship between representation and human perversity, Hitchcock "reinvented" the idiom of romantic irony in the medium of twentieth-century cinema. Inhabiting the form of popular romance and the ideal of transcendence through the romantic love it embodies, Hitchcock's romantic irony inscribes the lure and fascination of human perversity, which is veiled by a façade of normality, through a sophisticated level of stylistic self-consciousness.

But if we are going to explain the significance of Hitchcock's work, this explanation has to go beyond an evaluation of its immediate artistic merits.

Conclusion

After all, there are many other towering figures in twentieth-century cinema, including Anglo-American popular film, among whom Hitchcock certainly deserves a place, but not necessarily a preeminent place. The singularity of Hitchcock's importance as an artist is ultimately a historical one that lies, at once, in the nature of the influences Hitchcock absorbed and the pervasiveness of his own influence and the idioms that he perfected, an influence that is embodied in the adjective "Hitchcockian." Hitchcock is what John Orr has termed a "matrix" figure, one who distills one kind of aesthetic idiom inherited from nineteenth-century literary romanticism into another, the medium of twentieth-century popular film, via the influence of fin de siècle aestheticism and its modernist avatars.[3] By doing so, Hitchcock becomes, to my mind, quite simply the single most important director in the history of cinema, not to mention one of the most significant artists of the twentieth century. For the form of expression that he perfected has become, through the genres of the detective thriller, the romantic thriller, and the psychological horror film, the staple idiom for any director working within contemporary film and, more recently, television, to demonstrate their authorial flair and control over the medium.

Although I cannot prove the point here (for it would take another book at least as long as this one), I would argue that romanticism, in the form of romantic irony perfected by Hitchcock, is a pervasive mode of contemporary so-called "postmodern" visual fiction. This is not the place to enter into the history of this contentious term; suffice it to say that it has been used to describe, among other things, the interpenetration of modernist self-consciousness and self-reflexivity with the idioms of popular culture in a manner that undermines the historical divide between modernism and mass culture. Sometimes postmodernism is used to describe the direction taken by contemporary mixed-media artists after what some have described as the end of modernism, but it is also used, willy-nilly, to describe contemporary popular filmmakers such as Paul Verhoevon, Pedro Almodóvar, Dario Argento, Brian de Palma, David Fincher, and David Lynch. On this definition, Hitchcock, in a film like *The Lodger* or *Blackmail*, would be a postmodernist soon after the inception of modernism, which is surely not a very helpful idea! But perhaps more reflection upon the concept of romantic irony in the context of contemporary filmmaking practice will allow us to understand that some of what is now lumped together as postmodernist is, in fundamental ways, premodernist, or at least, as an aesthetic form, arising from the legacy of romanticism, which has developed parallel to modernism. The concept of romantic irony, I would suggest, provides a more precise and illuminating frame of reference than postmodernism for understanding the work of these and other filmmakers.

The historical dimension of romantic irony is also important for understanding criticism of Hitchcock's work. Any student who encounters the literature on Hitchcock cannot but surely be struck by the prevalence of psychoanalytic interpretations of his films that have consistently been produced from the 1970s to the present. How is this to be explained? One argument might point to the prevalence of explicit or implicit references to the psychoanalytic explanation of human action in Hitchcock's work, especially in his American films—overtly in *Spellbound* and *Marnie*; more covertly in works like *Rope, Suspicion, Strangers on a Train, Psycho,* and *The Birds.* However, Hitchcock's uses of psychoanalysis are not the same as his critics. Psychoanalysis in Hitchcock is as much a vehicle for emplotting romance as a form of explanation that is valorized for its own sake. As a "surface" feature of Hitchcock's films it is also subject to irony, like other elements of his work. Finally, from the standpoint of psychoanalytic theory and criticism, the psychoanalysis Hitchcock invokes appears naive. Hitchcock's use of psychoanalysis is part of a history of influence of the psychiatric profession on Hollywood screenwriters and screenwriting that still remains to be written, but it can scarcely explain why it is that psychoanalytic critics are drawn to Hitchcock. The reason, I would suggest, is a deeper one—namely, that the origins of psychoanalytic theory and Hitchcock's films can both be traced to late romanticism. If this is so, then it is no surprise that a psychoanalytic theory such as Slavoj Žižek's finds "confirmation" in the works of Hitchcock, although, of course, that "confirmation" tells us nothing about its truth.

Notes

Preface

1. David Bordwell, *Making Meaning: Inference and Rhetoric in the Interpretation of Cinema* (Cambridge: Harvard UP, 1989), 1–18. For a criticism of Bordwell's view with which I largely agree, see Berys Gaut, "Making Sense of Films: Neoformalism and Its Limits," *Forum for Modern Language Studies* 31:1 (1995): 8–23.

2. Susan Smith, *Hitchcock: Suspense, Humour and Tone* (London: BFI, 1999); Michael Walker, *Hitchcock's Motifs* (Amsterdam: U of Amsterdam P, 2005).

3. Claude Chabrol and Eric Rohmer, *Hitchcock: The First Forty-four Films* (1957), trans. Stanley Hochman (New York: Ungar, 1979).

4. Richard Allen, "Hitchcock and Cavell," in Murray Smith and Thomas E. Wartenberg, eds., *Thinking Through Cinema: Film as Philosophy* (Oxford and Malden, Mass.: Blackwell, 2006), 43–53.

1. Romantic Irony

1. John Belton, "Dexterity in a Void: The Formalist Esthetics of Alfred Hitchcock," *Cineaste* 10.3 (Summer 1980): 9–13.

Notes

2. Friedrich Schlegel, *Atheneum Fragments (A)*, paragraph 51, in *Philosophical Fragments*, trans. Peter Firchow (Minneapolis: U of Minnesota P, 1991). All subsequent citations are in the text.

3. Friedrich Schlegel, *Lyceum (L)*, paragraph 108, in *Philosophical Fragments*. All subsequent citations are in the text.

4. See Steven E. Alford, *Irony and the Logic of Romantic Imagination* (New York: Peter Lang, 1984), 35–46.

5. Friedrich Schlegel, *Ideas (I)*, paragraph 26 in *Philosophical Fragments*. All subsequent citations are in the text.

6. I draw this example from Jack Forstman, *A Romantic Triangle: Schleiermacher and Early German Romanticism* (Missoula: U of Montana P, 1977), 6.

7. Hans Eichner, *Friedrich Schlegel* (New York: Twayne, 1970), 53.

8. Friedrich Schlegel, *Dialogue on Poetry*, trans. Ernst Behler and Roman Struc, in *Dialogue on Poetry and Other Literary Aphorisms* (University Park: Pennsylvania State UP, 1968), 86.

9. Gary Handewerk, *Ethics and Irony in Narrative: From Schlegel to Lacan* (New Haven: Yale UP, 1985), 44.

10. See Alfred Edwin Lussky, *Tieck's Romantic Irony* (Chapel Hill: U of North Carolina P, 1932), 69.

11. D. C. Muecke, *The Compass of Irony* (London: Methuen, 1969), 164–77.

12. Lilian Furst, *Fictions of Romantic Irony* (Cambridge: Harvard UP, 1984), 230.

13. Anne Mellor, *English Romantic Irony* (Cambridge: Harvard UP, 1989), 18; Clyde de L. Ryals, *A World of Possibilities: Romantic Irony in Victorian Literature* (Columbus: Ohio State UP, 1990), 7–8.

14. Raymond Immerwahr, "The Subjectivity or Objectivity of Friedrich Schlegel's Poetic Irony," *Germanic Review* 26 (1951): 190–91.

15. John Francis Fetzer, "Romantic Irony," in Gerhart Hoffmeister, ed., *European Romanticism: Literary Cross-Currents, Modes, and Models* (Detroit: Wayne State UP, 1990), 22. This typology is close to one developed by Allen Wilde, who makes a three-fold distinction between realist, modern, and postmodern irony using the terms "mediate," "disjunctive," and "suspensive irony," in *Horizons of Assent: Modernism, Postmodernism, and the Ironic Imagination* (Baltimore and London: Johns Hopkins UP, 1981), 9–10.

16. Solger, quoted in Ernst Behler, "The Theory of Irony in German Romanticism," in Frederick Garber, ed., *Romantic Irony* (Budapest: Akadémiai Kiadó, 1988), 71.

17. Gurewitch, quoted in Furst, *Fictions of Romantic Irony*, 226.

18. For a detailed analysis of kissing in Hitchcock, see Sidney Gottlieb, "Hitchcock and the Art of the Kiss: A Preliminary Survey," in Sidney Gottlieb and Christopher

Notes

Brookhouse, eds., *Framing Hitchcock: Selected Essays from the Hitchcock Annual* (Detroit: Wayne State UP, 2002), 132–36.

19. He writes that Hitchcock's aestheticism "instead of being 'decadent,' amoral and idly sham-aristocratic, is moral, robust and 'democratic.'" Raymond Durgnat, *A Long Hard Look at "Psycho"* (London: BFI, 2002), 3.

20. François Truffaut (with Helen Scott), *Hitchcock*, rev. ed. (New York: Simon and Schuster, 1984), 73.

21. Belton, "Dexterity in a Void," 10.

22. See V. I. Pudovkin, *Film Technique and Film Acting*, trans. and ed. by Ivor Montagu (New York: Grove Press, 1970), 168.

23. For further discussion of this issue see Richard Allen, "*The Lodger* and the Origins of Hitchcock's Aesthetic," *Hitchcock Annual* (2001–2002): 55.

24. Hitchcock makes explicit reference to Pudovkin's account of the Kuleshov experiment in the course of discussing *Rear Window* in his interview with François Truffaut (see Truffaut, *Hitchcock*, 214–16); see also Hitchcock's discussion of "pure cinema" in "On Style: An Interview with *Cinema* Magazine," originally published in *Cinema* 1.5 (August-September 1963) and reprinted in Sidney Gottlieb, ed., *Hitchcock on Hitchcock* (Berkeley: U of California P, 1995), 288–89. The unreliability of reminiscences is noted by William Simon apropos of Orson Welles in a review of Irving Singer's *Three Philosophical Filmmakers*, *Hitchcock Annual* (2004–2005): 21.

25. Lesley Brill, *The Hitchcock Romance: Love and Irony in Hitchcock's Films* (Princeton: N.J.: Princeton UP, 1988), 56.

26. Robin Wood, *Hitchcock's Films Revisited*, 2d ed. (New York: Columbia UP, 2002), 84.

27. James Naremore, "Hitchcock and Humor," in Richard Allen and Sam Ishii-Gonzales, eds., *Hitchcock: Past and Future* (London and New York: Routledge, 2004), 22–36; Susan Smith, *Hitchcock: Suspense, Humour and Tone* (London: BFI, 1999), 49–75.

28. Bill Krohn, "*Suspicion* (Ambivalence)," *Hitchcock Annual* (2002–2003): 79–83.

29. Most famously Laura Mulvey in her 1975 essay, "Visual Pleasure and Narrative Cinema," reprinted in *Visual and Other Pleasures* (Bloomington: Indiana UP, 1989), 14–26.

30. Truffaut, *Hitchcock*, 261–62.

31. This is part of sixteen sequences from Hitchcock's home movie collection filed as item number 2990–1 in the Margaret Herrick Library of the Academy of Motion Pictures Arts and Sciences, Los Angeles, California.

32. See Robert Stam and Roberta Pearson, "*Rear Window* and the Critique of Reflexivity," in Marshall Deutelbaum and Leland Poague, eds., *A Hitchcock Reader*

(Ames: Iowa State UP, 1986), 193–206. Stam and Pearson provide a fine summary of the self-reflexive aspects of *Rear Window*, but assuming an identity between the film spectator and the rear window voyeur, they fail to conceptualize how *Rear Window* affords the spectator a critical distance upon the activity of voyeurism in the very act of invoking it.

33. Michael Walker, *Hitchcock's Motifs* (Amsterdam: U of Amsterdam P, 2005), 88.

34. Smith, *Hitchcock: Suspense, Humour and Tone*, 70, 102.

35. Raymond Bellour, *The Analysis of Film* (Bloomington: Indiana UP, 2001), 228.

36. Walker, *Hitchcock's Motifs*, 91.

37. John Fawell, *Hitchcock's "Rear Window": The Well-Made Film* (Carbondale: Southern Illinois UP, 2001), 99–101.

38. Smith, *Hitchcock: Suspense, Humour and Tone*, 3.

39. See William Rothman, *Hitchcock: The Murderous Gaze* (Cambridge: Harvard UP, 1982), 65.

40. Paula Marantz Cohen, *Alfred Hitchcock: The Legacy of Victorianism* (Lexington: U of Kentucky P, 1995), 67–85.

41. Walker, *Hitchcock's Motifs*, 95–96.

42. Tom Cohen, *Hitchcock's Cryptonymies*, vol. 1 (Minneapolis: U of Minnesota P, 2005), 26. Perhaps, following an assumption made in an editorial remark in the Truffaut interview book, Cohen claims to spot Hitchcock in the crowd that pursues the Avenger at the denouement of the film, though I like others am skeptical, for this figure is too old to match Hitchcock's profile. It is unfortunately characteristic of Cohen's chapter, one that is key to the argument of his book, that he builds an interpretation of Hitchcock's two "cameos" on the basis of one role that is not a cameo, in the sense that his later roles were (and why would Hitchcock lie about this?), and on a later alleged cameo that is arguably not Hitchcock at all.

43. For a detailed analysis of this sequence, see Charles Barr, *English Hitchcock* (Moffat, U.K.: Cameron and Hollis, 1999), 36–38.

44. Barr, *English Hitchcock*, 41.

45. Brill, *The Hitchcock Romance*, 20. Brill draws attention to the constitutive relationship between romance and artifice in Hitchcock's work and rightly singles out the concluding sequence of *North by Northwest* to illustrate this. However, Brill believes that the role of irony in Hitchcock's work has been overstated, and seeks to privilege the narrative of romantic renewal not as a form of irony in Hitchcock's work but as an antidote to it. In Brill's analysis of *North by Northwest*, irony along with the human perversity that it expresses is largely absent. However, in my analysis, irony with its source in human perversity is not an optional feature of Hitchcock's narratives of romantic renewal but constitutive of their form.

46. Truffaut, *Hitchcock*, 47.

47. As Patrick McGilligan reports it: "A naughty girl herself, Kelly juggled two or three affairs during the filming of *Dial M for Murder*, much to the director's delight. 'That's Gryce!' [*sic*] Hitchcock was wont to exclaim privately. 'She fucked everyone! Why, she even fucked little Freddie, the writer!' " McGilligan, *Alfred Hitchcock: A Life in Darkness and Light* (New York: HarperCollins, 2003), 471.

48. Sarah Berry, " 'She's Too Everything': Marriage and Masquerade in *Rear Window* and *To Catch a Thief*," *Hitchcock Annual* (2001–2002): 95–96.

49. I thank Bill Paul for pointing this out to me.

50. Cohen, *Alfred Hitchcock: The Legacy of Victorianism*, 99–113.

51. Brill, *The Hitchcock Romance*, 219.

2. Suspense

1. See Patrick McGilligan, *Alfred Hitchcock: A Life in Darkness and Light* (New York: Harper Collins, 2003), 276.

2. Two significant exceptions are Susan Smith's *Hitchcock: Suspense, Humor and Tone* (London: BFI, 1999); and Christopher Morris, *The Hanging Figure: On Suspense and the Films of Alfred Hitchcock* (Westport, Conn.: Praeger, 2002).

3. Ian Cameron, "Hitchcock and the Mechanics of Suspense 1," *Movie* 3 (October 1962): 6.

4. Noël Carroll, "Toward a Theory of Film Suspense," in *Theorizing the Moving Image* (New York: Cambridge UP, 1996), 101. Carroll restates the argument of this essay in more formalized language in "The Paradox of Suspense," in Peter Vorderer and Hans J. Wulff, eds., *Supsense: Conceptualizations, Theoretical Analyses, and Empirical Explanations* (Mahwah, N.J.: Lawrence Erlbaum, 1996), 71–92.

5. Carroll, *Theorizing the Moving Image*, 106–107.

6. Alfred Hitchcock, "Lecture at Columbia University (1939)," in Sidney Gottlieb, ed., *Hitchcock on Hitchcock* (Berkeley: U of California P, 1995), 272.

7. Gottlieb, ed., *Hitchcock on Hitchcock*, 272–73.

8. I borrow the term "shared suspense" from Susan Smith. See Smith, *Hitchcock: Suspense, Humour and Tone*, 20–22.

9. François Truffaut (with Helen Scott), *Hitchcock*, rev. ed. (New York: Simon and Schuster, 1984), 73 (emphasis in original).

10. Smith, *Hitchcock: Suspense, Humour and Tone*, 18–20.

11. Truffaut, *Hitchcock*, 73. Susan Smith's excellent discussion of suspense in Hitchcock is marred by her failure to reference sources other than the Truffaut interviews.

Notes

12. Meir Sternberg, *Expositional Modes and Temporal Ordering* (Baltimore and London: Johns Hopkins UP, 1978), 65.

13. Raymond Durgnat, *A Long Hard Look at "Psycho"* (London: BFI, 2002), 169.

14. See Steven Schneider, "Maufacturing Horror in Hitchcock's *Psycho*," *Cine-Action* 50 (October 1999): 71.

15. See Deborah Knight and George McKnight, "Suspense and Its Master," in Richard Allen and Sam Ishii-Gonzales, eds., *Alfred Hitchcock: Centenary Essays* (London: BFI, 1999), 108. For Hitchcock's comments on suspense and romance, see Gottlieb, ed., *Hitchcock on Hitchcock*, 72.

16. One might be reminded of the words of the old English music hall song: "My old man said, 'Follow the van, don't dillydally on the way!' "

17. Smith, *Hitchcock: Suspense, Humor and Tone*, 19.

18. Truffaut, *Hitchcock*, 109.

19. Cameron writes of the film: "Hitchcock builds up his suspense in sections, which depend on various complications. At times we almost forget the predicament of the little boy." "Hitchcock and the Mechanics of Suspense 1," 5.

20. Truffaut, *Hitchcock*, 272.

21. Truffaut, *Hitchcock*, 73.

22. Carroll, *Theorizing the Moving Image*, 122.

23. Carroll, "The Paradox of Suspense," 79.

24. I thank Sid Gottlieb for this suggestion.

25. Victor Perkins, *Film as Film* (Harmondsworth, Eng.: Penguin, 1972), 89–90.

26. Sigmund Freud, "Jokes and Their Relation to the Unconscious" (1905), in *The Standard Edition of the Complete Psychological Works of Sigmund Freud* (hereafter, *SE*), trans. James Strachey in collaboration with Anna Freud, vol. 8 (London: Hogarth Press and the Institute of Psycho-Analysis, 1953–1974), 229.

27. Sigmund Freud, "Humour" (1927), in *SE* 21:162.

28. For detailed discussion, see Smith, *Hitchcock: Suspense, Humour and Tone*, 50–54.

29. James Naremore, "Hitchcock and Humour," in Richard Allen and Sam Ishii-Gonzales, eds., *Hitchcock: Past and Future* (London and New York: Routledge, 2004), 27.

30. Thomas M. Bauso, "*Rope*: Hitchcock's Unkindest Cut," in Walter Raubicheck and Walter Srebnick, eds., *Hitchcock's Rereleased Films: From "Vertigo" to "Rope"* (Detroit, Mich.: Wayne State UP, 1991), 233.

31. Smith, *Hitchcock: Suspense, Humour and Tone*, 57–71.

32. Truffaut, *Hitchcock*, 127.

33. André Bazin, "Hitchcock vs. Hitchcock," in Albert J. LaValley, ed., *Focus on Hitchcock* (Englewood Cliffs, N.J.: Prentice Hall, 1972), 65.

34. Truffaut, *Hitchcock*, 72.

35. See Gaylyn Studlar, *In the Realm of Pleasure: Von Sternberg, Dietrich, and the Masochistic Aesthetic* (Urbana: U of Illinois P, 1988). Unfortunately, Studlar's argument about von Sternberg's aesthetic takes place in the context of constructing a theory that the film spectator him/herself is a masochist, which is as absurd as the theories of the sadistic spectator that Studlar is arguing against.

36. Michael Walker notes that while women in Hitchcock may eavesdrop, they are not cast as voyeurs. See Walker, *Hitchcock's Motifs* (Amsterdam: U of Amsterdam P, 2005), 164–70.

37. The female gaze in *Rebecca* is noted by John Orr in *Hitchcock and Twentieth Century Cinema* (London and New York: Wallflower Press, 2005), 84–88. I have also elaborated upon it in detail in "Daphne du Maurier and Alfred Hitchcock," in Robert Stam and Alessandra Raengo, eds., *A Companion to Literature and Film* (New York: Blackwell, 2004), 298–325.

3. Knowledge and Sexual Difference

1. Herbert Brean, "A Case of Identity," *Life* (June 29, 1953), 97–100, 102, 104. The story was first dramatized as "A Case of Mistaken Identity" on *Robert Montgomery Presents*, broadcast on January 11, 1954. Marshall Deutelbaum notes that there are similarities between the Hitchcock and Montgomery versions that suggest Hitchcock's familiarity with the earlier adaptation. See "Finding the Right Man in *The Wrong Man*," in Marshall Deutelbaum and Leland Poague, eds., *The Hitchcock Reader* (Ames, Iowa: Iowa State UP, 1986), 209.

2. Brean, "A Case of Identity," 102.

3. This is noted by David Sterritt in *The Films of Alfred Hitchcock* (New York: Cambridge UP, 1993), 76–77.

4. See Thomas Leitch, "The Outer Circle: Hitchcock on Television," in Richard Allen and Sam Ishii-Gonzales, eds., *Alfred Hitchcock: Centenary Essays* (London: BFI, 1999), 59–71.

5. François Truffaut (with Helen Scott), *Hitchcock*, rev. ed. (New York: Simon and Schuster, 1984), 103.

6. The film bears some affinities in this respect to *I Confess* (1953), in which a celibate priest, played by Montgomery Clift, is wrongfully accused of the crime of murder. He cannot clear his name even though he knows who did the murder, because this knowledge was communicated to him in the secrecy of the confessional. Again, *I Confess* is a "wrong man" story that is preoccupied with the consequences of wrongful accusation and imprisonment, though here the "coercion" is one that is bred by conscience.

7. Aristotle, *Poetics*, trans. by S. H. Butcher (New York: Hill and Wang, 1961), 11:2.

8. Terence Cave, *Recognitions: A Study in Poetics* (Oxford: Oxford UP, 1988), 250.

9. Cave, *Recognitions*, 251.

10. See Thomas Elsaesser, "The Dandy in Hitchcock," in Allen and Ishii-Gonzales, eds., *Alfred Hitchcock: Centenary Essays*, 3–13.

11. See, for example, Donald Spoto, *The Dark Side of Genius: The Life of Alfred Hitchcock* (New York: Da Capo Press, 1999), 16.

12. See Alfred Hitchcock, "*Rear Window*," in Albert J. LaValley, ed., *Focus on Hitchcock* (Englewood Cliffs, N.J.: Prentice Hall, 1972), 43–44.

13. Christopher Morris, *The Hanging Figure: On Suspense and the Films of Alfred Hitchcock* (Westport, Conn.: Praeger, 2002), 40–46.

14. Thornhill's name is also an in-joke on the name of David O. Selznick, whose "O" also stood for nothing. He added it to his name to give it the right sounding ring.

15. I thank Rahul Hamid for the idea of "secular Catholicism" in Hitchcock in an unpublished paper entitled "Hitchcock as a Catholic Director."

16. I shall defer discussion of the less visible but extremely important figure of the female dandy in Hitchcock until chapter 4.

17. *Greenmantle* was a book that Hitchcock expressed interest in filming, and he began development of a project to adapt Buchan's *The Three Hostages*. See Sidney Gottlieb, "Unknown Hitchcock: The Unrealized Projects," in Richard Allen and Sam Ishii-Gonzales, eds., *Hitchcock: Past and Future* (London: Routledge, 2004), 85–106.

18. Influential analysis of female subjectivity in Hitchcock from this period are offered by Laura Mulvey in "Visual Pleasure and Narrative Cinema," reprinted in *Visual and Other Pleasures* (Bloomington: Indiana UP, 1989); by Raymond Bellour in his essays on Hitchcock collected in *The Analysis of Film* (Bloomington: Indiana UP, 2001); and by Tania Modleski in *The Women Who Knew Too Much: Hitchcock and Feminist Theory* (New York: Routledge, 1989).

19. See Patrice Petro, "Rematerializing the Vanishing 'Lady'": Feminism, Hitchcock, and Interpretation," in Deutelbaum and Poague, eds., *A Hitchcock Reader*, 122–33.

20. See Michael Walker, "The Stolen Raincoat and the Bloodstained Dress: *Young and Innocent* and *Stage Fright*," in Allen and Ishii-Gonzales, eds., *Alfred Hitchcock: Centenary Essays*, 187–204.

21. See Phil Hansen, "The Misogynist at Rest: Women in Hitchcock's *Lifeboat*," *Hitchcock Annual* (1996–1997): 110–16.

22. On the transformation of James Stewart's persona, see Amy Lawrence, "American Shame: *Rope*, James Stewart, and the Postwar Crisis in Masculinity," in Jonathan Freedman and Richard Millington, eds., *Hitchcock's America* (New York: Oxford UP, 1999), 55–76.

23. For a discussion of female knowledge and agency in *Rear Window*, see Elise Lemaire, "Voyeurism and the Postwar Crisis in Masculinity," in John Belton, ed., *Alfred Hitchcock's "Rear Window"* (New York: Cambridge UP, 2000), 57–90.

24. Lesley Brill, *The Hitchcock Romance: Love and Irony in Hitchcock's Films* (Princeton, N.J.: Princeton UP, 1988), 279.

25. William Rothman, *Hitchcock: The Murderous Gaze* (Cambridge: Harvard UP, 1982), 53.

26. It should be noted that while the object of investigation by the women in these films is a brooding, incipiently villainous male character, sometimes the object of investigation by a woman is herself a woman, a "wrong woman," who is in some way associated with the male villain, as in *Rebecca*, *Stage Fright*, and, in a minor way, *Vertigo*, where the character of Midge Wood plays the role of the female investigator.

27. Mark Crispin Miller, "Hitchcock's Suspicions and *Suspicion*," in *Boxed In: The Culture of TV* (Evanston: Northwestern UP, 1988), 241–78.

28. For the affirmative interpretation, see Maurice Yacower, *Hitchcock's British Films* (Hamdon, Conn..: Archon Books, 1977), 126; for an ironic interpretation see Rothman, *Hitchcock: The Murderous Gaze*, 99. For a detailed critical discussion of this film, see Richard Allen, "Sir John and the Half-Caste: Identity and Representation in Hitchcock's *Murder!*," *Hitchcock Annual* 13 (2004–2005): 92–126.

29. Allan Lloyd Smith provides a valuable psychoanalytically oriented analysis of the mother's secret in "*Marnie*, the Dead Mother, and the Phantom," *Hitchcock Annual* (2002–2003): 164–80.

30. Why does Judy put on the necklace? We might surmise that she has finally capitulated entirely to Scottie's madness or we might, equally, impute to her an intention, perhaps an unacknowledged or unconscious one, that Scottie will recognize who she really is.

31. I thank Dana Polan for drawing my attention to the importance of these shots.

32. This is noted by Peter Swaab, in "Hitchcock's Homophobia? The Case of *Murder!*," *Perversions* 4 (Spring 1995): 21.

33. Rothman, *Hitchcock: The Murderous Gaze*, 53.

4. Sexuality and Style

1. Walter Pater, *The Renaissance* (Glasgow: Collins, 1961), 210–11.

2. Pater, *The Renaissance*, 208.

3. Ibid.

4. Kenneth Clarke, "Introduction" to Walter Pater, *Renaissance*, 11.

Notes

5. Pater, *The Renaissance*, 128.

6. See Alfred Hitchcock, "On Style: An Interview with *Cinema*," in Sidney Gottlieb, ed., *Hitchcock on Hitchcock* (Berkeley: U of California P, 1995), 285–302.

7. Alan Sinfield, *The Wilde Century: Effeminacy, Oscar Wilde, and the Queer Moment* (New York: Columbia UP, 1995), 98.

8. Ellen Moers, *The Dandy: Brummell to Beerbohm* (New York: Viking, 1960), 174.9. This distinction between Apollonian and Dionysian form is taken from Friedrich Nietzsche, *The Birth of Tragedy*, in Raymond Geuss and Ronald Spiers, eds., *The Birth of Tragedy and Other Writings*, trans. by Ronald Spiers (New York: Cambridge UP, 1999), 1–116. Nietzsche's book is itself a source of aestheticist ideas, and it is a work that mediates romantic irony and aestheticism. Furthermore, Nietzsche's concept of the *Übermensch* or superman who ranged beyond the framework of orthodox morality was certainly au courant in the 1920s and permeates the Hannay novels of Buchan, and through Buchan informs Hitchcock's characterization of the dandy. The relationship between Nietzsche's ideas, as filtered through their historical context, and Hitchcock's films, deserves more extended treatment.

10. In Poe's tale the well-being of the woman whose portrait is being painted is neglected by the painter, who is obsessed with completing his portrait of her. However, Poe's moral is clearly the triumph of artistic form over life itself. It is the picture itself that kills the thing that it represents.

11. Peter Conrad, *The Hitchcock Murders* (London: Faber and Faber), 67.

12. For a detailed discussion of Wilde's influence on Hitchcock, see Ken Mogg, "Alfred Hitchcock: Master of Paradox," at www.sensesofcinema.com/contents/directors/05/hitchcock.html.

13. Sigmund Freud, "Fragment of an Analysis of a Case of Hysteria" (1905), in *The Standard Edition of the Complete Psychological Works of Sigmund Freud* (hereafter, *SE*), trans. James Strachey, vol. 7 (London: Hogarth Press and the Institute of Psycho-Analysis, 1953–1974), 50.

14. Chasseguet-Smirgel's careful reading of Freud on perversion has been largely ignored by humanities scholars. Most salient, in this context, is *Creativity and Perversion* (New York: Norton, 1984). See also Chasseguet-Smirgel, *The Ego Ideal: A Psychoanalytic Essay on the Malady of the Ideal* (New York: Norton, 1985). By invoking Chasseguet-Smirgel as a Freudian, I mean to emphasize the fact that she elaborates a logic implicit in Freud's views, and therefore one that should be understood and assessed historically, alongside and in relation to Wilde's elaboration of the same themes.

15. See Sigmund Freud, "On Narcissism" (1914), in *SE* 14:73–104. Freud, as far as I am aware, does not discuss the figure of the dandy explicitly.

Notes

16. Thomas Elsaesser, "The Dandy in Hitchcock," in Richard Allen and Sam Ishii-Gonzales, eds., *Alfred Hitchcock: Centenary Essays* (London: BFI, 1999), 10–11. Elsaesser's essay directly inspired the argument of this section.

17. Martin Green, *Children of the Sun* (New York: Basic Books, 1976), 14.

18. Green, *Children of the Sun*, 12.

19. On the Byron legend, see Fiona McCarthy, *Byron: Life and Legend* (New York: Farrar, Straus, and Giroux, 2002), 525–74

20. François Truffaut (with Helen Scott), *Hitchcock*, rev. ed. (New York: Simon and Schuster, 1984), 82.

21. I explore the influence of du Maurier on Hitchcock in full in Richard Allen, "Daphne du Maurier and Alfred Hitchcock," in Robert Stam and Alessandra Raengo, eds., *A Companion to Literature and Film* (New York: Blackwell, 2004), 298–325.

22. See Robin Wood, *Hitchcock's Films Revisited*, 2d ed. (New York: Columbia UP, 2002), 336–57.

23. This is the profound weakness of Robert Corber's nonetheless informative book, *In the Name of National Security: Hitchcock, Homophobia, and the Political Construction of Gender in Postwar America* (Durham, N.C.: Duke UP, 1993). Erroneously, to my mind, Corber casts Hitchcock as a ventriloquist of homophobic Cold War ideology.

24. Examples of such actors include Ivor Novello (*The Lodger*); Farley Granger (who plays a homosexual in *Rope* and the ultra-straight Guy in *Strangers on a Train*); Montgomery Clift (*I Confess*), who Hitchcock also wanted in *Rope*; Anthony Perkins (*Psycho*); and even Cary Grant himself, who was rumored to be homosexual.

25. For a discussion of Dietrich's role in relation to lesbian desire, see Patricia White, "Hitchcock and Hom(m)osexuality," in Richard Allen and Sam Ishii-Gonzales, eds., *Hitchcock: Past and Future* (London and New York: Routledge, 2004), 221.

26. Raymond Durgnat, *The Strange Case of Alfred Hitchcock* (Cambridge: MIT Press, 1978), 61.

27. Elsaesser, "The Dandy in Hitchcock," 5. However, it is also worth remembering that in the early years in England, Hitchcock would entertain reporters in dressing gown and silk pajamas, rather in the manner of Noël Coward. See Leonard Leff, *Hitchcock and Selznick: The Rich and Strange Collaboration of Alfred Hitchcock and David O. Selznick in Hollywood* (Berkeley: U of California P, 1987), 13.

28. See James Eli Adams, *Dandies and Desert Saints: Styles of Victorian Masculinity* (Ithaca, N.Y.: Cornell UP, 1995), 195.

29. See Thomas Leitch, "The Outer Circle: Hitchcock on Television," in Allen and Ishii-Gonzales, eds., *Alfred Hitchcock: Centenary Essays*, 65–69.

30. Quoted by John Russell Taylor in the E! Channel documentary *True Hollywood Stories: Alfred Hitchcock* (1999). I thank Ken Mogg for this reference.

Notes

31. David Freeman, who worked with Hitchcock on his last script, reports that one day Hitchcock confessed to him, "You know, David, that Alma and I do not have relations. Haven't for years" (*The Last Days of Alfred Hitchcock* [New York: Overlook Press, 1999], 29). Patrick McGilligan states categorically that Hitchcock was impotent, citing among other things a joke by Hitchcock that he had only ever had sex once, to conceive Pat; a comment by *Marnie*'s writer and close family friend Jay Presson Allen that Hitchcock was "functionally impotent"; and a comment in response to Truffaut's observation about the intimacy and passion of his sex scenes: "I'm a celibate, you know. I'm not against it, but I just don't think about it very much" (*Alfred Hitchcock: A Life in Darkness and Light* [New York: HarperCollins, 2003], 177).

32. John Russell Taylor reports that during the shooting of *The Blackguard* in German, director Graham Cutts, who was accompanied by his wife, was having an affair. This led to absences from the set and de facto directorial decision-making by Hitchcock. Taylor, *Hitch: The Life and Times of Alfred Hitchcock* (New York: Da Capo, 1996), 57.

33. The shot from *Blackmail* is an early attempt on Hitchcock's part to evoke the sense of psychological dislocation later realized more completely in the combined tracking and zoom point-of-view shot that evokes Scottie Ferguson's vertigo in *Vertigo*.

34. Tania Modleski, *The Women Who Knew Too Much: Hitchcock and Feminist Theory* (New York: Routledge, 1989), 24.

35. See Sabrina Barton, "Hitchcock's Hands," in Sidney Gottlieb and Christopher Brookhouse, eds., *Framing Hitchcock: Selected Essays from the Hitchcock Annual* (Detroit: Wayne State UP, 2002), 174–75.

36. See Slavoj Žižek, *Looking Awry: An Introduction to Lacan to Popular Culture* (Cambridge: MIT Press, 1992), 88–97.

37. I discuss the "Hitchcockian Blot" in general, and this sequence in particular, in more detail, in chapters 5 and 6.

38. Durgnat, *The Strange Case of Alfred Hitchcock*, 203.

39. Ken Mogg notes the cannibalism motif and suggests a possible source for this in Huysman's novel *Against Nature*. See "Alfred Hitchcock: Master of Paradox" (cited in note 12).

40. Arthur Laurents, *Original Story by Arthur Laurents* (New York: Applause Books, 2000), 127. See also his comments in Walter Srebnick, ed., "Working with Hitchcock: A Screenwriter's Forum with Evan Hunter, Arthur Laurents, and Joe Stefano," *Hitchcock Annual* (2001–2002): 3.

41. I have not been able to find written corroboration of this, but more than one respondent from rural areas in the United States has confirmed this practice.

42. D. A. Miller, "Anal Rope," *Representations* 32 (Fall 1990): 130.

Notes

43. One character in *Jamaica Inn*, a bawdy smuggler, remarks that his public hanging "with the women watching" will "make 'em sit up." See Conrad, *The Hitchcock Murders*, 261.

44. See Amy Lawrence, "American Shame: *Rope*, James Stewart, and the Crisis in Postwar Masculinity," in Jonathan Freedman and Richard Millington, eds., *Hitchcock's America* (New York: Oxford UP, 1999), 67.

45. Laurents, *Original Story*, 131.

46. Stewart, quoted in Charlotte Chandler, *It's Only a Movie: Alfred Hitchcock, A Personal Biography* (New York: Applause Books, 2005), 169.

47. There are three instances of romantic encounters on a train in Hitchcock's work in addition to *Strangers on a Train*: *The 39 Steps*, *Suspicion*, and *North by Northwest*. In *The Lady Vanishes*, the couple is formed on the train although they meet before boarding.

48. Granger, quoted in Chandler, *It's Only a Movie*, 196.

49. I thank Bill Paul for drawing my attention to the importance of class envy and for his other comments on this film.

50. Federico Windhausen provides a shot-by-shot breakdown of this sequence in "Hitchcock and the Found Footage Installation: Müller and Girardet's *The Phoenix Tapes*," *Hitchcock Annual* (2003–2004): 210–12. I thank him for introducing me to this work.

51. Theodore Price, *Hitchcock and Homosexuality* (Metuchen, N.J.: Scarecrow Press, 1992), 367–80. Price reads homosexuality everywhere in Hitchcock's work, including *Torn Curtain*, even in places where it is not to be found. However, he does not discuss these three suspense sequences.

52. Truffaut, *Hitchcock*, 309.

53. Donald Spoto, *The Dark Side of Genius* (New York: Da Capo Press, 1999), 488.

54. See Robert Samuels, *Hitchcock's Bi-textuality: Lacan, Feminisms, and Queer Theory* (Albany: State UP of New York, 1998), 109–21, for an interpretation of *Rear Window* along "bi-textual" lines. For an earlier, baroque elaboration on the same theme, see Lee Edelman, "*Rear Window*'s Glasshole," in Ellis Hanson, ed., *Out Takes: Essays on Queer Theory and Film* (Durham, N.C.: Duke UP, 1999), 72–96. I earlier noted the range of homosexual actors that Hitchcock worked with. Fittingly, perhaps the least obvious of these is Raymond Burr himself.

55. See Lee Edelman, "Piss Elegant: Freud, Hitchcock, and the Micturating Penis," *GLQ* 2.1–2 (1995): 149–77.

56. Truffaut, *Hitchcock*, 262.

57. This structure of displaced looking is in fact invoked near the beginning of *Rear Window*. L. B. Jefferies looks across the courtyard at a helicopter buzzing the rooftops where two women are bathing topless, but they are concealed from Jefferies' gaze.

Notes

58. Truffaut, *Hitchcock*, 195.

59. Schiller, quoted in Leff, *Hitchcock and Selznick*, 63.

60. Rhona Berenstein, "'I'm Not the Sort of Person Men Marry': Monsters, Queers, and Hitchcock's *Rebecca*," in Cory K. Creekmur and Alexander Doty, eds., *Out in Culture: Gay, Lesbian, and Queer Essays on Popular Culture* (Durham, N.C.: Duke UP, 1995), 254.

61. Thanks to Ira Bhaskar for drawing my attention to this spiral pattern.

62. For a full analysis of the shower scene, see Philip Skerry, *The Shower Scene in Hitchcock's "Psycho": Creating Cinematic Suspense and Terror* (New York: Edwin Mellen Press, 2005), 281–332.

63. See Lee Edelman, "Hitchcock's Future," in Allen and Ishii-Gonzales, eds., *Alfred Hitchcock: Centenary Essays*, 239–62.

64. See Žižek, *Looking Awry*, 105–106. As Evan Hunter put it to me, somewhat ruefully, from a writer's point of view: "Hitchcock threw birds at my script!"

5. Expressionism

1. Lotte Eisner, *The Haunted Screen* (Berkeley: U of California P, 1969), 113

2. Donald Spoto, *The Dark Side of Genius* (New York: Da Capo Press, 1999), 68.

3. Thomas Elsaesser, *Weimar Cinema and After: Germany's Historical Imaginary* (New York: Routledge, 2000), 77.

4. Bettina Rosenblatt, "Doubts and Doubles: The German Connection," in Richard Allen and Sam Ishii-Gonzales, eds., *Hitchcock: Past and Future* (London and New York: Routledge, 2004), 44.

5. Rosenblatt, "Doubts and Doubles," 38

6. William Rothman, *Hitchcock: The Murderous Gaze* (Cambridge: Harvard UP, 1982), 84.

7. Evan Hunter's script of *Marnie* contains a scene in a cinema taken from the novel that focuses on a theft, but although much of his script seemed to make it into Jay Presson Allen's final screenplay for the film, this scene was left out.

8. Susan Smith provides a detailed analysis of this sequence in *Hitchcock: Suspense, Humor and Tone* (London: BFI, 1999), 11–15.

9. John D. Barlow, *German Expressionist Film* (Boston: Twayne. 1982), 136–37.

10. Descartes writes, "When looking from a window and saying I see men who pass in the street, I really do not see them, but infer that what I see is men … and yet what do I see from the window but hats and coats which may cover automatic machines." *The Philosophical Works of Descartes*, trans. Elizabeth Haldane and G. R. T. Ross (New York: Cambridge UP, 1931), 155.

Notes

11. Frances Guerin, *A Culture of Light: Cinema and Technology in 1920s Germany* (Minneapolis: U of Minnesota P, 2005), 163.

12. Sidney Gottlieb, "Early Hitchcock: The German Influence," in Sidney Gottlieb and Christopher Brookhouse, eds., *Framing Hitchcock* (Detroit: Wayne State UP, 2002), 44.

13. Elizabeth Weis, *The Silent Scream* (Rutherford, N.J.: Farleigh Dickinson UP, 1982), 45

14. See Charles Barr, *English Hitchcock* (Moffat, U.K.: Cameron and Hollis, 1999), 78–81.

15. Thomas Elsaesser notes the role of nature in Murnau's work, which he traces to the influence of what he calls the "naturalist" cinema of Scandinavian directors in *Weimar Cinema and After*, 228. Bettina Rosenblatt discusses the influence of Tieck on Murnau in "Doubts and Doubles: The German Connection," 47.

16. Ken Mogg suggests a wider salience of Schopenhauer's romantic philosophy for Hitchcock's work. See his MacGuffin webpage at www.labyrinth.net.au/~muffin.

17. See James McLaughlin, "All in the Family: Alfred Hitchcock's *Shadow of a Doubt*," in Marshall Deutelbaum and Leland Poague, eds., *A Hitchcock Reader* (Ames: Iowa State UP, 1986), 143.

18. My understanding of the film draws on Lesley Brill, *The Hitchcock Romance* (Princeton, N.J: Princeton UP, 1988), 283–91.

19. John Orr, *Hitchcock and Twentieth Century Cinema* (London: Wallflower Press, 2005), 58.

20. One explanation of the strangeness of this shot is that it is one of the many places where Hitchcock invokes film history. In this case it is Edwin Porter's film *The Great Train Robbery* (1903), in which an extradiegetic gun shot toward the audience by one of the characters was used as a framing device in the exhibition of the film.

21. Rothman, *Hitchcock: The Murderous Gaze*, 75.

22. For a detailed study of patterns and alternation in Hitchcock's work, see Raymond Bellour's *The Analysis of Film* (Bloomington: Indiana UP, 2001). For a critical discussion of Bellour's work on Hitchcock, see Richard Allen, "Hitchcock After Bellour," *Hitchcock Annual* (2002–2003): 117–48.

23. Rothman, *Hitchcock: The Murderous Gaze*, 279.

24. Sam Ishii-Gonzales, "An Analysis of the Parlor Scene in Psycho x2," *Hitchcock Annual* (2001–2002): 149–54.

25. Sabrina Barton "'Criss Cross': Paranoia and Projection in *Strangers on a Train*," in Cory K. Creekmur and Alexander Doty, eds., *Out in Culture* (Durham, N.C.: Duke UP, 1995), 221.

26. Barton "'Criss Cross,'" 222.

Notes

27. Lotte Eisner describes this film in *Murnau* (Berkeley: U of California P, 1973), 28–33; Theodore Price speculates on its influence upon Hitchcock in *Hitchcock and Homosexuality* (Metuchen, N.J.: Scarecrow Press, 1992), 322. For further discussion of the Janus face in Hitchcock, see Brigitte Peucker, "The Cut of Representation: Painting and Sculpture in Hitchcock," in Richard Allen and Sam Ishii-Gonzales, eds., *Alfred Hitchcock: Centenary Essays* (London: BFI, 1999), 146–48.

28. See Slavoj Žižek, "*Vertigo*: The Drama of a Deceived Platonist," *Hitchcock Annual* 12 (2003–2004): 69–70.

29. Dennis Zirnite, "Hitchcock on the Level: The Heights of Spatial Tension," *Film Criticism* 10.3 (Spring 1986): 4. For further discussion of Hitchcock's staircases, see Michael Walker, *Hitchcock's Motifs* (Amsterdam: U of Amsterdam P, 2005), 350–72.

30. Rothman, *Hitchcock: The Murderous Gaze*, 33.

31. See Robert Kolker, "The Man Who Knew More Than Too Much," in *The "Psycho" Casebook* (New York: Oxford UP, 2004), 205–255.

32. See, for example, Robin Wood, *Hitchcock's Films Revisited*, 2d ed. (New York: Columbia UP, 2002), 128; and Brill, *The Hitchcock Romance*, 205–206.

33. Thanks to Sid Gottlieb for drawing my attention to this example.

34. Ever since Lotte Eisner's *The Haunted Screen*, Spring-Heeled Jack has been identified with Jack the Ripper. The mistake is repeated by John Barlow in *German Expressionist Film* and Thomas Elsaesser in *Weimar Cinema and After*. Hitchcock scholar Theodore Price sees it as a direct source for Hitchcock's interest in the Jack the Ripper myth in *Hitchcock and Homosexuality*, and I repeat the mistake in my article "*The Lodger* and the Origins of Hitchcock's Aesthetic," in *Hitchcock Annual* (2001–2002): 53. For the record, Spring-Heeled Jack is not Jack the Ripper although he may have been an inspiration for Jack the Ripper's name. Spring-Heeled Jack, who first appeared in 1837, leaped out from hedgerows or from behind walls on unsuspecting victims, usually young women. Spring-Heeled Jack dressed up in a tight-fitting costume (which, according to one victim, "felt like oilskin"), a large helmet, and a black clock with a W inscribed on the back. He "breathed" a blue flame on his victims and scratched with his clawlike fingers at their faces and clothes. It is thought that the original Spring-Heeled Jack was an Irish nobleman, the Marquis of Watford, who was renowned for his sadistic practical jokes and scorn for women. "Sightings" of Jack continued as late as 1904 and the costume of the Batman was probably inspired by him. See Peter Haining, *The Legend and Bizarre Crimes of Spring-Heeled Jack* (London: Muller, 1977).

35. For further discussion of the carnivalesque in *The Ring* and *Strangers on a Train*, see Thomas Hennelly, Jr., "Alfred Hitchcock's Carnival," *Hitchcock Annual* 13 (2004–2005): 154–78.

Notes

36. The lyrics for "The Band Played On" are: "Casey would waltz with the strawberry blonde, and the band played on/He'd glide 'cross the floor with the girl he adored, and the band played on/His brain was so loaded he nearly exploded, the poor girl would shake with alarm/He'd ne'er leave the girl with the strawberry curls, and the band played on." (Thank you, Ken Mogg.)

37. See Barr, *English Hitchcock*, 129.

38. I thank Bill Paul for reminding me of this film.

39. There is further complex avian imagery in the film less immediately salient to Hitchcock. When the Professor is cuckolded, he is equated with a chicken and characterized as "birdbrained."

6. Color Design

1. See the quote from Bazin's reflections upon interviewing Hitchcock that opens this book, from "Hitchcock Versus Hitchcock," in Albert J. LaValley, ed.. *Focus on Hitchcock* (Englewood Cliffs, N.J.: Prentice Hall, 1972), 69. There is no doubt, in this context, that Hitchcock would have fully embraced digital technology and digital effects, for they would have allowed him to fully construct the narrative world of a film from his desk, not only in terms of the visual orchestration of the surface of the film but also in terms of the kind of navigation and penetration of space that he explores in *Vertigo*.

2. This was first pointed out by Ian Cameron in "Hitchcock 2: Suspense and Meaning," *Movie* 6 (January 1963): 9.

3. Natalie Kalmus, "Color Consciousness," in Angela Dalle Vacche and Brian Price, eds., *Color: The Film Reader* (New York: Routledge, 2006), 24. This article is reprinted from the *Journal of the Society of Motion Picture Engineers* 25.1 (1935): 139–47.

4. Kalmus, "Color Consciousness," 26.

5. Alfred Hitchcock, "Direction," in Sidney Gottlieb, ed., *Hitchcock on Hitchcock* (Berkeley: U of California P, 1995), 258. Originally published in Charles Davy, ed., *Footnotes to the Film* (New York: Oxford UP, 1937), 3–15.

6. Alfred Hitchcock, "Interview with Charles Thomas Samuels" (1972), in Sidney Gottlieb, ed., *Alfred Hitchcock: Interviews* (Jackson: U of Mississippi P, 2003), 136.

7. Kalmus, "Color Consciousness," 28.

8. Edith Head and Jane Kesner Ardmore, *The Dress Doctor* (Boston: Little, Brown, 1959), 153–54. This is quoted in Gorhem Kindem, "Toward a Semiotic Theory of Visual Communication in the Cinema: A Reappraisal of Semiotic Theories from a Cinematic Perspective and a Semiotic Analysis of Color Signs and Communication in the Color Films of Alfred Hitchcock" (Ph.D. diss., Northwestern University, 1977),

Notes

75. This dissertation is a valuable resource for thinking about color in Hitchcock's work.

9. Alfred Hitchcock, "Alfred Hitchcock Talking," in the journal *Films and Filming* (1959), quoted in Patrick McGilligan, *Alfred Hitchcock: A Life in Darkness and Light* (New York: HarperCollins, 2003), 567.

10. Kalmus, "Color Consciousness," 28.

11. Edward Branigan, "The Articulation of Color in a Filmic System: *Deux ou trois choses que je sais d'elle*," in Dalle Vacche and Price, eds., *Color: The Film Reader*, 170–82.

12. The shot seems to echo images from Antonioni's *Red Desert* (1964), where the dull industrial landscape articulates the desiccated emotional life of the protagonist.

13. "Hitchcock talks about Lights, Camera, Action: An Interview with Herb A Lightman," in Gottlieb, ed., *Hitchcock on Hitchcock*, 306.

14. Kindem, "Toward a Semiotic Theory of Visual Communication in the Cinema," 212.

15. Hitchcock, quoted in Donald Spoto, *The Dark Side of Genius* (New York: Da Capo Press, 1999), 22. According to Spoto, this memory dates from as early as 1905, when Hitchcock was six years old. This jade color is also strikingly rendered in at least two pre-Raphealite paintings. In William Holman Hunt's "Isabella and the Pot of Basil" (1867–68), Isabella inclines over a golden pot of basil containing the severed head of her lover while a jade light from frame left bathes her diaphanous gown in a deathly hue. In Dane Gabriel Rossetti's unfinished painting "Found" (1869?), a Hardy-esque country man in a smock tries to lift a fallen women of the city from the ground who is dressed in a violet shawl, her face a pasty jade green.

16. For further analysis of color in *Topaz*, see Lesley Brill, *The Hitchcock Romance* (Princeton, N.J.: Princeton UP, 1988), 188–90.

17. Donald Spoto, *The Art of Alfred Hitchcock* (New York: Doubleday, 1976), 364.

18. I explore the color scheme of *The Birds* in detail in Richard Allen, "Avian Metaphor in *The Birds*," in Sidney Gottlieb and Christopher Brookhouse, eds., *Framing Hitchcock* (Detroit: Wayne State UP, 2002), 281–309.

Conclusion

1. For an explicit discussion and defense of historical poetics against rival research paradigms, see David Bordwell, *On the History of Film Style* (Cambridge: Harvard UP, 1997), 116–57.

2. On "The Eve of St. Agnes," see Richard Allen, "Hitchcock, or the Pleasures of Metaskepticism," in Richard Allen and Sam Ishii-Gonzales, eds., *Alfred Hitchcock:*

Notes

Centenary Essays (London: BFI, 1999), 229–31. On "Lamia," see Robin Wood, *Hitchcock's Films Revisited*, 2d ed. (New York: Columbia UP, 2002), 66. On the "Rime of the Ancient Mariner," see John P. McCombe, "Oh, I see … ": *The Birds* and the Culmination of Hitchcock's Hyper-Romantic Vision," *Cinema Journal* 44.3 (Spring 2005): 70–71.

3. In *Hitchcock and Twentieth Century Cinema* (London and New York: Wallflower Press, 2005), John Orr proposes, after Gilles Deleuze, that David Hume's philosophy is the key influence on Hitchcock. Aside from the fact that this argument is based on scattered quotations, I find the argument unconvincing on at least three counts. First, Hume was a classical empiricist and hence a skeptic. Hitchcock, as I have argued, is not. He may be a skeptic about appearances but "knowledge by intuition" plays a central role in his work. Second, how is the historical connection to Hitchcock forged? If it is to be through the Scottish literary tradition from Robert Louis Stevenson to John Buchan, this has to be demonstrated. Third, like many discussions of film as philosophy, Orr's fails to account for Hitchcock's style.

Index

//// effect/motif. *See* expressionist
   iconography
39 Steps, The (1935), xv, 83, 273*n*47; black
   comedy/tonal ambiguity in, 17; and
   classical suspense, 48; "perversity" in,
   28, 29; as recognition narrative, 77; as
   romantic renewal narrative, 15, 29, 79,
   217; as romantic thriller, 13, 29, 118, 254;
   as wrong-man narrative, 28, 49, 78
Ackland, Rodney, 131
Acton, Harold, 126
aesthete: as decadent/effeminate, 121;
   gamesman-, 22, 23; gentleman-, 119;
   Hitchcock as, xiii, 12, 114, 120, 154, 250,
   252, 253. *See also* dandy-aesthete
aestheticism: and dandyism, 120–21, 126;
   defined, 117, 119–20; and disguised/
   displaced same-sex passion, 119–20;
   and explicit link to homosexuality,
   124; Hitchcock's mode of, xv–xvi,
   65, 70, 134, 140, 154, 244, 255, 258,
   263*n*19; linked to "perversity," 119–25,
   152; linked to romantic ideal, 12, 123;

and male beauty, 130, 139; relation
   to expressionism, xiv, 162, 167, 216;
   relation to romantic irony, xiv, 253,
   256–57, 270*n*9; relation to surrealism,
   158, 219, 250, 252; and threat to
   heterosexual romance, 118, 120. *See
   also* romantic irony; sexuality; Wilde,
   Oscar
Almodóvar, Pedro, 258
Anderson, Judith, 44
Andrews, Julie, 225
Argento, Dario, 258
Aristotle, 5, 75–76
artifice, 30, 118, 123, 183, 252; internal and
   external, 15–16, 26; and "perverse"
   sexuality, 15, 26
artwork/paintings/pictures/portraits,
   131–40. *See also* "Hitchcockian Blot"
Auber, Brigitte, 230
Ault, Marie, 170

Baker, Diane, 199
Ballet mécanique (1924), 15

281

Index

Balsam, Martin, 42

Bankhead, Tallulah, 89

Baring, Norah, 101

Barr, Charles, 26, 175

Barthelme, Donald, 8

Barton, Sabrina, 190, 191

Bass, Saul, 162, 199, 202, 204, 242

Battleship Potemkin (1925), 14

Bauso, Thomas, 62

Bazin, André, ix, 65, 220, 277*n*1

Beckett, Samuel, 8

Behler, Ernst, 10

Bel Geddes, Barbara, 19

Belle de Jour (1967), 245

Bellour, Raymond, 21

Belton, John, 3, 14

Benjamin, Arthur, 51

Bennett, Charles, 100, 101, 175, 254

Berenstein, Rhona, 157

Bergman, Ingrid: in *Notorious*, 12, 48, 89, 153; in *Spellbound*, 11, 93; in *Under Capricorn*, 232

Birds, The (1963), 182, 255; //// effect/motif in, 202–203, 239; chaos/shadow world in, 203; classical suspense in, 48; color design in, 222, 224, 228, 230, 233, 238–39, 242, 247, 248–49; death birds in, 183, 214–15, 216; the double/doubling in, 178, 215, 233; and horror, 70, 161, 162–63, 254; and ironic ambivalence, 221; lovebirds in, 183, 216, 233, 238, 248; as melodrama, 162; profile shot in, 194; psychoanalysis in, 259; relation to English romanticism, 256; role/force of nature in, 183–84, 215; the sublime in, 162; surprise in, 47; as suspenseful mystery, 47; and vicarious suspense, 47

black comedy/humor, xiii, 11, 31, 34, 134, 136, 161, 253; Freud on, 59, 61; and irony, 60–61, 252; and suspense, 17–18, 59–64, 66; and tonal ambiguity, 8, 17–18

Blackguard, The (1925), 134, 164, 272*n*32; artwork/paintings in, 132–33, 134

Blackmail (1929), 20, 106, 107, 152, 253, 258, 272*n*33; //// effect/motif in, 177, 201, 202; artwork/paintings in, 134–36, 139, 140; Bennett stage play, 100, 101, 175; black comedy in, 134, 136; chaos/shadow world in, 175; chase sequence, 149; the dandy in, 99, 100, 107, 134–35, 171, 201, 203; the double/doubling in, 171, 175, 178; expressionism in, 171, 174–78, 185, 254; Hitchcock cameo in, 21; "Hitchcockian Blot" in, 205, 206; and ironic inversion, 80, 217; irony in, 171, 175, 177; male forms of knowing in, 82; and "masculine" detection/coercion, 100, 103; as melodrama, 254; plot synopsis, 100–101; pursuit of knowledge in, 80, 99, 100; rectangular staircase in, 192–93, 203; staircase and banisters in, 200; wrong/ed woman motif in, 80

Blue Angel, The (1930), 215–16

Bordwell, David, xii, xiii, 256

Borges, Jorge Luis, 8

both/and logic. *See* romantic irony

Branigan, Edward, 225

Brean, Herbert, 73, 74

Brill, Lesley, xi, xvii, 15, 27, 36, 94, 240

Brisson, Carl, 184

Brontë, Charlotte, 94

Browne, Roscoe Lee, 241

Brummell, Beau, 120

Buchan, John, 28, 84, 85, 91, 257

buffoon/ery: author/Hitchcock as, 6, 167; irony as, 6; transcendental, 27, 167

Bulwer-Lytton, Edward, 121

Buñuel, Luis, 245

Burgess, Guy, 148

Burr, Raymond, 33, 273*n*54

Byron, Lord George Gordon, 11, 120, 126

Cabinet of Dr. Caligari, The (1919), 164, 165–66, 180, 208

Calhern, Louis, 99

Index

Index

De Banzie, Brenda, 90
de Marney, Derrick, 86
De Palma, Brian, 258
de Quincy, Thomas, 122
Descartes, René, 169
Destiny (1921), 164, 179, 200, 210, 215
Devane, William, 128
Dial M for Murder (1954), 185, 265*n*47;
    color design in, 229, 241
Dick, Douglas, 141
Dietrich, Marlene, 129
Disraeli, Benjamin, 121
divided two-shot, 196–97
Donat, Robert, 48
doppelgänger/double/doubling, xvi, 33, 52,
    73, 75, 113–14, 145–47, 237, 252–53; both/
    and logic of, 192; death birds as, 214–15,
    233; as expressionist, 16–17, 31, 34, 164–
    66, 168, 171, 175, 178–79, 181–82, 193–97,
    219, 254; Freudian interpretation of,
    178, 180–81, 182; of the hero/heroine,
    83, 97, 99, 145; Hitchcock as (character)
    double, 21–23; integrated into classical
    narrative/Hollywood style, 184, 186;
    as Jekyll/Hyde, 94, 95, 97, 193, 257. *See
    also* chaos/shadow world; expressionist
    iconography; shot/reverse-shot
    structure
doubled (multiple/ambiguous) endings,
    18–20; in Hitchcock's films and TV
    shows, 74
Douglas, Lord Alfred, 127
Downhill (1927), 127; expressionism in,
    170, 173, 254; and ironic inversion,
    13, 217; as melodrama, 254; plot
    synopsis, 170
Doyle, Sir Arthur Conan, 108
Dr. Mabuse (1922), 205, 206
Du Maurier, Daphne, 65, 68, 96, 127
Du Maurier, Gerald, 126, 127
Dunnock, Mildred, 183, 245
Dupont, E. A., 172, 208, 209
Durgnat, Raymond, xvii, 12, 62, 130, 141

Easy Virtue (1927), 67, 68, 127; as
    expressionist melodrama, 254; wrong-
    woman in, 89
eavesdropping, 66, 132, 143, 199
Edelman, Lee, xi, xvii, 153
Eichner, Hans
Eisenstein, Sergei, 14
Eisner, Lotte, 164, 276n34
Eliot, George, 8
Elsaesser, Thomas, xvii, 126
epistemology. *See* knowledge
Evelyn, Judith, 33
expressionism/ist aesthetic, xvii, 16–17, 79,
    112, 136, 164–217, 224; analytic/al, 15, 24,
    31, 65, 184–92, 254; aural, 16, 174, 175–76;
    black-and-white/shadow world, xvi,
    163, 195, 220, 221, 252–53, 255; and color
    design, 218–19, 220, 236, 242–43, 246;
    defined, 165, 218; German, 4, 15, 162–63,
    164, 173, 178, 218, 257; and modernity,
    168–70; moral psychology of, 165,
    167, 169, 219, 246–48; objective, 236;
    and relation to aestheticism, xiv, 162,
    167; and role/force/power of nature,
    178–84, 193, 208, 215; subjective, 171–78,
    185–86, 209, 220, 236, 242–43. *See also*
    chaos/shadow world; *doppelgänger*/
    double
expressionist iconography, 192–216; ////
    effect/motif (parallel line motif), 177,
    190–91, 192, 200, 201–203, 208, 210,
    219, 236, 237, 238, 239, 243; banisters
    (vertical lines), 200; death birds, 183,
    214–16; divided two-shot, 187, 196–97;
    "Hitchcockian Blot," 140, 203, 205–
    208, 237, 246, 249; Janus face/profile
    shot, 22, 186, 188, 193–94, 198, 201;
    lovebirds, 187, 188, 183, 213, 215–16, 233,
    238; merry-go-round (of chaos/death),
    208–13; merry-go-round (as circle
    of life/waltz), 211–13; mirror shot,
    191, 194–95; mullioned window, 155,
    193, 197–99, 201; precipitous staircase

Index

Hall, Radclyffe, 129

Hamilton, Patrick, 141

Handewerk, Gary, 7

Hayes, John Michael, 29

Head, Edith, 222

Hecht, Ben, 100

Hedren, Tippi: in *The Birds*, 47; in *Marnie*, 21, 130

Hellinger, Mark, 74

Helmore, Tom, 19

Herrmann, Bernard, 52, 74, 160, 162, 216, 246

Herzberg, Martin, 132

Hitchcock, Patricia, 22, 272*n*31

"Hitchcockian Blot." *See* expressionist iconography

Hogan, Dick, 141

homoerotic desire/homoeroticism/homosexuality, xvi, 84, 143, 150,151, 253; as anal-phallic sublime, 252; or bisexual/queer, 106–107, 126; and the dandy, 112–13; disguised, 147–48; and link to aestheticism, 124; as "perverse," 118, 125, 130, 141, 142, 145–46, 161, 252; in *The Picture of Dorian Gray*, 122; and suspenseful mystery, 70

Homolka, Oscar, 22

"horizontal" and "vertical" aspect/form/structure, 6, 8–9, 27, 31, 35, 38, 192; defined, 3–4, 72

horror film/genre, 11, 37, 43, 49, 70, 154, 254, 258; aesthetics/rhetoric of, 160–63, 234; modern, 51

Howard, Brian, 126

Hunt, William Holman, 219, 278*n*15

Huysman, Joris Karl, 122

I Confess (1953), 267*n*6

idealization, 12, 121, 122, 124, 130, 133, 137, 139–40, 154, 160, 161, 252

Immerwahr, Raymond, 8

interpretation, xii, xiii; divergent/diverse, xi, xiv, 256

irony, 4–5, 6–7, 74–75, 259; and ambiguity/ambivalence, 100, 161, 216; benign, 183; and black comedy/humor, 60–61, 64, 252; through color design, 232, 236; dialectical, 10; and expressionism, 171, 175, 177, 211, 254; inversion/reversal, 233; and inversion/subversion of morality, 54, 225; modern, 8, 9; and suspense, 39, 50–52; and suspenseful mystery, 58–59, 64; traditional, 8, 9. *See also* romantic irony

Ishii-Gonzales, Sam, 187

Jamaica Inn (1939), 127, 143; dandy in, 128, 129; female/feminine agency in, 86

Janus-faced (1920), 193

Jekyll/Hyde, 94, 95, 97. *See also* dandy; *doppelgänger*/double

Jourdan, Louis, 104

Kalmus, Natalie, 221, 222, 223, 225

Kammerspiel film, 168–69, 171–72, 180

Kandinsky, Wassily, 218

Keats, John, 11, 256

Keen, Malcolm, 23, 184

Kelly, Grace, 129, 265*n*47; in *Dial M for Murder*, 229; in *Rear Window*, 33; in *To Catch a Thief*, 12, 30, 130

Kieling, Wolfgang, 148

Kindem, Gorhem, 234

knowledge: and disenchantment/loss of innocence, 96, 98; vs doubt/self-doubt/skepticism/uncertainty, xv, 77–79, 88, 93; through female/"feminine" detection/faith/intuition, 81–82, 84, 89, 92, 93–98, 106, 113, 114; and gender difference, 75; and gender "inversion," 106–13; joint quest of, 84–93, 100, 106, 114; through male/"masculine" detection/coercion/reason, 81, 82, 84, 98–106, 113, 114; pursuit/quest/search for, xv, 71, 75, 79, 80; through recognition narrative/plot, xv, 70,

Index

Index

reverse-shot editing in, 186; subjective
expressionism in, 173–74; suspense in,
167; wrong/ed woman in, 80, 98–99,
101; and wrongful imprisonment,
77, 109
Murnau, F. W., 164, 165, 172, 179, 193,
197, 200

Naked City, The (1948), 74
Naremore, James, 17, 61
nature. *See* expressionism, role of nature
Newman, Paul, 148
North by Northwest (1959), xiv, 30, 35, 36,
37, 80, 108, 147, 250, 255, 273*n*47; ////
effect/motif in, 203, 238; and authorial
intervention, 27; black comedy/humor,
17, 59–60; character point of view in,
41, 45; classical suspense in, 45; color
design in, 199, 222, 223, 228, 228–29,
230, 236, 238, 239–40, 241, 247; crop-
dusting sequence, 148, 151–52; the
dandy in, 84, 112; the double/doubling
in, 16; female agency in, 89–90;
Hitchcock cameo in, 21; the kiss in, 11,
247; MacGuffin in, 78, 89; masculine
aesthetic in, 151–52; mullioned window
in, 198–99; and "perversity," 27–28;
rogue in, 128, 130; as romantic renewal
narrative, 15, 27–28, 33, 79, 123, 217, 221,
264*n*45; as romantic thriller, 11, 13, 118;
shared suspense in, 41; spiral motif in,
203; and surrealism, 253; suspenseful
mystery in, 45; tonal ambiguity in, 17;
and wrong/ed man, 78, 240
Nosferatu (1921), 164, 165, 166, 178, 179–80,
197, 200, 214, 215
Notorious (1946), 12, 57; //// effect/motif
in, 202; and classical suspense, 48; the
dandy in, 16–17, 109, 112; as domestic
melodrama, 81; the double/doubling
in, 16, 196; expressionism in, 173, 185;
female agency in, 89–90; as gothic
melodrama, 100; "Hitchcockian Blot"
in, 207; and identification with villain,
56; as joint quest narrative, 100; the
kiss in, 153; MacGuffin in, 78; and
"masculine" detection/coercion, 99–
100; as romantic renewal narrative, 99;
plot synopsis, 99; and shared suspense,
56–7; suspense in, 42; and wrong/ed
woman, 49
Novak, Jane, 132
Novak, Kim, 11
Novello, Ivor, 271*n*24; in *Downhill*, 127, 170;
in *The Lodger*, 23, 65, 127, 166
Number Seventeen (1932), 131

Ober, Philip, 60
Olivier, Laurence, 17
Olsen, Christopher, 52
Ondra, Anny, 20, 100
Orr, John, 184, 258, 278–79*n*3

Paradine Case, The (1947): and character
point of view, 105; the dandy in, 99; as
film noir, 103; and ironic ambivalence,
217; and "masculine" detection/
coercion, 103–104; masculinity in,
83; plot synopsis, 104; and wrong/ed
woman, 80, 99, 103
Pater, Walter, 119–20, 121, 124, 130–31, 132,
139. *See also* aestheticism
Pearson, Roberta, 20
Peck, Gregory, 255; in *The Paradine Case*,
83, 104; in *Spellbound*, 11, 81, 83
Perkins, Anthony, 13–14, 271*n*24
Perkins, Victor, 58
perversity. *See* sexuality
Phoenix Tapes, The (1999), 147, 150
Piccoli, Michel, 240
Pierrot le fou (1965), 225
Pilbeam, Nova, 86
Plato, 169
Pleasure Garden, The (1925): alternate
endings of, 18–19; the double/doubling
in, 16, 17

Index

Pleshette, Suzanne, 239

Poe, Edgar Allan, 122, 257, 270*n*10

poetics, xii–xiii, 251, 255–56

point of view, 9; audience/spectator/
viewer, xv, 39; character, xv, 13–14, 17,
20, 24, 31, 33, 34, 39, 40, 41, 44, 45, 53, 55,
66, 99, 100, 105, 106, 144, 155; narrative,
xv, 13–16, 33, 55, 108; objective and
subjective, 24; of the villain, 13, 53; and
voyeurism, 20

postmodernism, 256, 258–59

Powell, Michael, 224

Pressburger, Emeric, 224

Price, Theodore, 148, 150, 276*n*34

profile shot, 22, 186, 188, 193–94, 198, 201

Psycho (1960), 11, 51, 59, 80, 173, 192, 196,
199, 250; //// effect/motif in, 201, 202,
208; and artifice, 15–16; authorial
surrogate in, 22; avian imagery
in, 182, 187–90, 194; and character
identification, 55; and character point
of view, 13–14; classical suspense
in, 46; death birds in, 214, 215, 216;
divided two-shot in, 187, 196; the
double/doubling in, 178, 182, 184, 214,
215; expressionism in, 182; force/role of
nature in, 182; Hitchcock cameo in, 21;
"Hitchcockian Blot" in, 203, 207–208;
and horror, 11, 51, 70, 161–62, 163, 254;
and inverted/subverted morality, 55,
56; and ironic inversion, 13, 78, 217, 251;
Janus face in, 194; lovebirds in, 216;
mirror shot, 194–95; and murderer-
as-artist, 122; parlor sequence, 186,
187–90, 214; perverse desire/sexuality
in, 123, 161; psychoanalysis in, 259; and
shared suspense, 53, 55; shot/reverse-
shot structure, 186–90; shower scene,
12, 45, 122, 123–24, 162, 203; staircase
and banisters in, 200; spiral motif in,
203; suspenseful mystery in, 45–47;
and sympathetic villain, 110; vicarious
suspense in, 42

psychoanalysis, 76, 77. *See also* Freudian
psychoanalytic theory

psychoanalytic criticism/interpretation,
82, 259

Pudovkin, Vsevolod, 14

pure cinema, 14, 120, 146, 148, 150, 154, 158,
162, 175, 210, 250

queer aesthetic, 161

queer theory, xvii

Rains, Claude, 16, 109

Rear Window (1954), 3, 32, 211, 250, 273*n*57;
//// effect/motif in, 202; ambiguous
ending of, 35; authorial surrogate in,
22; black comedy/humor in, 34, 60;
and character point of view, 33–34,
185; classical suspense in, 46; color
design in, 197, 219, 220, 222, 229,
237, 242–43; the double/doubling
in, 34; expressionism in, 185; and
female/"feminine" forms of knowing/
faith/intuition, 81, 82, 92; Hitchcock
cameo in, 21–22; "horizontal" level
of, 35; and ironic ambivalence, 13, 33,
78, 221, 251; as joint quest narrative,
90–91, 92; and Kuleshov experiment,
263*n*24; MacGuffin in, 92; male forms
of knowing in, 82; masculinity in,
83, 90, 92; mullioned window in,
197–98; and perverse desire in, 35, 67,
152–53; and reflexivity, 34, 263–64*n*32;
surprise in, 46; surrealist aesthetic in,
219–20; villain as "vampire," 198; and
voyeurism/istic gaze, 20, 33–34, 67, 69,
152, 263–64*n*32

Rebecca (1940), 26, 104, 105, 107, 128,
130, 149, 235, 245, 253, 254; artwork/
paintings in, 137–38; authorial
surrogate in, 155, 157; and character
point of view, 14, 47; divided two-
shot in, 196; the double/doubling in,
17, 182; du Maurier novel, 65, 96, 127,

Index

130; expressionism in, 182, 186; female gaze in, 69; feminine aesthetic in, xvi, 68, 69, 149, 154–57; and "feminine" faith, 82, 95; force/role of nature in, 182, 198–99; as gothic melodrama, 81, 93; "Hitchcockian Blot" in, 207; irony in, 59; Jekyll/Hyde figure in, 84, 95; knowledge and disenchantment in, 98; masculine lesbian in, 129; mullioned windows in, 155, 182, 196, 198; plot synopsis, 96; pursuit of knowledge in, 80, 97, 154; the sublime in, 253; surprise in, 47; as suspenseful mystery, 44, 58–59, 69, 155; wrong/ed woman in, 269n26

recognition. *See* knowledge

Redgrave, Michael, 88

reflexivity, 3–4, 7, 8, 9, 34, 168, 257, 258, 263–64n32; and voyeurism, 20

Reinhardt, Max, 168

Renoir, Jean, 22

Reville, Alma, 85–86, 131, 272n31

Rigby, Edward, 87

Rilla, Walter, 132

Ring, The (1927): the dandy in, 209; the double/doubling in, 16; merry-go-round in, 209–10, 211; plot synopsis, 208–209; ring motif in, 193

Ritchard, Cyril, 20, 100

Ritter, Thelma, 60

Robison, Arthur, 166

rogue, 183; and dandy, 127, 128; defined, 95, 126; female, 129, 130; Hitchcock as, 131; and performance of gentlemanliness, 129

Rohmer, Eric, xiii

romantic ideal: defined, 10; as heterosexual love/romance, xiv, 11; linked to aestheticism, 12, 123, 253; and perversity, 72, 118, 251; undermined, 13, 36, 93, 96, 117

romantic irony, xiii–xiv, 3–4, 23, 26–37, 167, 251–59, 262n15; both/and logic

of, xiv, 5, 8, 9, 12, 17, 18, 59, 72, 154, 161, 192, 220, 251, 252–53; defined, 4–13, 117, 216–17; and the double or chaos/shadow world, xvi, 16, 75, 179; and doubt/misrecognition/skepticism vs knowledge/recognition, xiv, xv, 77; and gender difference, xiv; and horizontal and vertical form, 38; as ironic ambivalence/ambiguity/suspended judgment, xiv, 10, 13, 15, 31–35, 80, 81, 83, 216, 221, 251, 252; as ironic inversion/descent/downward spiral/negation, xiv, 10–11, 13, 35–37, 73, 80, 217, 221, 251; objective vs subjective, 7–9; and relation to aestheticism, xiv, 216, 252–53, 256–57, 270n9; as romantic renewal/redemption/transformation/transcendence, xiv, xvi, 10–11, 12–13, 15, 26–30, 31, 39, 73, 80, 81, 83, 93, 99, 123, 161, 183, 217, 220–21, 231, 251, 252, 255, 264n45; and tonal ambiguity, 8, 17–18. *See also* aestheticism; expressionism; horizontal and vertical form/structure; irony

romanticism, 4, 11, 163, 181, 258–59; British/English, xvi, 256–57; German, xvi, 164

romantic poetry, 5–6, 10

romantic thriller, xiv, 11, 13, 29, 49, 118, 254

Rope (1948), 80, 150, 153, 154; authorial surrogate in, 143, 155; black comedy/humor in, 62–63; character point of view in, 144; classical suspense in, 62–63; color design in, 194, 218, 235; the dandy in, 107, 112–13, 141; the double/doubling in, 113, 146; Hamilton stage play, 141; implicit homosexuality in, 112–13, 142; and inverted/subverted morality, 58, 62; Laurents screenplay, 142; the long take in, 122, 143–44; masculine aesthetic in, xvi, 141–45; masculinity in, 90; and murderer-as-artist, 122; plot synopsis, 58, 112; profile shot in, 194; psychoanalysis in, 259

Index

Rosenblatt, Bettina, 167

Rossetti, Dante Gabriel. *See* Dante

Rothman, William, xvii, 22, 94, 113, 167, 174, 186–87, 201

Rules of the Game (1939), 22

Ryals, Clyde de L., 8

Sabotage (1936), 246, 253; authorial surrogate in, 22; black comedy/humor in, 61; and classical suspense, 50, 61; as domestic melodrama, 81; Hitchcock on, 51; irony in, 50, 51; and inverted/subverted morality, 61; reflexivity in, 168; and self-conscious narration, 61; time-bomb sequence, 49–51, 61–62, 63

Saboteur (1942), 254; the dandy in, 84; reflexivity in, 168; tonal ambiguity in, 18

Saint, Eva Marie, 11, 89, 130, 222

Samuels, Charles Thomas, 221

Samuels, Robert, 153

Sanders, George, 128

Sayers, Dorothy L., 108

Schiller, Lydia, 156

Schlegel, Friedrich, 4–7, 8, 9, 10, 11, 27, 256

Schopenhauer, Arthur, 181

Schröder, Greta, 179

self-referentiality/self-reflexivity. *See* reflexivity

Selznick, David O., 130, 141, 268*n*14

sexual difference. *See* gender difference; knowledge

sexuality/desire: as deadly, 170; female, 135, 139, 242, 247; as Freudian joke, xv, 27; and Hitchcock's style, xvii, 65, 117–63, 244; as incestuous, 137; lesbian, 127, 129, 156; as masquerade, 130; as "perverse," xv–xvi, 11–12, 13, 14, 27–28, 31, 64–65, 66, 72, 95, 118, 120, 124, 125, 142, 144, 145–46, 150, 152, 154, 167, 233, 251, 252, 253, 255, 257; and suspense, 64–70. *See also* aestheticism; dandy; homoerotic desire/homoeroticism/homosexuality

Shadow of a Doubt (1943), xv, 33, 105, 128; //// effect/motif in, 201–202; black comedy/humor in, 60; chaos/shadow world in, 201–202; the dandy in, 60, 77, 95, 97, 107, 111; divided two-shot in, 196; as domestic melodrama, 81; the double/doubling in, 97, 178; expressionism in, 173, 181; and "feminine" faith, 82, 95, 97; as gothic melodrama, 81, 93, 95; and ironic ambivalence, 15, 217; Jekyll/Hyde figure in, 95, 97; knowledge and disenchantment in, 98; merry-go-round (of life and death) in, 210, 211–13; mullioned window in, 198; narrative point of view, 108; plot synopsis, 97; as recognition narrative, 77, 79; role of nature in, 181; spiral motif in, 213; staircase and banisters in, 200; surrealist aesthetic in, 212, 219; villain as "vampire," 97, 111–12, 181, 198, 202

shadow world. *See* chaos/shadow world

Shakespeare, William, 7

Shelley, Percy Bysshe, 11

shot/reverse-shot structure, 94, 185, 186–90, 190–92, 193, 210, 243. *See also doppelgänger*/double/doubling; expressionist iconography

Sinfield, Alan, 120

Skin Game, The (1931), 253

Slezak, Walter, 89

Smith, Susan, xiii, xvii, 17, 21, 22, 42, 49, 50

Solger, Karl Wilhelm Ferdinand, 10

Soviet montage, 14–15, 263*n*24

Spellbound (1945): expressionism in, 186; and "feminine" faith, 82, 93–94; Hitchcock cameo in, 21; the kiss in, 11, 94; masculinity in, 83; plot synopsis, 93–94; psychoanalysis in, 93–94, 259; as romantic renewal narrative, 93; shot/reverse-shot structure in, 94; surrealist aesthetic in, 219; wrong/ed man in, 81, 93–94

Index

spiral motif. *See* expressionist iconography

Spiral Staircase, The (1946)

Spoto, Donald, 131, 148, 241

Stafford, Frederick, 223

Stage Fright (1950): authorial surrogate in, 22; and female/feminine agency/forms of knowing, 81, 86, 89; femme fatale in, 129; wrong/ed woman in, 269*n*26

staircase motif. *See* expressionist iconography

Stam, Robert, 20

Stannard, Eliot, 127

Sternberg, Meir, 43

Sterne, Laurence, 7, 8

Stevenson, Robert Louis, 193, 257

Stewart, James, 83, 90, 255; in *The Man Who Knew Too Much* (1956), 52; in *Rear Window*, 3; in *Rope*, 58, 144; in *Vertigo*, 11, 94

Strangers on a Train (1951), 33, 120, 149, 154, 196, 253, 273*n*47; //// effect/motif in, 202, 210; artwork/paintings in, 136–37; authorial surrogate in, 22; and black comedy/humor, 66; and character point of view, 17, 66; and classical suspense, 48; the dandy in, 16, 57, 77, 83, 107, 111, 112, 122, 128, 137, 210; the double/doubling in, 21, 145, 146–47, 178, 181, 190–92, 253; expressionism in, 173, 185, 190–92; fairground sequence, 122, 137, 147, 210–11; female gaze in, 69; Hitchcock cameo in, 21, 22; "Hitchcockian Blot" in, 206; and identification with villain, 56, 66; implied homosexuality in, 145–46; and inverted/subverted morality, 57–58; and ironic ambivalence, 13, 251; irony in, 211; masculine aesthetic in, 145–47; merry-go-round in, 210–11, 212; opening sequence, 190–92; and perverse desire/sexuality, 137, 152; plot synopsis, 57, 145; psychoanalysis in,

259; and sexualized suspense, 66; and shared suspense, 56; shot/reverse-shot structure in, 190–92, 210; villain as "vampire," 211; voyeurism in, 210; wrong/ed man in, 49

Street, The (1923), 169, 170, 172, 205, 208, 209

Stuart, John, 19

Studlar, Gaylyn, 68; and "masochist" aesthetic, 69

sublimation. *See* Freudian psychoanalysis

sublime, 151, 254; anal-phallic, 252; apocalypse, 162; artwork as, 124; feminine, 70; and feminine aesthetic, 155, 160, 253, 255; phallic, 70, 252; and surrealism, 253; in suspenseful mystery, 68–69

surrealism/ist aesthetic, xiv, xvi, 158, 212, 245, 253, 257; and color design, 219–20, 250, 252, 255; and relation to aestheticism, 219, 250; and sublime, 253

suspense, xiii, xiv–xv, 120, 148, 149, 154, 167, 196, 252, 257; and black comedy/humor, xiv–xv, 17–18, 59–64, 72, 252; classical, xv, xvi, 39–40, 41, 43, 44, 45, 46, 48–58, 61, 141; vs curiosity, 43; defined, 38; eroticized, 96; Hitchcock as aesthete/"Master" of, 38, 70; Hitchcock on, 14, 40, 41–42, 43, 46, 48, 53–54, 67; and irony, 39, 252; objective, 40–41, 42; and pursuit/quest/search for knowledge, 70, 72; and romantic irony, 37, 38–39, 72; and sexuality, 64–70; shared, 41, 53, 55, 56, 64; subjective, 24, 40–41, 42, 43, 44; through suppressive narration, 41, 42–3, 44, 45; vs surprise, 41–42, 46; vicarious, 42, 49, 51, 53, 55. *See also* morality

suspenseful mystery, xv, xvi, 45–47, 58–59, 69, 147, 155, 254–55; defined, 43–44, 58; and feminine aesthetic, 68, 255; irony in, 58–59, 64; and masochistic aesthetic, 69; vs surprise, 46, 47

Index

noir, 103; "Hitchcockian Blot" in, 206; and ironic inversion, 13, 35–37, 78, 221; Janus face in, 195; the kiss in, 11, 159–60; knowledge and disenchantment in, 105; and "masculine" detection/coercion, 103–104, 106; masculinity in, 83, 90; and masquerade, 130, 139, 157, 194, 195; mirror shots in, 195; perverse desire in, 118, 233; plot synopsis, 35–36; profile shot in, 194; pursuit of knowledge in, 80; as recognition narrative, 77; relation to English romanticism, 256; romantic ideal in, 118; shot/reverse-shot structure in, 159; spiral motif in, 193, 203–205, 213, 242; the sublime in, 70; surprise in, 47; surrealist aesthetic in, 158, 219–20, 245; suspenseful mystery in, 45, 46, 47, 69; the "vertigo" shot, 157, 158–59, 206, 272n33; voyeurism in, 69; wrong/ed woman in, 80, 99, 103, 105, 269n26
von Sternberg, Josef, 68–69, 215
voyeurism, 20, 25, 66–68, 69, 82, 210, 264n32

Wainewright, Thomas, 122
Walker, Michael, xiii, 21, 22, 89
Walker, Robert, 16
Waltzes from Vienna (1934), 211
"warning series." *See* color design
Warning Shadows (1923), 166–67, 168
Waxworks (1924), 209
Weimar cinema/directors, 164, 168–69, 171, 180
Weis, Elizabeth, 174
Who Killed Cock Robin? (1935), 168
Wiene, Robert, 164
Wilde, Oscar, 119, 130–31, 133, 134, 137, 143, 257, 270n14; and aestheticism-dandyism link, 120–26; "Pen, Pencil

and Poison," 122; *Picture of Dorian Gray, The*, 121, 122–23, 125, 126, 131, 257. *See also* aestheticism; artwork/paintings; dandyism
Wilding, Michael, 232
Wilson, Josephine, 88
Winston, Irene, 33
Witty, Dame May, 88
Wood, Robin, xi, xvii, 128
Wordsworth, William, 233
Wright, Theresa, 79
wrong/ed man motif, xv, 28, 48–49, 72–75, 77–80, 83, 85, 89, 95, 99, 100, 106–107, 113, 267n6
wrong/ed woman motif, 48–49, 72, 77, 80, 89, 98–101, 103, 105–106, 113, 269n26
Wrong Man, The (1956), 113, 253; the double/doubling in, 73; expressionism in, 173; and "feminine" faith, 82; Hitchcock's prologue, 73; and ironic ambivalence, 73; irony in, 74–75; as joint quest narrative, 92–93; as melodrama, 75; plot synopsis, 73; precipitous staircase in, 192; and wrongful accusation/imprisonment, 77, 79

Young and Innocent (1937), 88, 90, 254; female/feminine agency in, 85, 86, 89; and female forms of knowing, 81; "feminine" faith in, 93; "Hitchcockian Blot" in, 207; as joint quest narrative, 86–87; MacGuffin in, 78, 87; plot synopsis, 86–87; as recognition narrative, 77; as romantic renewal narrative, 83, 87, 217; wrong/ed man in, 78, 86, 93

Zirnite, Dennis, 200
Žižek, Slavoj, xvii, 140, 162, 205, 259

FILM AND CULTURE
A series of Columbia University Press
Edited by John Belton